Bridging the
Sacred and the Secular

Selected Writings of
John Courtney Murray, S.J.

D1479323

Bridging the
Sacred and the Secular

Selected Writings of
John Courtney Murray, S.J.

EDITED BY
J. LEON HOOPER, S.J.

GEORGETOWN UNIVERSITY PRESS / WASHINGTON, D.C.

Georgetown University Press, Washington, D.C.
© 1994 by Georgetown University Press. All rights reserved.
Printed in the United States of America
10 9 8 7 6 5 4 3 2 1   1994
THIS VOLUME IS PRINTED ON ACID-FREE OFFSET BOOK PAPER

Library of Congress Cataloging-in-Publication Data

Murray, John Courtney.
   Bridging the sacred and the secular : selected writings of John
Courtney Murray / J. Leon Hooper, editor.
          p. cm. — (Moral traditions and moral arguments series)
       Includes bibliographical references.
       1. Sociology, Christian (Catholic) 2. Democracy—Religious
aspects—Catholic Church. 3. Freedom of religion. 4. Catholic
Church—Relations. 5. Catholic Church—Doctrines. I. Hooper, J.
Leon. II. Title. III. Series.
   BX1753.M96   1994
   261.8--dc20
ISBN 0-87840-561-5 (cloth)   0-87840-571-2 (paper)
                                                          94-9698

Contents

Editor's Preface

Moral Traditions & Moral Arguments, as a series, presents systematic, scholarly accounts of major themes in Christian ethics in order to critically examine those insights that, perduring through the ages, have shaped and continue to shape Christian lives and communities. These books are intended to provide scholars with a precise understanding of moral traditions as well as an appreciation of their contribution to contemporary life.

Weston School of Theology   JAMES F. KEENAN, S.J., ED.

Preface

The selection and organization of this collection is a response to several claims made by John Courtney Murray, shortly before his death on August 16, 1967. Scanning over two millennia of Western social history, yet with an eye on modern democratic societies, he broadly concluded that "[a] work of differentiation between the sacral and the secular has been effected in history." Further, the Second Vatican Council, particularly in its *Declaration on Religious Freedom* and *Pastoral Constitution on the Church in the Modern World*, had recognized and endorsed modern forms of this differentiation. Yet, he continued,

> . . . differentiation is not the highest stage in human growth. The movement toward it, now that it has come to term, must be followed by a further movement toward a new synthesis, within which the differentiation will at once subsist, integral and unconfused, and also be transcended in a higher unity ("The Declaration on Religious Freedom: Its Deeper Significance," 1966e, p. 593).[1]

It was now time to generate "new perspectives" within which the sacred and the secular might be (re)integrated.

What Murray in the 1960s designated by the terms "secular" and "sacred" covered a full set of distinctions or differentiations that he had

---

1. Most citations throughout this volume follow a modified Chicago style. Any citation listing a (title), year, and, perhaps, page (but no name, as in the citation for this quote) belong to Murray. Fuller bibliographical information can be found in the accompanying Murray Bibliography. References to all other authors use the author/date style, if they are cited in the Secondary Bibliography. All works that are not listed in either bibliography will appear in full form within the text or notes.

earlier injected into several American public arguments, and had mar-shalled to his defense of civil religious freedom. At its most concrete, incarnate level, the distinction was another expression of what he called Gelesian dualism or Christian constitutionalism—a dualism that he first characterized as "state" and "church," and later as "society" and "church." At the theological level, its earlier cognates were the paired terms "temporal" and "spiritual," the "natural" and the "revealed," or "nature" and "grace." In the realm of morals he distinguished between "natural law" and "divine law," and between "temporal means" and "spiritual means." At the level of reflective (academic) awareness he sharply distinguished between "philosophy" and "theology." For most of his publishing life he spelled out—and sharpened—these distinctions in the face of secularists and religious alike who sought to brand institu-tions and cultures that were so differentiated as immature, tainted by religious rebellion or by superstition, or as outright evil. To paraphrase Genesis 1, Murray looked over these distinctions and their resulting social differentiations, and saw that they were good. Yet they could not be the final word on Western social history. Those legitimate and neces-sary differentiations were hardening into ramparts, and society stood in danger of collapsing into social incoherence.

How a Christian—particularly, a Roman Catholic—might reinte-grate the temporal and the spiritual, civil society and the church, within "larger perspectives" remains a problem that troubles both the church and civil society itself. For those who claim to "do ethics in the Murray tradition," the problem is compounded by Murray's own publication record. Until recently, the two available collections of Murray's writings fell neatly on either side of his secular/sacred differentiation.[2] On the side of the secular stood *We Hold These Truths: Catholic Reflections on*

---

2. One further work was published in book form, namely, *The Problem of Religious Freedom* (1964e). It has been out of print for a number of years, but was reissued as one of four articles in his 1993: *Religious Liberty: Catholic Struggles with Pluralism*, 127–97. The issue of religious freedom does not fall on only one side of the nature/grace bifurcation. While Murray argued that the freedom eventually endorsed by the Council developed in the temporal (natu-ral) sphere, his argument was directed to believing Catholics and was based on the Christian premise of Gelesian social dualism (i.e., that civil society and the church each had independent foundations in God's creative and redemptive will, respectively). His work on religious freedom, then, can offer some source material for constructing a bridge between the sacred and the secular, although the foundations for that bridge are in his writings on Christian Humanism.

the American Proposition 1960c; hereafter (WHTT). The articles that make up *WHTT* were written between 1950 and 1959 and deal, as the title suggests, with Roman Catholic reactions to, and possible actions toward, American culture and institutions.[3] Although consciously Roman Catholic in spirit, those essays were not, in Murray's understanding, theological. Instead he proposed the "tradition of reason" or, under another name, "natural law philosophy" as the only viable basis for civil unity within religiously pluralistic America—whether the America under discussion was that of its founding or the United States at mid-twentieth century. Throughout that work he insisted that natural law discourse be kept distinct from the theological affirmations of any particular religious community.

In contrast to *WHTT, The Problem of God* (1964c) is an all out Catholic theological reflection on the development of trinitarian theology, leading to a dialectic engagement with modern social atheism. For those unfamiliar with Catholic scholastic treatments of theological doctrine and, particularly, the understanding of that development as proposed by Bernard J. Lonergan, S.J., this work verges on the incomprehensible. Those who appeal to Murray for enlightenment on the present moral state of America, therefore, tend to ignore this and Murray's other theological works. In practice, and sometimes in theory, the differentiations that Murray endorsed are turned into dichotomies by many who claim to continue his work.[4]

---

3. See 1960c in the Murray Bibliography for a history of *WHTT*'s various chapters. Chapters that were previously published are also listed earlier in the bibliography, with comments on the amount of editing that they received to reach their final *WHTT* form.

4. In the late 1970s (see Hollenbach et al., 1979) this bifurcation solidified into a debate whether the church should approach public social discourse with the language of natural law only or with a combination of natural law and revealed languages. By this time the church was more consciously bringing biblical insights to social issues, exemplified most starkly in some liberation theologies. The argument, insofar as it sought grounding in Murray's work, pivoted on whether he had endorsed solely an incarnational humanism or an eschatological and an incarnational humanism. (These two forms of Christian humanism will be discussed more fully in the Introduction to Part III.) Those who favored a more consciously biblical approach to social issues argued for the equal validity of both forms of Christian humanism; those worried about a negative impact that particularistic Roman Catholic perspectives might have on public debate argued for exclusive appeal (within public arguments) to incarnational humanism. Those endorsing incarnational humanism generally tended toward political neo-

Granted that Murray did clearly distinguish between his natural law and his theological writings, does he offer any perspectives that might help the citizen/believer integrate nature and grace, society and the church, natural law and trinitarian theology? Does he offer any methods that might lead to mutually informative approaches to questions concerning God and the human good? In fact, Murray pursued two distinct paths toward a new integration, or two languages that can mediate between the sacred and the secular.

First, for much of his life Murray had argued that natural reason, unaided by grace, could arrive at a spirituality that might unite people who otherwise could not theologically understand one another. Murray insisted that the right use of reason could delineate a notion of God that was necessary to, and sufficient for, contemporary social living (see Introduction, Part 4). He, and some who rely on him, appeal to this "natural theism" as a mediating language between civic life and Catholic faith (McElroy, 1989).

Second, Murray's treatment of what he called "Christian humanism" offers a distinct second source for the task of reintegration. By that term, Murray meant an explicitly theological viewpoint that expressed a specific Roman Catholic stance toward nature and grace, reason and revelation. That stance was, in its first 1940 expression and in its continued development, the principal ground from which Murray criticized both Protestant and Catholic theological approaches to American social issues. As will be apparent in the last two sections of this collection, the foundational premises of his understanding of Christian humanism—as later augmented by more nuanced understandings of reasoning in both

---

conservatism (see Weigel, 1985), thus restricting languages of faith to the internal life of the church.

I argue that this particular way of configuring Murray's understanding of the two humanisms misses what is fundamentally at stake in his humanism discussions. The choice for him was not between reason and faith or natural law and theology. Fundamentally his two humanisms differed in the sharpness with which they distanced themselves from the works of human hands, whether institutions or cultures. Murray eventually opted for a critical, but appreciative, stance toward civil culture—as an aspect of Catholic appreciation for the role of reasoning even in matters of faith. Murray's overall discussion leaves open the question of purely natural law or mixed languages in public argument (one has to go elsewhere for his own insistence on only natural law languages). He does, however, insist on the interpenetration of nature and grace, denying finally that human reasoning belongs to only one of those realms.

temporal and theological matters—grounded his late attempts to speak theologically with atheists and non-Catholics.

Both natural theism and Christian humanism offer distinct advantages and disadvantages. Natural theism, with its somewhat deistic, abstract notion of God, advances a generalized theistic affirmation to which most Americans can give assent and then move toward a discussion of social goals and methods. However, the problem that natural theism poses is the flip side of its generality, namely, its lack of a value-ladened and tradition-deep content that can enrich "a naked public square." Further, some claim that natural theism finds its primary unity in a negation that enforces or legitimates contemporary social polarities, rather than bridges them. And, in fact, natural theism is chronically plagued by its inability to grant any legitimate social space to the modern pragmatic or dogmatic atheist. It offers no bridges for spanning that particular social gap.

Christian humanism, particularly in the form that Murray claimed for the church, starts out with the distinct disadvantage of being particularistic, of being a stance that (Murray claimed) was based on an explicitly Roman Catholic understanding of nature and grace, of God the Creator and God the Redeemer. The advantage of Murray's Christian humanism, however, is its ability to place up front a tradition-deep theological stance, thereby informing public civil argument with a needed value-rich content. Its principal weakness is obviously its need to face an American society that is permanently suspicious of confessional religious languages.

The selection and arrangement of this collection is based on two judgments. First, Murray's articles on Christian humanism, including as they do rich trinitarian materials, offer a coherent, principled grounding for his later attempts at theological dialogue with both the atheist and the non-Catholic. They highlight the integrity of these late moves—an integrity that is not immediately apparent in a natural theism perspective. Second, Murray's humanism writings, now with their focus on reasoning as common to both the realms of nature and grace, appear better suited to the post-conciliar task of integrating the sacred and the secular. They best highlight two key analytic lines that are common to Murray's strictly natural law writings and his theological work.

The first line is Murray's deepening appreciation of just how thoroughly any form of human knowing is dependent on its social environment. This dependence is not simply a matter of being locked into the perspectives of one's culture or religion. In his natural law writings,

Murray argued that a distinctive, and new, notion of human dignity had emerged within the Anglo-American tradition. In his theological writings, there were many forms of human reasoning by which the church came to understand the God who became human in the person of Jesus Christ. These insights and perspectives were not simply matters of deducing implications from more general propositions. Rather they were breakthroughs to new meanings that were occasioned by cultural and institutional changes within concrete historical societies. All this falls under the label of the historicity of human knowing, which, stands in contrast to classicist understandings of human knowing. I will more fully outline this historicity/classicist distinction in Part 3.

A second common ground between Murray's late natural law and theological writings has variously been described as a "turn toward interiority" and "turn toward the self."[5] In the late sections of WHTT Murray clearly appeals to Lonergan's notion of four cognitional operations to explain how America can move from the "naive realism" of its founding to the "critical realism" necessary for its ongoing development. In his *Problem of God* he searches out common cognitional structures that can supply a basis for a dialectical conversation with atheistic existentialism and Marxism. In his conciliar and postconciliar discussions of Catholic approaches to the modern world, Murray tried to distinguish clearly between doctrine and theology, appealing to Lonergan's distinction between the cognitional operations of judgment and understanding. In all these cases, Murray explored structures and operations of the knowing citizen/believer in search of a common grounding for secular and religious conversation.

This collection begins with articles that fall within the strictly natural law orientation of WHTT. In the first two articles, Murray spells out his distinction between civil law (policy) and generalized, publicly held value commitments (consensus). He also establishes a necessary link between policy and consensus. The remaining articles in Part I address questions of national consensus and the imposition, through legal coercion, of particular moral viewpoints.

---

5. A "turn toward interiority" is a Lonergan term (as developed in *Method in Theology* (New York: Herder and Herder, 1972). This move to ground moral and truth claims in human cognitional and emotive sources has recently been traced through Western thought by Charles Taylor, *Sources of the Self: The Making of the Modern Identity* (Cambridge, MA: Harvard University Press, 1989) in a manner that I believe, is consistent with Lonergan's thought.

The several articles of Part II are clearly outside a strictly natural law philosophy. They follow Murray's ongoing but changing understanding of Christian humanism, particularly the version of humanism that he considered the strength of the Roman Catholic community. These articles establish a basis for interpreting the remaining articles of the collection.

The last three sections take up Murray's own late attempts at generating higher perspectives. Part III concerns the internal life of the Roman Catholic Church. It begins in Murray's judgment, where the Second Vatican Council left off, namely, in recognition of the church's own embededness in history, then moves to his later recommendations for the internal life of the church. Parts IV and V address the problems of social atheism and ecumenical theological discussions, respectively. Each begins with an early article in which Murray rejects the possibility of theological conversation with the atheist and the Protestant. The remaining articles then trace Murray's entry into theological discussions, the possibility of which he had earlier rejected.

In introductions to the five sections and the particular articles, I had two tasks: first, to direct the reader to other writings in which Murray treated the issue or argument under discussion; and second, to outline the overall contours of Murray's approach to the various topics as it shifted over the thirty years of his professional writings. By far the most important discussion is the introduction to Part III. There I trace through Murray's use of the term "doctrine" in both his natural law and theological writings. I will indicate how Murray gradually found a common ground for both his philosophical and theological work in the historicity and cognitional operations (interiority) that are common to both. Thus he was able to bridge the two realms—a bridge that might be of use to us.

Acknowledgments

Bridging distinctions that have turned into ramparts is a complicated business. At the very least it requires funding, for which I thank Lilly Endowments, Inc., and particularly Sister Jeanne Knoerle, S.P., their Program Director for Religion. Their generous grant covered the preparation of this collection and a symposium that is becoming a collection, tentatively entitled "Doing Ethics in the Murray Tradition." Then it requires a public voice, for which I thank Georgetown University Press and its director, Dr. John Samples. And, finally, Murray's call for "movement toward a new synthesis, within which differentiation[s] will at once subsist, integral and unconfused, and also be transcended in a higher unity," requires hope. While this last requirement is often in short supply, Woodstock Theological Center has for twenty years been guided by faith in the God who can surprise us not only in the unforeseen future but also in the depths of our past. My thanks to Woodstock's staff, fellows, and director, James Connor, S.J., for risking hope both in that past and future.

PART I

Civil Law:
National and International

The articles in this section deal with civil law and are further subdivided according to the juridical order that they address; that is, as they take up questions of (1) international law, (2) American constitutionalism, and (3) the penal restraint or constraint of particular actions. Within the venerable distinction between applications (or policy) and theory, all three orders touch on questions of applications—the making of good civil law. In the two discussions of international law, Murray elaborates and adds specificity to Pope Pius XII's call for rebuilding the post-war, international order. The article on American constitutionalism addresses the question of state distribution of tax dollars to private education. The third set of articles struggle with problems concerning the legal enforcement of specific ethical judgments within a pluralistic society.

Yet none of these arguments are entirely restricted to policy considerations. In all three Murray presumes that equitable and reasonable applications can only be shaped and enforced within commonly shared, general commitments, or, in other words, that policy is always dependent on theory.[1] In each argument, he defends or proposes a set of theoretical truths that are necessary for policy formation. Murray's

---

1. I use the terms "theory" and "consensus" interchangeably. For Murray, theory includes not only the products of academic reflection, but also the generalized value commitments that are held by a community. It is this "consensus" (on general commitments) that transforms a mass of individuals into a people. Constitutional law, then, is theoretical insofar as it expresses the general commitments of a nation. It becomes policy to the degree that it spells out how those commitments are to be embodied in specific social institutions. In Murray's use of the phrase, "We Hold These Truths," the truths held in consensus are theoretical, that is, general claims that then direct policy considerations. For Murray's contrast between "consensus" and "public opinion," see note 6.

reasons for insisting on a specifically *natural law* consensus for juridical discussions are discussed throughout this collection. Suffice it here to suggest one such reason, namely, that all three types of law belong to the temporal, not the eternal, order. They find their intelligibility in the realm of nature, not (immediately) in that of grace. In these articles Murray lays out what he considers are the substantive components of consensus—a series of propositions that permeate his later articles in *WHTT*.

Prudential Construction of an
International Order

The two articles included here demonstrate an early, subtle shift in Murray's approach to social ethical issues—from an almost exclusive concern with society's general truth claims to at least equal focus on its juridical order. In 1940 Murray had argued that only the Christian doctrines of Incarnation, Trinity, and the Cross could provide an adequate defense of Western liberties.[2] However, in "The Pattern for Peace" (1944b), he claims that a natural law consensus suffices for international reconstruction. While the difference between these arguments is striking, both remain primarily at the level of culture. In the second article, "The Juridical Organization" (1944a), Murray's attention shifts from consensual requirements for justice to institutional requirements, that is, to juridical structures that must embody the people's moral commitments. In the following year, he began his first religious liberty argument, yielding his subsequently enduring judgment that the establishment of Catholicism is always a juridical, and therefore a contingent, non-ideal, act (see, e.g., "Freedom of Religion, I: The Ethical Problem" [1945b] and "Notes on the Theory of Religious Liberty" [1945e].[3]

A further aspect of this first debate deserve attention. The environment within which these juridical concerns first arose had a lasting

---

2. See part II, "The Construction of a Christian Culture" (1940).

3. 1945e is a memo to Archbishop Mooney outlining a three-part argument that was to proceed in the following fashion: first, a natural law ethical argument, then a theological argument, then a political argument that would rely on either the natural law argument alone or a combination of the natural law and theological arguments. The style here is deductionistic. But even here Murray maintains that practical wisdom is needed to move from either or both of the theoretical realms to practical embodiment. Murray published the first, the natural law argument, in *Theological Studies* (1945b), but later abandoned this deductionistic style of argument in favor of a more historical study of the church's endorsement of Establishment and Intolerance. These two articles also stand in interesting contrast to Murray's mid-1950s studies of East/West relations. There Murray argued from the impossibility of arriving at a common juridical structure or a common understanding between the two, to strategies for dealing with that complete lack of mutual intelligibility, particularly regarding the use of nuclear deterrence. See his "Confusion of U.S. Foreign Policy" (1958c), *WHTT*, 221–247; and "Morality and Modern War" (1959b), *WHTT*, 249–73. I discuss this reading of international relations in the introduction to Part III.

impact on Murray's understanding of the human person. Toward the end of the Second World War, a debate swirled within Roman Catholicism concerning the manner and degree to which Catholics could participate with non-Catholics in social reconstruction.[4] Those favoring close participation cited the extensive destruction left by the war—the repair of which required the cooperation of "all men of good will." Arguing against close participation was the danger that Roman Catholics might become "indifferent" to Catholic social teaching and, particularly, to Catholic doctrinal claims. No one argued, however, that participation in international reconstruction was unnecessary. New institutions had to be created.

With others who favored close forms of cooperation, Murray sharply distinguished the goal of social reconstruction—namely, civil laws—as products of practical reasoning, and asserted that practical reasoning was the particular charism of the laity, not the clergy or the theologian. With this distinction, he grounded a relative degree of lay autonomy in the social order (understood as the temporal realm), while he consigned and preserved control of moral and theological meaning to the church hierarchy (understood as a realm that was permanent).[5] In all these debates, then, Murray understood human law to be a contingent, practical reality that stood (initially) in stark contrast to the orders of permanent truth, that is, to the foundational principles of natural and

---

4. Three forms of cooperation were debated, varying in the degree to which they encouraged people of different faiths to mix together in their work for justice. One envisioned parallel organizations with no common working together; a second, parallel organizations with sporadic or ongoing coordination through the leadership of each; a third, organizations of mixed-faith membership with daily interaction between people at all organizational levels. For Murray's outline of the counterpositions in the debate, see "Current Theology: Christian Co-operation" (1942b) and "Current Theology: Co-operation: Some Further Views" (1943a).

5. For the epistemological manner by which Murray granted lay autonomy, see: "Toward a Theology for the Layman: The Problem of its Finality" (1944b) and "Toward a Theology for the Layman: The Pedagogical Problem" (1944c). For a study of why this manner of distinguishing lay activity failed to achieve the autonomy that Murray sought, see Hooper, 1983, pp. 26–30.

divine law. Human law is a product of practical reasoning, not theoretical reasoning—an object of public opinion, not of consensus.[6]

This understanding of an active, constitutive human role in forming civil laws proved important for Murray's later understanding of the social responsibilities that fall to all members of human society. Here are responsible agents who are constructively and imaginatively to shape morally adequate institutions—institutions demanded by ever changing social environments. Later Murray's focus would shift again from the juridical and institutional to the realms of philosophical and theological meaning, finding even in the latter a need for fresh and new ways of understanding moral and religious truth claims. From the beginning, however, Murray's laity could never be purely passive implementors of philosophical or theological agenda; they had to exercise their own distinct form of creative wisdom. Subsequent sections of this collection will take up Murray's development of constructive moral agency and its role in the construction of an ethically adequate public philosophy, then a public theology, within the church and between churches.

---

6. At his clearest Murray used the term "public opinion" as governing decisions at the level of application or particular policy choices and "consensus" as commonly held, general value commits. This usage crystallized in his appropriation of Adolf Berle's phenomenology of the American business community. See *WHTT*, 102–3.

The Pattern for Peace and The Papal Peace Program

JOHN COURTNEY MURRAY, S.J.

The "Declaration on World Peace," issued simultaneously on October 7, 1943, by Catholic, Protestant, and Jewish leaders has been widely hailed as a significant document. A major feature of its significance would seem to lie in the fact that it proves beyond doubt the truth of our Holy Father's conviction that there is an immense body of right-thinking men, of all religious faiths, who are in agreement with him as to the religious and moral bases necessary for a new world order. Properly speaking, the Declaration did not aim at bringing Catholics, Protestants, and Jews together on a program for peace and world reconstruction. Rather, it simply registered the fact that they already stand together on fundamental points of cardinal importance. It was based on ideas that had already been publicized in Catholic, Protestant, and Jewish pronouncements, independently issued. And it simply discovered to a larger audience what had been known to students—that these pronouncements reveal a remarkable agreement in thought and program. The Declaration did not, of course, contain the full Catholic program, nor, for that matter, the full Protestant or Jewish program, nor even a full statement of the points of agreement in the three programs. However, the Declaration did contain a common program, a clear-cut pattern for peace impressive in itself, and destined to impress because it was agreed on by an authoritative array of America's religious leaders.

Originally published as "The Pattern for Peace and the Papal Peace Program," a pamphlet of the Catholic Association for International Peace (Washington, D.C.: Paulist press [1944]). Another version of this article, with some alterations, can be found as "Co-operation Among All Men of Good Will, Murray Archives, file 12-764. This latter was in turn published as "La Cooperacion Interconfessional Para la Pax," *Verbum* [Guatemala] (January 9, 1945), and in *Vida: Revista e Orientacion* 7 (1944): 757–71. For a discussion of the "Pattern for Peace," see Pelotte, 1975, 14–16.

In another respect, too, the document was of deep significance to all who had been following closely the work of the Pope for a just peace. It was an effort to make the agreement of religious men with regard to the conditions of peace and world order a powerful force for influencing both the counsels of the statesmen who will formulate the peace, and the views of the common people who (it must have hoped) will dictate its terms. Such an effort has been explicitly desired by our Holy Father. He expressed to the late Cardinal Hinsley his lively satisfaction over the famous Joint Letter to the *Times* of December 21, 1940.[1] In its own way, the Declaration shows that Catholics in the United States are following the lead of the Holy Father in seeking allies among all men of good will in their efforts to win the peace by insuring beforehand that it will be a just one. Catholic participation in the act of its issuance, therefore, can be given a legitimate place within the framework of the Pope's total peace program. As a matter of fact, it must be situated within this framework in order that its importance for Catholics may be rightly understood, and neither overestimated nor underestimated. The present report attempts to sketch, in very brief fashion, this larger framework.

THE NEED OF A NEW ORDER

With the utmost clarity Pius XII has seen (what many, even among Catholics, are still missing) that, beneath the military conflict now rending the nations, a war of even more colossal proportions has been engaged: "a great spiritual combat in which the stakes are the construction, nay, the very soul of the society of tomorrow."[2] And he has made it very clear that "for a Christian who is conscious of his responsibility toward even the least of his brethren there is no such thing as slothful tranquility, no question of flight, but of struggle, of action against every inaction and desertion" (n. 1838). For the issue in this war of spirits is truly cosmic. It is "a war on the darkness that comes of deserting God, and on the coldness that comes from strife between

---

1. For text of this letter Appendix F in *America's Peace Aims* (C.A.I.P. 1941).

2. *Principles of Peace*, edited for the Bishop's Committee on the Pope's Peace Points by Rev. Harry C. Koenig (Milwaukee: Bruce Publishing Co., 1943), n. 1838. The ensuing parenthetical numerals in the text are references to paragraphs in this book.

brothers. It is a fight for the human race, which is gravely ill, and must be healed in the name of conscience ennobled by Christianity" (n. 1863). Christ, as Pius XII solemnly stated in *Summi Pontificatus*, is once again crucified, and a chill darkness covers the earth. By Christ he means His members, every human person; and the crucifixion is not simply on the cross of total war but on the whole order of human life, dechristianized and dehumanized in its spirit and its institutions, which made total war possible, and even inevitable.

The Pope has assisted intimately at this crucifixion. In the passion of humanity no one in all the world has shown himself more compassionate than he: "The watchword, 'I have compassion on the multitude,' is for Us a sacred trust which may not be abused; it remains strong and impelling at all times and in all human situations, as it was the distinguishing mark of Jesus. The Church would be untrue to herself, ceasing to be a mother, if she turned a deaf ear from every class of the human family" (n. 1827). Moreover, the Pope knows that these cries are not for sterile sympathy. He hears "cries that rise from the depths and call for justice and a spirit of brotherly collaboration in a world ruled by a just God" (n. 1839). The common voice of humanity is articulate in his ears, and he hears it demanding "a new order."

It is indeed striking to note how often he has spoken of the desire of "the people," "of all peoples," for a new order. And for his part, viewing "the ruins of a social order which has given such tragic proof of its ineptitude as a factor for the good of the people" (n. 1860), the Pope acknowledges the justice of the demand. In 1940 he said: "We have to face today a fact of fundamental importance. Out of the passionate strife of the parties concerning peace and war aims, a common opinion emerges. It is that all Europe, as well as the separate nations, are in such a process of transformation that the beginning of a new period is clearly recognizable. . . . It is true that opinions and aims diverge; yet they agree in their will to establish a new order, and in their conviction that a return to the old order is neither possible nor desirable" (n. 1640). The conviction, he adds, is justified, and it is "especially strong in those strata of society which live by the work of their hands, and which are doomed to experience the hardships of national or international disturbances more than others. Still less can it be ignored by the Church, which, as the Common Mother of all, is bound to hear and to understand the outcries of suffering mankind"

(n. 1641). In a word, therefore, Pius XII has put the full authority of the Church behind the popular will to a new world order.[3]

THE NEED OF COLLABORATION
TOWARDS A NEW WORLD ORDER

But the construction of that new order is a task of such immense difficulty as to appear almost impossible to human strength. The ultimate agent of its accomplishment must, therefore, be the Holy Spirit of God, whose power alone is equal to it. This truth bases the Holy Father's incessant pleas for prayer and sacrifice. But he knows, too, that in the order of human instruments, two things are indispensable.

The first is spiritual leadership. Its primary function is to clarify the conscience of the world with reference to spiritual root of the present disorder in the temporal sphere, and authoritatively to lay down the religious and moral bases of the new order. The Pope has undertaken to provide this leadership, conscious of the fact that it is his Apostolic duty, and conscious, too, of the fact that, as he has said in more than one place, many even outside the Catholic Church are looking to him for leadership. Notably in his four great Christmas Allocutions of 1939–1942, he has been at pains to express "thoughts which are meant as an appeal to the conscience of the world, and a rallying cry to all those who are ready to ponder and weigh the grandeur of their mission and responsibility by the vastness of this universal undertaking" (n. 1859). No Pope in modern history has spoken so openly to all humanity, and in the name of all humanity; nor has any Pope ever made it so clear that behind his assumption of leadership is singly and solely the driving force of "a deep, all-embracing, unchanging affection . . . an immense desire to bring them (all the peoples of the world) every solace and help which is in any way at Our command" (n. 1827).

But leaders can only lead. Consequently, the second thing indispensably necessary for the construction of a new world order is

---

3. EDITOR NOTE: The notion of an international will for a new world order first appeared in Murray's 1940 address (see Part II, p. 111–113). This rising will toward order will eventually be transformed, under the inspiration of Pope John XXIII, into a rising recognition of, and respect for, human dignity.

world-wide collaboration. It is obvious that a host of statesmen and experts in all fields will have to collaborate on the technical details of the new structure. But the Pope regards it as no less obvious that the more fundamental religious and moral aspects of the new order will require the collaboration of an even wider circle, that must include all men of good will.[4] Hence he has taken the initiative in inviting this collaboration. Three such invitations, contained in the Christmas Allocutions of 1939, 1941, and 1942 are particularly solemn. Impressive in themselves, they are still more impressive because they occur in the midst of the Pope's formal announcement of his peace program; their issuance, and acceptance, seem to be clearly conceived by him as necessary to the successful execution of his program. Hence they are phrased with an urgency whose imperiousness reflects the Pope's insight into the fact that the cause of humanity itself is at stake, and his conviction that worse disaster can only be averted by instant and unified action. Other texts of similar tenor may be found, but it will be sufficient here to quote these three:

> If ever there was a purpose worthy of the collaboration of all noble and generous spirits [he is speaking of a just international peace and order], if ever there arose flaming courage for a spiritual crusade, in which with new truth the cry "God wills it" might resound, it is surely this high purpose and this crusading struggle, which should enlist all unselfish and greathearted men in the endeavor to lead the nations back from the muddy cisterns of material and selfish interests to the living fountain of divine law, which alone is powerful to create that enduring moral grandeur of which the nations and humanity, to their own serious loss, have for too long a time felt the absence and the need (n. 1498).

> The destruction brought about by the present war is on so vast a scale that it is imperative that there be not added to it the further ruin of a frustrated and illusory peace. In order to avert so great a calamity, it is fitting that in the formulation of the peace there should be assured the cooperation, with sincerity of will and energy, with the purpose of a generous participation,

---

4. See also *Intercredal Co-operation* by Parsons and Murray (C.A.I.P. 1943).

not only of this or that party, not only of this or that people, but of all people, yes, the common good, which requires the collaboration of all Christendom in the religious and moral aspects of the new edifice that is to be constructed (n. 1755).

It is for the best and most distinguished members of the Christian family, filled with the enthusiasm of crusaders, to unite in the spirit of truth, justice, and love, at the call of "God wills it," ready to serve, to sacrifice themselves. . . . With this lofty purpose before us [the freeing of the human spirit in the social order], we turn from the crib of the Prince of Peace, confident that His grace is diffused in all hearts, to you, beloved children, who recognize and adore in Christ your Savior; We turn to all those who are united with Us at least by the bond of faith in God; We turn, finally, to all those who would be free from doubt and error and who desire light and guidance; and We exhort you with suppliant, paternal insistence not only to realize fully the dreadful gravity of this hour, but also to meditate on the vistas of good and supernatural benefit which it opens up, and to unite and collaborate toward the renewal of society in spirit and truth (n. 1843).

THE PAPAL IDEA OF CO-OPERATION

The point now is to analyze the papal idea of cooperation. In order to understand it, one must grasp its motive, its objective, its bases, the persons to be engaged in it, and the unity which it establishes among them.

The Motive: Compassionate Charity

First of all, the Pope understands this collaboration to have its motive in "that universal love which is the compendium and most general expression of the Christian ideal, and which, therefore, bridges the gap between us and those who have not the blessing of sharing the same faith with us" (n. 1497). The moral conscience of mankind has been outraged, its sense of justice violated; and above all its belief in human fraternity and solidarity shocked by the present state of affairs; together these three human and Christian sentiments have created a common will to establish a new and better order. The Pope supposes this common will to be already in existence; he appeals to it, and especially to its main inspiration, that compassion on the multitude which every man of conscience and good will must today experience. The Pope, therefore, wants a cooperation "in a spirit of truth, justice, and love" (n. 1842); above all, he wants a cooperation in charity—an alliance in a common will to a common good.[5]

The Goal: Peace, the Work of Justice

Secondly, this cooperation in charity has a very definite objective. This point is of cardinal importance; for the objective of the cooperation determines its whole character, and vindicates its legitimacy. There is, for instance, a kind of cooperation that is aimed simply at the creation of amity, tolerance, mutual understanding, better human relationships, etc., between men of different creeds. This is not precisely the type of cooperation which the Pope has in mind. He has, indeed, recalled to his children the demands of "the inspired teaching of the Apostle, who, while he inculcates the need of resolution in the fight against error, also knows that we must be full of sympathy for those who err, and open-minded in our understanding of their aspirations, hopes, and motives" (n. 1839). But he has not explicitly concerned himself with the problems in social psychology created by religious division. When he speaks of cooperation, he is concerned with getting one particular thing done—an immense thing, but a sufficiently definite thing.

He has many formulas for it: the establishment of "a new and just international and national order giving security" (n. 1641); "a future peace that will assure the loyal and sincere consent of all peoples" (n. 1654); "a new edifice of fraternal solidarity among the nations of the world, an edifice built upon new and stronger foundations, with fixed and stable guarantees, and with a high sense of moral sincerity which would repudiate every double standard of

---

5. EDITOR NOTE: Murray's use of the term "charity" is somewhat ambiguous. Charity is of course a theological virtue, grounded in revelation and having a theological content. He had previously ruled out the possibility of charity (understood as a theological virtue) as a common motivational source for Catholics, Protestants, and Jews, insisting that civil friendship (understood as a natural virtue) can sufficiently motivate cooperation (see "Current Theology" [1942b] and "Current Theology: Co-operation: Some Further Views" [1943a]). Further on in this text Murray will make clear that he believes intercredal cooperation can be based only on natural law, and therefore natural virtue.

morality and justice for the great and the small, or for the strong and the weak" (n. 1655); "a fraternal and harmonious union of nations bound together in friendship" (n. 1668); "a new international order which will guarantee to all peoples a just and lasting peace, and which will be a bountiful source of well-being and prosperity" (n. 1757); "a new order founded on moral principles" (n. 1758); "an international order of friendly relations and collaboration such as conform to the demands of God's law" (n. 1828); "a society which is pervaded and sanctioned by religious thought" (n. 1833); "justice and a spirit of brotherly collaboration in a world ruled by a just God" (n. 1839); "the renewal of society in spirit and truth" (n. 1843); "a complete rehabilitation of the juridical order . . . resting on the supreme dominion of God and safeguarded from all human whims . . . an order which stretches forth its arm, in protection or punishment, over the unforgettable rights of man, and protects them from attack" (n. 1854); "the bringing back of society to its center of gravity, which is the law of God . . . [and to] the service of the human person and his common good ennobled in God" (n. 1860); or finally, in the most revealing and characteristic formula, "a new order . . . founded on that immovable and unshakable rock, the moral law, which the Creator Himself manifested in a natural order, and which He has engraved with indelible characters on the hearts of men" (n. 1757).

From these many formulas, the one identical objective of cooperation emerges quite clearly. It has two distinguishing notes: (1) it is a spiritual objective, but (2) it remains within the temporal order. It is a spiritual objective because it involves a return to the principles of justice and charity made mandatory by God's law. It remains within the temporal order because it concerns the establishment of these principles as the bases of man's political, economic, and social life in this world. Were it not a spiritual objective, our Holy Father could not authoritatively summon the Church to its attainment. Because it remains within the temporal order and does not extend into the realm of religious worship, ecclesiastical faith and order, etc., he can and does invite the cooperation of all men of good will in its attainment. Concretely, therefore, the cooperative effort aims at the establishment of the order of justice, dictated by the natural law, at the heart of a new political and socio-economic order in national and international life. Or in a briefer formula: it is to be a cooperation in charity to do the work of justice which is peace—the ordered tranquility of the earthly city of man.

The Basis: Four Truths of the Natural Order

Thirdly, in the perspective of this goal, the bases of the cooperative effort—the set of religious and moral principles which support it—become clear. There are four such principles: (1) a religious conviction as to the sovereignty of God over nations as well as over individuals; (2) a right conscience as to the essential demands of the moral law in social life; (3) a religious respect for human dignity in oneself and in others—the dignity with which man is invested inasmuch as he is the image of God; and (4) a religious conviction as to the essential unity of the human race.[6] In terms of these four truths the natural order of justice between men and nations is set up, made obligatory, and sanctioned. They form the essential bulwarks of that "holy land of the spirit, which is destined to sustain in its foundations the unchangeable norms and laws on which arise a social construction of solid internal consistency" (n. 1842). And the Christmas Allocutions of 1939 to 1942 have been primarily concerned with drawing out the essential implications and consequences of these four truths in the national and international field. One must accept the conclusion that the Pope has wished to formulate in terms of these four truths (which, he knows, are held within all religious groups) both a philosophy of human society and a general program of social reform which will command the assent and support of all men of right conscience and good will.

We must not be blind to this fact because of another fact—that the Holy See has surrounded this nuclear platform with a fuller, more intimately Catholic philosophy and program. This latter will always remain the basis of distinctively Catholic social action. But, viewing the world situation with concrete realism, our Holy Father recognizes that Catholic social action alone, for all its intrinsic resources, is simply not up to the enormity of the task that confronts it with frightening urgency. Hence he has characterized the task as "a universal undertaking for the common good," requiring the "collaboration of all Christendom in the religious and moral aspects of the new edifice." And the problem is to provide a sound basis for this necessary collaboration.

---

6. EDITOR NOTE: These four truths are foundational to Murray's present understanding of a natural law ethic and appear to be prerequisites to participation in the type of reconstruction he envisions. The problem of natural law's theistic premise will be considered in Part IV.

This problem was met consciously and squarely in the Christmas Allocutions of 1939 to 1942. They provide the needed basis—a social theory and a social program based on the four truths mentioned. All these are, indeed, truths of what we call the natural order. But we may not doubt their power to found a just social order; no such doubts appear in the papal documents. Moreover, we must remember that the Gospel and the natural law are not, as it were, two alternative foundations for social reconstruction. The natural law exists within the Gospel; and a social order which would conform to the demands of the natural law would already be fundamentally Christian. Therefore a Catholic program of cooperation on the basis of the natural law would be in perfect harmony with the program of Catholic operation on the basis of the integral Gospel.

An Invitation to All Men of Good Will

Fourthly, in view of the bases of cooperation it is clear to whom the invitation to cooperate was issued, namely, to all men who believe in God; for belief in God necessarily entails acceptance of the moral law and of human dignity and equality. It may be well to emphasize that the invitation was issued to all men who believe in God. Its purpose was not to bring together religious groups in their corporate entities as religious groups, or to effect a "reunion of the churches." There can be no thought of setting up a sort of "super organization" that would somehow consider itself an interdenominational "church." On the contrary, the idea is to bring together persons of right conscience and good will on the basis of those religious and moral principles which are the spiritual source of social order, and which the Pope recognizes to be held by persons within all religious groups. Consequently, in the idea of cooperation in charity for the work of justice which is peace there is no suggestion of "equating churches," or of countenancing the idea that a man may freely choose from among a variety of ecclesiastical allegiances, as if all were equally valid for eternal salvation.[7] In

---

7. EDITOR NOTE: Here Murray is perhaps ingenuously trying to deflect the charge of indiffentism. At issue was indifferentism understood as the belief that Catholic doctrine did not offer the best possible or solely feasible grounds for social reconstruction. Murray deflects the problem toward questions of eternal salvation and the church's role in advancing that salvation, avoiding the question of indifferentism toward Catholic social doctrine. For a listing of possible meanings to the term "indifferentism," see Hooper, 1983, 13.

fact, the question what is necessary for eternal salvation, and what are the "fundamentals of religion as such," did not come into view at all. The only problem with which this type of cooperation deals is that of the rescue of mankind from damnation to injustice on this earth; and it aims simply at reinforcing "the genuine fundamentals of all social life" (n. 1829).

All men have equal right to justice in the temporal order, and all men who acknowledge this right and its essential religious foundations have a common obligation and responsibility to see that it is respected. On this basis the Pope appeals to all these men. However divided they are religiously, they are all on the side of God—and hence at one another's sides—in one clearly drawn respect, namely, in the marshalling of hosts for the "great spiritual combat wherein the stakes are the construction, nay, the very soul, of the society of tomorrow." For he says, "vile unbelief, which arrays itself against God, is the most dangerous enemy of a new order which would be just; on the other hand, every man who believes in God is numbered among His champions and knights" (n. 1763).

There is, moreover, a hierarchy in the ranks of God's host; for, he adds, "those who have faith in Christ, in His divinity, in His law, in His work of love and brotherhood among men will make a particularly valuable contribution to the reconstruction of the social order." And to his own children the Pope (tacitly in the place cited, where he was speaking to all the world, but explicitly in other places) reserves the place of special privilege—the privilege of bearing the highest responsibility.[8] They have the responsibility for a more unified effort, a more courageous spirit of enterprise, more persevering, patient, and intelligent labor, more profound prayer and sacrifice, for the common good of mankind.

The Bond of Unity: Spiritual and Civic

Fifthly and finally, the papal concept of cooperation has one distinguishing mark, consequent upon all the rest, namely, the unique type

---

8. EDITOR NOTE: This note of the Catholic faith placing more stringent demands on Catholic social witness will reemerge in Murray's thought after the council, in a demand also placed on the church as a whole to respect human dignity even within the church (see "The Unbelief of Christians," in this collection).

of unity which it asserts among the men who cooperate. Their bond of unity is certainly not simply a community of political ideals or economic interests. At the other extreme, it is not a bond of ecclesiastical unity, such as binds together the members of the same church. Nor again is it simply a bond of civic unity, like the civic virtue of patriotism, which binds together Catholic, Protestant, and Jewish Boy Scouts, or soldiers in the armed forces. On the contrary, this bond of unity is unique, because of the uniqueness of the objective set before the cooperative effort—the establishment of spiritual order, based on belief in God and the moral law, in the sphere of earthly civilization. To accomplish this task men come together into a unity constituted on the basis of certain religious and moral principles (and therefore into a spiritual unity), but constituted for the purpose of a common effort in the temporal order (and therefore into a civic unity). Because the unity is civic, it leaves intact the uniqueness of the Church as the Body of Christ and the sole ark of eternal salvation; cooperation does not create any interdenominational unity among "religions." And because the unity is not only civic but spiritual, it forms an effective principle for "a new ordering of private and public life, rooted in the divine law" (n. 1736).

On this latter point the Pope insists. The basic principles for the remedy of the world's present social miseries can, he says, "be followed in their entirety and bear their fullest fruits only when statesmen and people, employers and employees are animated by faith in a personal God, the Legislator and Judge to whom they must one day give an account of their actions" (n. 1763). Sheerly humanitarian sentiment is not enough. The Pope has directed an "appeal to all" for a "fuller religious consciousness" (n. 1767), in the conviction that the "impulse and the pattern for a renewal of society must come from a general movement back to the altars from which innumerable generations of our faithful ancestors received the moral power to master their life's task; back to faith in God, in the light of which each individual and each community find their proper measure of right and duty, back to the wise and unshakable norms of a social order which, in affairs of national as well as international import, erect an efficacious barrier against the abuse of liberty and the misuse of power" (n. 1752).

An immediate fruit of this movement toward "a fuller religious consciousness" will be the rediscovery by all men of their own essential spiritual unity as human persons, moral and responsible agents, all under the sovereignty of God. Only on such a widely operative sense of human unity can the peace of the world be securely built.

THE FORM FOR THE PATTERN OF PEACE

In spite of its brevity, the foregoing analysis of the papal idea of cooperation in charity among all men of good will to do the work of justice which is peace should illustrate the fact that the Catholic participation in the issuance of the Pattern for Peace may legitimately claim a place in the total Catholic program. At this point, however, a comment is needed on the precise form of the cooperation implied in its issuance.

The Pattern for Peace was not issued as a joint statement in the strict sense of the term. Rather, it was conceived as an identical statement issued simultaneously by Protestant, Catholic, and Jewish leaders, with three distinct preambles, which introduced it respectively to the three audiences, and which expressed for each its motive and meaning. At the same time, the document was released to the whole nation and to all the world, with the full power of an impressive agreement. The Pattern for Peace was, as it were, a perfectly synchronized three-front-attack against all secularist thinking on the problems of peace.

This formula for the issuance of the Pattern proved satisfactory to all the signatories. And here an important point must be made. By its supreme authority, the Holy See has established for Catholics the legitimacy and necessity of cooperation in charity with all men of good will towards a just peace. It has not, however, determined the precise form that this cooperation should take in particular regions. In a sense, this is a distinct, because more concrete, problem.[9] And on the Catholic side its solution is left to the judgment of the bishops. In all this matter one must have in mind St. Paul's distinction (I Cor. 10:23) between the "lawful" and the "expedient" (or, as he explains, that which "edifies"). The lawfulness of the cooperation with which we are concerned has been established, as we have seen, by the

---

9. EDITOR NOTE: For Murray's spirited debate with Catholic University's Paul Furfey over the form that cooperation should take, see: 1943b: "Current Theology: Intercredal Co-operation: Its Theory and Its Organization"; 1943e: "To the Editor"; and 1945f: "On the Problem of Co-operation: Some Clarifications: Reply to Father P. H. Furfey."

authority of the Holy See; and it is explained by a simple analysis of the papal recommendations—their principles and purposes, the whole idea and concern behind them. But the expediency of this cooperation—or better, its edifying value, its constructive usefulness for the life of the Church and all humanity—depends also on other factors, notably on a prudent judgment as to the workability and the probable effects of cooperation as initiated in some concrete form in some particular set of circumstances. Questions of pastoral prudence therefore enter; and on such questions Catholic must look to the judgment of the bishops, who are invested with pastoral authority.

On their part, the bishops are guided by a twofold concern. First, there is a necessary concern for the unity of the Church and the integrity of her faith. Whenever the problem of cooperation with men of other religious beliefs comes up, consideration must be given to the possible danger of thereby fostering an indifferentist view of religion. Perhaps significantly, Pius XII has not called attention to this danger when urging the united action of religious men towards a "new order founded on moral principles." Nevertheless, our American scene has its own religious peculiarities. And the general principle of St. Paul is valid—that what is done with a clear conscience by the strong and well instructed may be "a stumbling block to the weak" (I Cor. 8:9). It is, therefore unfortunately necessary at times to be weak for the sake of the weak (ibid., 9:22), and to hold back from bold and decisive action up to the full limits of the law. In our case, the real problem is whether the bishops can stimulate their priest to explain the Catholic idea of cooperation so fully that all reasonable fear of scandal or misunderstanding will be eliminated. We say, all reasonable fear; for there will always be people of limited intelligence who misunderstand, and of unbalanced enthusiasm who exaggerate.

The second guiding principle for decisions in this matter will be equally necessary Catholic concern for the common good of humanity, even in its temporal life. This concern is imposed upon us by our love of Christ, who came to save, not only individual souls, but the whole order of human society.[10] This concern for civilization is itself

---

10. Editor Note: Lest one get the impression that Murray nurtured some mitigated form of millenialism, it would be helpful to check 1948g: "The Roman Catholic Church" where Murray claimed Roman Catholic interest in the social arena primarily in terms of its effects on the salvation of souls.

an obligatory act of the virtue of charity. And at the present moment it is tremendously active in the heart of the Church; innumerable utterances of the Holy See have endeavored to wake it in the hearts of all the faithful.

Consequently, there must be a judgment on the necessity of certain types of cooperation among all men of good will, if society is to be so "pervaded and sanctioned by religious thought" that the common good of the earthly city may be effectively insured. Serious attention must be given to the question whether grave damage may not accrue to the life of humanity, if we stand aside from the efforts of other religious men in the direction of world peace, even under pretext of pursuing our own more complete program. Finally, it must be honestly considered whether religious forces will be actually effective in shaping the world of tomorrow, if they are not somehow united in their action.

We may suppose that, in consequence of a balanced consideration of all these values, and others, the peculiar formula for issuing the Pattern for Peace received episcopal approval. It was likewise acceptable to Protestant and Jewish leaders; in all this matter, we shall do well to remember that difficulties over cooperation are not felt just on one side; and it is important, too, to realize that the exigencies of the Catholic conscience, to which we must be strictly obedient, can at times impose no small demands on the charitable patience of those who do not share our faith. For the sake of giving tribute where tribute is due, it should be said that in the discussions over the Pattern the necessary concerns of the Catholic conscience met with generous respect.

While on the subject, we may recall the breadth of episcopal approval given to the Pattern. In the statement released to the press on November 13, 1943, by the Administrative Board of the National Catholic Welfare Conference at the direction of the Archbishops and Bishops who attended the annual meeting of the hierarchy, this was said: "It is heartening to note the wide agreement on the moral postulates of the just peace among religious leaders otherwise divided by the deep cleavage of fundamental doctrinal differences. This significant and hopeful agreement has recently been evidenced in the three parallel statements on world peace issued by American religious groups. This pattern for peace fashioned on the moral law has attracted nationwide attention, and will, we hope, be carefully studied by all men of good will." Here, too, we may recall the clear-cut statement made in the Detroit Cathedral on March 13, 1944, by Archbishop Mooney,[11] Chairman of the Administrative Board of the N.C.W.C: "Last October, men of authority in widely differing American religious groups with impressive accord gave wide publicity to a pattern for peace which in its every line is in fundamental agreement with the ideas and ideals of the Pope. I commend this statement for study and discussion in our schools and colleges, in meetings of our Catholic societies, and in every forum through which public opinion may be enlightened."

THE PATTERN AND THE PUBLIC CONSCIENCE

In the last phrase, Archbishop Mooney signalized the peculiar value of the Pattern for Peace—it is an instrument for the enlightenment and formation of public opinion on the peace. In this connection, an insistent theme in the thought of Pius XII must be recalled. The Pope has repeatedly emphasized—what other religious leaders have likewise emphasized—that the primary source of modern social disorder has been the decay of moral conscience on the part of those who govern, and a similar decay on the part of those who are governed. Significantly, his fatherly indictment has been almost universal; he has not succumbed to the easy fallacy of many of our Catholic publicists, who seem to concentrate exclusively on the faults of "those without"; "A great part of mankind, and—let us not shrink from saying it—not a few of those who call themselves Christians, have to some extent their share in the collective responsibility for the growth of error and for the evil and lack of moral fibre in the society of today" (n. 1859). In his latest Christmas Allocution, on December 24, 1943, he reverted to, and pointedly developed, the same theme. His conclusion has always been the same: the first step towards a new order must be penance, a

---

11. EDITOR NOTE: Archbishop Mooney, at about this time, encouraged Murray to address the question of religious freedom, since the Catholic position on the First Amendment was a stumbling block to cooperation in social reconstruction. Murray's response to Mooney's request was a long memo that dealt with the problem in three parts (1945e). Only the first part of his argument reached final form and publication (1945b). Murray then abandoned this line of delineating and defending the Catholic position of religious liberty.

change of heart, expiation, and prayer: "supplications must be raised to heaven that a new spirit may take root and develop in all peoples, and especially in those whose greater power gives them wider influence and imposes on them additional responsibility" (n. 1655).

It is important to note the Pope's preoccupation with this latter class. More than once he has dwelt upon the fact that in the organization of peace, "there will be required broad intellects and wills strong in their purposes, men of courage and enterprise; but above all there must be men of conscience, who in their plans, deliberations, and actions are animated by a lively sense of responsibility, and who do not shrink from submission to the holy laws of God" (n. 1753). To the interior action of prayer and penance there must be added a persuasively educative action on the leaders of nations; their ideas of human society must be formed, and their moral purposes shaped and strengthened, in order that their leadership of others may indeed be towards "a new edifice of fraternal solidarity among the nations of the world."

The Pope has seen too much of the world not to realize the decisive social influence still wielded by the ideas of the relative minority which is "on top"; "security, reorganization, progressive improvement cannot be expected and cannot be brought about save by the return of large and influential groups to correct notions about society. . . . From these influential circles, which are more capable of penetrating and appreciating the beauty of just social norms, there will pass on and infiltrate into the masses the clear knowledge of the true, divine, spiritual origin of social life" (n. 1829).

Nevertheless, the Pope has an equally exact appreciation of an important feature of the democratic idea—the power of public opinion. Consequently, to an educative action upon men with power and responsibility—one thinks of men not only in government, but in universities, in industry, in trade unions, in the newspaper, radio, and publishing business, etc.—there must be added an even more important effort to reach and reform public opinion throughout its strata. More than once the Pope has indicated his conviction that the peace will be stable and lasting to the extent that it is a people's peace. It is consequently necessary that the people should have impressed upon them the fact that peace, "in its ultimate and deepest significance, is a moral and juridical act" (Christmas Allocution, 1943). The moral and juridical sense of the people—their reverence for the law of God and for the rights of men and nations—must be developed, and made articulate. It must become literally a structural element of public opinion. The people's concept of justice, and their cry for it, must exert a pressure from below upon the leaders upon whom they depend for the creation of the machinery for justice. And this pressure must be exerted from every possible direction, from the university seminar down to the last cracker-barrel forum in the smallest village. On this point the thought of Pius XII is explicit: "Such a new order, which all peoples desire to see brought into being after the trials and ruins of this war, must be founded on that immovable rock, the moral law . . . that moral law whose observance must be inculcated and fostered by the public opinion of all nations and all States with such a unanimity of voice and energy that no one may dare to doubt it" (n. 1757).

At this point, we may reflect upon ourselves. It would be idle to maintain that public opinion is unanimous, organized, and energetically articulate on the relevance of the moral law to world peace. We ourselves surely come under the indictment levelled by the paternal authority of the Pope against countries afflicted with "religious anaemia," which are in too great a part living in a "moral vacuum, which no artificial substitute for religion [shall we interject, for example, 'Democracy'?], no national myth [for us, 'the American Century'?]. and no international myth ['The Century of the Common Man'?] is able to fill" (n. 1747). It is unfortunately too true that large sections of our people are among those "whose ideas of social life have been impregnated with a purely mechanico-materialistic character" (n. 1748).[12]

There is, therefore, an immense work to be done toward the education of the public conscience in the United States. Moreover, it is an eleventh-hour task. And in the practical order, an extremely pertinent question faces us: Are we Catholics actually in a position by ourselves to sensitize the public conscience to the views of our Holy Father—which are fundamentally the views of all right-thinking men of good will—with regard to the postulates of a just world order? Shall we singlehandedly be able to reeducate the public conscience, and make it utter genuinely moral demands with such a unanimity of voice and energy that no one will dare to stand against these demands?

It is rather obvious that such a feat is quite beyond our present powers. In fact, it would seem that we have not yet been able to draw considerable sections of our Catholic citizens away from several con-

---

12. EDITOR NOTE: See "The Return to Tribalism" (1961b) in Part II of this collection for parallels in Murray's own arguments.

ceptions fundamentally opposed to our own high Catholic thought—
away, for instance, from adherence to outworn concepts of unlimited
sovereignty, national isolationism, economic individualism, interracial prejudice. It was dismaying to note that as late as the fall of 1943
the Denver National Opinion Research Center found that more Protestants than Catholics believed that peace action is a legitimate function
of the Church. This, in spite of the fact that it was in a broadcast to the
United States that Pius XII stated unequivocally that "the peace of the
world is also a missionary aim of the Church "(n. 1604).

Here the great practical value of the Pattern for Peace emerges
into view. We have to recognize, as sheer matter of fact, that large sections of public opinion were not reached by the Christmas Allocutions of Pius XII. But they can be reached by the Pattern. As
Archbishop Mooney said in the sermon already referred to, "its every
line is in fundamental agreement with the ideas and ideals of the
Pope." And through it they will come in contact with at least the fundamental lines of Catholic thought on the new order. This thought
was framed for all men of good will. Consequently, by lending their
authority to the Pattern, the Bishops of the National Catholic Welfare
Conference took a significant step towards the achievement of one of
the major objectives of the papal peace program—the reawakening of
the public conscience to the demands in the social order of the sovereignty of God, the moral law, the dignity of man, and the unity of the
human family.

THE IMPACT OF THE PATTERN

All these experiments[13] have shown the possibility of organized effort
at arousing the sentiment of whole communities in support of a peace
founded on moral ideals. In each case, the organizational formula was
acceptable to Catholics, since it was kept entirely clear that the focus
of the gatherings was on goals in the temporal order for whose
achievement all men of good will have a common responsibility. The
end in view was cooperation in charity to do the work of justice
which is peace, national and international. Obviously, any organiza-

---

13. EDITOR NOTE: I have edited out an extended exposition of uses
made by the Pattern by the popular press and local groups in shaping their
own cooperative efforts.

tional formula for such common or parallel effort will have to be made to suit the particular exigencies of a local situation. The point is that we now have evidence to show that such formulas can be worked out, and that results are of no small value.

CATHOLICS AND THE PATTERN

Of late, Catholics have become increasingly aware that they have the duty of affording leadership—an active support of the Pope's own leadership—towards the solution of religio-social issues in the present world crisis. Moreover, they are beginning to see that this leadership has a twofold aspect. First, there is the effort intelligently to explain the integral Catholic program, and vigorously to work for its realization. Secondly, there is the will to take the initiative in cooperative efforts, or at least take part wholeheartedly in joint initiatives, according to formulas approved by their bishops, towards making religious and moral principles operative in the social order. The fact is beginning to emerge that both forms of leadership have their sanction in the works and deeds of the Holy See. And it is being seen that complete loyalty to the full content of our own program does not entail, as its counterpart and consequence, a standing aside from the immense work for peace and justice that is being inspired by fundamentally Christian principles in other religious groups.

The presence of the Pattern for Peace on the American scene puts to us the serious question: Under whose leadership will these seven principles be transformed into vital, dynamic forces that will inspire all American thinking on the problems of world order—the thinking of our statesmen and of our common people? In the concrete world of affairs, leadership belongs to those who exercise it. In the practical order, it is of little avail to assert leadership as a matter of right, if one is not prepared to assume it as a matter of fact. No one, of course, will doubt the necessity of impressing on the Catholic conscience its duty and responsibility to give leadership. But it would be unfortunate to see develop, as a consequence of this necessary educative effort, a situation in which we would fall between two stools—on the one hand, a reluctance to co-operate with sound initiatives from without, and, on the other hand, an unwillingness or inability to offer any initiatives of our own. Such a result would be sterile. The dilemma might be avoided by one means—a large-hearted, as well as prudent, appreciation of the full demands of Christian charity in the present crisis, which concretely would mean a willingness to co-operate in joint initiatives in behalf of the Pattern.

THE DEMANDS OF CHARITY

In all this matter, it is ultimately to the demands of charity that we must continually return. The Pattern for Peace was itself an act of charity—an expression of vital and operative concern for the needs of suffering mankind. It must not, therefore, be allowed to fail of the proper finality of all charity—the kindling of a still warmer flame. Surely we Catholics should be smitten by a more profoundly compassionate concern for mankind, into whose very soul a sea of sorrow has come, when we see in the common phrases of the Pattern how deep this compassion is in the hearts of our Protestant and Jewish brethren. As our Holy Father has pointed out, only this compassionate charity, mutually felt, can avail to bridge the gap—otherwise so distressingly real, and, at the moment, the same faith with us. Moreover, only this compassionate charity can supply the dynamic for action as well on distinctively Catholic lines as on the co-operative lines suggested by the Pattern.

We must, in a word, ruthlessly subject ourselves to experience the piercing effects of which speak out in almost every line of Pius XII's utterances—an experience, wholly Christlike, of intimate self-identification with all the woe that war has brought upon the race of men, members of Christ and our brothers. Only out of such an experience will be born the spiritual energy for the immense peace-making effort—thought, love, and action—that is demanded of us. Initially, such an experience would compel us to reject, as intolerably self-complacent, any notion that our efforts have been at all adequate either to the desperateness of the situation or to the urgency of the Pope's pleas for action. "The call of the moment," he said in his 1942 Christmas Allocution, "is for action—not for lamentation over what has been, but for reconstruction of what is to arise, and what must arise, for the good of society" (n. 1842). Our lamentations have been probably satisfactory, in volume and pitch. Not so our action. And what our Holy Father wants is action. In his cry for it he voices both the anguish of humanity and his own profound sense of the moment's critical urgency. Again in his 1943 Christmas Allocution this favorite thought appeared: "There has perhaps never in the history of mankind been a time so capable as the present of great and beneficial progress no less than of fatal defects and errors." And his conclusion is always the same: action—united courageous action: "To action, then! To work, beloved children! Close your ranks! Let not your courage fail you. Do not remain inactive in the midst of ruins, but come into the open to build a new world for Christ" (ibid.).

This is not a rhetorical flight, but a considered command. And the lines of action have been made entirely clear: first, there is the cooperation of Catholics with one another, in the full unity of faith and love, towards the peace of Christ in the reign of Christ; and, supporting it, there is the cooperation of Catholics with all men of good will, in the unity of a common love of God and man, towards the reign of justice in a world at peace.

The Juridical Organization of the International Community

JOHN COURTNEY MURRAY, S.J.

As the Temples of Justice reopen throughout the land, the cosmic struggle to achieve the work of justice that is peace is entering more deeply into a new phase. The military victory of our arms is now assured; now we are growing increasingly concerned with the juridical victory that must crown the triumph of our arms. History has taught us that peace does not lie sheerly in the triumph of force, but in the permanent, ever renewed triumph of law over force. And this triumph is won only by the superior energies of the human spirit, by high political intelligence operating under the guidance of a profound moral sense. "In its ultimate and deepest significance," Pius XII has said, "peace is a moral and juridical process."

One encouraging evidence that this truth is beginning to be grasped lies in the mounting conviction that the peace of the world will not be assured unless the community of nations is somehow juridically organized. I wish to speak this morning in support of this conviction.

Let me first communicate to you one of my own anxieties on the subject. In his address at the opening of the Dumbarton Oaks conference, our Secretary of State said: "No institution . . . will endure unless there is behind it considered and complete popular support." He was absolutely right; in fact, he stated an idea that is pivotal in the program of Pius XII. Its undeniable truth gives birth to my anxiety. American public opinion, in common with great reaches of public opinion throughout the world, does seem to have marshalled itself

---

A sermon given at a Red Mass (a yearly liturgy for Catholic lawyers) in New York City. Originally published as "The Juridical Organization of the International Community," *The New York Law Journal* (October 9, 1944): 813–14. Also published as "World Order and Moral Law," *Thought* 19 (December 1944).

behind the idea of a general international organization, and is prepared now to promote and support it. The view is widely accepted
that America must not go back to the pacifist isolationism of the
decades following the First World War, nor go on to the imperialist
isolationism that may present itself as her future temptation. This fact
is most heartening; there is a promise of peace in it. But it leaves room
for some misgivings. For the question rises: Have we, as a people,
grasped the true nature of the necessity for the juridical organization
of the international community? What are the bases of the present
public opinion? What is the power behind it? What shocks can it
endure? What is its promise of permanence? Is it a thing of the surface, a mood of the moment, a sentiment born of the emotional shock
of total war? Or is it a settled conviction, whose roots are sunk in the
solid conclusions of political intelligence and moral science? These
are the questions we must anxiously ask.

For my part, I am convinced that there is little hope for a general
international organization, and consequently little hope of lasting
peace, unless we, as a people, with the peoples of the world, firmly
grasp that the juridical organization of the international community is
an unescapable demand of social justice, a true and genuine moral
imperative, laid upon the collective conscience of states and peoples
by the moral law, and sanctioned by the sovereignty of God. The reason is plain; no other motive than a moral imperative has the abiding
and compelling power to support statesmen and peoples in their
gigantic task of organizing a peaceful world.

Let us make no mistake about it. What the nations today are
undertaking is a new beginning, which will end no man knows
where. The creation of juridical institutions that will guarantee an
order of justice and peace is a long, long task that will meet with
many setbacks. In its prosecution there will be mistakes, deceptions,
discouragements. Hostility to the very idea will break out in willful
men and selfish nations. At times, no doubt, the goal itself will almost
vanish from our view. Consequently, our common purpose to organize an international order of justice must be founded on a motive
that will remain compelling under every change in national mood
and world circumstance, that will not crumble in hours of thwarting
and disillusionment, that will be as valid in one nation as in another,
and that will be as operative in future generations as in our own.

We shall find this indestructible, ever-urgent motive only in the
unchangeable moral law, written in the collective conscience of

mankind, and dictating to it its permanent obligation to further, by means of international organization, the moral and juridical process that is peace.

For my part, I do not feel assured that present sentiment for a general international organization is based on a sense of moral obligation. Hence, my anxiety is lest it falter and fade. If it fades, the counsels of statesmen will have lost their surest guide and support, and the world will have lost its hopes of peace.

If you share my conviction and anxiety, you will be prepared to accept the suggestion I make this morning. The suggestion is that you and I have a responsibility for the enlightenment of the public conscience concerning this critical moral issue. We have, therefore, a duty to see the issue clearly ourselves.

As a help to a clear vision of the issue, I must take up one preliminary question. On what manner of international organization does this moral imperative fall? First, it does not fall on the creation of what is called a "world-state," a supernational government under which national sovereignties would be more or less destroyed. Apart from the fact that this political conception is unrealizable, now or ever, it has no basis as far as I can see, in Catholic political and moral science. Basically, it looks to me like the projection on the international plane of the individualistic liberal illusion that has contributed to the wreck of national society itself.

On the national plane, this illusion denies that there are any institutions that mediate between the isolated individual and the state. In its extreme form, this illusion is found in the famous Chapelier law (1791) of the First French Republic, which insisted that politics takes account of only two goods, the private good of the individual and the public good of the state, and which consequently denied to French citizens the right to prosecute by institutional, organized action the intermediate special goods of particular groups, such as the church, the professions, the laboring class, etc. On the international plane, the same illusion would have no really sovereign political institutions mediating between the individual—the world-citizen—and the world-state. It asserts that each of us is directly and primarily a member of humanity, before being a member of a racial or national group.

In both its forms this theory stands in opposition to the Catholic doctrine of the organic state, which maintains the natural necessity for a corporative organization of society, based on the principle that there is a natural sociability among the members of particular groups within a state and among the member of a national community. This natural sociability is based on certain common aspirations, interests and needs; and it creates the right to pursue by organized action the ends that are of value to the group. Catholic doctrine, therefore, would maintain that national states, with their proper sovereignty, are natural political units; they exist by natural necessity and right, and they may not be merged into a community of world citizens under some supranational government.

On the other hand, the moral imperative of which I speak will not be content with the establishment merely of what is called "continuous international conference." Catholic political and moral realism regards this minimalist conception of international organization as falling short of the demands of human nature. A continuous international conference, its advocates say, would create an atmosphere favorable to peaceful relationships among the nations, and would serve as an instrument of friendly cooperation. Perhaps it would do these things. They are very valuable and necessary things. But they are not all that must be done. We must create among the nations an atmosphere of peace, a disposition to collaborate. But, following the imperatives of our social nature, we have above all to create an international juridical order. Men are not effectively kept at peace by atmosphere, but by law, and by forces operating under law. Men and nations do not collaborate unless there is a compelling necessity for them to do so. When the compulsion of war is passed, another kind of compulsion will be needed—the juridical compulsion of an international organization. Writing about the Federal Council of Churches' fourth Pillar of Peace, President Dodds of Princeton said: "It is through social and political institutions that ideas are made to march. Unless the idea of international collaboration is embodied in political institutions, it will remain a pious platitude." With Pius XII, I should prefer the term "juridical" institutions; but at any rate, the statement is most true.

I believe, therefore, that our moral imperative falls on a mode of international organization that stands somewhere between the minimalist continuous international conference and the maximalist world-state.

It demands that the international community be organized in terms of its natural political units (the sovereign states); and it demands that the international community be *truly organized*, that is, juridically organized. Its essential demand is for juridical institutions in the international field that will control, not destroy, national sovereignties. Demanding these institutions, it demands that there should exist in the international scene a coercive power adequate to protect the juridical order and to vindicate it in case of violence—a coercive power that would be at the service of an international institution, to be employed in the interests of the common good.

I do not think that the moral law itself makes more than these two demands concerning international security. It is for political intelligence, guided by moral law, further to determine the form of these juridical institutions, and the exact manner in which the sword is to be put at their disposal. Nevertheless, in making these two demands, the moral law takes us very far along our way—much farther than many men of inferior vision and excessive timidity (which they may prefer to call political realism) are willing to go.

These demands lead, for instance, to the conclusion that a limit must be placed on one right of which sovereign national states have always been exceedingly jealous—the right to arm without limit, and to regard the determination of their national rights, and the armed defense of these rights, as exclusively a national affair. On the contrary, the moral and juridical process that is peace must be made to evolve to the point where national states can trust themselves to the international protection of their rights, just as the citizen now trusts himself to the protection of the organs of the state.

Recall the frontier days in America, when each citizen carried the law on his hip, in the form of a six-shooter. We look on those days as uncivilized; for civilization means the juridical organization of community life, which outlaws six-shooters on every man's hip, because the defense of the individual's rights and liberties has become a collective and organized defense under juridical guarantees. Today each nation claims the right to carry the law on its hip, in the form of armaments whose size and quality it presumes to determine for itself. But this is an uncivilized state of affairs, that must give way under the progressively more perfect organization of the international community. Civilized international life demands that the community itself should guarantee the rights of its members, and itself apply coercive measures in case of their violation.

I am not, of course, suggesting that national states should be stripped of all their armaments, in exactly the same way as individuals were once deprived of their six-shooters. There is an analogy here, because the national state within the international community retains a sovereign right to be armed, which it would be absurd to attribute to the individual within the national state. But I am suggesting that within the framework of a new order based on moral principles and made secure by juridical institutions restrictions must be placed on the present arbitrary sovereignty of the state in the whole matter of armaments and national defense.

One disastrous temptation must be removed from every nation— the temptation to think that it may carry an immense six-shooter on its hip, arbitrarily declare itself to be the law, and enforce in its own case whatever it thinks to be justice. We have had evidence enough to know how real this temptation is and how tragic for humanity are the consequences of yielding to it.

The international community, therefore, through the organized action of its members, must move on to a state of civilization in which, in Benedict XV's words, the material force of arms will be replaced by the moral force of right as the primary means for the defense of national rights, and in which the secondary means of such defense—armed force—will be employed only at the instance of an international institution and under its control.

The great jurist, Guido Gonella, has said that the limitation of armaments and its correlative problem, the use of armed force in national defense, "is the problem of the future, the touchstone of the political and moral maturity of the community of peoples." Its solution is obviously bound up with the solution of the problem of international security through juridical institutions that will act to forestall and settle disagreements by means other than force, or if these means fail, by themselves employing force under law. And pressing for the solution of both these related problems is a moral imperative laid upon the collective conscience of mankind.

So much, therefore, for the object of our moral imperative. Before going farther, let me introduce an important distinction. In all this matter, there are two questions involved. First, ought international juridical institutions be established? Secondly, will they work? Much depends on which of these two questions receives prior discussion. I should insist on putting the first question first; for it is by right the first question. If there is a categorical moral imperative for the establishment of these institutions, it follows that they must be established, and they must be made to work. It follows further that they can be made to work, if only men have the common will to make them work. This is my full case.

Let us now look more closely at this moral imperative itself: does it exist? What are the reasons for it? For the sheer fact of its existence, we have the consensus of the highest and the best moral authority. The idea that the community of nations can and should be juridically organized is a part of the best Catholic political and moral thought, however slow many Catholics have been in realizing the fact. The moral authority of Pope Benedict XV was set squarely behind the idea, in the Encyclical *Pacem Munus Dei,* issued in 1920, at the critical moment of the life of the League of Nations.

The principles of Pius XI on social justice, though formulated chiefly on the national plane, clearly dictate the idea. And Pius XII, often and categorically, has called for international juridical institutions, most recently in his radio address on September 1, on the fifth anniversary of the war. Implicit and explicit in the statements of the Holy See is the idea that the juridical organization of international life is not simply a political expedient but a necessary thing deriving from the moral law. The Christian principles held by Protestant bodies have led them to the same conclusions. The Oxford Conference in 1937, the Federal Council of Churches through its Commission to Study the Bases of a Just and Desirable Peace, the Council of Bishops of the Methodist Church, the General Assembly of the Presbyterian Church, the various unions of Congregationalists—all these organs of Protestant moral opinion have emphasized the idea. Like emphasis had been laid on it by the official utterances of the Synagogue Council of America, the Central Conference of American Rabbis, the Rabbinical Assembly of America, and other Jewish organizations. Finally, last October, Catholic, Protestant and Jewish leaders joined in issuing the seven-point Pattern for Peace, whose fifth point sets down, as one postulate of the moral conscience of mankind in the matter of peace, "the organization of international institutions" with judicial functions. There is no doubt that the best moral thought of America and of the world is solidly behind the idea.

Nor is it too difficult to show that this high moral thought rests on solid reasons. The basic argument may be simply stated. The international community has historically emerged as a natural society (a society that exists by the law of man's social nature), with its own proper good. The law of nature therefore demands that this society be organized in a properly human way for the prosecution of its common good. This properly human mode of social organization is juridical organization—a rational system for the control of possibly conflicting freedom through juridical institutions. Upon the free will of men and nations, therefore, devolves an obligation from natural moral law to establish such institutions. Let me now evolve this argument, at least in skeleton fashion.

We start from an empirical fact that has been remarked repeatedly of late—the fact of international solidarity. It is surely a fact that today the nations live in a state of most intimate association and organic interdependence. Their distinct lives are woven into one texture that may not be torn at any part without the whole texture being torn. The good of one is the good of all; and the good of all rebounds to the good of each. This is particularly true in the economic sphere; it is recognized today that any attempt at an autarchic national economic system would not only be suicidal but murderous. It is no less true in the political sphere: Hitler has proved that no foreign policy can be pursued uniquely in the national interest without embroiling the whole world in conflict.

Secondly, we have to ask ourselves, how did this fact of international association and solidarity come into being? Here two answers are possible. One may say, first, that international association has come about purely and solely because the nations have freely decided to associate. This is the individualistic theory of contractualism.

Its first premise is that the individual states are absolutely prior to international society. Simply by their own free wills they determined to create international society and to bind themselves to membership in it for as long as they like. Freely they pledge their cooperation to one another, in whatever measure and for whatever time they choose. Their association is purely voluntary, unconditioned save by their own contracting wills, on which no limits may be placed save those that the contracting parties choose to assume. International society, therefore, is simply the result of a multilateral contract, over whose genesis, modification or dissolution the wills of the individual states are absolutely sovereign.[1]

---

1. EDITOR NOTE: This location of the source of the political order in arbitrary contractualism or will (often based on self-interest) was a standard target of Roman Catholic criticisms of the (Anglo-American) West. Murray appealed to such a criticism in 1940, there finding contractualism's source in Puritanism (see pp. 111 and 103–5). By 1946 he sharply distinguished between American and French contractualism (see 1946a), and by 1950 he found an unrecognized communitarian base behind even Lockean political theory (see *WHTT*, 302–20).

This contractualist theory, therefore, regards international life simply as a mass of contractual relations (treaties, agreements, etc.), each of which is separately regulated by the interested parties in a manner suitable to their own sovereign choice. They are juridical relations, of course, but they are governed solely by the norms of commutative or contractual justice, and they stand under no higher control or supervision. Consistently, the advocates of this theory regard international law as having a purely statutory character; it is a purely voluntary law, in whose determination the sovereign wills of states are the sole agents; it exists solely because they have agreed it should exist, and it exists subject to no conditioning from other sources than their own sovereign wills.

Such is the contractualist theory. It is right inasmuch as it says that international association has been developed, and must always be developed, by the free action of men and nations within the process of history. It is also right inasmuch as it says that contractual agreements have had, and must always have, a place within the international juridical order. But it is shallow and false inasmuch as it attempts to found international society and the international juridical order ultimately and solely on acts of the free national will. As a matter of sheer fact, they are founded on an unescapable natural necessity that exists antecedently to any free choice, and that morally binds that free choice.

Take an analogy. Properly speaking, brothers and sisters do not create the system of relationships that we call brotherhood and sisterhood. The system itself is natural, an institution of nature. Once within it, boys and girls may freely choose to act as brothers and sisters, but when they do so they merely acknowledge a duty to be what they are by nature. Nor is it entirely up to them to decide just how they are to act as brother and sister; there are certain brotherly and sisterly ways of acting that are determined by nature itself. For the family is a natural institution; hence there is an order of piety—a whole system of filial obligations—inherent in its structure.

The analogy is not perfect, but it has a point. The point is that international society is also, though analogously, a natural institution. Properly speaking, nations did not create the dynamic system of relationships that is the international community solely by sovereign acts of their national wills. This community has gradually come into being by a natural process, by the operation of a law resident in the very

being of national states and manifested by the historic development
of their organic interdependence. I mean the natural law of human
sociability,[2] which expresses itself as well on the international plane
as on the domestic and national planes.

Nations were sociable before they decided to associate. They are
by nature brothers and sisters, members of a family, dependent on
one another, destined to help one another. They may refuse the obligations of family life, the obligations of mutual respect and mutual assistance; but they do not cease to be a family; they only become an
unhappy family. They may freely will to cooperate, but when they do
so, it is by a will to perform a duty—a duty to themselves and to their
welfare, which cannot be secured without cooperation; a duty to the
family itself as a whole and to its common good. For the family exists
by right of nature; it has a common good, and it can claim the cooperation of its members toward this common good.

This is what I imply in saying that international society is a natural society. Two important conclusions must be noted. First, it is not
entirely up to the individual nations to decide by arbitrary act of their
sovereign wills just how, or how far, or for how long they will cooperate. The ultimate norm of their cooperation is already fixed. It is not
the self-interest of the individual nations, but the common good of the
family of nations, the preservation of the order of justice on which the
family of nations, as a natural institution, is built. Think again of
domestic society, in which the ultimate norm of cooperation among
brothers and sisters is the preservation, at whatever cost to personal
pride and convenience, of the order of piety on which the family is
built. The second conclusion is that it is not entirely up to the individual nations, simply by a manifestation and agreement of their sovereign wills, to determine the whole fundamental law that will give
existence to the international community. On the contrary, the law of
nature itself gives existence to the international community, and it is
for the community as such, by its social will, acting through legitimate institutions, to give expression and clarification and effect to the

2. Editor Note: For a 1950 exposition of Murray's natural law theory,
see "The Natural Law" (1950a), which became, with little editing, the concluding chapter, "The Doctrine Lives: The Eternal Return of the Natural Law," of
WHTT, 295–336.

natural law of nations by its enactment in positive statutes, or, in other words, to develop the *ius gentium* into a body of positive international law.

So much for the premise of our argument—that international society is an institution of nature itself—and for two of the immediate conclusions from it. From this ground, we can see what is the primary act of national freedom, the initial exercise of national sovereignty, in relation to the international community. It is the free acceptance of the obligation to make the family of nations a good family. The first question put to free national wills is not whether to have an international society or not to have it. That question has been already settled by nature itself; international society is a social fact. The nations have the power to make it good or bad; but they also have the obligation to make it good.

The sole questions that remain are, when is international society good, and how shall it be made good?

The answer is that international society will be good when the order of justice inherent in its very constitution is secure, and when this security is achieved by means consonant with the freedom and dignity of man. Order and security, humanly achieved—this is the common good of the family of nations. Concretely, this means security through juridical institutions that will guarantee the protection of rights and the performance of duties—if necessary, under the sanction of the employment of coercive force. The only properly human means of directing, controlling and harmonizing a multitude of free human wills, in the interests of a common good, is a system of juridical control—the control of law, or at least of force employed under law. The law of our social human nature, therefore, demands the creation in the international community of such a human system of control. The juridical institutions that will exercise it are the object of a moral imperative.

I do not think it possible for anyone seriously to question the moral argument for juridical institutions as the means of international security. The objection raised is what is called a "practical" objection. These institutions, it is said, will not work.

To this I quickly give a practical answer: "Then no lasting peace is possible." And since this is the practical conclusion of the objection, I think that those so-called "practical" men who spread it abroad are doing a disservice to the cause of peace. They are shallow realists, prophets of despair. Because, if we despair of organizing an international order based on justice, we despair of the moral nature of man.[3]

There are only two ways to peace. The first is a system of power—power unified in one nation, or power balanced between nations; in either case, power set above international law, because consecrated to the interests of individual nations. This system certainly has not worked, nor will it. The second is a system of law—international law set above all national power, and employing the power of nations, not primarily in their defense, but in defense of itself and of the order over which it stands guard. This system has to be tried. If it won't work, then we must resign ourselves to the barbarism of a third World War.

But this alternative is not only humanly unthinkable, but also divinely forbidden. The conclusion is that this system of international law above all national power must be made to work. The only question left is, how shall it be made to work?

First, it shall be made to work if the system is organized as soon as possible. The decision on this general international organization must be made, and the framework set up, with the least possible delay. And anything and anybody who would cause delay must be pushed aside resolutely, in the name of the common good of the family of nations.[4]

---

3. EDITOR NOTE: Murray did later "despair of organizing an international order based on justice," at least in the sweeping form suggested here (see my discussion of East/West relations Part 3). He later, nonetheless, insisted that the U.S. could pursue an international policy consistent with the "dictates of reason," even in the face of a not fully effective international consensus or juridical organization.

4. EDITOR NOTE: In a 1955 critique of American Catholicism, Murray noted "[t]he hostility of many Catholics, and the indifference of many more, to the idea of an organized international community. More is involved than rational patient criticism of the institutions that presently embody the idea—the UN and its many agencies. Criticism of this kind is altogether proper. The puzzling thing is the opposition to the international idea itself." Murray cited this as one example of Catholic tendencies to deny Catholic responsibilities for the social order. He found the ideological grounding for this tendency in a misinterpretation of the Catholic claim that it is "the one true church" ("Special Catholic Challenges" [1955d, 198]).

Secondly, this system shall be made to work if we do not expect miracles from it, and hence lose our faith in it when they are not immediately forthcoming. Let us be clear about one thing. The peace that will follow the war will not be an ideally just peace. It probably will be riddled with injustices. That is why I insisted that our support of international juridical institutions must be founded on a sense of moral imperative.

We are not obligated to the impossible. And, as a sheer matter of fact, with national passions blazing as they do, and with our international ignorance what it is, an ideally just peace in the proximate future would be a miracle of divine grace that surely we have not deserved. But our moral imperative does extend to what is possible at the moment. Consequently, it extends, first, to the establishment, at least in provisional form, of juridical institutions that will embody and advance the moral and juridical process that is peace. This, I believe, is possible. Secondly, at every moment of the future, our moral imperative will oblige us to the persevering, intelligent effort to keep this machinery going, no matter how it creaks and groans, and to improve it in the light of experience. These things, too, are possible. Thirdly, our moral imperative will oblige us now and always not to give ear to unregenerate nationalists who will most surely, but most arbitrarily, claim to be the judges of the justice of the peace and who will oppose our support of a general international organization, because, they will say, it may fasten on the world an unjust peace. Our practical answer to them must be that there is no other way to redress the injustice that will undoubtedly occur, but our fundamental answer must be that we are morally obligated to this way.

Finally, international institutions will work steadily in the direction of a peace more and more just, if we—all of us—bear constantly in mind our own collective responsibility to make this work. Here is the critical point from which I started out and with which I conclude.

In the nature of things, there will never be in international society an authority as strong and as centralized as the authority that keeps order in the national state. International relations cannot be policed as thoroughly as the relations between individual citizens. In the nature of things, the processes of international life must be kept peaceful and orderly, not so much by minute regulation in terms of statutory law, as by the controlling power of the idea of justice itself.

Moreover, juridical institutions can only embody the idea of justice, and the origin of its processes. They can't create their own soul;

they cannot supply the vital energies needed for their own functioning. They depend for their very life upon the living moral energies in the soul of the international community. And the soul of the international community is the love of justice in the soul of its peoples. Only if this love of justice flames shall we have peace.

Moreover, this love of justice must not only flame inwardly, it must be made so articulate in public opinion that it will effectively sway the counsels of statesmen. Enduring peace cannot be founded in their often uncertain counsel, nor even on juridical institutions. Its sole foundation is the law, "whose observance, "Pius XII said, "must be inculcated and fostered by the public opinion of all national states with such a unanimity of youth and energy that no one may dare to doubt it." Enlightened public opinion sensitized to the demands of the law, and influencing political decisions—this is the keystone in the arch of peace. And the responsibility for holding firm under every strain is yours and mine.

Constitutional Law

While Murray attempted to defend American constitutionalism as a legitimate growth of Christian constitutionalism (against counterclaims within his own church), he was also engaged in an intra-American debate over historical and contemporary interpretations of the First Amendment. Here the firm wall separating church and state could, in secularist proclamations, sound like a product of Enlightenment laicism or, in Protestant calls, like outgrowths of Protestant ecclesiologies.

To my reading, Murray's constitutional argument took three distinct tacks that differed from one article to the next more in emphasis than in substance. First he argued that the founding fathers adopted the First Amendment for the sake of public peace. Here the primary drive behind the Amendment was a pragmatic attempt to preserve public order in a religiously divided society. As such, the Amendment was primarily a product of practical reasoning, not of theory, although grounded in a founding consensus that was compatible with Murray's notions of the externality of civil law and of the incompetence of the natural law state in religious matters. His early responses to the Supreme Court's *McCollum* and *Everson* decisions followed this emphasis. The following articles more or less pursue this line of argument:

- 1946e: "Separation of Church and State." *America* 76 (December 7, 1946): 261–63.
- 1947b: "Separation of Church and State: True and False Concepts." *America* 76 (February 15, 1947): 541–45.
- 1947c: "The Court Upholds Religious Freedom." *America* 76 (March 8, 1947): 628–30.
- 1948a: "Religious Liberty: The Concern of All." *America* 77 (February 7, 1948): 513–16.

Second, Murray's increasing concern with secularist and atheistic readings of America's present and past, and debates about the relative priority of the non-establishment and free exercise clauses of the First Amendment, led to his insistence that the Amendment was instituted with the clear, principled intent of protecting and encouraging diverse religious expression (now within a stronger notion of governmental incompetence in religious matters). At this point Murray also attempted to counter the reading of Protestant ecclesiologies back into the First Amendment. For this type of argument, see:

1948b: "Dr. Morrison and the First Amendment." *America* 78 (March 20, 1948): 683–86.

1949b: "Reversing the Secularistic Drift." *Thought* 24 (March 1949): 36–46.

1949i: "Law or Prepossessions." *Law and Contemporary Problems* 14 (Winter 1949): 23–43.

Third, faced with what he read as Protestant sympathies with secularism and as an inadequate Protestant juridical theory, Murray admitted to a founding Protestant consensus for the First Amendment, but argued that now the pluralistic composition of America's faiths placed a requirement on the government that it allow diverse, public religious expression, particularly in public schools. The shift here is from the past consensus to the present consensus. Two *WHTT* articles are based on the notion that at least three faiths (Catholic, Protestant, and Jew) now had legitimate places in the public forum:

1956b: "The School Problem in Mid-Twentieth Century." In *The Role of the Independent School in American Democracy*. Ed. William H. Conley. Milwaukee: Marquette University Press, 1956. 1–16. Reprinted as chapter 6, "Is It Justice?: The School Question Today," *WHTT*, 143–54.

1958e: "The Making of a Pluralist Society." *Religious Education* 53 (November–December 1958): 521–28. Edited for chapter 5, "Creeds at War Intelligibly: Pluralism and the University," in *WHTT*, 125–39.

Murray always maintained that withholding public funds from church affiliated schools was unjust. Some of his most uncivil writings were directed at those, Christian or not, who attempted to firm up the wall of separation by denying such funding. In his last article written on the subject, however, his principal concern has shifted to the state of the public debate about the role of Catholic schools in the American educational establishment and the role of Catholics (and other believers) in public education. In the following article, he attempts to get the partisans talking to one another, paralleling similar concerns and methods in his treatment of other specific social issues, as highlighted in the next subsection.

Federal Aid To Church-Related Schools

JOHN COURTNEY MURRAY, S.J.

Congressional hearings rarely make interesting reading. Last year's hearings on federal aid to education are a notable exception. As Hugh Douglas Price recently remarked, it became obvious during the dispute over education "that the subject was more in the class with civil rights than with such mundane matters as minimum wage, housing and urban redevelopment, or social security coverage."[1] As a result the arguments presented by many Congressional witnesses turned on issues fundamental to our society and our Constitution. The question of the inclusion of church-related schools in federal aid to education was, of course, only one of the "high temperature issues" before Congress, and far from deserving sole credit or blame for the defeat of federal aid last year. Nevertheless, it was one of the critical issues and deserves careful study, especially through analysis of the principal arguments on both sides.

At the outset, it is important to recognize the differences in terminology of the various parties. Those who oppose any inclusion of church-related schools in federal aid to education tend to speak of "aid to public schools" and "aid to parochial schools." Those who favor the inclusion of church-related schools tend to speak of "aid to education" and of "public and private nonprofit schools," including in the latter nondenominational as well as church-related institutions.

These differences in terminology have an important bearing on the solution of the constitutional issue. "Aid to parochial schools," by

EDITOR NOTE: Originally published as "Federal Aid to Church Related Schools." *Yale Political: A Journal of Divergent Views on National Issues.* 1 (1962): 16, 29–31.

1. Hugh Douglas Price, "Race, Religion, and the Rules Committee," in *The Uses of Power: 7 Cases in American Politics* (ed. Alan F. Westin: New York: Harcourt, Brace, 1962), 70.

its very terms, smacks of unconstitutionality. "Aid to education in all qualified schools" has quite a different ring. Opponents of public funds for the improvement of education in church-related schools emphasize their religious character. Proponents emphasize the public character. Since both characteristics are real, the fundamental constitutional problem remains the coordination of civic and religious interests in one society.

The constitutional issue, of course, is only one of the levels of debate. The other is the policy issue. Assuming for the moment that inclusion of all schools meeting reasonable public standards is constitutional, should the federal government include "parochial schools" (if you are against them) or "private nonprofit schools (if you are for them)? Once again, "parochial schools" evokes the image of direct and purposeful government support of religion, with all its evil memories in history. "Private nonprofit schools" evokes the image of free enterprise, parental and academic freedom, and the historical collaboration of our government with privately managed institutions dedicated, at least in part, to the public welfare.

It is not surprising, therefore, that one of the head-on collisions in the current debate is precisely on the issue of religious freedom. Last year, to mention only a few groups, the National Council of Churches, the National Lutheran Council, the Baptist Joint Committee on Public Affairs and the American Jewish Congress testified through their spokesmen that it would violate the religious freedom of their members to make public funds to church-related elementary and secondary schools. Some groups hesitated on the issue of loans, but on grants there was unanimity. Most of the groups also claimed that such a violation of their religious freedom would violate the Constitution, as plainly interpreted by the Supreme Court. All claimed that such a violation was bad public policy.

On the other side, the groups that supported at least some kind of participation in federal aid by the private nonprofit schools claimed that the religious freedom of their members would be diminished if participation were denied. Orthodox Jewish groups like Agudath Israel and Torah Umesorah, the nondenominational Citizens for Educational Freedom, and the National Catholic Welfare Conference all argued that it was in the public interest for the government to respect the freedom of parental choice, especially when religious beliefs motivate that choice. Only one of these organizations, however, Citizens for Educational Freedom, went to the extent of arguing that exclusion of the private nonprofit schools would be unconstitutional.

This direct clash over religious freedom means that someone must lose the argument. With or without the Constitution, Baptists argue that public funds for education in church-related schools will violate their conscience, and Catholics argue that the denial of funds will violate theirs. Which concept of religious freedom is written into the Constitution? Which concept is in the public interest?

It seems manifest that the First Amendment neither can nor does protect the citizen's pocketbook in the same way as it protects his beliefs. The Jeffersonian principle that it is "sinful and tyrannical" to expend tax funds for the propagation of religious beliefs has not meant in our courts and legislatures that an expenditure of tax funds for nonreligious public purposes becomes unconstitutional if the expenditure violates some citizen's conscience. If the citizen's individual beliefs are offended by the religious consequences of nonreligious legislation, the law protects his conscience but exacts the taxes. In our pluralistic society, to subject the constitutionality of nonreligious expenditures to the conscience of each individual would mean anarchy. The 5-4 split in the Everson decision of 1947 rests substantially on the refusal of the majority to extend the Jeffersonian principle to the point where resulting benefit to religion would automatically and invariably invalidate governmental spending programs.

Is it possible, however, to classify a federal aid to education program as "nonreligious" if it includes church-related schools? There is an emphatic "No" on one side and an equally emphatic "Yes" on the other. Speaking for the National Council of Churches, Dr. Gerald Knoff testified that the Protestant Churches "see the general public service argument as being wholly inapplicable to these schools." Church-related schools are primarily and intrinsically ecclesiastical instruments; any public service they perform is a by-product. Moreover, to argue that the schools should be helped because they perform a public service is implicitly to argue that whatever performs a public service should receive public funds. If schools are to be assisted on this ground, so should the churches themselves be aided, because their contribution to the public welfare is equally undeniable. The absurdity of the consequence demonstrates the falsity of the argument.

On the other side of the issue, the argument was pressed home that the nation has a clear nonreligious interest in the education (for this life, at least) of all our children, whatever schools they may attend. One out of every seven American school children is in a private nonprofit school; in our major metropolitan areas the percentages go as high as 44 (Pittsburgh). To exclude seven million children from the government's effort to promote educational excellence and marshal the talents of the nation cannot be justified in terms of any educational or defense policy. The only possible ground, it was insisted, on which these children could be excluded from the benefits of federal assistance is a religious ground: every other consideration urges their inclusion.

It was in this area, I think, that the arguments on both sides tended most to ignore one another. There was no clear reply to the objection that it is absurd to propose public assistance for every activity that contributes to the public weal. The proponents of the inclusion of church-related schools failed to present detailed evidence in support of their claim that exclusion from federal assistance would imperil the public service they are now performing. It may seem obvious that exclusion from federal aid would harm the private nonprofit schools, but obviousness is no substitute for available evidence. Moreover, from the national viewpoint, it is not enough to prove that the national nonprofit schools will be hurt. The point is: Will the nation be hurt? In part this can be shown by reasoned argument on the pluralistic nature of our society and the traditional rights of parents, teachers, and students. In part it must be shown by statistical and economic evidence demonstrating the practical impossibility of shifting seven million children from private nonprofit to public schools within our lifetime without grave educational disruption. The theory that the public schools are open to all is a myth at the level of practice. Every major city in the United States would be crippled tomorrow if the private nonprofit schools shut their doors. We cannot marshal our intellectual resources for the conflict we are in without assisting education in private nonprofit schools.

Just as the private school proponents failed to meet the objection to their public-service argument, so their opponents failed to meet the harm-to-the-nation argument. Some, indeed, insisted that what is unconstitutional cannot be for the public welfare; but this begs the question on constitutionality. Others argued that inclusion of church-related schools would mean the destruction of the public school system. I do not exaggerate. The American Humanist Association testified that, if private nonprofit schools were included in the legislation, the public schools would be "weakened and decimated." The National Council of Churches spoke of "destroying" the public school system, or at least of "weakening" it so gravely "that it could not possibly adequately meet the educational needs of all the children of our growing society." The Baptist Joint Committee on Public Affairs spoke of "intolerable educational chaos."

Such opinions of the weakness of the public schools can stir only amazement and incredulity. Apparently, it is the conviction of some of the most important Protestant leaders in the country that the only force keeping the public schools in existence is the law that limits public funds to their systems. "Remove that limitation," they say, "and the system will collapse."

The fact is that the public schools continue to satisfy the vast majority of American parents. If they did not, the limitation of public funds to their support would have been changed long ago. The best evidence of this is the situation in the South, where several states have introduced tuition grants to provide an escape from desegregated public schools. It is deplorable that this path to educational freedom should also provide flight from racial justice. But the real significance of this legislation is plain: the people will change the financing of education when the public schools no longer satisfy them.

The public schools have flourished because most American parents want them for their children. Similarly, the private nonprofit schools have flourished because millions of other American parents want them badly enough to pay for them. If anyone thinks that Catholic schools exist in this country solely because the Catholic Church wants them, he gravely misjudges the sentiments of the people. The argument that Catholics send their children to Catholic schools because of some prescription of canon law is as absurd as the contention that Americans send their children to school because of the compulsory education laws. Parents send their children to school because they want them educated. Parents send their children to this or that school, if they can afford the choice, because they want them educated this or that way.

At the root of the argument over federal aid to education and private nonprofit schools lies the problem of the coordination of the interests of three societies: parents, churches, and civil society.[2] Both the public schools and the private schools presently achieve some measure of coordination; both need to achieve a greater coordination. There is a tendency in the public schools to become merely instruments of the state. There is a tendency in the private nonprofit schools to become merely instruments of some church. Both tendencies have to be guarded against, because education is not the responsibility merely of parents, or merely of the state, or merely of the church. It is the responsibility of all three.

In this connection it is important to notice that the proponents of private nonprofit schools, while they urge religious considerations, do not urge a religious test for participation in federal aid. The test they urge is purely educational: any qualified school should be eligible. If the private nonprofit schools were proposing the inclusion only of church-related institutions, it could be said with justice that they were seeking a preference of "religion" in the traditional sense. What they are doing, however, is to argue that the religious character of a school is constitutionally irrelevant so long as the school meets proper academic standards. Ironically, it is the champions of the public schools who are proposing a religious test.

It may seem paradoxical that religious interests should be defended by an argument that would banish religion from consideration at the level of law. Nevertheless, this same paradox is written into our Constitution. Religious liberty is protected by a triple prohibition; no religious test for public office; no national creed; no prohibition of free exercise. These prohibitions make religion a matter of conscious legal concern, but the way law manifests that concern, in most instances at least, is by not making religious tests. Except in certain special areas, such as chaplains and the tradition of tax exemptions, religion is protected by being deliberately ignored.

---

2. EDITOR NOTE: This manner of viewing the public school system as an arena within which three sets of interests meet first surfaced in Murray's thought, as best I know, in a series of exchanges with Robert MacIver on a project dealing with freedom of speech within state universities (1954a, Correspondence with Robert MacIver, dating from 1952 through 1954, Murray Archives, file 2–147). For those who presently wish to move beyond Murray to explore the forms in which confessionally explicit languages might be brought into the public forum, Murray's work on religion in public schools offers some guidelines.

Religious considerations, however, have already played too important a part in the debate over federal aid to education. The structure of the argument has become lopsided, for lack of proportion between the interests of all three institutions intimately concerned with education: parents, civil society, and the churches. When all is said and done, two solutions are currently being proposed for the coordination of these societies at the federal level. One would have the Federal Government imitate the choice of the States and limit public support to those who send their children to public schools. The other would have the Federal Government provide the same benefits to all parents and children through all academically qualified schools, public or private, nondenominational or church-related. The great questions faced by the American public are: Which solution is in the national interest? Which will provide the nation with the greater number of well-educated students? Which will show greater respect for parental, religious, and academic freedom?

Civil Restraint and Constraint

Murray considered the genius of the Anglo-American juridical tradition to be expressed in the jurisprudential maxim "as much freedom as possible; as much coercion as necessity." The adoption of the maxim was grounded in a "great act of faith" in the moral capacities of the American people, i.e., in the recognition of their human dignity (see *WHTT*, p. 30). Murray offered variously three or five indices for the application of restraint or constraint on a citizen's freedom, namely, public peace, general moral norms, and justice, to which he later added the further norms of national security and public welfare.[1]

Murray also argued that any and all attempts to change juridical structures affect two distinct areas of social, moral concern. The first of course pertains to the actions that are to be demanded or restricted. Here juridical reform attempts to control or encourage specific types of behavior. A second order of concern, however, involves the way a people understand the juridical system as a whole. Bad laws encourage disregard for law and the government that enforces that law; good laws evoke compliance and virtues that are necessary for living within a complex, modern society.

In the following essays Murray attempts to address both areas of juridical concern. Increasingly his own focus shifted from specific issues to the manner in which those issues were pursued in the public forum, and to the way juridical practices might encourage or curtail a proper practice of juridical reasoning. Before the Second Vatican Council Murray's juridical attention was directed toward American society and the American Catholic community. After the council he also encouraged his church itself to act in the civil juridical forum in a manner that reflected "its" complex theory of jurisprudence.

---

1. The first three criteria surfaced in his discussion of censorship in "Questions of Striking a Right Balance" (1956f) and can also be found in his conciliar defense of religious freedom (see *Religious Liberty* [1993] and "The Problem of Religious Freedom [1964e], p. 145). The two added criteria surfaced in his nuclear deterrence arguments (in testimony before the Rockefeller Project, Murray Archives, file 8–593, pp. 28–29), although the "general welfare" criterion first appeared in Murray's treatment of Leo XIII, particularly of *Rerum Novarum* (see p. 80 of Murray's suppressed Leonine article, published in 1993 as "Leo XIII and Pius XII: Government and the Order of Religion" [1955c]).

The Problem of Free Speech

JOHN COURTNEY MURRAY, S.J.

Murray wrote the following article at the same time he was pursuing an extended study of Leo XIII's endorsement of Establishment and Intolerance. Note Murray's concern with presenting a proper theory of jurisprudence (neither pragmatic nor relativistic), something that he claimed Leo XIII and Protestants in general lacked. Here his affirmation of Anglo-American conceptions of the limited state is fairly well established, as is his distinction between society and state. He had not yet developed fully his criteria of public peace (that would become clearer in his "Questions of Striking a Right Balance" [1956f]). Therefore it is not surprising that his dealing with the question of the state's positive action for the preservation of a national heritage is somewhat weak. Notes belonging to the editor of *Philippine Studies* are so indicated.

The contemporary communist challenge to Western society has had at least one good result. It has furnished an impulse toward formulating more articulate theories of democratic institutions. In the United States the tendency has generally been to rest content with purely

---

Originally published as "The Problem of Free Speech." *Philippine Studies*. 1 (September 1953): 107-24. The following note was attached:

The Philippine Constitution is so closely modelled upon the Constitution of the United States, that any light thrown upon the American document must necessarily aid to an understanding of its Philippine counterpart. The constitutional right of free speech has during the past year in the Philippines been the subject of acrimonious debate, and therefore we have invited an internationally known authority to discuss its understanding in the American system.

pragmatic and utilitarian views; but now the need is felt for an intellectually more respectable philosophy of the rather vague thing called "the democratic way of life." There is a growing realization that if the institutions of a free society are to be effectively defended, it is essential to have a genuinely philosophical understanding of them. No mere "love" of them will suffice, unless the love is grounded in intelligence. This need for philosophical understanding is notably felt with regard to the institution of free speech.

This article does not pretend to discuss the problem of free speech in all its amplitude. My limited purpose is, first, to comment briefly on the present legal situation in the United States and, secondly, to make some equally brief reflections on the institution of free speech from a philosophical and Catholic point of view.

THE LEGAL SITUATION

A multitude of cases involving freedom of speech, both religious and political, have been decided by the Supreme Court of the United States. It is not a question here of analyzing them in detail. I do not write as a lawyer. The following comments are those which suggest themselves to a lay mind after a study of the cases of major importance that have been adjudicated by the Supreme Court.

The initial impression is one of confusion and uncertainty. The nine judges are not unanimous in their decisions. Often those who agree with the decision of the Court disagree with the Court's reasoning. And even the dissenters do not always agree on the reasons for dissenting. It is clear that the Court feels itself to be confronted by a vexing problem which grows continually more complex in consequence of an intensified clash of ideas, and in consequence too of the multiplication of media of communication. Moreover, the Court does not seem to be at all sure that even the principles of solution have yet been formulated with requisite definiteness.

In any event, it is not difficult to define the general climate of feeling in which the decisions of the Court are conceived. It is a climate of anxious concern to provide the fullest possible protection to the individual in the expression of his individual opinions, however singular, heterodox, bizarre, and even offensive they may be. The individual and his right to express whatever ideas and even feelings he may have—this seems to be the focus of the Court's concern.

This attitude has not lacked critics even within the Court itself. A criticism of it is implied in the dissent of Mr. Justice Jackson in the *Kunz*[1] case:

> Essential freedoms are today threatened from without and within. It may become difficult to preserve here what a large part of the world has lost—the right to speak, even temperately, on matters vital to spirit and body. In such setting, to blanket hateful and hate-stirring attacks on races and faiths under the protection for freedom of speech may be a noble innovation. On the other hand, it may be a quixotic tilt at windmills which belittles great principles of liberty. Only time can tell. But I incline to the latter view. . . .[2]

Later in the same dissent he cites Lord Russell: "The problem, like all those with which we are concerned, is one of balance; too little liberty brings stagnation, and too much brings chaos." Mr. Justice Jackson adds: "Perhaps it is the fever of our times that inclines the Court to favor chaos. My hope is that few will take advantage of the license granted by today's decision."[3] The point seems to be sound. Concern for an individualistic freedom of utterance, when it becomes excessive, encourages license and not liberty, chaos and not ordered freedom.

Despite these criticisms, however, the prevailing attitude of the Court has been, as described above, a preoccupation with the individual's right of expression. And that is the first important thing to be observed about the legal position of free speech in the United States.

---

1. *PS* EDITOR NOTE: A New York City ordinance required a permit from the police commissioner in order that a minister might preach in public places. Kunz received a permit in 1946, which was revoked in November of that year after a hearing which indicated that he had ridiculed and denounced the religious beliefs of others. Subsequent permits were denied him; and then, after speaking without one, he was arrested for violating the ordinance. In reversing his conviction the U.S. Supreme Court found the ordinance unconstitutional in application, inasmuch as the ordinance gave an administrative official discretionary power to control in advance the free speech of citizens of New York City. Such a law the Court decided was clearly invalid as a prior restraint of First Amendment liberties.

2. *Kunz* v. *People of New York*, Mr. Justice Jackson, dissenting, 71 S. Ct. 315.

3. *Id.* at 325.

LEGAL THEORY OF THE COURT

The second point regards the legal principles that guide the Court's decision. What are they? The central principle is that government has no right to place prior restraints on the individual's right to speak. The principle has often been stated. Thus, for instance, in the *Kunz* case:

> We have here then an ordinance which gives an administrative official discretionary power to control in advance the right of citizens to speak on religious matters on the streets of New York. As such, the ordinance is clearly invalid as a prior restraint on the exercise of First Amendment rights.[4]

Mr. Justice Frankfurter in his concurring opinion in the *Kovacs*[5] case gives, in a subordinate clause, a simpler statement of the principle: "So long as a legislature does not prescribe what ideas may be noisily expressed and what may not be, nor discriminate among those who would make inroads upon the public peace, it is not for us, etc."[6] In still simpler terms, government is not the patron of one idea over any other idea; it is simply the patron of freedom for all ideas.

FIRST BASIS: PRAGMATISM

One must then further ask, upon what ultimate grounds is this legal principle based? The answer is a bit difficult, because two different lines of thought appear. The more common line is pragmatic. It is, for instance, contained in a statement of Mr. Justice Roberts, made in 1940, to which the Court later makes frequent reference:

> In the realm of religious faith, and in that of political belief, sharp differences arise. In both fields the tenets of one man may

---

4. *Id.* Ct. 314.
5. *PS* EDITOR NOTE: The Court upheld the conviction under a Trenton, New Jersey, ordinance prohibiting the unlicensed use of sound trucks emitting raucous noises. Such legislation, the Court held, involves no violation of constitutionally guaranteed liberties for freedom of speech does not require legislation to be insensible to claims by citizens to comfort and convenience.
6. *Kovacs* v. *Cooper*, Mr. Justice Frankfurter, concurring, 69 S. Ct. 459.

seem the rankest error to his neighbor. To persuade others to his point of view, the pleader, as we know, at times resorts to vilification of men who have been or are prominent in church and state, and even to false statement. But the people of this nation have ordained in the light of history that, in spite of the probability of excesses and abuses, these liberties are in the long view essential to enlightened opinion and right conduct on the part of citizens of a democracy.[7]

This statement makes no pretense to be philosophical. It starts from the fact of existent diversity of religious and political beliefs, alludes vaguely to past experience in the control of opinion, and suggests that the most practical expedient is for the law to take the side of freedom of utterance. If any principle is invoked, it is simply that of the lesser evil: the abuse of freedom is a lesser evil than the curtailment of freedom. Underlying the statement is that general distrust of secular government as a judge of ideas, which has been an American characteristic. Also underlying the statement is the unargued confidence, current since the French Revolution, that under conditions of full freedom, reason and truth will somehow prevail and result in enlightened opinion and right conduct.

These pragmatic considerations, and especially this idealism, undergird the further Court doctrine, which extends the above statement, that freedom of speech, like the other freedoms of the First Amendment, enjoys a "preferred position" within a free society. This doctrine leads to the conclusion once stated by the Court: "Only the gravest abuses, endangering paramount interests, give occasion for permissible limitation [of First Amendment freedoms]."[8] Actually, the main dispute within the Court has centered on the question, when does an abuse become grave enough, or when is a paramount interest sufficiently endangered, to permit legal limitation of free speech? Or, what comes to the same thing, what are the standards whereby to judge between liberty (and its permissible abuses) and license (with its intolerably injurious consequences)?

---

7. Cited by Mr. Justice Black, dissenting, *Feiner v. People of State of New York*, 71 S. Ct. 315.

8. *Thomas v. Collins*, 65 S. Ct. 315.

SECOND BASIS: RELATIVISM

Although the general attitude of the Court is pragmatic (to the point indeed of a rather doctrinaire pragmatism), the temptation has been felt, notably by Mr. Justice Frankfurter, to go further and seek some philosophical ground. This ground is found in the philosophy of Mr. Justice Holmes: "The ideas now governing the constitutional protection of freedom of speech derive essentially from the opinions of Mr. Justice Holmes."[9] Mr. Frankfurter goes on to give the essence of the matter. He makes Holmes's distinction between "liberties which derive from shifting economic arrangements" and "those liberties of the individual which history has attested as the indispensable conditions of an open as against a closed society." The former are fairly readily subject to curtailments by laws and courts. The latter have a specially sacrosanct and inviolable character:

> But since he [Holmes] also realized that the progress of civilization is to a considerable extent the displacement of error which once held sway as official truth by beliefs which in turn have yielded to other beliefs, for him the right to search for truth was of a different order than some transient economic dogma. And without freedom of expression thought becomes checked and atrophied. . . . Accordingly, Mr. Holmes was far more ready to find legislative invasion where free inquiry was involved than in the debatable area of economics.[10]

In other words, Mr. Frankfurter would found constitutional freedom of speech upon the philosophic ground of Holmes's dogmatic relativism of truth—upon the denial that truth in any absolute sense exists, and upon the consequent assertion that the highest, most untouchable value is the search for truth, not truth itself. Mr. Justice Jackson, for all that he belongs to the conservative wing of the Court in this matter, seems to embrace the same philosophy, though less forthrightly:

> As a people grows in capacity for civilization and liberty, their tolerance will grow, and they will endure, if not welcome,

---

9. *Kovacs* v. *Cooper*, Mr. Justice Frankfurter, concurring, 69 S. Ct. 458.
10. *Ibid.*

discussion even on topics to which they are committed. They regard convictions as tentative and know that time and events will make their own terms with theories by whomever and by whatever majorities they are held, and many will be proved wrong. But on our way to this idealistic state of tolerance the police have to deal with men as they are.[11]

The implication seems to be that for the moment the old song is right in maintaining that "a policeman's lot is not a happy one," but that the years (or centuries) to come will see an improvement, after the triumph of a relativist philosophy.

It would seem that, as the issue of free speech has pressed itself upon the Court in these latter years, the impulse to find a theory for this freedom has made itself felt. The only trouble is that the theory upon which the Court seems to fall back, as upon the ultimate ground and justification of its practical decisions, is a false and disastrous philosophical relativism. Worse still, it is the particularly shallow kind of relativism proposed by Holmes—the theory of the "free market" as applied to ideas, which maintains that all ideas are free and equal, that each must be left to make its way in the unlimited competition of the market place, and that those which survive, for the length of time that they survive, are "true." In this theory the sole function of law and government is to protect the freedom of the market; it has no interest in the goods—the ideas and opinions—that pass through the market, and it does not care which ideas survive and which ideas perish.

LIMITATIONS OF FREEDOM

Both the pragmatism and the relativism of the Court lead it to extend individual freedom of speech to the utmost limit. However, there is a limit; the right of free speech is not altogether absolute. The classic rule was stated by Holmes in the *Schenck*[12] case:

---

11. *Terminiello* v. *City of Chicago*, Mr. Justice Jackson, dissenting, 69 St. Ct. 909.

12. *PS* EDITOR NOTE: Conviction for violation of the Espionage Act of 1917 upheld because distribution of a pamphlet calculated to cause insubordination among inducted members of the military services constitutes a conspiracy to obstruct military induction. Such a conviction, the court held, does not abridge free speech as conceived under the First Amendment, for the question in every case is whether the words are used in such circumstances and are of such a nature as to create a clear and present danger that they will bring about the substantive evils that Congress has a right to prevent.

The most stringent protection of free speech would not protect a man in falsely shouting fire in a theatre and causing a panic. It does not even protect a man from an injunction against uttering words that may have all the effect of force.[13]

This concept was later amplified by Mr. Justice Murphy in the *Chaplinsky* case:

There are certain well-defined and narrowly limited classes of speech, the prevention and punishment of which have never been thought to raise any constitutional problem. These include the lewd and obscene, the profane, the libelous, and insulting or "fighting" words—those which by their very utterance inflict injury or tend to incite an immediate breach of the peace.[14]

There are therefore certain kinds of speeches which one is not legally free to make. However, the Court has found itself in trouble in the application of this rule. The difficulty lies in the reconciliation of this rule with the rule against prior censorship of opinions. The *Kunz* case illustrated the difficulty. Reversing the decision of the New York Court of Appeals, the Supreme Court invalidated an ordinance of New York City which made it unlawful to hold public worship meetings on the streets without first obtaining a permit from the city police commissioner, because this ordinance invested restraining control over the right to speak on religious subjects in an administrative official without providing appropriate standards to guide his actions. The fact, however, was that Kunz's speeches were highly injurious and insulting to Catholics and Jews. The Court overlooked this fact in ruling in favor of Kunz. However, in his dissent, Mr. Justice Jackson questioned the decision of the Court on the grounds that this kind of provocative language, uttered on the public streets, cannot claim constitutional protection. He denied Kunz's contention that he was simply exercising his constitutional rights, and implied that Kunz had no right to demand that New York City "must place its streets at his disposal to hurl insults at the passerby."[15]

---

13. *Schenck v. United States*, 39 S. Ct. 247.
14. *Chaplinsky v. State of New Hampshire*, 62 S. Ct. 766.
15. *Kunz v. People of State of New York*, Mr. Justice Jackson, dissenting, 71 S. Ct. 317.

Mr. Jackson also raised the important question whether such a "freedom," granted to Kunz and his kid, would not constitute a violation of the religious freedom of others:

> Is official action the only source of interference with religious freedom? Does the Jew, for instance, have the benefit of these freedoms when, lawfully going about, he and his children are pointed out as "Christ-killers" to gatherings on public property by a religious sectarian sponsored by a police bodyguard?[16]

Finally, Mr. Jackson puts a pertinent question:

> In streets and public places all races and nationalities and all sorts and conditions of men walk, linger, and mingle. Is it not reasonable that the city protect the dignity of these persons against fanatics who take possession of its streets to hurl into its crowds defamatory epithets that hurt like rocks?[17]

PRINCIPLE OF ORDERED LIBERTY

Actually, the Court has made an effort to avoid an anarchic concept of liberty and to defend a concept of "ordered liberty." Ordered liberty is limited by a decent respect for the rights of others. It is also limited by the police power of the state, whose proper extension is to all the needs of public order: "The police power of a state extends beyond health, morals and safety, and comprehends the duty, within constitutional limitations, to protect the well-being and tranquillity of a community."[18] The principle of the rights of others was invoked in the *Kovacs* case:

> The right of free speech is guaranteed every citizen that he may reach the minds of willing listeners, and to do so there must be opportunity to win their attention. . . . Opportunity to gain the public's ears by objectionable amplified sound on the street is no

---

16. *Id.* at 319.
17. *Id.* at 325.
18. *Kovacs* v. *Cooper*, 69 S. Ct. 451.

more assured by the right of free speech than is the unlimited opportunity to address gatherings on the streets. The preferred position of freedom of speech in a society that cherishes liberty for all does not require legislators to be insensible to claims by citizens to comfort and convenience. To enforce freedom of speech in disregard of the rights of others would be harsh and arbitrary in itself.[19]

The principle of public order was stated by Chief Justice Hughes in the Cox[20] case: "Civil liberties, as guaranteed by the Constitution, imply the existence of an organized society maintaining public order, without which liberty itself would be lost in the excesses of unrestrained abuses."[21] This principle, like the preceding one, does indeed furnish some standard of limitation upon the right of free speech. And the Court has conceived its function to be that of "balancing" the requirements of the various rights and interests involved in particular cases.

CONCRETE NEEDS YIELD TO ABSTRACT THEORY

However, although the outcome of the balance is not seldom unpredictable, one has the impression that the balance is always somewhat loaded. There seems to be the following difficulty. On the one hand, the problem of the rights of others and of the requirements of public order is posited in the concrete. Whether these rights will be violated and whether public order will be disturbed depends largely upon the concrete content of the utterance, the circumstances in which it is made, the dispositions of the hearers, etc. On the other hand, the individual's right to freedom of utterance is initially conceived in abstract, not to say doctrinaire, fashion; so too is the supporting rule

---

19. *Id.* at 454.

20. *PS* EDITOR NOTE: The Supreme Court affirmed a judgment of conviction for violation of a statute prohibiting organized parades on public streets without a permit. The issue of a permit was subject to reasonable discretion determined by public safety and convenience as to time, place and manner of such use of the streets. Authority to so control the use of public highways is not inconsistent with civil liberties in the opinion of the Court.

21. *Cox* v. *State of New Hampshire*, 61 S. Ct. 762 (1941).

that there may be no prior government censorship of utterance, and by consequence (as the Court tends to insist) no prior licensing of the right to speak. The "load" in the balance consists of the Court's predominant disposition to apply, at times a bit ruthlessly, the abstract doctrinaire rules, under greater or less disregard of the particular demands of the more concrete balancing principles. It is this disposition which gives point to Mr. Justice Jackson's warning to the Court in his dissent in the *Terminiello*[22] case:

> The Court has gone far toward accepting the doctrine that civil liberty means the removal of all restraints from these crowds and that all local attempts to maintain order are impairments of the liberty of the citizen. The choice is not between order and liberty. It is between liberty with order and anarchy without either. There is danger that, if the Court does not temper its doctrinaire logic with a little practical wisdom, it will convert the constitutional Bill of Rights into a suicide pact.[23]

AMERICAN CONSTITUTION AND FREEDOM

So much for a description of the current legal situation in the United States. Obviously, one must reject the relativistic philosophy of truth which the Court has recently come to allege in support of its attitude and decisions. However, it should be noted that this philosophy was

---

22. *PS* EDITOR NOTE: Arthur W. Terminiello addressed Christian Veterans of America in Chicago, Feb. 7, 1946. His speech occasioned a violent riot. He was arrested, convicted and fined $100.00. By a five-to-four decision the Supreme Court reversed the Illinois judgment convicting petitioner for violation of a Chicago ordinance. This ordinance provided that anyone could be convicted of disorderly conduct if in public speaking he should contribute to "any improper noise, riot, disturbance, breach of the peace or division tending to a breach of the peace." In charging the jury the trial judge stated that "breach of the peace" includes a speech which "stirs the public to anger, invites disputes, brings about a condition of unrest or creates a disturbance." The Supreme Court held the ordinance invalid on grounds of vague delineation of the crime, without reaching the further question whether the content of the speech carried it outside the scope of constitutional guarantees.

23. *Terminiello* v. *City of Chicago*, Mr. Justice Jackson, dissenting, 69 S. Ct. 911.

not originally and inherently implied by the First Amendment provision that "Congress shall make no law . . . abridging the freedom of speech or of the press." No philosophical doctrine about the nature of truth lay behind this restriction of governmental power. Such theory as did lie behind it was purely political. The first premise was a sharp distinction between state and society, that is, between the voluntary and the coercive aspects of social existence. This distinction involved a subordination of the state to society, and a concept of the state (meaning primarily the law, and government as the agent of law) as simply instrumental to the purposes of society, and indeed instrumental only to a severely limited number of these purposes. The problem of truth, especially of religious truth, was removed from the area of governmental or legal concern and deposited in the area of society, there to be solved, if possible, by the processes of freedom, and not by the enactments of law.

In a word, American government was to have no truths to teach; the teaching of the truth was to be done by associations, including the Church, within society. Again, government was to have no power of deciding between conflicting beliefs and no function of protecting the teaching of one rather than of another. Its sole functions were to be, first, the protection of individual and social freedom to seek the truth and to teach it, and secondly, the protection of public order, including an order of minimal public morality, against abuses of freedom. It is in the light of this theory of government that the American institution of free speech must initially be judged, having in mind that these restrictions on governmental power were imposed by popular consent. It may be well to remark that, in proposing a relativist philosophy of truth as the basis of the First Amendment, the Supreme Court is being false to the tenor and spirit of this part of the Bill of Rights, which expressly forbids government in any of its branches to adopt and impose any such sectarian philosophy.

The special character of the American system might perhaps be illustrated by comparison with the Constitution of Eire. The pertinent provision runs thus:

> The State guarantees liberty for the exercise of the following rights, subject to public order and morality: The right of citizens to express freely their convictions and opinions. The education of public opinion being, however, a matter of such grave import

to the common good, the State shall endeavor to ensure that the organs of public opinion, such as the radio, the press, the cinema, while presuming their rightful liberty of expression, including criticism of Government policy, shall not be used to undermine public order or morality or the authority of the State. The publication or utterance of blasphemous, seditious or indecent matter is an offence which shall be punishable in accordance with the law.

This constitutional provision reveals the concept of the state that the Irish Constitution contains. It reflects the Continental idea rather than the British or American one. It does not indeed go so far as to accept the concept of *l'Etat enseignant* ("the state as a teacher") characteristics of France under the ancient and restored monarchies under Napoleon and under the Republic, and of Germany under the "enlightened despots." However, it goes farther than the British and American concept of government. It grants to the state that manner of negative power of teaching by which official state agencies may decide what shall not reach the public mind. The premise of this grant of power to the state is the grave importance of the education of public opinion to the common good.

This principle is, of course, recognized in the American system; indeed it is insisted upon. However, the American conclusion from the principle seems to have been the contrary of the Irish conclusion. Behind the constitutional law of the United States is the conviction that public opinion is so important that the task of educating it may not be entrusted to government, either by way of positive teaching or by way of censorship. This task is committed to all kinds of free agencies within society. Even the public school system is not a state system in the Continental sense; its educational content is not determined by government.

There is no space here to criticize at length the American theory of free speech (in so far as there is a theory) or other contrasting theories. The interested reader will find a brilliant critique of freedom of speech, as based upon the philosophical and political theories of eighteenth and nineteenth-century rationalism, in an article by a Protestant author, Gerhart Niemeyer, "A Reappraisal of the Doctrine of Free

Speech."[24] The author's argument is that this theory of free speech, when consistently applied in institutional practice, tends to discredit and destroy the three assumptions on which it is based—the pre-eminent value of truth, the concept of "the people" as a structured moral entity with a genuine "will," and the ideal of rationality and reasonableness as the supreme social good. I shall not attempt to summarize the argument; but I must say that it is made with complete success. The author's positive thesis is that all ideas are not free and equal, that there is a distinction between right and wrong uses of speech in public life, and that there must be some official attitude of patronage and favor toward the ideas that form the moral basis of society.

MORAL BASIS OF COMMUNITY

Actually, this seems to be the essential Catholic thesis. Perhaps I can briefly set it forth in two propositions, which answer two distinct questions. The first question is philosophical and moral: is there a moral basis of human community? Leo XIII's answer is clear:

> There are certain natural truths—such as the principles of nature and the further principles which are immediately deduced from them by reason—which constitute, as it were, the common patrimony of the human race. And upon this patrimony, as upon a most firm foundation, morals, justice, religion, and indeed the social unity of the human community rest.[25]

This notion of "the human heritage" is a favorite one with Leo XIII. He opposes it to the rationalist notion of "free thought," which regarded all ideas as equal, and equally open to question. In contrast, the Pope asserts the Catholic thesis that there are certain privileged

---

24. *Thought*, XXV (1950), 251–74. The article was a paper read before a panel of the American Political Science Association in December 1950. The panel held sessions for three days on the whole problem. The general result was considerable dissatisfaction with current theories and with alternative theories.

25. Encyclical, *Libertas*.

ideas. The ideas that make up the human heritage furnish man with his basic understanding of himself as a person and as a social and political being. To destroy them would be to destroy the foundations of freedom and justice in human association. Hence, their position within society is privileged.

The notion of an inviolable human heritage of ideas furnishes the primary criterion by which to distinguish right and wrong uses of public speech. Man is not morally free to destroy the very spiritual substance of his social life: ". . . it would be wicked and stupidly inhuman to permit [this human heritage] to be violently attacked and dissipated with impunity."[26] Be it noted that the duty of preventing this wickedness and folly devolves in the first instance upon the community itself, whose existence as a human community depends on the preservation of its intellectual and spiritual heritage. The community must make this moral demand on all its members, that they respect this heritage.

GOVERNMENT AND MORAL BASIS

Here the second question rises—a political question: what is the function of the state—of law and government—with regard to the preservation of this heritage? This is a much more difficult question, since it involves not merely abstract considerations of truth and error, right and wrong, but also concrete problems of political prudence. At least one must say, with Niemeyer: "There ought to be no public neutrality in questions concerning the moral basis of society, whether one approaches them from the point of view of moral obligation or from that of vital political interest."[27] The official attitude must be partisan, not neutral; it must take a side, in favor of the heritage. This attitude of favor follows from the principle that the state has a positive function in the perennial struggle between truth and error, right and wrong. To deny this principle would be to adopt a concept of the state that is unhistorical as well as immoral, and is furthermore impossible; for the political and legal action of the state is inevitably in some moral direction, inescapably on the side either of good or evil. (I

---

26. Loc. cit.
27. *Thought*, XXV (1950), 272.

might add that no such absurd concept of the state figures in the American system, as a host of early and later documents witnesses.)

This much is certain. But the complications begin when one asks how far, and with what degree of detail, this official attitude of patronage of the truth should be translated into specific laws and positive governmental action, e.g., of censorship or indoctrination. In a sense, this is an administrative problem—a problem of setting up norms and procedures for applying in practice the distinction between right and wrong uses of public speech. It is also a very concrete problem, whose solution greatly depends on circumstances.

The general principle holds good in any set of circumstances: official public neutrality with regard to the moral laws of community life is absurd and dangerous. But only practical wisdom and political prudence, which take close cognizance of the needs, the sensitivities, and the cultural level of the body politic, will be able to translate this general principle into specific laws and procedures that will further the common good.

I might only add that for democratic societies today the crucially important thing is to come to a common awareness of the general principle. Difficult and annoying problems of free speech are indeed raised by sectarian fanatics, like the Jehovah's Witnesses.[28] But the real problem is raised by Communism. This activist ideological movement hurls its challenge at the very spiritual substance of so-called "free societies," which are free precisely because their roots are in the Christian tradition, whatever may have been their subsequent departures from that tradition. The basic communist denial is directed against the human heritage of which Leo XIII spoke. The basic communist drive is to substitute a new idea of man for the idea contained in the human heritage. And the question is, how shall the free society, remaining free, protect itself against this fundamental searching challenge?

My hope is that the Philippines may show the way towards a solution of this crucial, complicated question. I think it is a good

---

28. To follow these cases through the American courts in like wandering through a legal wilderness. The Court has reversed and re-reversed itself several times. And the reasonings have widely varied. This is why the present article makes no attempt at detailed discussion of these cases.

hope, for two reasons. First, the Philippine state is committed to a political ideal of freedom. Second, the Filipino people are still largely faithful to the Christian idea of man, in itself and as the spiritual basis and substance of the political community. This second point is the important one. Other Western societies have become vulnerable to Communism in proportion as they have put their faith simply in the forms of freedom, in matters of process, procedure, method, to the neglect of the substance of freedom, which is of the religious and spiritual, not the political, order. To this extent they have lost the sense of the political community as a spiritual and moral community. They have lost touch, as it were, with their own soul—the soul that was infused in them by their participation in the human and Christian heritage. This loss of soul is their weakness. But the Filipino people has not lost its Christian soul or its grip upon its heritage of Christian wisdom. And if the Filipino people wed their ancestral Christian wisdom to their hard-won political wisdom, there is hope that they will show triumphant leadership in today's crisis.

The Bad Arguments
Intelligent Men Made

John Courtney Murray, S.J.

In 1956 Murray published "Questions of Striking a Right Balance: Literature and Censorship" (1956c), which became one of his most republished articles and eventually chapter 7, "Should There Be a Law: The
Question of Censorship" in *WHTT*. The problem guiding the article was
a boisterous national movement, often led by Roman Catholics, to
restrict access to "adult" literature. Murray offered four procedural rules
for dealing with the problem:

> (1) each minority group has the right to censor for its own mem-
> bers. . .; (2) no minority group has the right to demand that govern-
> ment should impose general censorship. . . [where] judgments of
> harmfulness [are not shared generally]; (3) any minority group has
> the right to work toward the elevation of standards of public
> morality . . . by the methods of persuasion and pacific argument;
> (4) no minority group has the right to impose its own religious or
> moral views on other groups, through the use of the methods of
> force, coercion, or violence (1956f, 168).

To Murray's apparent chagrin, those rules were picked up by John Fischer in a broadside against some methodologies used by Catholics. The
following is Murray's response to Fischer's editorial.

From his "Editor's Easy Chair" (Harper's, October, 1956) John Fischer
looks out and sees "immeasurable damage" being done "to the American way of life and to the very foundations of democratic govern-

---

EDITOR NOTE: Published as 1956a: "The Bad Arguments Intelligent Men
Make," *America*. 96 (November 3, 1956): 120–23. This and the Fischer article
that provoked it were published as appendixes in *Catholic Viewpoint on Censorship*, ed. Harold C. Gardiner, S.J. (Garden City, N.Y.: Hanover House, 1958),
157–92.

ment." This has become a familiar vision, many of us share it. But we frequently differ on the question, who or what is doing the damage?

In Mr. Fischer's view the damage is being done by "a little band of Catholics" who are "conducting a shocking attack on the rights of their fellow citizens" through the medium of an organization called the National Organization for Decent Literature, which undertakes to "censor" certain publications.

I take a rather broader view. I see a large band of people, of all faiths, who are conducting a shocking attack on the reason of their fellow citizens through the medium of passionately irrational argument about important public issues. I believe that nothing is more damaging to democracy than lack of rationality in public argument. The foundations of our society are indeed laid in an identifiable consensus. But they are more importantly laid in a reasonable disposition to argue our many disagreements in intelligent and temperate fashion, using restrained language, avoiding misstatements, overstatements or simplifications, and endeavoring to define issues with precision in the light of all the relevant principles and facts. I believe that whatever corrupts rational public argument corrupts democracy.

It has seemed to me that censorship is one of the public issues that are being deformed by bad argument, emanating from all sides. Hence on May 4, 1956, in a talk given before the Thomas More Association in Chicago and printed in the organ of the Thomas More Book Shop, *Books on Trial*, I made an attempt at a contribution to good public argument on this difficult subject. Part of my argument consisted in stating four practical rules that should govern the action of minority groups in a pluralist society, in their legitimate efforts to improve public morality. These rules were not original. I had seen them stated in substance in a news release of a paper given at Marquette University on March 1956 by Prof. Vernon J. Bourke of St. Louis University.

Mr. Fischer quotes my statement of these four procedural rules in support of certain conclusions of his own with regard to the activities of the National Organization for Decent Literature. Perhaps Mr. Bourke will undertake to say whether, and how far, Mr. Fischer's conclusions follow from the four norms of action for whose formulation, in language somewhat different from my own, he should be given the credit. (At the time of my writing there was no printed source to which I could refer the reader for Mr. Bourke's excellent paper. It has since appeared in the volume *Problems of Communication in a Pluralistic Society*, Marquette University Press, 1956.) My own major concern is with the broader question—the quality of public argument. My question is whether Mr. Fischer has made a contribution to rational public argument on the issue of censorship. I am afraid my answer must be No.

Consider the preliminary question of language. In his opening paragraph Mr. Fischer asserts that a "little band of Catholics" is "engaged in an un-American activity which is as flagrant as anything the Communist party ever attempted—and which is in fact very similar to Communist tactics." Does one open a rational public argument by two such attacks on the reason of the reader? That tired old cussword, "un-American activity"—has it not gone the way of all cusswords, into meaninglessness? And the tactic of slapping the label "Communist" on your adversary's position—have we not agreed that this is a tactic of unreason? As for the later argument by epithet (the NODL is "lynching" books), one hardly expects to find it in *Harper's*, however much it may be used on the hustings.

The more substantive question is this: has Mr. Fischer done justice to the NODL's own understanding of its purposes and methods, as these are stated in its explanatory literature?

The literature is easily obtainable from the central office (31 East Congress St., Chicago Ill.). On reading it, one would come, I think, to the following conclusions. The NODL is simply a "service organization," not an "action group." Its major service consists in offering to "responsible individuals and organizations an evaluation of current comic books, magazines and pocket-size books." This is the famous "NODL list." The evaluation of these types of publications (only these) is done singly from the standpoint of what is objectionable as juvenile reading. The standards of evaluation are nine in number. All of them are common-sense norms; none of them are special tenets of any type of "group morality." Methods of review vary for each type of publication. Five reviewers vote on each item. The purpose is to "encourage the publishing and distribution of good literature," as well as to discover what is unfit for adolescents.

NODL also distributes information about ways of organizing decent-literature campaigns on the community or parish levels. It is clearly stated that the list is merely an expression of a publication's nonconformity with the NODL code and that "the list is not to be used for purposes of boycott or coercion." The procedures seem to rest on the suppositions that the ordinary merchant is a responsible man; that he would welcome some assistance in ridding his shop of stuff that responsible parents fairly judge to be unfit for their children; that if he accepts the assistance, he is to be commended; that if he rejects it, he is to be left alone. (NODL says; "Instruct your committee workers to leave silently if the owner, manager or clerk refuses cooperation.")

The general conclusion, on the basis of its own statements about itself, would be that the NODL looks to voluntary reform, through cooperation between parent-citizens and merchants, in an area where a special problem of public morality exists. That problem arises out of the ready accessibility to boys and girls of a rather immense amount of cheap literature that is objectionable on common-sense grounds of morality and taste.

Consider now Mr. Fischer's description of the NODL. "Its main purpose is to make it impossible for anybody to buy books and other publications which it does not like." "Its chief method is to put pressure on newsdealers, drug stores and booksellers to force them to remove from their stocks every item on the NODL blacklist." It "deliberately prefers to ignore the established legal channels for proceedings against books which it thinks improper. Its chosen weapons are boycott and literary lynching." It is embarked upon a "campaign of intimidation."

Something is wrong here. When Mr. Fischer describes the NODL he is obviously not describing the same thing that NODL describes when it describes itself. Thus you have reproduced the perfect pattern—the perfectly wretched pattern—of so much American public argument at the moment. There is really no argument at all—at least not yet. The two sides are not talking about the same thing. Hence the exchange proceeds to the customarily futile end. On the basis of his own description Mr. Fischer asserts that NODL "is *compelling* [emphasis his] readers, of all faiths, to bow to its dislikes, by denying them a free choice in what they buy." Hence he defines the issue thus: "The real issue is whether any private group—however well-meaning—has a right to dictate what other people may' read."

To Mr. Fischer's charges the NODL would, I expect, reply to this effect: "But we are not compelling anybody to do or not do anything. We are not doing any such arbitrary thing as making our own 'dislikes' the coercive standard for the reading of the general public. We are not trying to do any 'dictating.' And as for denying to readers of all faiths a free choice in what they buy—that is not the real issue at all."

Thus the argument fulfills the customary American pattern. The next step is for the contestants to retire from the field, either in sorrow or in anger or in both. Thereafter their partisans move in, epithets are bandied; labels are exchanged; non sequitur's proliferate. Until finally, both sides mutter disgustedly, "So's your old man." And there is, for a time, a sullen silence.

Maybe the argument could be rescued from this dismal end, to which most arguments in America seem to be condemned. Mr. Fischer could have rescued it, but he didn't. The NODL could have obviated the need for rescue, but it hasn't. The point where rescue begins is, of course, a fact. Mr. Fischer notes the fact, but he abuses it to advance his own purposes. The NODL must surely recognize the fact, but it has not acted on the recognition, to the detriment of its own purposes. The fact is that in half-a-dozen or more cities and towns the police have made use of the NODL list in order to threaten, coerce or punish dealers in reading matter.

Unquestionably, officers of the law have full right to use the weapons of law, which are coercive. The point in question, however, is their use of the NODL list. This puts NODL in an ambiguous position. It cannot expect to have the thing both ways. It cannot, on the one hand, protest that "the list is not to be used for purpose of boycott or coercion," and, on the other hand, fail to protest against the use of the list by the police. It has to choose its cooperators—either the merchant or the police. It cannot choose both; for the choice is really between opposed methods of cooperation—the method of voluntary cooperation as between equal citizens, or the method of coercion as used by the police.

If NODL consents to the use of its list by the police, it creates an ambiguity that its critics may rightly seize upon, as Mr. Fischer did; what is worse, it obscures from public view its own "idea," the altogether valid idea of voluntary reform. On the other hand, if NODL does not consent to the use of its list by the police, it should say so—publicly, and on every necessary occasion. Surely part of its service must be the supervision, conducted on its own principles, of the uses to which its list is put.

There is another inappropriateness here. Officers of the law must operate under statutes which in this matter are, or ought to be, narrowly drawn. On the other hand a voluntary reform precisely because it is voluntary, may be based on the somewhat broader categories of commonsense judgment. The latter are employed by the NODL, rightly enough. But for this very reason it is not right for the police to use NODL's judgment forcing the law. The law must have its own standards minimal enough to sustain the challenge of due process.

In this connection another fact must be noted. The fact is that on NODL lists there appear some twenty-odd works that either have received literary honors or at least have been acclaimed by serious critics. Doubtless high-school teachers could not, without absurdity, make them required reading for their students. But the police cannot, without equal absurdity, make them prohibited reading. Such stultification of the law is itself immoral.

There is a third fact of some consequence. The history of censorship has been a history of excess. The NODL has the problem of the local zealot, operating far from the central office in Chicago, and way outside the four pages of sensible procedures sent out from it. He or she "has the zeal of God indeed, but not according to understanding" (Romans 10:2). Such zealots are righteous, usually indignant, people. They have a cause. They want results. What they lack is St. Paul's "understanding," which bears, he said, on "the *way* of justification."

I shall not labor the analogy. The point of it, in our case, is that the zealot at times fails to see how his zeal for results may betray him into the use of methods that will in turn betray his cause. Mr. Fischer, for example, in his zeal for his own cause, which is a good one, fell into a bad method of argument. Among other faults, he fails to distinguish between the "idea" of the NODL which is the substantive issue, and the applications of the idea, which raise issues of procedure. In good "liberal" fashion he assigns the primacy to the procedural over the substantial. Contrariwise, in good Catholic fashion, the local zealot for the NODL cause assigns the primacy to the substantive over the procedural. He, or she, wants the newsstands "cleaned up"; and he, or she, in some instances doesn't greatly care how.

At that, Mr. Fischer is more nearly right. In this sensitive area the question of procedure is all-important. Part of the service of NODL to its own cause should be what I can only call a service of fraternal correction. It should somehow find a way of rebuking, or at least disavowing, the local zealot who violates, or goes beyond, the cooperative procedures, none of them coercive, which it officially stands for. (As for Mr. Fischer maybe I have myself done him some service of intellectual charity?)

At this point, with all the ambiguities at least sorted out, if not cleared up, we could begin the rational public argument. The starting-point would be a fact—the existence of a "real national problem" (Mr. Fischer's words). Then the questions arise. For instance, does Mr. Fischer adequately measure the dimensions of the problem? He says:

A good many tawdry and disreputable magazines, paper-bound reprints and comic books have been offered for sale on a lot of newsstands. A few publishers unquestionably have tried to base their sales appeal on sex and violence; the pictures and text on the covers of their publications often hint that the contents are far more salacious than they are in fact.

He adds that "law-enforcement agencies in some cities have not been vigorous in enforcing the statutes against obscene publications." And that's it.

Or is it? Others would maintain that this is an astonishing understatement of the real national problem. They see the problem much more ominously large. A major issue in public morality has arisen; the morals of youth are particularly involved in it; the problem is growing. They further see a causal line between bad magazines, etc., and immorality. And they feel it imperative to "do something" about the bad literature.

When these last statements are made, they start up the current argument between sociology and common sense. The sociologist expresses professional doubt about the causal line between bad reading and immorality; he finds insufficient evidence for it. The commonsense view asserts that the causal line is sufficiently established by the nature, content, tendency, etc., of the literature itself. At least a strong presumption is thus created; and it furnishes reason for action, until— and maybe after—all the Ph.D. theses, pro and con, have been written.

The word "action" disturbs the jealous advocate of civil rights. He therefore comes up with his own causal line—between any attempt at suppressing any kind of literature and the subversion of the foundations of the Republic. The commonsense view expresses doubt about this causal line. There is, it says, insufficient evidence that any such alarming consequences will follow if the action taken is rational and prudent.

Here the real issue begins to appear: what kinds of action, as taken by whom, are rational and prudent in the circumstances? And what promise of effectiveness do they offer?

Mr. Fischer has his own program of action, which deserves consideration. He recommends two positive courses. The first is self-regulation by newsdealers, book sellers, and other merchants. They should, he says, "set their own house in order; they should refuse to sell any publication which—in their own untrammeled judgment—falls below their own standards as responsible businessmen."

A question of fact occurs here: how effective so far has the principle of self-regulation been in the solution of our real national problem? The evidence suggests a discouraging answer. Some efforts in this direction have been made, always under the pressure of public opinion; but their slim success bases little hope for the future. Second, the principle itself may be, and has been, called in question. For instance, in a report entitled *The Freedom to Read*, written for the National Book Committee, Richard McKeon, Walter Gellhorn and Robert K. Merton say this:

> The dangers of police censorship are obvious; but we are convinced that the dangers of a code of self-censorship are even greater. It provides the means by which all kinds of restrictions can be put on freedom of expression, and it places the freedom to read in the hands of a group which does not even have the accountability to the public which a chief of police has (p. 70).

I don't necessarily endorse this judgment; but it may suggest that Mr. Fischer is on shaky ground.

There are other questions too. What, I might ask, is the right of a newsdealer to "untrammeled judgment"? Is his judgment, as a matter of fact, untrammeled? And whether it is or not, why should one trust it as a means of solution for our real national problem? Is he a better critic of literature, a better judge of morality, than the average parent? How is one even to know what his "standards as a responsible businessman" are? And if they could be known, is there to be no possibility of public judgment on them? On what title is this Olympian immunity claimed? One would like to know.

The second positive course is the action of law—legislative and court action. I am inclined to think that Mr. Fischer's confidence in the efficacy of legal action as a corrective in this difficult field of printed media will be astonishing to students of the law. If I mistake not, it is pretty generally admitted that the present legal picture is a muddle. It is further admitted that the difficulties encountered in trying to straighten it out are immense. There are the two sacred legal doctrines that must be protected—prior restraint and due process.

Furthermore, there are certain adverse high-court decisions that seem to have reduced the law to a state of practical impotence, not least in the two crucial areas of obscenity and violence.

What is even more decisive, even if the law could be lifted to the full height of its legitimate potency, it would still be largely impotent to cope with the new problem of mass media, whose crude subtleties seem to defeat the subtle crudities of the law. The grounds for accepting the relative ineffectiveness of law in this special field, where the moral issue is not justice, are both theoretical and practical—to be found both in the art of jurisprudence and in the lessons of history.

Mr. Fischer suggests two manners of action—one private, the other public—whose possibilities ought by all means be explored and exploited. But in the course of rational public argument it would, I think, appear that his program of positive action is inadequate to the real national problem that confronts us. His negative demand is more acceptable. He wants organizations of private right to stop campaigns of coercion. So do I. Mr. Fischer's reasons are, I think, doctrinaire; further argument would have to illuminate the fact, if it is a fact. Whereas, I, as a Catholic, am not a doctrinaire.

In my Chicago lecture I said that

> . . . it is not possible to prove the position, taken by some, that an action like the boycott of a moving picture is somehow "unrightful," or "undemocratic" or "unconstitutional." No one can show that such an action lies beyond the limits of a primeval American right to protest and object. The action may indeed be strenuous; but the American right to protest and object is permitted to run to some pretty strenuous extremes. This said against the doctrinaire, it remains true that methods of action which verge upon the coercive exhibit some incongruity when used by citizen-groups in the interests of morality in literature or on the screen. Even if they raise no issue of abstract right, they do raise the concrete issue of prudence, which, equally with justice, is one of the cardinal virtues.

I hold to this position now, against Mr. Fischer (I think), and also (I think) against the NODL in its present ambiguous situation—certainly in its representation by local zealots and by the secular arm of the police.

I further hold to my previous position that private agencies such as the NODL can perform an indispensable public function in the promotion of public morality—provided they understand what their function is. It is not to supplant the coercive function of the agencies of public law. It is to represent, soberly and honestly, the principle of voluntary reform, to be accomplished on the basis of social cooperation—that sincere cooperation which in America is always ready to be stimulated but often needs stimulation.

This principle of reform is altogether valid in itself. Its applications call for prudence—concretely, as I have previously said, for "men and women of prudence, who understand the art of procedure, and understand too that we are morally bound, by the virtue of prudence, to a concrete rightness of method in the pursuit of moral aims." For the rest, the rationality of this method of social reform will be understood, and its pitfalls will be avoided, if we can all somehow hold to high standards of public discussion. In this respect the editor of *Harper's* has failed. But his failure is less reprehensible than that of Catholics who miss their present opportunity—and duty—to perform the instant task, which is to inject the Catholic tradition of rationality into a mass democracy that is rapidly slipping its moorings in reason.

Memo to Cardinal Cushing on Contraception Legislation

John Courtney Murray, S.J.

In the mid-1960s Richard Cardinal Cushing asked Murray for recommendations concerning a Catholic response to a Massachusetts law that would decriminalize the supplying of artificial contraception devices. At this time Murray apparently maintained the natural law immorality of artificial contraception. Here, however, he argued that Catholics ought not oppose the law and that they ought to offer appropriate witness to both the morality of contraception and the public uses of civil law. For Murray's later judgments concerning contraception, see "Toledo Talk" in the appendix to this collection.

In my opinion, Catholics may and should approve amendment of Sections 20 and 21 of Chapter 272 of the *General Laws* of Massachusetts.[1]

The necessary amendment would permit doctors and responsible agencies to give contraceptive information to those who request it, and hence permit the sale of contraceptives on such responsible

---

No previous publication. Found as "Memo to Cushing on Contraception Legislation" Murray Archives, file 1–43.

1. EDITOR NOTE: Massachusetts General Law 272, §20 imposed penalties of not more than three years jail or $1,000 fine for advertizing or dissemination of information directed to inducing miscarriages or preventing conception. §21 imposed similar penalties for "selling, lending or giving away an instrument or other article intended to be used for self-abuse, or any drug, medicine, instrument or article whatever for the prevention of conception," and also any advertizement or information distribution concerning such practices. The May 10, 1966, passage of General Law 272, §21A approved physician distribution of contraceptive means by way of prescription and the dissemination of contraception information by qualified health personnel. It still did not allow direct advertisement or distribution of such devices through vending machines.

recommendation. Whether the amendment should go farther than this is not now so clear.

There are, I think, two general lines of argument.

1. The first argument is based on the differential character of law and morality and on the distinction between public and private morality.

It is not the function of civil law to prescribe everything that is morally right and to forbid everything that is morally wrong. By reason of its nature and purpose, as the instrument of order in society, the scope of law is limited to the maintenance and protection of public morality. Matters of private morality lie beyond the scope of law; they are left to the personal conscience.

An issue of public morality arises when a practice seriously undermines the foundations of society or gravely damages the moral life of the community as such, in such wise that legal prohibition becomes necessary to safeguard the social order as such. So, for instance, offenses against justice must be made criminal offenses, since justice is the foundation of civil order.

Moreover, the scope of law is further limited to the protection and maintenance of relatively minimal standards of public morality. A minimum of public morality is a social necessity. On the other hand, the force of law is coercive (*disciplina cogens metu poenae*), and men can normally be coerced into the observance of only minimal standards.

These norms of law hold with particular force for a free society, in which government is not paternal and the jurisprudential rule obtains: "As much freedom as possible; as much restriction and coercion as necessary."[2]

Furthermore, the measure of public morality that can and should be enforced by law is necessarily a matter of public judgment,

---

2. EDITOR NOTE: This double phase was at the heart of Murray's argument for civil religious freedom (at this time under discussion at the Second Vatican Council). In Murray's 1964e: "The Problem of Religious Freedom" (1964e) "the maxim was presented as an outgrowth of an Anglo-American "great act of faith in the powers of the people to judge, direct, and correct" the government. That is, the maxim emerged within a particular historical society. In Murray's last argument for religious freedom, he linked the maxim immediately to a notion of the human person, prior to and formative of government (see 1968: "The Human Right to Religious Freedom" [1968] in *Religious Liberty: Catholic Struggles with Pluralism* [1993].

especially in a democratic society. The people whose good is at stake have a right of judgment concerning the measure of public virtue that is to be enforced on them, and concerning the manner of public evils that are to be repressed.

Again, by reason of the function of law, there must be a reasonable correspondence between the moral standards generally recognized by the conscience of the community and the legal statutes concerning public morality. Otherwise laws will be unenforceable and ineffective and they will be resented as undue restrictions on civil or personal freedom.

In certain cases, the law may be "ahead" of the public conscience, or some segments of it; so, for instance, in the matter of racial equality. Here, however, justice and constitutional guarantees are at stake. On the other hand, in the field of sex morality the public educative value of law seems almost nil. For instance, it is useless to attempt to suppress fornication, or even adultery, by law.

In our present case, the crucial issue is whether contraception is an issue of public morality or of private morality. The question is disputed among Catholics.

I think that the case for affirming contraception to be matter of private morality is sufficiently conclusive in our present circumstances. It is not merely that the practice is in fact widespread, or that so many people do not consider it to be wrong. The more decisive reason is that the practice, undertaken in the interests of "responsible parenthood," has received official sanction by many religious groups within the community. It is difficult to see how the state can forbid, as contrary to public morality, a practice that numerous religious leaders approve as morally right. The stand taken by these religious groups may be lamentable from the Catholic moral point of view. But it is decisive from the point of view of law and jurisprudence, for which the norm of "generally accepted standards" is controlling.

It may be argued that contraception raises an issue of public morality because it has public consequences—an effect on the birth rate, on family morality, on the rise of hedonism, etc. On the other hand, it does not seem that these public consequences can be controlled by law. It further seems that the effort at legal control results in other social evils—contempt for the law (already widespread), religious strife within the community, etc.

The conclusion is that amendment of the birth-control statutes is permissible and even advisable on grounds of a valid and traditional theory of law and jurisprudence.

2. The second—and secondary—argument derives from the concept of religious freedom. The forthcoming conciliar declaration will assert that the concept includes a twofold immunity from coercion.

First, a man may not be coercively constrained to act against his conscience. Second, a man may not be coercively restrained from acting according to his conscience, unless the action involves a civil offense—against the public peace, against public morality, or against the rights of others.

But the practice of contraception involves no such civil offense. Therefore the principle of religious freedom should obtain. And laws in restraint of the practice are in restraint of religious freedom.[3] I call this argument secondary because it supports the prior argument, that contraception is a matter of private morality.

So much for the case favoring the amendment. There remains, of course issues of prudence.

First, the amendment should be put through with as little public agitation as possible. Let there not be another referendum, which stirs popular passions, raises false issues of power and prestige, and divides the community on the moral issue when it should be united on an issue of law and civil freedom.

Second, Catholics must make publicly known the grounds of their approval, namely, that they, like all citizens, are bound on the principles of law, jurisprudence, and religious freedom.

Third, Catholics themselves must be made to understand that, although contraception is not an issue of public morality to be dealt with by civil law, it remains for them a moral issue in their family lives, to be decided according to the teaching of the Church. Because contraception is made legal it is not therefore made moral, any more that it should be made illegal simply because it is immoral.

Catholics might well take this public occasion to demonstrate that their moral position is truly moral, that is, it is adopted freely, out of personal conviction and in intelligent loyalty to their Church.

---

3. EDITOR NOTE: Unless Murray were here ready to claim that judgments concerning contraception arise out of revealed sources, not from natural law analysis, it is difficult to see what this religious liberty appeal adds to his first argument, except to highlight the fact that judgments concerning contraception differ from denomination to denomination, and that Catholics should hesitate when, as mentioned above, leaders of other religious communities differ from Catholic magisterial judgments.

Selective
Conscientious Objection

JOHN COURTNEY MURRAY, S.J.

In a 1958 address on nuclear deterrence, Murray admitted the partial validity of a relative nuclear pacifism, partially valid in that it pointed to the extremely deadly potential of a full scale nuclear war, partially invalid because it did not take into account the valid insights of two other viewpoints (*WHTT*, p. 250). The other two were the recognition that a tremendous gulf between the East and West (suggesting to some the possibility of a Holy War), and the insight of others that an international order of law, embodied in the United Nations, ought to make war impossible. While Murray had, in 1944, called for just such an international order of law, and criticized some Roman Catholics for opposing the U.N., in this 1958 article he commented that the U.N was at present too weak to morally outlaw defensive war for the sake of justice. He then proceeded through a rather tortured argument that Pius XII, in the latter's application of the principle of proportionality, had not ruled out limited nuclear war (p. 259). He continued that Pius had prohibited any Catholic pacifism (p. 264). He finally concluded that the church must help break the American temptation of thinking of war in terms of either total surrender or total defeat, or the temptation of thinking of the use of force as amoral or immoral. Murray's main point once again was the need to construct a social environment in which the nation could distinguish between force and violence, limited and total nuclear war and to think morally about the issue across the present polarization of viewpoints.

An address given at Western Maryland College, June 4, 1967. First published as pamphlet entitled "Selective Conscientious Objection" by *Our Sunday Visitor* (Huntington, IN: Our Sunday Visitor, Inc.). Republished as "War and Conscience" in *A Conflict of Loyalties: The Case for Selective Conscientious Objection*, 19–30, ed. by James Finn, (New York: Pegasus, 1968).

The following article was an address, given at Western Maryland College on June 4, 1967, just weeks before Murray's death. Here he affirms the moral validity of selective conscientious objection. Once again his preoccupation rests on the quality of debate that ought to result from the conscientious objector's obligation to defend his position in the public forum. Amid the sharpening polarities brought on by that war, he had his doubts whether such a public debate could be effected.

The nation is confronted today with the issue of selective conscientious objection, conscientious objection to particular wars, or as it is sometimes called, discretionary armed service.

The theoretical implications of the issue are complex and subtle. The issue raises the whole question of war as a political act and the means whereby it should be confined within the moral universe. The issue also raises the question of the status of the private conscience in the face of the public law and national policy. In fact, the whole relation of the person to society is involved in this issue. Moreover, the practical implications of the issue are far reaching. Selective conscientious objection, as Gordon Zahn has pointed out, is an "explosive principle." If once admitted with regard to the issue of war, the consequences of the principle might run to great lengths in the civil community.

My brief comments on this far-reaching principle are here directed, for reasons that will appear, both to the academic community, especially the student community, and to the political community and its representatives.

A personal note may be permissible here. During the deliberations of the President's Advisory Commission on Selective Service, on which I was privileged to serve, I undertook to advocate that the revised statute should extend the provisions of the present statute to include not only the absolute pacifist but also the relative pacifist, that the grounds for the status of conscientious objector should be not only religiously or non-religiously motivated opposition to participation in war in all forms, but also to similarly motivated opposition to participation in particular wars.

This position was rejected by the majority of the Commission. No Presidential recommendation was made to the Congress on the issue. There is evidence that the Congress is not sympathetic to the position of the selective objector and is not inclined to accept it. This does not mean that the issue has been satisfactorily settled. The public argument goes on and must go on. It is much too late in the day to defend the theory of General Hershey that "the conscientious objector by my theory is best handled if no one hears of him." The issue is before the country and it must be kept there.

It is true the issue has been raised by a small number of people, chiefly in the academic community—students, seminarians, professors, not to speak of ministers of religion. But this group of citizens is socially significant. It must be heard and it must be talked to. I recognize that in many respects the issue has been raised rather badly, in ways that betray misunderstanding. Moreover, mistakes have been made about the mode of handling the issue. Nevertheless, the student community is to be praised for having raised a profound moral issue that has been too long disregarded in American life.

The American attitude toward war has tended to oscillate between absolute pacifism in peacetime and extremes of ferocity in wartime. Prevalent in American society has been an abstract ethic, conceived either in religious or in secularized terms, which condemns all war as immoral. No nation has the *jus ad bellum*. On the other hand, when a concrete historical situation creates the necessity for war, no ethic governs its conduct. There are no moral criteria operative to control the uses of the force. There is no *jus in bello*. One may pursue hostilities to the military objective of unconditional surrender, and the nation may escalate the use of force to the paroxysm of violence of which Hiroshima and Nagasaki are forever the symbols, even though they were prepared for by the fire-bomb raids on Tokyo and by the saturation bombing of German cities. And all this use of violence can somehow be justified by slogans that were as simplistic as the principles of absolute pacifism.

These extreme alternatives are no longer tolerable. Our nation must make its way to some discriminating doctrine—moral, political, and military—on the uses of force. Perhaps the contemporary agitation in the academic community over selective conscientious objection may help in this direction. It has contributed to a revival of the traditional doctrine of the just war, whose origins were in Augustine and which was elaborated by the medieval Schoolmen and furthered by the international jurists in the Scholastic tradition and by others in the later tradition of Grotius.

This doctrine has long been neglected, even by the churches. Now we begin to witness its revival. We are also beginning to realize that it is not a sectarian doctrine. It is not exclusively Roman Catholic;

in certain forms of its presentation, it is not even Christian. It emerges in the minds of all men of reason and good will when they face two inevitable questions. First, what are the norms that govern recourse to the violence of war? Second, what are the norms that govern the measure of violence to be used in war? In other words, when is war rightful, and what is rightful in war? One may indeed refuse the questions, but this is a form of moral abdication, which would likewise be fatal to civilization. If one does face the questions, one must arrive at the just war doctrine in its classical form, or at some analogue or surrogate, conceived in other terms.

The essential significance of the traditional doctrine is that it insists, first, that military decisions are a species of political decisions, and second, that political decisions must be viewed not simply in the perspective of politics as an exercise of power but of morality and theology in some valid sense. If military and political decisions are not so viewed, the result is the degradation of those who make them and the destruction of the human community.

My conclusion here is that we all owe some debt of gratitude to those who, by raising the issue of selective conscientious objection, have undertaken to transform the tragic conflict in South Vietnam into an issue not simply of political decision and military strategy, but of moral judgment as well.

The mention of South Vietnam leads me to my second point. The issue of selective conscientious objection has been raised in the midst of the war in Southeast Asia. Therefore, there is danger lest the issue be muddled and confused, or even misused and abused. In South Vietnam we see war stripped of all the false sanctities with which we managed to invest World War I and World War II, and to a lesser extent even Korea. The South Vietnamese war is not a crusade. There is not even a villain of the piece, as the Kaiser was, or Hitler, or Hirohito. Not even Ho Chi Minh or Mao Tse-tung can be cast in the role of the man in the black hat. We have no easy justifying slogans. We cannot cry, "On to Hanoi," as we cried "On To Berlin" and "On To Tokyo." This war does not raise the massive issue of national survival. It is a limited military action for limited political aims. As we view it in the press or on television it almost seems to fulfill Hobbes' vision of human life in the state of pure nature, "nasty, brutish, and short"—except that the war in South Vietnam will not be short. In the face of the reality of it, all our ancient simplisms fail us. The American people are uncomfortable, baffled, and even resentful and angry.

To state the problem quite coldly, the war in South Vietnam is subject to opposition on political and military grounds, and also on grounds of national interest. This opposition has been voiced, and voiced in passionate terms. It has evoked a response in the name of patriotism that is also passionate. Consequently, in this context, it is difficult to raise the moral issue of selective conscientious objection. There are even some to whom it seems dangerous to let the issue be raised at all.

At this juncture I venture to make a recommendation in the common interest of good public argument. The issue of selective conscientious objection must be distinguished from the issue of the justice of the South Vietnam war. If this distinction is not made and enforced in argument, the result will be confusion and the clash of passions. The necessary public argument will degenerate into a useless and harmful quarrel. The distinction can be made. I make it myself. I advocate selective conscientious objection in the name of the traditional moral doctrine on war and also in the name of traditional American political doctrine on the rights of conscience. I am also prepared to make the case for the American military presence and action in South Vietnam.

I hasten to add that I can just about make the moral case. But so it always is. The morality of war can never be more than marginal. The issue of war can never be portrayed in black and white. Moral judgment on the issue must be reached by a balance of many factors. To argue about the morality of war inevitably leads one into gray areas. This is the point that was excellently made by Mr. Secretary Vance in his thoughtful address to the Annual Convention of the Episcopal Diocese of West Virginia on May 6, 1967. It is evident here that our national tradition of confused moral thought on the uses of force does us a great disservice. It results in a polarization of opinion that makes communication among citizens difficult or even impossible. As Mr. Vance said, "In America today one of the greatest barriers to understanding is the very nature of the dialogue which has developed over the issue of Vietnam. It is heated and intolerant. The lines on both sides are too sharply drawn." I agree.

By the same token rational argument about selective conscientious objection will be impossible if public opinion is polarized by all the passions that have been aroused by the South Vietnam war. The two issues, I repeat, can and must be separated.

Another difficulty confronts us here. The issue about conscientious objection seems to have been drawn between the academic

community and the political community—if you will, between poets
and politicians, between scientists and statesmen, between humanists
and men of affairs, between the churches and the secular world. It is,
therefore, no accident that the dialogue at the present moment is in a
miserable state. One may seek the reason for the fact in the differences
in the climate of thought and feeling that prevail in the two distinct
communities, academic and political. In consequence of this difference in climate each community, in a different way, can become the
victim of the intellectual and moral vice that is known as the selective
perception of reality.

It has been observed that the commitment of the intellectual
today is not simply to the search for truth, but also to the betterment
of the world—to the eradication of evil and to the creation of conditions of human dignity, first among which is peace. One might say
that he has assumed a prophetic role, not unlike that of the churches.[1]
This is most laudable. The danger is lest the very strength of the
moral commitment—to peace and against war—may foreclose
inquiry into the military and political facts of the contemporary
world—the naked facts of power situations and the requirements of
law and order in an imperfect world, which may justify recourse to
the arbitrament of arms. The problem is compounded if the so-called
"norms of nonconformism" begin to operate. In that case opposition
to war becomes the test of commitment to the ideals of the academic
community.

On the other hand, the politician is no prophet. He may and
should wish to shape the world unto the common desire of the heart
of man which is peace with freedom and justice. But he is obliged to
regard the world as an arena in which historical alternatives are
always limited. He must face enduring problems, which may seem
intractable, and which demand continuing decisions and acts. His
actions cannot be based on a careful balancing and choosing between
the relativities that are before him.

In a word, for the prophets and for the intellectual, war is simply evil. For the politician it may well appear to be the lesser evil. This
too is a conscientious position—the choice of the lesser evil is part of

---

1. EDITOR NOTE: This prophetic role of the academic community is not
unlike Murray's description of the eschatological humanist in "Is It Basket
Weaving," *WHTT*, 175–97.

the human pursuit of the good. But it is very different from the prophetic position. In any event, it is not surprising that the politician and the prophet fail to communicate. It must also be remembered that the politician creates the situation within which the prophetic voice may be safely heard. There is much wisdom in the statement of Paul Ramsey: "The right of pacifist conscientious objection can be granted for the fostering of the consciences of free men, only because in national emergencies there are a sufficient number of individuals whose political discretion has been instructed in the need to repel, and the justice of repelling, injury to the common good."

I might add a practical point. The intellectual, whether he be student or professor, sets a premium on being provocative. His task is to challenge all certainties, especially easy certainties, and therefore to challenge the authorities on which certainties may depend. He wants evidence, not authority, and besets a high value on dissent. All this is excellent and necessary. But there is danger in thrusting this scale of evaluation into the political community. It is not merely that the intellectual provokes reaction; he provokes an over-reaction on the part of the representatives of the political community, and thus he may easily defeat his own cause.

The advocacy of selective conscientious objection in the midst of the South Vietnamese war is provocative, and the political response to it has been an over-reaction. If you want the evidence you need only read the record of the hearings in Congress, both Senate and House, on the revision of the Selective Service Act, when the issue of conscientious objection was brought up. The claim that the selective objector should be recognized was met with response that all conscientious objection should be abolished.

All this amounts simply to saying that we face a most difficult issue. It might be of some value to try to locate some of the sources of the difficulty. Strictly on grounds of moral argument, the right conscientiously to object to participation in a particular war is incontestable. I shall not argue this issue. The practical question before all of us is how to get the moral validity of this right understood and how to get the right itself legally recognized, declared in statutory law. (I leave aside the question whether the right is a human right, which ought to receive sanction in the Bill of Rights as a constitutional right.)

I have made one practical suggestion already. The issue of selective conscientious objection must be argued on its own merits. It is not a question of whether one is for or against the war in Vietnam, for or against selective service, much less for or against killing other people. The worst thing that could happen would be to use the issue of conscientious objection as a tactical weapon for political opposition to the war in Vietnam or to the general course of American foreign policy. This would not be good morality and it would be worse politics. Perhaps the central practical question might be put in this way: Do the conditions exist which make possible the responsible exercise of a right of selective conscientious objection? The existence of these conditions is the prerequisite for granting legal status to the right itself.

There are two major conditions. The first is an exact understanding of the just war doctrine, and the second is respect for what Socrates called "the conscience of the laws." I offer two examples, from among many, where these conditions were not observed.

Not long ago a young man in an anti-Vietnam protest on television declared that he would be willing to fight in Vietnam if he knew that the war there was just, but since he did not know he was obliged to protest its immorality. This young man clearly did not understand the just war doctrine and he did not understand what Socrates meant by the "conscience of the laws."

Similarly, in a statement issued by a Seminarians' Conference on the Draft held not long ago in Cambridge, there appears this statement: "The spirit of these principles [of the just war doctrine] demands that every war be opposed until or unless it can be morally justified in relation to these principles." Socrates would not have agreed with this statement nor do I. The dear seminarians have got it backward.

The root of the error here may be simply described as a failure to understand that provision of the just war doctrine which requires that a war should be "declared." This is not simply a nice piece of legalism, the prescription of a sheer technicality. Behind the provision lies a whole philosophy of the State as a moral and political agent. The provision implies the recognition of the authority of the political community by established political processes to make decisions about the course of its action in history, to muster behind these decisions the united efforts of the community, and to publicize these decisions before the world.

If there is to be political community, capable of being a moral agent in the international community, there must be some way of publicly identifying the nation's decisions. These decisions must be declared to be the decisions of the community. Therefore. if the decision is for war, the war must be declared. This declaration is a moral and political act. It states a decision conscientiously arrived at in the interests of the international common good. It submits the decision to the judgment of mankind. Moreover, when the decision-making processes of the community have been employed and a decision has been reached, at least a preliminary measure of internal authority must be conceded by the citizens to this decision, even by those citizens who dissent from it. This, at least in part, is what Socrates meant by respect for the "conscience of the laws." This is why in the just war theory it has always been maintained that the presumption stands for the decision of the community as officially declared. He who dissents from the decision must accept the burden of proof.

The truth, therefore, is contrary to the statement of the seminarians. The citizen is to concede the justness of the common political decision, made in behalf of the nation, unless and until he is sure in his own mind that the decision is unjust, for reasons that he in turn must be ready convincingly to declare. The burden of proof is on him, not on the government or the administration or the action as a whole. He does not and may not resign his conscience into the keeping of the State, but he must recognize that the State too has its conscience which informs its laws and decisions. When his personal conscience clashes with the conscience of the laws, his personal decision is his alone. It is valid for him, and he must follow it. But in doing so he still stands within the community and is subject to its judgment as already declared.

Only if conceived in these terms can the inevitable tension between the person and the community be properly a tension of the moral order. Otherwise, it will degenerate into a mere power struggle between arbitrary authority and an aggregate of individuals, each of whom claims to be the final arbiter of right and wrong.

This is the line of reasoning which led me to argue before the National Advisory Commission on Selective Service that one who applies for the status of selective conscientious objector should be obliged to state his case before a competent panel of judges. I was also following the suggestion of Ralph Potter that the concession of status to the selective objector might help to upgrade the level of moral and political discourse in this country. It is presently lamentably low. On the other hand, Paul Ramsey has recently suggested that the matter works the other way round. "A considerable upgrading of the level of political discourse in America is among the conditions of the possibil-

ity of granting selective conscientious objection. At least the two
things can and may and must go together." He adds rather sadly:
"The signs of the times are not propitious for either." I agree.

Those who urge the just war doctrine as the ground for selective
conscientious objection must understand the doctrine itself. They may
not naively or cynically employ it as a device for opting out from
under the legitimate decisions of the political community, or as a tactic for political opposition to particular wars. Rightly understood, this
doctrine is not an invitation to pacifism, and still less to civil disobedi-
ence. There is a further requisite for legal recognition of selective conscientious objection. It is the prior recognition of the difference
between moral objection to a particular war and political opposition
to a particular war. This seems to be the sticking point for the political
community. It brings into question the whole ethos of our society in
the matter of the uses of force.

Historically, we have been disposed to regard the intuitive ver-
dict of the absolute pacifist that all wars are wrong as having the force
of a moral imperative. The same moral force is not conceded to the
judgment of the conscientious man, religious or not, who makes a
reflective and discriminating judgment on the war in front of him.
The general disposition is to say that objection to particular wars is
and can only be political and, therefore, cannot entitle anyone to the
status of conscientious objector.

Here again there is a misunderstanding of the just war doctrine.
In fact there seems to be a misunderstanding of the very nature of
moral reasoning. The just war doctrine starts from the moral principle
that the order of justice and law cannot be left without adequate
means for its own defense, including the use of force. The doctrine
further holds that the use of force is subject to certain conditions and
its justice depends on certain circumstances. The investigation of the
fulfillment of these conditions leads the conscientious man to a consideration of certain political and military factors in a given situation.
There is the issue of aggression, the issue of the measure of force to be
employed in resisting it, the issue of probable success, the issue of the
balance of good and evil that will be the outcome. The fact that his
judgment must take account of military and political factors does not
make the judgment purely political. It is a judgment reached within a
moral universe, and the final reason for it is of the moral order.

There is some subtlety to this argument. But that is not, I think,
the reason why the political community refuses to assimilate or

accept it. The reasons are of the practical order. The immediate reason is the enormous difficulty of administering a statute that would provide for selective conscientious objection. The deeper reason is the perennial problem of the erroneous conscience. It may be easily illustrated.

Suppose a young man comes forward and says: "I refuse to serve in this war on grounds of the Nuremberg principle." Conversation discloses that he has not the foggiest idea what the Nuremberg principle really is. Or suppose he understands the principle and says: "I refuse to serve because in this war the United States is committing war crimes." The fact may be, as it is in South Vietnam, that this allegation is false. Or suppose he says, "I refuse to serve because the United States is the aggressor in this war." This reason again may be demonstrably false. What then is the tribunal to do?

Here perhaps we come to the heart of the difficulty and I have only two things to say. First, unless the right to selective objection is granted to possibly erroneous consciences it will not be granted at all. The State will have to abide by the principle of the Seeger case, which does not require that the objection be the truth but that it be truly held. One must follow the logic of an argument wherever it leads. On the other hand, the political community cannot be blamed for harboring the fear that if the right to selective objection is acknowledged in these sweeping terms, it might possibly lead to anarchy, to the breakdown of society, and to the paralysis of public policy.

Second, the reality of this fear imposes a further burden on the consciences of those who would appeal to freedom of conscience. Selective objection is not a trivial matter. As Ralph Potter has said: "The nation is ultimately a moral community. To challenge its well-established policies as illegal, immoral, and unjust is to pose a threat, the seriousness of which seem at times to escape the critics themselves, whether by the callowness of youth or the callousness of usage." It must be recognized that society will defend itself against this threat, if it be carelessly wielded.

The solution can only be the cultivation of political discretion throughout the populace, not least in the student and academic community. A manifold work of moral and political intelligence is called for. No political society can be founded on the principle that absolute rights are to be accorded to the individual conscience, and to all individual consciences, even when they are in error. This is rank individualism and to hold it would reveal a misunderstanding of the very nature of the political community. On the other hand, the political community is bound to respect consciences. But the fulfillment of this obligation supposes that the consciences of the citizens are themselves formed and informed.

Therefore, the final question may be whether there is abroad in the land a sufficient measure of moral and political discretion, in such wise that the Congress could, under safeguard of the national security, acknowledge the right of discretionary armed service.

PART 2

Christian Humanism

In *We Hold These Truths* Murray claimed that natural law philosophy grounds, and offers the best hope for, the American experiment. As we saw in the last section, Murray eventually judged that natural law theory provides a sufficient, non-theological foundation for social cooperation among peoples of different faiths—especially concerning juridical immunities and enforcement, the deeper commitments of American Constitutionalism, and American foreign policy. The development of Murray's natural law thinking, then, is central for understanding WHTT's approach to questions of public meaning and policy.

The articles in this and subsequent sections move beyond the claim that the public forum ought to be guided exclusively by natural law theory. They approach the possibility of confessionally specific, theological languages entering the public forum—shaping both general value commitments and policy determinations. Advancing the discussion to the possibility of public theological discourse, however, does not demand a thorough rejection of the Murray of WHTT. Even in WHTT he provided an entry point for this contemporary "state of the question," namely, his discussion of "Christian Humanism." Two articles in WHTT betray his use of Christian humanism to bridge his own (exclusive) natural law considerations and strictly Catholic trinitarian theology. Both rely on his understanding of reasoning within the context of faith, as presented in his Christian humanism studies. Here I will briefly outline those two arguments and situate the collected articles of this section in relation to WHTT.

The first WHTT article addressed a quite specific institutional problem; the second, a more theoretical question concerning the Christian's general stance toward human society. In "Creeds at War Intelligibly: Pluralism and the University" (WHTT, Chapter 5),[1] Murray called for the teaching of America's religions in state schools by believers. In

---

1. First published as "The Making of a Pluralist Society." *Religious Education.* 53 (November–December 1958): 521–28.

that teaching, he hoped that all students would be exposed to "episte-molog[ies] of religious truth" and "the various systems of belief, pre-cisely as systems, in their inner organic consistency (whatever it may be), and in their relation to other areas of human knowledge (insofar as these relations are intellectually discernible)" (p. 137). He further argued that the state had no right, particularly in the schools, to ignore or suppress the faith commitments of the American people. In effect, then, Murray's 1958 treatment of the educational forum anticipated our contemporary concerns with a broader, societal-wide theological con-versation and offers hints of the ethical and virtue requirements for that larger discourse. The last article in this section, "On the Future of Humanistic Education" (1964b), continues that analytic line, now per-meated by Bernard Lonergan's cognitional theory.

On the theoretical side, in "Is It Basket Weaving? The Question of Christian and Human Values" (WHTT, Chapter 8),[2] Murray spelled out the groundings for his educational recommendations—groundings that are explicitly theological. In the original 1953 article, he distinguished between two distinct types of Christian humanism: eschatological humanism and incarnation humanism, and granted equal validity to both. In this section, "The Christian Idea of Education" (1955b) and edited portions of his "Liberal Arts College and the Contemporary Cli-mate of Opinion" (1959a) appear to claim incarnational humanism as the special charism of Roman Catholicism.

Those familiar only with the Murray of *We Hold These Truths* may see in the first two articles of this section a triumphalism that Murray eventually overcame. The first, "The Construction of a Christian Culture" (1940a), is a previously unpublished series of talks given in 1940. In them Murray argues that the necessary (and only sufficient) groundings for the freedoms that Americans hold dear are to be found in the explic-itly Catholic doctrines of the Incarnation, the Trinity, and the Cross. Par-ticularly in the humanism of the Cross, Murray searched for sources of social healing in the face of a disintegrating Europe and a materialistic America. The second article, "Toward a Christian Humanism" (1941b), is similar in theological expectations to the first, without, however, its explicit, sharp criticisms of America. Although Murray eventually claimed the sufficiency of natural law languages, the concerns of this 1940 address never fully left him, as is evident in the conclusion to "The Return of Tribalism" (1961d), which is also included here.

2. Previously published as "Christian Humanism in America" (1953a).

The Construction of a Christian Culture

John Courtney Murray, S.J.

PORTRAIT OF A CHRISTIAN

The original title for these three talks was "The Concept of a Christian Culture." But I have changed it to "The Construction of a Christian Culture." For my desire is to present you not merely with a thesis, but with a task.[1] I shall attempt to outline for you the basic ideas upon which a Christian culture must be built; a firm grasp on them is the essential preliminary to all effective action. But it is not enough to have grasped the idea of a Christian culture; that idea must be given shape in the world of human life.

The task of constructing a culture is essentially spiritual, for culture has its home in the soul. It is difficult to describe in itself, but is very manifest in its effects. Its proper effect is to bring order into human life, the order proper to a human life, namely, a spiritual order, that alone makes a life authentically human. For a human life, like a body, is humanized in that it is brought under the direction of an intelligence that is conscious of itself and of its spiritual destiny, and in that it is brought under the domination of a will disciplined enough to maintain order among its subservient instincts and actually to import to the whole of life a spiritual purpose.[2]

Three talks given in February 1940 at St. Joseph's College. Original text in Murray Archives, file 6–422. I have omitted about one-fourth of the original text to remove redundancies and material not applicable to our present topic. I have also supplied some transitional phrasing, where needed.

1. Editor Note: Murray wrote in the margins of a long section directed to St. Joseph students that they were to be an elite, a "fifth column," in the task of social reconstruction. For a similar vision of Catholic action, see "Operation University" (1946b).

2. Editor Note: One objection Murray had to the work of Scheeben was its deminishment of the role of human intelligence in redemption (see *Matthias Scheeben on Faith: The Doctrinal Dissertation of John Courtney Murray* [1937, published 1987]).

Culture, then, means man's effort to be fully human and hence his effort to bring spiritual order and spiritual purpose into his life. It follows therefore that the proper instruments for the construction of a culture are intelligence and will, man's two spiritual powers. Do not think [intelligence and will] weak equipment. Intelligence and will were, so to speak, all that God himself had wherewith to create us and this world of ours; and it is solely by their use that he rules his creatures and guides them to their appointed spiritual destiny. The Word and the Spirit, as Irenaeus said, are the two hands of God, and in sharing them with you, he shares with you his omnipotence. And omnipotence ought to be enough for any task.

And notice this: it is not within the province of intelligence and will actually to create a spiritual order for human life; in fact, they do not have to. That spiritual order already exists; it is objective, "given." It is for man to discover it by his intelligence and submit to it by his will. Consequently, all man's cultural effort is at bottom an effort at submission to the truth and the beauty and the good that is outside him, existing in an ordered harmony, whose pattern he must produce within his soul by conformity with it.

Our first question must be: what is the actual problem confronting us here today in America? What have we actually to do?

It would seem that our American culture, as it exists, is actually the quintessence of all that is decadent in the culture of the Western Christian world. It would seem to be erected on the triple denial that has corrupted Western culture at its roots, the denial of metaphysical reality, of the primacy of the spiritual over the material, of the social over the individual.

Hence in view of the fact that American culture is built on the negation of all that Christianity stands for, it would seem that our first step toward the construction of a Christian culture should be the destruction of the existing one. In the presence of a Frankenstein, one does not reach for baptismal water, but for a bludgeon.

And truly, American culture does present itself as something of a monster, the like of which has surely never been seen on this planet. Its most striking characteristic is its profound materialism; it would seem to be orientated almost wholly to matter and the things of sense.

It has had, in fact, one dominating ideal: the conquest of a material world, with the aid of science, a conquest that has made one promise: a more abundant life for the ordinary man and woman, the abundance being ultimately in physical comfort. It turns out one typical product: the "homo oeconomicus," the business man, in a business suit, whose dreams of paradise are of a land in which there is no red ink.

It has given citizens everything to live for and nothing to die for. And its achievement may be summed up thus: it has gained a continent and lost its own soul. Say rather that it has lived so much on the surface that it has lost contact with its soul.

A profound religious truth is at the basis of democratic theory and practice, namely the intrinsic dignity of human nature, the spiritual freedom of the human soul, its equality, as a soul, with others of its kind, and its superiority to all that does not share its spirituality.

Yet, that truth, which we sum up in the Kantian phrase: "the individual man is an end in himself," has been corrupted to the point of blasphemy. And that is a blasphemy whose punishment is death. That corrupted belief, widespread, is the destruction of all spiritual order, all social order, all order within the individual personality and hence the ruination of all genuine human culture.

[How did America succumb to those temptations?] Briefly, the process was this: the ideals of humanist democracy, received very largely from France in the revolutionary period, had been divorced from their proper religious setting in the Christian revelation, but still had the form of a philosophy. Later they were stripped of their intellectual content by the Calvinist spirit of the Northern States and made over into a moral postulate, that animated a program of economic individualism. And, finally, when Calvinistic moral earnestness had died out, they survived as a humanitarian emotion, three degrees removed from their original source of inspiration.

Thus from a philosophic doctrine, the idea of individual dignity and liberty became a moral postulate and, from a moral postulate, it became a mere emotion. And it is upon that idea, emotionalized into a caricature of itself, that we are trying to live today, very dangerously. For if democracy as a doctrine is dangerous, as an emotion it is big with disaster.

Let me speak briefly of the second stage, which was the decisive one. I blame for it the Calvinistic Puritanism[3] of the Northern States. Consider three things. First of all, the fact that the Calvinist soul was

---

3. EDITOR NOTE: Murray claims he does not want to blame this development on Calvin, for "whose intellectual qualities and religious genius I have rather an admiration." For a later treatment of American Protestantism, see "Morality and Foreign Policy, Part I & II" (1960a), in *WHTT*, 273–94.

probably unique in the history of souls for its abhorrence of what we term humanism. Puritanism, as a religion, was exclusively a culture of the will, imposing an inhumanly rigid ethical discipline, professedly anti-intellectual and on principle contemptuous of all aesthetic and sensuous culture. Democracy as a basis for a genuinely humanist way of life had no meaning for it.

Secondly, consider the fact that Max Weber in his much-controverted, but still essentially sound book, *Die protestantische Ethik und der Geist des Kapitalismus*, has pointed out, that Calvinism brought one thing into the world that was "unquestionably new: the valuation of the fulfillment of duty in worldly affairs as the highest form which the moral activity of the individual could assume" (Weber-Parsons, p. 80). To the English or American Puritan, business activity for profit was a definitely religious *"Beruf,"* vocation, a divine call, towards which he had an ethical obligation; his success in it was the evidence of his "election," the source of his "certitude of salvation," the single goal of his religious striving.

For a combination of moral earnestness and business acumen one can find no equal to John Milton's "unscrupulous merchants" in the Puritan circles of England in the late 18th century, or to certain early American industrialists, with their peculiarly pious ruthlessness. Even the history of the Standard Oil Co. reveals those qualities.

If you wish the typical American incarnation of the Calvinist spirit, just at the time when it was beginning to decay, take Benjamin Franklin and his *Necessary Hints to Those Who Would be Rich*, or his *Advice to a Young Tradesman*, or even his *Autobiography*—books that have been of incalculable influence in forming the culture of America.

Consider lastly the unprecedented inner loneliness of the Calvinist soul, bred into it by its dogma of predestination, the belief that man follows his path alone to a destiny decreed for him from eternity, alone, isolated, beyond the help of anyone or anything. This inner loneliness, accentuating the all-importance of the individual, was moreover still further emphasized by persecution that roused in the Calvinist breast an angry spirit of protest against external authority.

In terms of three qualities of the Puritan soul, its anti-intellectualism and anti-humanism, its this-worldly morality, its intense individualism, you will, I think, find a major (though obviously not in itself adequate) explanation of the transformation of early American ideals of democracy. They were dehumanized, deintellectualized, moral-

ized, clothed with fierce emotion and made the justification for the
unregulated activity of the individual in the field that absorbed him—
business, economic life. Thus American culture became doubly material: material in its body, its economic order, and material in its soul,
emotional individualism.

Now, if the foregoing analysis has any validity, our cultural
problem should be as clear in its outline as it is urgent in its demands
for a solution. It is, I said, a problem of construction, and the point of
insertion for our effort, has, I hope, been made clear. At the basis of
our culture is a spiritual idea, a religious truth that has been impoverished and deformed. The truth, I mean, that man is a person, sacred,
inviolable, gifted with the divine prerogative of freedom and charged
with all the responsibilities of that gift, that reach horizontally out to
the farthest confines of human life and vertically up into the heart of
eternity.

The world owes that truth to Christianity; it did not exist before
Christ; it came to earth in him.[4] The Hellenic mind, intellectualist,
abstract and at bottom determinist, had but a slight apprehension of
it; the Oriental mind today, save where it has been influenced by Western teaching, still does not apprehend it.

And if we have it, it is because of Him who said: "If you remain
in my word, you will truly be my disciples and you will know the
truth, and the truth will make you free" (John 8:32). Christianity is
throughout, as von Hügel finely said, "the revelation, through the Person and example of its Founder, of the altogether unsuspected depth
and inexhaustibleness of human personality and of this personality's
analogue in God" (*The Mystical Element in Religion, I*, p. 26).

It is this vision of the Christian soul, stamped in the image of the
Most Blessed Trinity, given us in Christ, that we must give to America. It alone will fill up the spiritual void that exists at the center of
our culture and that explains its materialism and profaneness; it alone
will be the interior vital principle that will give to our democracy and
its economic achievements a spiritual purpose and hence a permanent vitality.

---

4. EDITOR NOTE: Compare this assertion to Murray's later claims that
the church had little role in modern developments of human dignity (see,
e.g., "The Declaration on Religious Freedom," [1966c] in this volume, Part 3).

Here, then, is the solution for our cultural problem that I wish to propose. I would take as the creative principle of our Christian culture the full, metaphysical theology of the Incarnation. The Incarnation, I mean, not as understood by Paul Elmer More or Mr. Middleton Murray, but as understood by Cyril of Alexandria and the Council of Ephesus, and by Leo the Great and the Council of Chalcedon. Hence the theology that regards Christ, not as the incarnation of the ethical ideals of humanity, but as the Incarnation of the Son of God, His subsistent Word and Image.

To develop this thesis, let me first state the theology of the Incarnation and then draw out, briefly, its cultural significance. Thus I shall, I think, be tracing the portrait of a Christian, whose strong and gentle, beautifully human features we must strive to engrave upon the countenance of America.

"In the beginning was the Word, and the Word was with God, and the Word was God. . . . And the Word was made flesh and pitched his tent among us. Of this fullness we have all received." So St. John states the fundamental fact of Christianity. And St. Paul: "When the fullness of time was come, God sent his Son, born of a woman. . . . that we might receive the adoption of sons" (Gal 4:4–5).

And this faith of John and Paul received its classic formulation at the Council of Chalcedon (fourth ecumenical) in the year 451. This faith of Chalcedon was formulated by the universal Church with anguished accuracy, for upon the exactness of its phrases the life of mankind depends: Christ is God, perfect in divinity, Christ is man, perfect in humanity; Christ is not two, but One. God is one with man and man is one with God. God is still God and man is still man, yet they are one: The Word was made Flesh, the Son of God was born of a woman.

And the primary cultural significance of this theology is that it is in this light that man, as St. Thomas said, now dares to think worthily of himself. Think of the consequence: now a Humanity can and must be adored. Let me put it thus strongly: the dreams of all idolaters have come true: a thing of flesh and blood has become so one with the divine that before it "every knee must bend, in heaven, on earth, and under the earth" (Phil 2:11). Chalcedon does not shrink before that conclusion; rather, it smites with its anathema Nestorius, who would not adore the man, Christ Jesus, with the same adoration that he gave to the Person of the Word. Equally Chalcedon teaches, in the eighth of the Cyrilline anathemas, one worship and one hymn of praise goes up to Emmanuel, God with us, for the Word has become Flesh. A human nature has become adorable and has launched, on metaphysical foundations, the cult of man.

What philosopher's theory of the dignity of man can rival this? Yet it is no theory, but a sober historical fact.

But there is more. The Incarnation is not only a revelation of what man is, but of what he can become, if he chooses to lay hold of the new divine energy (grace) that has been put at his disposal through the Humanity of Christ. I mean that man can become lord of creation and like to God: "for to as many as received him, he gave them power to become the children of God," (John 1:12) enjoying the freedom of his house on earth, having access to the mansions of his own blessed immortality.

Thus in Christ man received the answer to the two fundamental questions that vexed the mind of pagan antiquity and that must, in fact, vex any human mind that reflects upon itself. The first was this: how shall man achieve "salvation" from the tyranny of destiny, the *eímarméne*, the iron law of fate that apportions him a place in the scheme of things entire? How shall he achieve the spiritual freedom that he obscurely knows to be his birthright, but that he feels himself powerless to seize? How shall he rescue himself from beneath the hoofs of Time and break the chains that bind him to the wheel of matter? The second question is correlative: how shall man become like unto the gods, perfect in their perfection, sharing their changeless beatitude, quaffing the nectar of immortality?

The anguished note of these two questions shaped all philosophical and religious thought. To find the answer to them were directed all the philosopher's contemplative effort and all the solemn initiations of the mystery cults.

But one answer never entered their heads: that God himself should raise them to his blessed freedom and immortality, by coming down to them, to share in time their slavery and thus to shatter it, to grapple in combat with their death and thus to overcome it. It was the historical fact of the Incarnation that certified the eternal hope, somehow native to the human soul, of becoming like to God.

Secondly, the Incarnation answered the spiritual desire that, in spite of thwartings, man has always cherished, namely, the dream of becoming master of the world of nature and master too of the dark powers of evil whose presence in the world he has never ceased to feel. Through the Incarnation, which teaches man his proper dignity,

comes to him his long-sought enfranchisement from all earthly servi-
tudes. Now there is divinity in man; how shall he serve what is
beneath him?

Do you see emerging now the portrait of a Christian, the man
who believes in God made man? The first of his features is a noble
Christian pride, born of his likeness to God and God's likeness to
him; born too of his position as master of material things, in that he is
one with God, who has all creatures beneath his feet. In the power of
this Christian pride man puts forth his noblest effort, to make himself
master of creatures in fact, as he is their master in right; to control
them, to order his love for them, to free himself from the seduction of
their charms, to direct them toward the cause of humanity.

It was this Christian pride that the great Leo taught his flock:
"Realize, O Christian, your dignity; you have been made to share in
the divine nature; then betray not your nobility, by conduct unbecom-
ing it; go not back to your former baseness." So too, in the name of
this pride Gregory Nazianzen sent his people into battle with their
fiercest enemy, against whose dominion they must always struggle:
"Trusting in the seal set upon you, say (to the devil): I also am the
image of God; I have not yet, like him, been thrust down from the
glory of heaven because of pride; I have put on Christ; by baptism I
have claimed him for my own: do thou adore me!" (Orat. 40, 10).
There are the authentic accents of a Christian man, commanding adoration from the devil himself, an adoration due him of right, because
he is clothed with Christ.

Beside those ringing words, how cheap and vacuous sound the
voice of the modern liberal humanitarian, shouting of his freedom
and his individual dignity. The Christian man has a reason in history
to believe in his dignity and his spiritual freedom. And I very much
fear that unless the liberal humanitarian leaves off shouting long
enough to think out for himself a reason for it, his shouts will soon be
drowned out by the clankings of the chains he is forging for himself.

One last point that has been shown to man in the theology of the
Incarnation. It is this: that now man, since he is capable of divinity, is
capable also and, for the first time, of full humanity. Old Aristotle saw
truly: a man cannot and will not be perfectly human unless somehow
he becomes divine.

Now however that the "semen Dei," as St. John calls it, the germ
of divinity has entered his nature, man is free to develop all the

hidden possibilities of his nature, in fact, to shatter its limitations and make himself over in the image of Christ, "perfect in humanity."

Hence that powerful expansion of humanness that has characterized the Christian era. Man has asserted his freedom to love and to use all things human, because all things human have been sanctified for him in Christ, in whom, as the Council of Florence teaches, "nothing of God is separated from man, and nothing of man is separated from God" (D 708).

It is to the Word of God made Flesh that humanity owes its pride in being human, its joy in human life, and its dreams of ever fuller humanity. But notice: this pride and joy and aspiration have within themselves that which protects them from excess and self-destruction. They are tempered by an inner austerity. The theology of the Incarnation does indeed inspire the Christian with a deep sense of his dignity as a man; but no less strongly does it wake in him the consciousness of his nothingness were he merely a man, apart from God who makes him all he is. Consequently the dignity of the Christian is the most noble of all human dignities, being the dignity of a profound humility.

Here, then, is the second feature in the portrait of a Christian: his lowliness before God, his utter dependence upon God. That trait was given its proper expression by Him who was "perfect in humanity," and who nevertheless said: "Why do you call me good? There is One who is Good, God" (Luke 18:20). And He too drew its last consequences: "I am in the midst of you as one who serves" (Luke 22:27).

I must be content with having set before you thus briefly these two essential characteristics of the Christian soul, stamped upon it by its belief in God-made-Man. They must be expressed in paradox. The first is a pride in human nature that is willing to serve the lowliest of humanity; the second is a humility that exalts itself in a refusal to serve aught that is not God. He who is thus lofty and thus lowly can truly call himself a man, a Christian man, for he reflects the image of the perfect Man, Christ Jesus.

Briefly to sum up. I said that our first effort toward the construction of a Christian culture in America must be to rescue from its debasement the essential idea upon which a democratic culture must be erected, the idea of the dignity of human nature and of man's spiritual freedom. That idea has been sentimentalized into a dangerous caricature of itself; it has become a mere instinct, a thing "felt," a visceral stirring, not an intellectual conviction. Instead of being a spiritual force at once inspiring and controlling, a humanizing, ordering force, it has become the servant of selfish impulse, the all-sufficient excuse for lawless economic life. In a word it has become materialized and in the process it has lost its proper power to create a personal and social life that might justly be termed human and Christian.

We must, I said, rescue that idea, spiritualize it, by bringing it once more in to contact with its sources in Christian history and Christian truth. Only he who believes in the fact of God made Man will have a true spiritual idea of man's essential dignity and freedom. Only he will be effective in redeeming our culture from its soulless mechanism and in transforming it into a way of life authentically human. Only he will be able to eradicate from the face of American culture the ugly features of the economic man and to imprint upon it the gentle, noble, divinely-human features of the Man, Christ Jesus.

II. PERSONALITY AND THE COMMUNITY

A second major cultural problem confronts us today in America, as it confronts the whole world. It is, in fact, the most acute of all contemporary problems. I call it that of personality and the community.

In its main political form, it is termed the conflict between Democracy and Statism, between the theory that asserts the right of the individual to rule his own life and the opposing theory that asserts the right of the State to rule it for him.

The democratic theory advances the claims of the individual: his autonomy and liberty. The statist theory advances the claims of society: order and obedience to authority. In the concrete, these claims would seem to be antagonistic and, as a matter of fact, they do conflict.

We know the solution (political and cultural) that their conflict has received in Europe. Our problem is to decide what solution it will receive here in America. Shall we embrace democracy or statism? If it were merely a political problem, the answer is clear. We do embrace democracy. We repudiate and execrate statism with all the power of our American and Christian souls. I take that answer as self-evident.

But the deeper cultural problem is not answered simply by a dedication of ourselves to the political ideals of democracy. For dictatorship, as history abundantly proves, is the natural and inevitable way out of the disorder that is engendered by a regime of undisciplined individual liberty. It is but one step from a regime of liberty that recognizes no law that is not its own creation to a regime of law that recognizes no liberty that is not its own concession. Contemporary totalitarianism is the logical outcome of individualism as the modern man has understood it.

Hence, if our dedication to democracy means nothing but a rededication of ourselves to the ideals of individualism, as conceived in a system of naturalistic and materialistic philosophy, then we are dedicating ourselves to ruin. We are completely misconceiving the problem that confronts us; we are closing our ears to the lessons of history and covering our eyes before the realities of the present moment.

We stand today at a turning point in history (cf. Christopher Dawson, "Modern Dilemma" [p. 100]). The change may be briefly characterized thus: the age of individualism has ended and the age of collectivism has begun.

When I say that the age of individualism has ended, I mean that age which was dominated by a false theory of personality, whose essential tenets have been these. It makes the sovereign liberty of the individual the source from which all things flow: truth, religion, morality, the family, society. It reduces to a vanishing point all dependence of the individual upon those who share his human nature and upon God who is the author of human nature. It teaches that the development of personality requires that the individual free himself from all constraints upon his liberty, that he refuse to recognize any law that he does not impose upon himself. Its concept of society and of humanity has been of a mass of individuals, mathematically equal in their rights, whose mutual relations are established simply in terms of contracts, entered into with sovereign freedom, to be dissolved with sovereign freedom, whenever they become distasteful or cease to serve self-interest.[5]

Hence its essential denial has been that humanity is one, one in nature, antecedent to any contractual unities; one in its common origin, one in its common destiny, one in the obedience it owes to a common truth and law of life, one in its responsibility to a common Master, God.

When I say that the age of collectivism has begun, I am also registering a fact. For the 20th century has made one cataclysmic discov-

---

5. Editor Note: For a later discussion of Lockean contractualism, see *WHTT*, pp. 302–320.

ery: that mankind is one and that the individual man lives in the collective life of humanity. He is what he is in dependence upon the totality of man. He is not an isolated phenomenon, but a social being, the termination of a human genealogy, the product of a family, a race, a soil, whose life is maintained by exchanges with his fellows—a being whose mind and character are formed by tradition and environment. The individual is what he is, in what is most essential to him, only by being the very same his fellows are: a man among men.

The causes of this new sense of human unity are many. Most prominent is the fact that now the economic life of man has become one: a whole country cooperates in sustaining the life of its citizens, the whole universe in sustaining the life of a country. Secondly, the natural barriers between man and man, space and time, have been annihilated: the airplane, newspaper, and radio has made distant continents next-door neighbors, the world is a geographical unit.

Truly, today no man is alone; there is such a thing as humanity. Each of us is but a trifling part of it. It exists, it is real, it is one. Such is the discovery of our times. It has profoundly affected the mentality of men; it has caused the major preoccupation of today to be, not the life of the individual, but the collective life of humanity. It has created a new will in man, the will to unite with that which he recognizes as himself and more than himself. It has given birth to a new spirit, that of human solidarity.

True it is that the most obvious manifestations of this new spirit are bizarre, outrageous, extreme, even inhuman: Bolshevism, Nazism, Fascism, nationalisms of all sorts, plans for collective security, dreams of international federations of states. But their fundamental significance is that they are signs of the times that betray the powerful leaven at work in the soul of humanity;[6] they are all forms of social organization, of social regeneration; they are all attempts at a new order, based on humanity's new experience: that the individual was not made for isolation, but for community, that it is not good for man to be alone, for alone he perishes and, if he would live, he must insert himself into the life of his fellow man. Only in union with humanity can he save himself.

---

6. EDITOR NOTE: "Signs of the Times" is a term John XXIII would use later to indicate an international demand for human dignity, understood as the responsible exercise of the democratic and economic rights of all peoples.

The cultural problem that confronts us is the problem of reconciling the new collectivism with the old individualism, in such a way that we shall lose none of the genuine human values in each. In searching for a reconciliation, we must reject the worship of the idol of the past, the individual man who sets himself apart from the human community, and the idol of the present, the collective man who sets himself over the individual.

And we must seek the solution of our problem by regarding man as he has been made in the image of God, a personality, living in community. Hence, neither liberalistic individualism nor pagan totalitarianism, but Christian personalism. To the development of this idea of Christian personalism, I must now turn.

My thesis: as the traditional theology of the Incarnation must be the first creative principle of our Christian culture in that it gives us the Christian idea of the dignity of human nature and its natural superiority over the material world, so the traditional theology of the Trinity must be the second creative principle, for it gives us the Christian idea of personality and its relations to the community.

Is not that natural? It is precisely this vision of God as a Trinity in Unity that is of the very essence of Christianity. It consequently must inspire all our efforts at the construction of a Christian culture (cf., Basil of Caesarea: *adv. Eunom.*, 2, 22; PG 29, 620).

The Christian is he who begins his prayers: "In the name of the Father and of the Son and of the Holy Spirit," for that formula sums up his belief in God, a Trinity of Persons in a Unity of Nature. Hence it sums up, too, his belief in himself, a human person, in a unity of nature with all men, who he calls his brothers, every one, for that they are all the sons of God, in Christ Jesus.

The parallelism is perfect. It is a man's vision of God that gives him his vision of himself and illumines for him the whole of life. This was the chief part of the Son's doctrinal mission to earth, to lift a little the impenetrable veil that hides from man the Face of God and answer a little the fascinating question with which man has always been tormented: What is God? What is his life? What is the secret of his being? How is man in His image?

And his answer was simply this, that God is truly a Father, who has a Son, and a Spirit, too, who is also the Spirit of his Son. On this answer our Blessed Lord looked back at the Last Supper, when in his High-priestly prayer he summed up his work: "I have made thee known upon earth, I have finished the work thou gavest me to do. . . .

I have manifested thy name to the men whom thou gavest me out of the world" (John 17: 4–6). Nor was it the name of God as Creator that he revealed, nor as the Father (in a metaphorical sense, i.e.) of men, whose designs on them are loving. The Jews of the Old Testament had called God by the names of Lord and Father. The new name of God, that makes the newness of the New Testament, was the name of Father in its proper, metaphysical sense: the Eternal Father of an Eternal Son, who is, as the Council declared, "of his very substance, true God of true God, begotten, not made, of one substance with the Father."[7] And the revelation was completed by the third Name, the Holy Spirit, "who proceeds from the Father and the Son, and, with them, is glorified and adored."

It is this vision of God, given us, not in a philosophic speculation, but in a living Person, the Incarnate Word of God, that is formulated theologically in that great "war-song of faith," as Cardinal Newman called it, the creed "Quicumque": "This is the Catholic faith: one God in a Trinity, and a Trinity in a Unity, do we venerate; neither confusing the persons, nor dividing the substance; for other is the person of the Father than the person of the Son, and other still is the person of the Holy Spirit; yet Father and Son and Holy Spirit are one divinity, in glory they are equal, in majesty coeternal."

This Christian vision of God is dark indeed with mystery, yet luminous in its darkness. For it sheds light upon the problem that so vexed the mind of the pagan philosopher, the problem of a solitary God, lofty, lonely, majestic but loveless. It was a feeling for this problem that made the Indian philosopher put in the mouth of the one Absolute he worshipped: "Ah, if I were Many!"

Herein precisely lies the cultural significance of the Christian notion of God. When the Christian raises his eyes to God, he sees not a solitary, separated individual, but a Community. He sees a triplicity of distinct persons, each with his own distinctive and characteristic personality, yet whose life is utterly and ineffably one: for these three, Father Son and Holy Spirit, have but one nature, one mind, one will.

---

7. EDITOR NOTE: By 1963 Murray granted a priority to the "existential (biblical) problematic" (see *The Problem of God, Yesterday and Today* [1964c]), without, however, missing a beat on the importance of later Trinitarian doctrinal development (see "The Status of the Nicene Creed as Dogma" [1966j] in this collection).

Such is by definition a community, a unity of life amid a diversity of personalities.

The nature of God is infinitely One; yet at the very interior of his unity, as at once its fruit and its consecration, arises a mysterious plurality, three distinct Personalities, perfect as personalities, perfect, too, in their community. Such is the mystery of God's infinitely perfect spirituality.

I do not say that human reason can comprehend this mystery. My point is that faith here can touch, though it cannot see, the profound truth that is verified also in human life and that constitutes it basic paradox: personality is achieved in community, it is in communion with others that one finds oneself.

Traditional Christian theology teaches that the whole personality of the Father is simply his Fatherhood, as the whole personality of the Son is his Sonship. That is, each is but a subsistent relation to the other: each is turned wholly to the other. And it is precisely by perfectly "relating" himself to the others that each is constituted a person. Their mutual relations oppose them to each other and thus distinguish them from each other, with a distinction that is real. But, just as unity is not confusion, so distinction is not separation: the relation that distinguishes the Father from the Son also binds them together with a living link and situates each at the interior of the other. A relative demands its correlative.

Let me put it in ordinary language, very defective. The Father, in order to be what he is, Father, "needs" the Son. It is in the Son that the Father "finds" himself. And he "finds" himself precisely in giving to the Son all he has, the one divine nature, in an eternal act of love, called generation. The Eternal Father is but an eternal generosity toward his Eternal Son and, by this generosity, he is both one with the Son in nature and distinct from him in personality.

And the whole mystery is summed up in the classic phrase of Hilary: "Unum sunt qui invicem sunt": They are one who are wholly for each other. It is the paradox of personality and the community realized in the plane of infinity: each of the divine persons is himself by being wholly "for" the others, and each of the divine persons is one "with" the others because wholly "for" the others.

You see the consequence: the perfection of personality and the perfection of community are achieved by one and the same movement, an active self-giving of each to the other. This active self-giving has the name of love; and hence the mystery of God, as St. John saw, is a mystery of love: perfect personalities in perfect community.

Now, all this may seem very rarefied and abstract. Let me then give some concreteness by drawing out its cultural consequences.

The first is this: both liberal individualism and totalitarianism are a sin against the Christian God, as revealed to us in Christ. Liberal individualism sins against his Unity and totalitarianism against his Trinity. For individualism would shatter the community in the name of the individual, and totalitarianism would suppress the individual in the name of the community.[8] Consequently both are blasphemies: as Christians we are forbidden to destroy personalities in the name of unity, nor disrupt community in the name of personality. Both of these opposing cultures, then, are based on a theological error; neither is capable of offering man a full human life. For a full human life is made in the image of God's life: a life of full selfhood, that is found in community with others.

And the way to it is clear to the Christian soul that has penetrated into the revelation of personality given it in the mystery of the Trinity and learned the difference between individualism and personalism. If individuality as such is simply itself and nothing more, personality is not only itself, it is a limitless desire to be more than itself. Your individual is but the cow in the pasture, seated placidly in the midst of the herd, but immeasurably alone, contentedly closed in her private self, wholly absorbed in her individual cud. But your person is the man on the windswept hill of earth, conscious of his spiritual self and its absolute value, yet restless within himself, looking up into heaven and longing to give himself into communion with the Infinite Truth and God for which his restless heart was made, and looking out, too, over the world and longing to give himself into communion with all that shares with him a human spirit.

Personality is all openness. What counts for the person is not its "self," but the "other," for it is in the other that it finds itself. The psychologists have established the fact. The infant wakes to the consciousness of self through experiencing the otherness of things around it. "The you is earlier than the I."

---

8. EDITOR NOTE: For a structuring of the problem of atheism that parallels this dialectic tension, see "The Unbelief of the Christian" (1969) in this collection.

That is the point that the individualist—that willful child who has wrecked the world and shattered himself to pieces—never understood, that the dignity of personality is not in its freedom but in its obedience, in its free submission to the demands of objective order, religious, moral, social.

The individualist never understood the meaning of person. In the original Latin it meant one who played a role, who was cast in a part, one of the "dramatis personae." And that meaning still holds. To be a person is to be entrusted with a role in the great drama being played out on the stage of earth—humanity's search for union with itself and with God. And when the curtain is rung down, we shall each be rewarded, not according to the brilliance of our ad-libbing, but according to our fidelity to our role and the support we lent to the other members of the cast.

The individualist, in a word, never understood the profound solution given once and for all to the problem of personality by Him who knew the heart of man as no one else has known it: "He that tries to find his soul, shall lose it, and he that loses his soul for my sake shall find it" (Matt 10:39; cf. Luke 17:33: "Whosoever shall seek to secure his life shall lose it, and whosoever shall lose his life shall preserve it"). A man must lose his individual self, which is limited, isolated, immersed in the material, in order to find his true self, which is spiritual, large and wide and free, because it is lived, as God lives his life, in a community of spirit with others.

Curious paradox: the more united you are to others, the more completely you are yourself; the more you give to others, the more you have yourself; you possess yourself only by giving yourself away; you find yourself by losing yourself.

Curious paradox, but one that may not be spurned with impunity; for its converse also holds true. If you refuse to lose yourself, if you seek yourself alone, in isolation from others, then you will indeed find yourself alone, in isolation with others. But that is, by very definition, what both God and man mean by Hell, whether in this world or in the next—the place where the soul is isolated.

Through the Passion, Death and Resurrection of Christ, the Spirit of Love and Unity, and the Spirit too of Personality has been given back to the world, to dwell in man and, through his alliance with man, to renew the face of the earth. It is the Spirit of Christ, in dwelling in man, that gives meaning and direction to the whole historical process, making it the progressive realization of the prayer of

Christ, made on the eve of his death: "that they, the men for whom I am about to die, may all be one, as thou, Father, in me and I in thee, that they may be one in us" (John 17:21).

The spiritual unity of all men with each other, with the Father, through the Son, in the Holy Spirit, that is the goal of history. In the collective destiny of humanity, each human person has a share and toward it each individual and each nation has a responsibility. The realization of that universal human unity is the proper role of personality.

One final point: in the material unification of the world that is the achievement of the 20th century, in the creation of a unified economic life, no nation has had a greater share than America. And we were, I think, whether we knew it or not, cooperating with the Spirit of God, as were Roman engineers when they built the roads on which Christianity travelled throughout the Empire.

But we as a nation and each one of us as a human person miss our rendezvous with destiny, if we do not strive to complete our work by consecrating ourselves to the spiritual unification of mankind. For economics will never unite men permanently nor solidly. Their principle of unity must be spiritual; it must be the attachment of all men and nations to a common source of life that may express itself uniquely in each. And that source of life is Christ; he alone is the life of the world. And only by his Spirit, the Spirit of Love, dwelling in them and leading them, shall men be both united into one and personalized.

Our duty and our vocation, then, is clear. We must use our liberty to teach the world how to obey; we must put forth that Christian effort to lose ourselves that we may find ourselves. The lot of each of us is linked to all that bears the name of man; and we shall only save ourselves by helping to gather into one the scattered children of God.

III. THE HUMANISM OF THE CROSS

These lectures have been inspired by one conviction, namely, that Christian truth is the guardian of human life, so a return to the full Christian truth is the only remedy for the inhumanities of the present world. A Christian culture can only be erected on the basis of Christian theology. We have already considered two dogmas of that theology and their link to our society.

Today we come to what is undoubtedly the crucial cultural problem confronting us. I use the word crucial in its original sense, since I mean the problem of the Cross. We must make the momentous decision as to whether or not we shall admit as a creative principle of our culture the Christian dogma that historically man has been redeemed by the Passion, Death and Resurrection of our Blessed Lord and that apart from sharing in that redeeming death there is for him no redemption. Let me first of all, then, explain the problem.

Any culture obviously professes to be a humanism, that is, a development of man into full humanity, the expansion of his human energies and the creation by them of patterns of life that will satisfy man's vital needs, above all, his vital need for the happiness to be found in personal, free, creative effort.

But a Christian culture professes a technique for the humanizing of man that has always been found a stumbling-block. It proposes the development of man by self-denial, the expansion of his energies by self-discipline, the satisfaction of his vital need for happiness by self-oblivious service for others. And all this because a Christian culture would humanize man in this world by teaching him resolutely to look beyond its horizons into the perspectives of eternal life in the next world. A Christian culture is, in fact, wholly dominated by the idea of another world, to which this world is wholly relative. Consequently it is dominated by the idea that self-renouncement, a certain withdrawal of self from the things of sense, is the indispensable instrument of true human perfection.

The Christian hierarchy of cultural values is erected in obedience to the principle: "Seek ye first the Kingdom of God and his justice and all these things, the things necessary for an adequately human life in this world, will be added unto you" (Matt 6:33). And the humanizing efforts of Christian humanism are controlled by the paradox: "He who loveth his life shall lose it; and he who hates his life in this world (that is, he who prefers to it the higher life beyond the grave) shall keep it unto life everlasting" (John 12:25).

Yet, since the 18th century belief in the reality of another life has progressively declined and the surviving measure of belief has been almost totally inoperative as a cultural force. Man has increasingly regarded himself as self-sufficient, an absolute, unrelated to any transcendent God. He has regarded his temporal life as self-contained, an absolute, unrelated to another life beyond the grave.

In a word, culture may be defined as an earthly idealism, the search for earthly felicity, based on the belief in the indefinite perfectibility of human nature and its assured power to control the world.

Western man, in J. Maritain's words, has devoted himself to "a courageous and untiring effort to make human life yield its maximum
earthly output" (*Essays in Order, I, Religion and Culture*, p. 14). The
boundaries of his efforts were the limits of this earth.

Europe today should indeed make us distrust the redemptive
value of earthly idealism and weigh the ultimate, inhuman consequences of banishing the idea of Heaven in our efforts to set the world
right. And let us beware of the temptation to which the unthinking
cede when viewing Europe from what we fondly hope is a safe distance. Right here among us is error, basically the same error that has
convulsed European civilization. I mean the error of earthly idealism.
Would anyone be so venturesome as to assert that the modern principle, "Everything in this life," has not dominated American culture in
its origins and development? Would anyone seriously challenge Mr.
Christopher Dawson's statement that "The Communists may have
deified mechanism in theory, but it is the Americans who have realized it in practice"? (*Essays in Order, I, Christianity and the New Age*, p.
167). Would anyone undertake to prove that self-renouncement and
the subordination of the body to the soul are characteristic American
virtues? Above all, would anyone presume to say that the doctrine of
the soul's immortality is a vital, controlling factor in American life and
that the idea of a future life tempers and qualifies the ordinary American's devotion to life, liberty and the pursuit of happiness?

Moreover, if we survey the results of America's earthly idealism,
as pursued, for several centuries, I doubt if anyone will be satisfied
with them. Ours is a land of immense material comfort, so much so
that the very word "comfort" is used in Italy and France to designate
a peculiarly American thing, which they do not possess, nor even consider very desirable.

On the other hand it is a land of immense suffering, of a peculiarly soul-destroying kind. Poverty in no country in the world, save
perhaps England, which is as materialistic as we are, is so destructive
to personality as it is among us. For in a land where money is the
passport to happiness, the lack of it means a cramped and narrow life,
generative of rebellion, or of apathy.

America has raised the standard of living to historically
unknown heights; it is extremely doubtful if it has raised the quality
of life to anything like a proportionate degree. We have multiplied
our needs endlessly and thereby multiplied our sorrows. We preach
the abundant life for all. In late years we have imposed upon a grow-

ing number of people the worst kind of asceticism, that which they have no grace to support. We have sought first our kingdom of earth and we begin to discover that in the process millions upon millions have been disinherited from both the Kingdom of earth and the Kingdom of God. It is time for us to examine our earthly idealism and see if it really be the way to our ideal, the full, free, human life. For we have no grounds for confidence that our national earthly idealism will be immune from the fate that has overtaken other brands.

A nation is not like an individual. An individual can somehow live without a faith or a spiritual purpose or a care for his immortal soul. For he can be a parasite on society, his life sustained by the spiritual powers it contains. But a nation that loses faith and purpose and soul is doomed.[9] And our national faith is today the heritage of a diminishing number; soon there may be but an Isaian remnant left. We must remember that "remnant of Israel" saved itself indeed, but it did not save Israel.

How, then, shall we be saved? How shall we assure ourselves and others of this full, free human life that is our natural aspiration?

We begin by remembering that historically mankind has been saved. By his Passion, Death, and Resurrection Christ accomplished the redemption of mankind. God did not leave the task to human powers, which were entirely inadequate to it; he descended in human form and took it in hand himself. Nor did he do it by beautiful sermons, by proposing brilliant economic programs or techniques of social adjustment. Rather, he did it by being obedient unto death, even unto the death of the Cross. Christian theology has attached the redemption of mankind to the Passion and Death of Christ; and it is this theology of redemption that must be made the third and greatest creative principle of our Christian culture.

Obviously a total exposition of the theology of the Redemption is impossible here. I must omit its inner mystical meaning, the total dedication of mankind in sacrifice to God by Christ, the Head of Humanity, who carried us all in himself. Let me merely select several aspects of the mystery that have a cultural significance of the first order.

First, we recall that the mystery of Christ is primarily a mystery of resurrection, the definitive revelation to humanity that death is not

---

9. EDITOR NOTE: See "The Return to Tribalism" (1961d) also reprinted in this section.

an end, but a beginning, that the soul of man is immortal and that no man has the power to slay it.

St. Matthew tells us that on the first Easter morning there was an earthquake when, through the unbroken seals of his tomb, the Man who had been crucified came forth, gloriously alive, into the sweet light of dawn. Well there might have been an earthquake, for an idea burst upon the world in a new clarity. To Plato, the greatest mind of pagan antiquity, the immortality of the soul had been, as he called it, a "glorious risk": *kalos gar o kindunos*. A costly risk, as he saw, for it entailed upon man the renouncement of the pleasures of the flesh and the goods of the world, by the practice of temperance, justice, courage, and love of the truth—virtues imposed on man by the hope of an eternal life, wherein virtue would have its recompense in a blessed beatitude.

But what to Plato had only been a glorious risk, an enchanting hope, became in Christ a thrilling certainty. The first Christians on the first Easter evening touched with their own hands the solid flesh of a Man who had been dead and who rose again, never more to die. And by that touch they reached the certainty that the great mind of Plato had failed to achieve, that they, too, would rise again.

Such is the first cultural significance of the fact of man's redemption, inasmuch as it is a mystery of Resurrection. It carries the condemnation of all that I have called earthly idealism, the theory that a man can be a man, even though he does not live now in the light of a life to come. It was from the error of earthly idealism that Christ redeemed man by rising from the dead. Henceforth the risen Christ and his immortal life is man's ideal of manhood.

The second cultural significance of the dogma of redemption is this: that if the mystery of Christ is primarily a mystery of life and resurrection, it is also a mystery of crucifixion and death. The two mysteries are inseparably linked and they both find expression in the same word: the *Pascha Domini*, the "passage of the Lord," from death to life, from total self-renouncement to total self-achievement, from self-loss to self-finding, from the darkness and isolation of Calvary to the light and reunion of Easter.

If you realize the meaning of this passage, you will see, I think, the concrete task that lies before you, individually and as a group, in the construction of a Christian culture. With its double movement, the redemption of self unto personal freedom will be accomplished and the redemption of humanity unto union with itself.

The final paradox is that, when our hearts are lifted up to God in the desire of his pure light, then only are we truly in contact with the earth and able to exert upon the earth a redemptive action. Only the heart that is lifted from the earth can give to life on earth a meaning and a value, and rescue it from the tragedy of so many lives, futility. Only when our dwelling is in the heavens can we hope to fulfill our vocation on earth. Only when in the presence of God we possess ourselves can we give ourselves away to others.

And if we do not understand the world and why it was made, what right have we to meddle with it? If we do not know that man is made in the image of God, how dare we live with him or attempt to fashion his life?

But the Christian humanist has a vantage point from which to view the world and understand his work in it. He stands on Calvary, the place where God met all mankind and blessed them as his children, bought with the blood of his Son. From Calvary one can truly see the earth in its full reality: beautiful, splendid, heroic, mean, sordid, ugly, thrilling, heart-breaking, backbreaking.

The place where the Son of God once pitched his tent, to be warmed by its sun and to pray beneath its blanket of stars, to eat its bread and to drink the fruit of its vines, to feel its affection and the blast of its hate, to give it words of truth and life and to be crucified by its raging injustice. A queer world indeed, but he loved it and he still loves it. On it he lavishes the gifts of his own Spirit of Love, for on it he sees stamped the image of his face.

Have you ever seen that image—tearstained, bloodstained, defiled with spittle, whitened and drawn beneath the anguish of pain, injustice and loneliness, but a holy Face. For it is the face of the Son of Man, as it shall be until the end of time. Perhaps if we withdrew into thoughtful prayer long enough, we could catch the vision of the Face of the suffering Son of Man reflected in the world. It would illuminate for us the highest and holiest task of the Christian humanist—to share something of the sufferings of the sons of men, to seek some measure of union with their age-long crucifixion—that thus made over into the image of the Son of Man crucified on Calvary, he may have some share in the world's redemption, Man's passage into the possession of God.

Towards a Christian Humanism: Aspects of the Theology of Education

JOHN COURTNEY MURRAY, S.J.

Perhaps my first word should be in explanation of the title of this paper. Naturally it suggests two questions: What is Christian humanism? and: What has theology to do with education? Both are large questions, and consequently my answers to them must be suggested rather in outline than in detail. Moreover, the second question demands a previous answer; it is the more fundamental, and the more controversial.

However, in the circumstances my approach to it must be positive, not controversial. To those who oppose denials to the affirmations I shall make, I shall have to answer in the words of the greatest of Christian controversialists: "You are contending for a partisan view; you are contending in order to remain a partisan. I am contradicting you that you may possess the whole (truth). Understand, this is a dispute for the sake of union, a dispute in charity."[1]

My starting point, then, is that assumed by the Christian educator when he begins his task, namely, that Christian theology is the architectonic science that furnishes the basic postulates of the theory of Christian education, specifies its objectives, invests the whole process with a distinctive atmosphere, and gives unity and hence intelligibility to its concrete program. In a word, I assume that Christian theology gives to Christian education what Newman would call its "idea." And I am concerned with showing how this is so.

Presented at the 17th Annual Convention of the Jesuit Philosophical Association of the Eastern States, September 4–6, 1940. Originally published as 1941b: "Toward a Christian Humanism: Aspects of the Theology of Education" (1941b) in *A Philosophical Symposium on American Catholic Education*, 106–15, ed. H. Guthrie and G. Walsh (New York: Fordham University Presss, 1941).
 1. "St. Augustine, *Sermon on the Ordination of a Bishop*, No. 11.

First of all, I shall briefly state the theological premise, or set of premises, on which the theory of Christian education is predicated, and draw some of their consequences; then I shall indicate the total quality or style of life unto which the Christian educator, in consequence of his inspiration, endeavors to form his subjects. From a discussion of these two points, perhaps the idea of Christian humanism may at least begin to emerge.

The first point, namely, the theological inspiration of Christian education, is not easily put. For it is both extraordinarily simple and extraordinarily complex.

As a first step in its exposition I might risk a platitude, and say that the office of the educator is, in general, simply to assist humanity in the realization of itself. The educator is not the master of humanity, but its servant, or, if you will accept the metaphor, its midwife. He assists in bringing humanity to birth in those who freely offer themselves to his ministrations. The educator's effort is simply to evoke and ally himself with energies that are larger than his own, since they are the energies of life itself, existent in the social mass, and surging to absolutely unique expression in each of its component individuals. If he is properly reverent toward his task, he must conceive himself and his activity in essentially instrumental terms. In a word, he is not humanity's creator, but simply its educator. And his words to his charges should properly be these: "My little children, of whatever age, with you I am continually in labor, till humanity be formed in you."

However, it is characteristic of the Christian educator that he feels his instrumental role to be double. He is not only the servant of the life-forces of humanity as such—its desire for truth and beauty and goodness, for personal integrity and social usefulness, for self-mastery and mastery of the human environment; he is also, and primarily, the instrument of a higher energy, a force of the specifically divine order, that is at work in the world. He conceives all his activity in essentially theological terms, as a cooperation with the grace of Christ, as a mingling of his own energies with *energeia hagiastike* of the Greek Fathers, the sanctifying energy that is the Holy Spirit of God operative on the life of humanity.

And his directive conviction is that only by allying himself strongly with the "power of the Most High" may he hope to achieve his educational objective, the formation of a whole man, ready for the whole of life. This conviction follows naturally from his acceptance of the paradox that expresses the very idea of Christianity, namely, that the Spirit of Christ is the agent properly creative of humanity in the full sense, since he is the agent of its divinization, its regeneration to a new life, higher than human, its reformation into the image of Christ. Consequently the formula that exactly expresses both the meaning of his labors and their anguish is that of St. Paul: "My little children, with you I am continually in labor, till *Christ* be informed in you" (Gal 4:19).

That is, in truth, a resounding formula, that flings wide echoes. However, it will be sufficient here to single out its central assertion, namely, that to be a whole man, one must be a Christian, baptized into Christ, fashioned in His image, made a member of the Body of which He is Head, brought into the human community that is animated interiorly by His Spirit and organized visibly under the hierarchs to whom His prophetic, priestly, and kingly mission has been historically communicated. "Whole man, Christian, Catholic": the equivalence of these three terms is the basic tenet of the Christian educator.

I am aware, of course, that this assertion of their equivalence is to the secular educator quite fantastic, and highly irritating. Dean Holmes, in the *Atlantic Monthly* for July 1940, was the latest to indicate that assertion as the rock of cleavage between non-Catholic and Catholic educational theory.

Yet this audacious assertion presents itself as a simple logical necessity to one who accepts the fact of the Incarnation; the Christology of Chalcedon is its sole and sufficient justification. In fact, one has only to elaborate the implications of Chalcedon in order to demonstrate the whole idea of Christian education. Naturally enough; for the Person of Christ, who is God and man and One, is the concrete principle of intelligibility in regard to all things Christian.

Consequently, the position of the Christian educator can at least claim the merit of an internal consistency. Ultimately, it is based on the fact that, whether men wish it or not, whether they believe it or not, an event has occurred in history: God, remaining always God, has become man; humanity, in Christ, has been made one with the Word of God; Christ, in His unity, is all that God is, and all that man is.

As a consequence of this fact, a change has occurred, not only in man's relations to God, but at the interior of humanity itself. The change is manifold, but its essence is this: the fact of the Incarnation effected the sanctification of human nature in its entirety *precisely by* its elevation to a higher, divine plane of being. Hence it affirmed on the one hand the validity of all things human, while affirming on the other hand their insufficiency. And both affirmations are of far-reaching consequence in the field of human education. Some brief development of the point must be suggested.

First, the fact of Christ affirms the validity of all things human, for Christ was *perfectus homo*, perfectly human. In Him our nature remained all that it was and all that it could hope to be; the Word of God destroyed nothing in it by making it His own. In Him, then, we too are still men, and we must resolve to be men, human in the word's fullest sense. Indeed, our resolve to be men has now a new and higher motive, the fact that God himself was and is a man, *unus ex nobis*, of our very kind. Integral humanism is henceforth a primal Christian law. We need not and we must not mutilate our nature, nor reject even the smallest of human values. Christ despised nothing in our nature, but took it all, just as it was, rejecting only that which would diminish it, namely, sin. He assumed a body, a soul, a will, an intelligence, a sensibility; he made his own human nature's total capacity for thought and prayer and love and suffering.

Hence our affirmation of human nature must be equally total and sincere. The soul of a man must be set at the summit of the hierarchy of human values, and the free exercise of his spiritual powers must be protected from tyrannous encroachments. The human personality must be enthroned in a unique sacredness; to subject it to the dominion of matter or of mechanism, or to dedicate it exclusively to the creation of purely temporal values must be regarded as a profanation of its immortal dignity. Human reason must not be debased by concessions to sentimentalism, and the science that it creates, though no longer queen of human life, remains still in her own order Lady Paramount. *Intellectum valde ama* is a Christian precept.

Furthermore our affirmation of human nature does not fall only on its spiritual part; we reverence, too, the animal element in our organism. We make the surrender of the body unto humanity's highest act of love the object of a Sacrament, and a channel of holiness. Matter and material goods have their claim to our respect. We recognize that historically the Church's first great doctrinal combat was in defence of matter against Gnostics. *Materia capax salutis*, we assert with Irenaeus, for God is the Creator of visible things as well as invisible things, and Christ was *visibilis in nostris*. We put a blessing on man's natural and incessant endeavor to become master of his material environment. We recognize in science and in its interest in empirical phenomena a human and hence a holy impulse. And we know that if it does not stop halfway it can bring man to the Word of God who dwelt among us in a world of harvests and storms and birds and lilies, and who thus made known His will that even the material world should share in the deification He brought to the sons of men. We are not enemies of material progress as such, for we know that it can be integrated into the total purpose of the Incarnation, and we are conscious that since matter touched divinity in the Person of Christ it is itself hallowed and can sanctify.

Integral humanism, then, is our ideal. We reaffirm with a new note of joy the whole program of the Greeks. Far more than they, we are captured by the splendor of humanity, for we see far more deeply than they into its dignity. We elevate our veneration for man to the status of a religious cult, for in every man we reverence the nature God has taken as His own. And we feel that the first step in our religious effort to become like unto God is to become men, for the Son of God was and is Himself a man.

Nevertheless, together with this new, joyous, great-hearted love for all that is human, Christ imposes also a recognition that the merely human is not enough. By the fact of the Incarnation our nature remained indeed all that it was, but it lost its independence. It is no longer closed in itself, a complete whole, with all its obligations determined and all its possibilities defined by its own intrinsic possibilities. By assuming a human nature God manifested His idea of what it means to be a man: it means to be more than man. In His own Person He showed that humanity is itself when it is one with God. And henceforth not to dream of being more than man is to refuse to be totally human, for it is to refuse humanity's predestined ennoblement, divinization by the grace of Christ.

Here is the crucial point. By the fact of the Incarnation the problem of human life has been posited in new terms. Individuals, it is true, may decline to accept them, but they remain for all that the only valid statement of the problem. The problem is not: How to be human? but: How to be human divinely? Man's aspirations after self-completion must carry him to acceptance of the divinizing grace of Christ, or they are doomed to sterility. Historically man's nature has been opened to a share in divinity; it cannot close itself, and it attempts to do so on peril of self-destruction. The naturalist idea, the idea of human nature as an entity, self-sufficient and all-sufficient, is not only a profanation of the love of God for man, it is an unreality, a contradiction, that nullifies its own affirmation of nature by its denial of anything more than nature. All its achievements, in spite of their multitude and magnificence, have brought it no nearer to its own ideal of humanism; they are but the Augustinian *splendida vitia*, and their net result has been to make of human life the shell of emptiness that we hear rattling all around us. It is certainly no accident that the century and a half which has witnessed its domination should have culminated in military barbarism, that makes humanity its victim.

For the second great law of human life was laid down in the fact of the Incarnation. The splendor of the humanity of Christ, that has waked the admiration of centuries, was the consequence of its union with the Person of the Word: Christ was perfect man because He was perfect God. And so He is to us the Way to perfect humanity. All our hopes of that grand achievement are conditioned by our willingness to abdicate our own proud self-sufficiency, and to recognize that He is our fulfillment. We must go out of ourselves, out of our natural land, like Abraham, that we may come into the land that we view from afar as our heritage, wherein we shall find humanness at last—our humanity realized by a union with God, through Christ, in His Holy Spirit, as the humanity of Christ was realized, made existent, by its union with the Person of the Word.

Thus, Christology dictates that the first step in our program of humanism must be the great act of self-abnegation which the naturalist refuses to make: we must lose ourselves to find ourselves; we must go out of humanity in order to possess it; to be human we must consent to be made divine. Integral humanism is not solely a personal achievement; it is initially a gift of God, the gift of His own Spirit who sets upon us the seal, the character, of Christ. When Christ is formed in us, then we shall be men.

All this is paradox, certainly. But it cannot be condemned as idle theory by anyone who thoughtfully reviews the course of history. We stand now at the end of what has been aptly termed "the era of good paganism," whose ideal was a humanism closed in itself, and consciously divorced from all religious, much less supernatural, inspiration. Its program has been the restless pursuit of human values for their own sake, and as ends in themselves; above all, it has set itself to remedy the scandal that Rousseau publicized in *Emile*: "Man was born free, and is everywhere in chains." And we have seen the program come to its ghastly term in a paganism worse than that of Greece and Rome. For the Greek was human enough to aspire after the salvation of his humanity through a deification: *soteria* and *theiosis*

were to him correlative terms. But the modern pagan has grown too
petty for such noble aspiration. And for all his bravado he feels
within himself a despair that the Greek never knew. For he has sinned
as the Greek never did: he has vowed himself unto himself, and the
vow has recoiled as a curse upon his own head. He presumed to
make himself the agent of humanity's redemption, and he has doubly
damned it. He called unto his aid all the resources and techniques of
materialism, and he finds himself the prisoner of matter, the victim of
estrangement that matter tends to produce between man and himself,
and between man and man. And if you listen closely, you may hear
him cry: "Unhappy man that I am, who shall free me from the body
of this death?" (Rom 7:24). In fact, so profound is his misery here in
America that he is willing to hearken even to the voice of a political
leader, doubtfully competent in the ways of Western civilization, who
dares promise to lead him out of "doubt, negation, and disunity."

So much, then, for the theological inspiration of the Christian
educational ideal and program; it is incarnate in the Christ of Chalcedon, who is both God and man and One.

And in the light of its inspiration the ideal itself emerges
instantly; the Christian educator has to cooperate with the Spirit of
Christ in fashioning a human personality whose life will be both
divine and human and one. That is by definition the Christian humanist: the man who, in the image of Christ, respects and develops in himself the two natures, divine and human, and who makes of them a
unity.

To the production of Christian humanists the whole of Christian
education is directed. In initiating the process, the Christian educator
takes into his hands a *human* personality that is *baptized*. He must visu-
alize it as a unity; its two aspects, human and baptized, cannot be separated. And his aim is simple in itself, but enormously complex in its
achievement. First, he has to assist the grace of baptism, the grace of
likeness to Christ, to achieve its own intrinsic finality, the union of
this whole personality with God, the transformation of its whole
being into that of a child of God, the catching up of all its life in to the
life-stream of the Son of God, Christ Jesus, that in Him it may set
solely toward the Father.

Secondly, he has to assist this particular bit of humanity realize
its uniquely *human* self in its full, divinely-planned beauty, that it may
be a fit vessel of divinity. For it is not to offer to the divinizing action
of the Holy Spirit a humanity that is empty, impoverished, discolored.

Finally, he has to assist this human personality in what is unquestionably its most difficult task, the joining of the two elements of its life into an organic unity, into *one* life, that is humanly divine and divinely human. For the Christian humanist is not to be conceived as a man *and* a Christian. His Christian life and his human life are not two lives, but one theandric life. His life of grace is simply the life of a human soul, transfigured by grace. In a word, the Christian humanist, in the image of Christ, must be one in selfhood. Hence grace must appear in him, not as something along side of nature, but as the elevation and perfection of nature; it is not a new soul, a complete substance, that issues in an independent life, quite other than his human life. Rather, it is simply a new *quality* of soul, that shows itself in a new and essentially superior style of human life. As Christ was God and man and One, so Christianity in its inmost idea cannot be otherwise conceived than as a way of being human, divinely. Similarly, humanism must appear in the Christian humanist, not as an isolated phase of his activity, or as an independent sphere of interest, but as the organic complement of his life of grace. It is not a thing apart from grace, an autonomous, second self; it is that which grace inspires and informs, even as the body of man is not a thing apart from the soul, but that which the soul vitalizes and makes human.

To achieve this unity of grace and nature, in the full actuation of both, is the Christian humanist's proper triumph. It is a synthesis infinitely delicate, absolutely unique in each person, constantly resolving and being reconstituted. Blessed is the educator who can assist in its formation in his charges. For to be able to do so is a sign that he has achieved it in himself. And that is the achievement of few.

This paper would have to be expanded far beyond the bounds set, if I were to attempt to develop in fuller outline the three traits of the Christian humanist already indicated: his openness to the world and to all things human; his interior religious life, consciously and constantly turned toward the Father, in Christ, by His Holy Spirit; and his interior unity with himself and with all humanity. Let me, however, put some practical point to this exposition of theory, by stating the challenge that we, as Catholic educators, are compelled to accept, in virtue of the principles we assert and the aspirations we entertain.

It is, of course, true that our faith is susceptible of other demonstration than that afforded by the living arguments for it that we plan to fashion and send into the world. But perhaps our other demonstra-

tions would receive a more sympathetic hearing if our living arguments were more convincing. As Christian educators we make
profession of Christian humanism: that is the very essence of our spiritual tradition. And our educational first premise is that on which all
Christian humanism is built, namely, that to be a whole man is to be a
Christian and a Catholic.

We cannot, then, resent it when the secularist proposes to test
the truth of our premise by the product we turn out. He is not being
unfair when he says to our product: "I shall judge the validity of your
Christianity by the type of manhood it has wrought in you. Let us see.
Are you at peace with yourself? Have you resolved in yourself the
interior conflict that tears me apart? Are you able to resist the attrac-
tion of matter, and to save yourself from immersion in it? Do you
understand this world? Are you able to see a meaning in its history?
Do you love it, and all of us who live in it, enough to be willing to die
for salvation? Does the salvation of humanity mean anything to you
or are you only interested in saving yourself? You say you are a whole
man—are you?"

Surely a legitimate question. Our products have to meet it. And
consequently, do we not have to put it to ourselves? But its formulation, when put to ourselves, must be changed, if we are to be true to
our first premise. The world will question the humanity of our product; we must inquire into its Christianity. We want to make whole
men; well, then, are we making Christians and Catholics?

I myself have no way of knowing what the answer will be. But I
do feel that it is a good question.

The Christian Idea of Education

John Courtney Murray, S.J.

It is sometimes instructive to examine the dynamism of an idea in its first origins. I propose therefore to look at the Christian idea of education in its first institutionalized form, as it took shape in this Christian School of Alexandria in the early decades of the third century.

The forehistory of the school includes the name of Clement of Alexandria (who would himself deserve a special study) and also the more shadowy name of Pantaenus. Both of them conducted what we would today call "private schools." But the proper history of the School of Alexandria, as the first officially "church-related" school, begins with Origen, the gigantic intellect who towers over the third century and indeed over the whole of Christian antiquity.

His story starts, modestly enough, in A.D. 203, when Demetrius, Bishop of Alexandria, put him in charge of the diocesan catechesis, at the age of eighteen. Doubtless the bishop had no intention of starting an intellectual revolution; that is not the sort of thing that bishops ordinarily do. But Origen happened to be a genius. And a particular moment in history had arrived. The time was at hand when the Church, still preaching the Word of God in all the simplicity of its divine wisdom, had to move onward and outward into the complex world of human intelligence where many words, pretending to be

A talk given at St. Louis University, 1955. Published as 1955b: "The Christian Idea of Education," in *Eight Views of Responsibility in Government, Business, Education and the Church*. 35–42 (St. Louis: St. Louis University, 1955) and republished in this form as "The Catholic University in a Pluralistic Society," *Catholic Mind* 57 (May–June 1959): 253–60. Excerpts published as "The Unity of Truth," *Commonweal* 63 (January 13, 1956): 381–82. Significantly edited and republished in *The Christian Idea of Education*, 152–63 (New Haven: Yale University Press, 1957). The version of the text published here is consistent with the Fuller, 1957, printing.

wise, were being spoken. Origen was the man who spectacularly made this crucial move.

His initial task was spiritually thrilling but not intellectually ambitious. He taught the elements of Christian doctrine to catechumens preparing for baptism in the shadow of the edict of Septimius Severus which threatened death to Christian converts. In time, however, a problem arose that was also intellectually exciting. "When I devoted myself to the Word," Origen later wrote, "and the fame of my proficiency went abroad, there came to me adherents of the various schools of thought, and men conversant with Greek learning, particularly with philosophy. It seemed therefore necessary that I should examine the doctrines of the schools and see what the philosophers had said concerning the truth." In this simple, almost casual way Origen describes the beginning of the full-scale historic encounter between Christianity and the ancient world of intellect. Out of this encounter the first Christian school was born.

We can, without excessive fancy, construct Origen's problem. The men who came to him, wanting to be Christians, were living in the seething heterogeneity of contentious cultures, philosophies, and pieties that was third-century Alexandria. They had frequented the famous Museum and its fabulous library—the twin institutions that together had made Alexandria the capital of "the creative half of the Empire." These cultivated men—Egyptians, Jews, Greeks, Romans, Orientals—were troubled and confused as they heard Origen discourse on the Christian creed and on the history behind it.

Their philosophy raised questions about God and immortality, the finite and the infinite, the nature of morality, and the content of the good life. Their nascent discipline of philology created difficulties about the text of Scripture and its sense. The science of the Ionian epoch had known a revival in Alexandria, and consequently these men had questions about the Christian view of the material universe. They knew history and had theories about its meaning; they would therefore want to inquire into the Christian sense of history. They were skilled in politics and law and therefore were desirous to know the situation of the Church, visible as an institution with its own structure of government, in the face of the empire. The great desire for redemption from evil that had become central in all the religions of the time had touched them, and they had questions about the Christian interpretation of evil and the Christian meaning of redemption. Their Roman masters had fixed their minds on an ideal of citizenship;

but was there a relation between the service of an earthly city and a citizenship in the Kingdom of God? And did the ascetic otherworldliness of the Christian life leave a place for the art and music and literature that they had learned to love? They were men to whom Hellenism had taught the primacy of the life of reason; how then was their love of intelligence to he reconciled with the obedience of Christian faith and the acceptance of great mysteries?

In short, these men were asking one searching question. What was the relation between the Museum of Alexandria and the Church of Christ, between the human wisdom that lay accumulated in the scrolls of the library and the divine wisdom of which the books of the Bible were the repository? It was a most valid question that demanded an answer. A journey to Rome about A.D. 212 further convinced Origen that Christianity was challenging the best intelligence of the time and was in turn being challenged by it, either with hope or with hostility. Therefore on his return to Alexandria he reorganized his catechesis into a *didaskaleion*, a proper school, and embarked upon a new course.

Eusebius tells us that there were two levels in the new program. Origen put his average students through the general education of the freeborn Greek youth—in grammar, rhetoric and logic, in arithmetic, geometry (which included geography and some rudimentary biological science), astronomy (including what was known of physics), and music. These were the "Hellenic disciplines" (Eusebius), ἡ ἐγκύγλιοσ παιδεια, the "circle learning" of Francis Bacon, the arts and sciences that made the free man and the citizen, equipped with the intellectual tools on which civilization depends, possessed of the humanist heritage that man had so far accumulated. However, Origen struck a new note when he told his students, as Eusebius reports, "that this general education would be of no small help to them in the study and understanding of the divine Scriptures."

Origen broke the old "circle"; or, if you will, he included it in a circle of a wider sweep. He affirmed the old humanism to be valid still, but he denied its adequacy. The traditional *paideia* was to be retained; it was a true culture that enriched the mind. But it left the soul still in poverty, for now the materials for a higher culture were available in the doctrine of Christ. Therefore Origen's school had for its ulterior purpose the transmission of the Christian heritage of faith whose depository was the Church. And his general education stood in relation to this higher purpose; it would be "no small help" in the assimilation of Christian truth. The statement is laconic; and it raises many problems, with which Christian educators have struggled ever since.

It was, of course, no such simple matter as that of teaching people to read in order that they might read the Scriptures (itself an admirable idea). Nor was it the equally simple combination of two unrelated jobs that was recommended by the sturdy colonial American Calvinist when he said: "The Bible and figures—that's all I want my boy to know" (a better idea, at that, than just "figures"). Origen's purpose was the civilization of intelligence in order that it might be able to receive a fuller understanding of the doctrines that simple catechetical instruction by the Church had already made known to it.

Christian faith can of course be received into an intelligence altogether rude; on the other hand, it does not necessarily spring up in a cultivated intelligence. It is a gift of God. But what is given is truth, and the gift is made to a human intelligence. Therefore it makes on intelligence the demand that the truth, thus given, should be understood, insofar as intelligence can encompass its understanding. In this process of understanding a civilized intelligence is "of no small help." The civilization of intelligence is a humanistic and scientific process; the understanding of Christian faith is a religious and supernatural one. The processes are distinct, but they ought to be related; for they go on within the same one mind and soul. It was therefore the essential function of Origen's school to relate them, under the primacy of the process in which faith, a higher gift than intelligence, involves the Christian. Origen wanted his students to grow into an intelligent Christianity; but to this end it was necessary that intelligence itself should grow in them. And there could be no other means of growth than the acquisition of the intellectual skills, the assimilation of the body of knowledge, and the initiation into the traditions of civility, that made the society around them civilized.[1]

There was a further cognate task, reserved for those who were up to it. "When he perceived that any persons had superior intelligence," Eusebius writes, "he instructed them also in philosophic disciplines." Here Origen really came to grips with the problem of the day.

---

1. EDITOR NOTE: Murray tended to equate "the tradition of civility," "the tradition of reason," and the "natural law tradition." See his Introduction to WHTT, "The Civilization of the Pluralistic Society."

Christianity, he knew, was not the Grecian art of being human, or a sentimental touch of universal brotherhood added to a Roman ideal of citizenship; still less was it an ineffable, incommunicable, self-authenticating, individual inner experience of "salvation," that stood in no intelligible relation to what the Alexandrian Museum was thinking and saying. Christianity was fundamentally a Word, a doctrine, a *gnosis* (so Origen called it), something that one knows, and knows to be the law of life, normative in all the problems of human thought and purpose. Christianity of its essence presumed to occupy intellectual ground; and in third-century Alexandria it found the ground to no small extent already occupied.

There was the ancient lore of Egypt and the East; there was the revealed wisdom and sacred law of the Jew; above all, there was Greek reason and "all that the philosophers had said concerning truth." The problem was not some rude dispossession of these tenants of intellectual territory. The Library of Alexandria was not to be burnt, as Justinian later thought, in a stupidity of zeal rather Vandal or Mohammedan than Christian. The question, as Clement of Alexandria had already put it, was whether there is "one river of Truth"; whether the two Testaments are finally One; whether the Logos, the Word, Who had come as Christ to be the Light of the world, was not somehow also the light that had beckoned to the soul of Egypt, burst upon the prophets, and illumined the intelligence of Greece. The question was whether Christianity, like Christ, was the Truth in which all truths are ultimately One.

This was the ultimate question with which Origen's best students were put to wrestle, and he with them as their guide. He was, as Eusebius notes, "celebrated as a great philosopher even among the Greeks themselves." And his first step with his students is described by one of them, Gregory of Neocaesarea, a lawyer and later a bishop, in the famous *Panegyric of Origen* that was his valedictory to his alma mater and its master: "He introduced us to all schools of thought and was determined that we should be ignorant of no type of Greek doctrine," Stoic, Pythagorean, Platonist—all except the Epicureans, who, as atheists, had no answers to the questions a Christian might ask and asked no questions a Christian had not already answered. "Nothing," Gregory writes, "was forbidden us, nothing hidden from us, nothing inaccessible to us. We were to learn all manner of doctrine—barbarian or Greek, mystical or political, divine or human. We went into and examined with entire freedom all sorts of ideas, in order to satisfy ourselves and enjoy to the full these goods of the mind. When an ancient thought was true, it belonged to us and was at our disposition with all its marvelous possibilities of delightful contemplation." This was the first task—the acquisition of an all-inclusive knowledge. But with it went a more stringent task. Origen himself, Gregory says, "went on with us, directing us, pointing out to us all that was true and useful, putting aside all that was false." This was the work of discernment and order that is proper to the Christian intelligence. It is the task of making an inclusive knowledge also universal in the true sense—that is, "*uni-versum,*" turned into one, fashioned into a unity.

Gregory's account catches something of the spirit of the five years he spent with Origen. One feels the pulsation of that active energy upon whose release and discipline the success of the educational process depends. One recognizes the excitement inherent in the free search of the mind for truth, wherever it is to be found. But one recognizes too the greater excitement inherent in the mind's search for intellectual order, for the hierarchy in the order of truth, for the inner hidden unity that must somehow join in a many-splendored, differentiated pattern all the fragments of truth, human and divine, that the intelligence of man can encompass.

This was the highest responsibility accepted by the School of Alexandria—a responsibility for establishing intellectual order, for constituting the unity of truth, for communicating the Clementine vision that "there is one river of truth, but many streams fall into it on this side and on that." This is the Christian "view," in Newman's later sense of the word. What the human spirit endowed with Christian faith permanently needs is to view all its knowledges, acquired within the Church and within the Museum, as ultimately ordered into one. For to the Christian the word "truth," like the word "God," is a word that in the final analysis has no plural, despite all the distinctnesses that exist, unconfused, within the compass of its unconfined infinitude.

The tools for the achievement of this work of order and unity were philosophical, as the word itself was a work of intelligence. Nevertheless, this intellectual work was profoundly religious. Its ultimate dynamism was what Gregory calls "piety," a piety of intellect as well as a piety of will—a love of the truths that may he found amid all the chaos of philosophical opinion, and a will to subsume all these truths under "the Holy Word, the loveliest thing there is" (in Gregory's exquisite phrase). This love of the ordered wisdom of the Gospel, guiding intelligence—itself greatly loved—in all its free ranging, was for Gregory the glowing heart of his school experience. It remains forever the heart of the school experience, when the school is Christian.[2]

This brief sketch of the Christian School of Alexandria reveals, I think, the two related ideals that have traditionally been the inspiration of Christian education. There is, first, the ideal of the civilized intelligence, a certain ideal of rationality that embraces (a) a perfecting of the powers of man—his reason, imagination, and taste; and (b) a vision of things as they are, a view of reality that reaches to fundamental certainties. Second, there is the ideal of the unity of truth, a vision of the realm of truth as an order, a universe, all-embracing in its scope, unified in its character.

The first ideal was the basic inspiration of the Church's century-long efforts at popular education. These efforts began in the sixth century after the wreck of the imperial school system; they were renewed at the Carolingian renaissance, and again renewed as the Iron Age ran out under the impulse of the Cluniac reform. The efforts were slack enough at times, and always enormously hampered, not least by the stubborn other half of Aristotle's famous half-truth that "all men naturally desire to know." The Church which could not compel men to believe could hardly compel them to know. It could not even compel its priests to obedience to the canon law, whose origins were in A.D. 529, that they should establish schools in their parishes. Nevertheless, that the success was considerable is known to all except those to whom myths are important. In his classic three volumes on the medieval universities Rashdall has made it clear that the lofty apex of medieval education which was the university—populous, wide-

---

2. EDITOR NOTE: At this point the earlier St. Louis text outlines the contemporary disunity of learning within American culture, a divorce particularly between science and theology. Murray writes "Inherent in the system is the denial of the possibility of true metaphysical experience, as a Scholastic understands the term. Also inherent in the system is a denial that religious experience can have any intellectual content whatsoever. Any effort to give an intellectual structure to Christian faith is either sheer obscruantism or mere fantasy" ("The Catholic University in a Pluralistic Society," p. 258). Murray concluded that the main task of a Catholic university is to "represent the ideal of the unity of truth," that, while such unity "is never finally constituted: all past unities have proven fragile, incomplete," in the face of contemporary "disunity, disruption, conflict" (p. 259).

spread, and, for all its limitations, vigorously alive—rested on a broad base. In the later Middle Ages, he says, even the small-town boy "would never have to go very far from home to find a regular grammar school." In fact, Leach has estimated that there were relatively four times as many schools in pre-Reformation England as there were in 1864. One of today's accrediting associations would doubtless look down its nose at them; but its nose has a twentieth-century length. They remain an impressive embodiment of the perennially vital idea first launched in Alexandria—the relation between Christian faith and the civilized mind and manner.

The second aspect of Origen's idea is even more important. The first church-related school came into being in answer to an inner need of the human spirit as it was caught in the clashing encounter between Christianity and all the knowledge symbolized by the Alexandrian Museum. This encounter is permanently joined, for "the Museum" is a permanent institution and so too is the Church. They continue to present mankind with two forms of knowledge, each of which is autochthonous, subject in its growth to its own laws and to its own dynamism. One knowledge issues from reason and the experience of the senses; the other from divine revelation and the experience of faith. And what the human spirit endowed with Christian faith permanently needs is that these two knowledges should somehow be related in a universe of intellectual order. Out of this permanent inner need there springs the permanency of the dyad, Church and school. Actually, what Origen's school sought to provide was, in modern terminology, a unity of educational experience, issuing in that unity of intellectual and spiritual life which is by definition freedom and is likewise, when shared by a people, culture. The principle of unity was the primacy of "the Holy Word, the loveliest thing there is," and the sternest too. For this Word, the whole developed wisdom of the Church, requires to be made somehow relevant to every problem of intellectual discernment and moral decision that a school exists in order to raise.

This need of inner spiritual intellectual unity is doubtless felt most sharply on what we call the higher levels of education, when the full exigencies of "the liberal life" seek harmony with the full exigencies of the Christian life in terms of that most precarious of all syntheses, a Christian humanism. Nevertheless, the inner need is always there, inescapably to be met. What makes the difference is simply the principle (stated by Whitehead, agreed to by all sensible men) that no one is to be taught more than he can think about at the time. Your Christian, be he first-grader or graduate student, has always to enter more intelligently into the Church's life of faith and into the life of thought proper to the Museum. Between the two lives there is no automatic harmony. Indeed there seems to be a certain tension (which was deeply experienced, for instance, by John Henry Newman, who was continually caught between the visions of loveliness opened by human learning and the vision of the Word, the loveliest thing there is). Possibilities of seeming conflict are forever being disclosed, which center around changing foci. In these conflicts the growing mind is inevitably caught, and it is troubled and confused, as Origen's students were. Crises of growth are recurrent. The Christian school therefore undertakes to provide an area of experience in which the Church may meet the Museum in deliberate encounter.

The school is not the Church nor is it the home. It is a sort of city—an area both of protection and of prudent exposure. Within it all youth's confusions and crises may be consciously created, not simply allowed to happen, and then faced and solved under the guidance that only piety, in Gregory's sense, can give. It is a city of freedom in which intelligence may be released freely to grow. And it is a city of order in which the growing intelligence freely gives itself to the guidance of what is lovelier than itself to be led to the higher freedom with which the Word of God makes men free.

In his Bampton Lectures, *The Christian Platonists of Alexandria,* Charles Bigg says of the school there: "It may be doubted whether any nobler scheme of Christian education has ever been projected." It still is the essential Christian scheme, presenting the essential Christian school-ideal—a universal knowledge, founded on a broad basis of fact, integrated by a philosophic view, this view itself being then vitally related to the organic body of Christian truth. When it comes to the realization of the ideal, the most stubborn enemy has always been the sheer nobility of the ideal itself, which—even apart from hindering circumstances—tends to defeat performance. The failures of Christian education are normally multitudinous, sometimes scandalous, and occasionally spectacular. Even at its best a school is only a school, one milieu of influence among others, able to do only what a school can do. What matters in every age is the idea that inspires its efforts, and the integrity of these efforts.

The Liberal Arts College and The Contemporary Climate of Opinion

JOHN COURTNEY MURRAY, S.J.

The liberal arts college confronts today a most subtle and serious problem in the form of the climate of opinion that prevails in our contemporary world. Upon its success in meeting this problem depends in large part its value to the American community. This, in briefest statement, is my theme.

What is the most characteristic feature of the contemporary climate of opinion? I would call it the devaluation of intelligence; of the discount of rationality; or a disposition to doubt or deny the capacities of human reason; or a narrowing of man's mental vision; or a diminution of the powers of the mind and a consequent contraction of the dimensions of reality. All these formulas would be valid, but they are abstract. Perhaps it would be better to illustrate the phenomenon rather than attempt to define it. The areas of illustration are many.

First, there is philosophy. Our generation has witnessed the rise to dominance of the anti-intellectual philosophies, so called—the various forms of pragmatism and instrumentalism, of positivism and materialism, the cult of the history of thought rather than thought itself, and, of course, linguistic analysis, which is the philosophy to end all philosophy. All these modes of philosophical thought have one thing in common: they represent something less that the full use of the intrinsic capacities of intelligence; they include some refusal of the mind to rise to the full height of its powers. Concretely, they deny to human reason the power to affirm transcendent truth, to make the passage from the realities of the physical world of experience to the

Originally published as 1959a:"The Liberal Arts College and the Contemporary Climate of Opinion," a pamphlet produced by St. Joseph's College, from a talk given in November, 1959. A copy of the pamphlet can be found in the Murray Archives, file 6–480. I have cut two sections of the talk, as indicated in further notes.

higher realities of the metaphysical order where Truth is spelled with a capital and has a universal bearing and validity. These anti-intellectual philosophies are still dominant. Presently their ascendancy is being challenged by a new disposition to "return to metaphysics"; but they continue to set the climate of opinion. And in this climate intelligence is at a discount.

There is, secondly, the area of religion. It is widely assumed today that religion has nothing to do with the affirmation of truth. Religion does not touch the intelligence but only the heart. Religion is "experience," not knowledge. If you believe in God, it is said, He exists—for you. And to believe or disbelieve is simply a matter of choice, not of understanding. And even the choice is determined by sentiment or temperament: "I choose to see," Saroyan makes his Josiah say, "because I am by nature a religious man." Religion is not an area in which one seeks the truth in order to know it, to assent to it as true, and to consent to its implications for life. Religion has no warrant in the dictates of reason or in the facts of history. Its sole warrant resides in the experience that it "helps." In a word, the uses of intelligence are exiled from the world of religion, and thus intelligence itself is discounted. . . .[1]

It would be possible to illustrate from other areas of American life this same phenomenon—the same doubt or denial, explicit or implicit, of the capacities and responsibilities of reason. But what I have said may perhaps suffice. It would be further interesting to explore the historical origins of this phenomenon. But what I would have to say would take too long.

I must, however, pause a moment on the fact that the phenomenon itself has alarmed the Church. The consequence was the Encyclical *Humani generis*, issued by Pius XII in 1950. This document notes many prevailing errors with regard to particular Catholic doctrines, but its fundamental concern was with one pervasive error that is also a state of mind. What chiefly concerned the Church was the contemporary skepticism with regard to the inherent capacities of reason to reach the full measure of the truth that is accessible to it. Man's confi-

---

1. EDITOR NOTE: I have dropped the other areas that Murray here considered, namely, the fields of law and politics, since these topics were taken up in Part I. In his discussion of politics, Murray here relied on Max Ways, *Beyond Survival*, and Emmet Hughes, *America the Invincible*.

dence in his own reason has somehow been undermined. He can indeed confront quite confidently the realities of experience—the empirical realities that can be observed, explained, and managed by the methods of science. But in the face of the higher realities that only the philosophical intelligence can grasp by methods proper to itself man stands strangely paralyzed. He can cope with facts but not with ideas. He can take hold of practical problems, but basic theoretical issues escape him. He is at home in individual situations, but uneasy in the world of general principles. He can describe events, but his mind falters over their meaning. He can be certain enough about the present, the situation here and now, but he doubts whether he can know anything with certainty about the past, the record of history. About the terrestrial world and its secular affairs he is most knowledgeable, but in the face of God and eternity the temper of his mind is agnostic.

This state of mind, widespread today, is a matter of special concern to the Church. Throughout her history she has fought against rationalism, the error that exaggerates the autonomy of human reason and is too pridefully confident of reason's competence. But she has likewise been the champion of rationality, the defender of reason's true autonomy, the supporter of a due measure of confidence in the powers of human intelligence. In the doctrine of the Church, reason was darkened by original sin, but its darkness is not total. The phrase, "the light of reason," has a true meaning. So too has the other phrase, "right reason." The light of reason flickers and is feeble indeed, and it is difficult for man to sustain reason in its rightness. Nevertheless, reason is still a light whereby man can make right judgments. Faith, of course, is the fuller and steadier light, and the affirmations of faith have a greater solidity, because the authority of God sustains them. However, faith could be no light at all, if reason were not also a light. Faith supposes reason as grace supposes nature. If the genuine powers of reason are destroyed or undermined, the true notion of Christian faith suffers the same fate. Faith becomes irrational, unintelligible, indefensible—and unworthy of a man. Thus the destinies of Christian faith are linked with those of human reason.

Hence the Encyclical, *Humani generis*, emphatically asserted the statute of reason in the universe of truth. In particular, the Church reasserted the traditional doctrine on the four inherent capacities of human intelligence. First, reason can demonstrate the existence of God; God too belongs to the order of reason as the Supreme Reality that reason can reach. Second, reason can discern the structure of the moral order; there is a moral law that is "natural" to man, because its imperatives are those of "right reason." Third, reason can be certain about the historical foundations of Christian faith; the essential claim of Christianity to be a religion of events can be vindicated by reason with a due measure of historical certainty. Fourth, reason can achieve a limited but real understanding of the mysteries of faith by relating them to one another and to truths of the rational order.

Thus the Church convicts of error those who doubt or deny the capacity of human reason to reach certain truth in the orders of metaphysics, morals, and history. Thus the church opposes the irruption of the irrational that is characteristic of our day. Thus the church authoritatively marks up, as it were, the values of intelligence in a world in which they are at a discount. Thus, finally, the church defends, not only the Christian faith and its values, but also civilization and the basic values of the City of Man, which are the values of reason. The integrity of her own faith is the primary concern of the Church, but part of her faith is a belief in the essential integrity of human reason. Without this belief civilization itself would perish; for high philosophy, and just law, and intelligent politics, which are the sustaining forces of civilization, cannot survive in a climate of doubt or denial of the powers of reason.

If it be true to say that this doubt or denial is widespread in today's climate of opinion, it follows that a special problem is put to the liberal arts college. This spirit of distrust of intelligence that is characteristic of the climate must inevitably infiltrate the minds of youth. The task of the college is to dispel this spirit and instill in the youthful mind a due confidence in the powers of the mind. This confidence is not prideful; the mind that knows its own powers also knows its own limits. But without this due confidence man is something less than man; he has not grasped his true dignity, and he cannot achieve his full destiny. The Church has indeed spoken powerfully against the contemporary spirit of skepticism and agnosticism. But it remains for the college to take up the task of rolling back these forces. They have already been far too successful in their attack on the minds of an older generation. If a younger generation succumbs to them, the consequences will be most serious.

In more positive terms the task of the liberal arts college, as defined by the needs of the time, is the restoration of the Tradition of Reason. This is, in fact, the essential tradition of the liberal arts. It is

our patrimony from the past, which the college undertakes to trans-
mit as a legacy to the future. It has been laboriously amassed through
centuries by a work of critical constructive intelligence. But its only
depositary is the living minds of men, where it must be kept alive by
being taught and learned. The process of disciplined argument is the
price of its constant renewal. The Tradition is always "there"; but it
has always to be newly discovered in each generation. The truths it
contains are forever certain, but they have always to be newly understood. The truths are forever valid, but they must always be made
newly vital. The truths were "found" by men in the past, but they
have continually to be "pursued" by men in the present. And the Tradition as a whole, since it is a living thing, must develop, if it is not to
decay.

This task of conservation and development of the Tradition of
Reason is not only the proper task of the liberal arts college but also
the test of its value to the community. For this patrimony of rational
truth, and an underlying confidence in the power of reason to maintain its affirmations against the corrosive spirit of modern doubt, is
the source and warrant of the public philosophy of the West. The Tradition of Reason sustains the tradition of law and supplies the discipline of force that force may serve the rational purposes of law. The
order of freedom is defined by reason; so too is the order of justice.
Reason, in the end, sets limits to government by constituting an order
of human and civil rights. The rightness of reason is the final bulwark
of public morality. The restraints of reason give form and purpose to
the work of politics and direct the action of the state toward the common good. Not even religion will supply the lack, if reason fails in its
functions; for religion cannot form a civilization except as its truths
and precepts are mediated to the temporal order through a rational
philosophy. . . .[2]

---

2. EDITOR NOTE: Murray concluded with some general comments on
the "loyalty" of St. Joseph's College to the "Tradition of Reason."

The Return to Tribalism

JOHN COURTNEY MURRAY, S.J.

Is there some danger that a false, fallacious or fictitious unity might be foisted on the American people? I think there is! I think there are two dangers and both of them are clear and both of them are present.

One of them is historical; it is the product of the contemporary historical moment of world crisis. The other is more inherent, a derivative from the very nature of political society itself.

Let's think for the moment of the first danger, that which is induced by the present world crisis. The fact is, that, as of the moment, the United States is confronted by an enemy, an external enemy, the Communist empire, the Communist ideology, the whole revolutionary movement in history that is associated with the word "communism."

The danger is that this country may be driven into a unity based simply on negation, on anti-communism, and the danger of this is greater in proportion as the opposition to communism is more passionate and less intelligent. This would be a shame because such unity would be one born of fear, one born of a sense of menace. It is good indeed to know what we are against, but far more important is it for us to know what we are for.

Moreover, this enemy is a very special one; his tactics are those of infiltration and subversion. He can, therefore, and does become an internal menace in our country, and the danger, as we confront the menace of communism within our own borders, is that we may be driven to some manner of unity that I will characterize as "tribal."

Originally published as "The Return to Tribalism," *Catholic Mind* 60 (January 1962): 5–12, as "What Can Unite a Religiously Divided Nation?" *Catholic Messenger* 79 (May 4, 1961): 4, and in *Readings in Social Theology*, ed. E. Morgan, 191–201 (Dayton, Ohio: Pflaum Press, 1961).

The unity of a tribe, as you know, is based on kinship—on kin and kind—and the enemy tribe is the stranger. No matter who the stranger is, as a stranger, he is the enemy. The tribe seeks security in sheer solidarity, a solidarity that is absolutely intolerant of anything alien to itself. Those in the tribe speak in terms of "we" and "they." The members of the tribe tend to huddle, to get close together, to close up, to close ranks.

The tribe cannot deal with the stranger in any other terms or by any other means except those of force and violence. The ideal of the tribe, of course, is the ideal of the warrior. The tribe is essentially a war-making group.

Is there some danger of this "tribalism" in America? I rather fancy there is, and it appears in the debased concept of loyalty that has become current among us, especially in the more fanatic, the more passionate, and also, the more unintelligent opponents of communism.

Loyalty is a sentiment proper to the family, proper to the clan, proper to the tribe. It is something that one expects from one's friends. One finds it in the minor types of social groupings—the corporation, the union, the club. Loyalty is the sentiment that one shows toward one's kin and one's kind.

I don't think that loyalty is the proper bond of civil society. Good citizenship is tested by other standards and more rigid standards than the shifting standard of loyalty. Loyalty and disloyalty—I don't think it is at all useful to divide citizenship into these categories. Moreover, I am quite convinced that the dichotomy between "we" and "they" has no place whatever among the people temporal, within the body politic as such.

When the Constitution was being written, it started off: "We, the people"; it did not start off: "We, the tribe." We are not a tribe, we are a people. What is the danger here? Well, I suppose we have seen it, have we not? It is the danger of indicting ignorance and error and political stupidity, which are commodities hardly in short supply— the danger of indicting these things as disloyalty.

This is useless; it just doesn't get us anywhere at all. Moreover, it confuses the whole issue of communism because the issue of communism, if I understand it at all, is an issue first, of understanding, and secondly, of action based upon understanding. Moreover, all this tribal cultivation of loyalty leads to a stupidity that is itself dangerous. I mean the stupidity of mistaking the real domestic issue. Who is the real enemy within the gates of the city?

I suggest that the real enemy within the gates of the city is not the Communist, but the idiot. Here I am using the word "idiot" not in its customary, contemporary vernacular usage of one who is mentally deficient. No, I am going back to the primitive Greek usage; the "idiot" meant, first of all, the private person, and then came to mean the man who does not possess the public philosophy, the man who is not master of the knowledge and the skills that underlie the life of the civilized city. The idiot, to the Greek, was just one stage removed from the barbarian. He is the man who is ignorant of the meaning of the word "civility."

What is our contemporary idiocy? What is the enemy within the city? If I had to give it a name, I think I would call it "technological secularism." The idiot today is the technological secularist who knows everything. He's the man who knows everything about the organization of all the instruments and techniques of power that are available in the contemporary world and who, at the same time, understands nothing about the nature of man or about the nature of true civilization.

And if this country is to be overthrown from within or from without, I would suggest that it will not be overthrown by communism. It will be overthrown because it will have made an impossible experiment. It will have undertaken to establish a technological order of most marvelous intricacy, which will have been constructed and will operate without relation to true political ends; and this technological order will hang, as it were, suspended over a moral confusion; and this moral confusion will itself be suspended over a spiritual vacuum. This would be the real danger, resulting from a type of fallacious, fictitious, fragile unity that could be created among us.

There is, however, in second place, a more serious and more subtle danger. It derives from the very nature of political society. The danger would consist in the growth among us of a civil religion, that would somehow be a substitute secular faith, that would undertake to take the place of the traditional religious faith that has historically given substance to the civilization that we call Western.

The candidate, of course, for this post of being the civil religion of American society has already presented himself. It is, of course, democracy conceived as a quasi-religious faith.

Informed by this faith the political community becomes a kind of spiritual community, and its bond of unity is not simply the common obedience of all the citizens to the common law. Its bond of unity is rather a common mind among the citizenry. The citizenry are to

share the same organized view of reality and the same set of democratic values. And the organized view, this set of democratic values is
conceived to be transcendent to all the religious divisions that are
unfortunately among us.

Our diverse religions are to be judged not in terms of whether
they be true or false, but in terms of whether they be American or un-
American. And to this concept of democracy as a quasi-religious faith
there corresponds, of course, a philosophy of public education. The
common school is said to be the organ for the creation of this common
mind, the common faith. The highest function of the institutions of
public education is not simply to communicate knowledge, but to create unity.[1]

The school is supposed to be a sort of pastoral ministry of the
Democratic Church, whose function is to gather up all the flock into
one true fold—the one true democratic fold; and initiate them into the
common mind and faith. It follows then, as the democratic community is unitary, so the school system should also be unitary. There
should only be one kind of school, because only one kind of school
serves the public purpose. And this one kind of school, of course, is
the school that is separated, not only from the churches, but also from
religion itself.

From this school there must be outlawed all the traditional
tenets of traditional religion. And these tenets must give place to the
unifying tenets of the secular democratic faith. Well, you know all
about this and I think you will grant that we here confront a danger
that is clear and present enough.

The issue of divisiveness, of course, is thrust continually into the
question that confronts the greater part of the country at the
moment—the famous, historical school question. The issue of divisiveness is at once formidable and chiefly formidable because it is
formless, very hard to grapple with. I think, myself, it's unreal and
invalid.

Well, this development in America of the secular substitute for a
traditional religious faith is not something that we can scream and
yell about. As a matter of fact, I think the development is inevitable.

---

1. Editor Note: See the Introduction to "Federal Aid to Church Related Schools" (1962b) in this collection for a discussion of Murray's views on religion in public education.

Both in fact and in law there is no public religion in America today. There is no common religious faith. The law—the First Amendment— that copes with the fact is a wise law. But once one has affirmed the fact and also affirmed the wisdom of the law that copes with it, one still is left with an unanswered question, namely: "Can a political society do without a public religion?"

So far, the historical evidence would seem to argue for a negative answer. It has been pointed out that the chief phenomenon of modern times has been the development of secular civil religions.

We know about the political faith of Jacobin democracy; we know about the racist faith of German National Socialism (Nazism); we know more about the far more materialistic faith of Russian communism; and we know something, or are beginning to know something, about the more idealist faith in democracy as man's way of life and salvation. This development has been inevitable.

You know very well, of course, that the Church is socially incomplete without a Christian society somehow surrounding it. It is indeed quite possible for man to live an integral Christian life amid the conditions of a concentration camp. But the conditions of a concentration camp have never been the civilizational ideal of the Catholic Church or of any other Christian church for that matter.

The Church does strive, as it were, to complete itself, not ecclesiastically, mind you, but socially, by creating an ambience, an environment that could be called a Christian society.

In the same way, a political society is normally incomplete without some spiritual bond of unity. Society—secular society—must have some spiritual substance that underlies the order of law, the order of public morality and all other orders and processes within society. And if there be no such spiritual substance to society, then society is founded on a vacuum; and society, like nature itself, abhors a vacuum and cannot tolerate it.

It may be possible, as pointed out by Hilaire Belloc and others, that an individual can live without religion, but a society cannot. All the evidence of history points in this direction. Arnold Toynbee and Christopher Dawson have commented on the fact that civilization rests upon the conception of spiritual and moral order, and secular civilization necessarily must base itself upon some concept of a higher law, some concept of a doctrine that is sacred.

Nowadays, in the modern world, traditional religion is outlawed as the public religion by the doctrine of separation of Church and State. What then remains to fill the vacuum that otherwise would result at the heart of society?

You have only two things. You have the mystique of science, whose aim is to create a civilization that will be purely technological. But of course this would be the greatest mistake and the most stupid mistake that could possibly be made. It is a mistake that not even Soviet communism makes in Russia, because their technological civilization, in which they are desperately interested, is certainly not solely that. It claims a spiritual substance that is its animating force and dynamism, namely the dialectical materialism of Marx and Lenin.

The other candidate would be some political mystique, the unclarified concept of freedom, or what's meant by "democracy" or majoritarian rule, and there are those among us who would wish to try this experiment—to found society, namely, upon this unifying principle that is summed up in the rubric of Democracy.

I would suggest, therefore, that the question which confronts us is not whether we shall have a national unity—of course we shall! The only question is: what kind of unity and quality of unity shall we have? And on what will it be based, and what ends will it serve and pursue? And there is the related question, namely: What relation will be established between this national unity of ours and the religious pluralism and division that obtain among us?

There is another little point which I think adds further actuality to this question of the unity and division of our national life. You see, the fact is that, as of the moment, I should say, American culture is not pluralistic. American culture is unitary. American culture is uniform, and it is tending always to become more and more unitary and uniform.

Today, it has been pointed out by the sociologists, man leads the most organized life that man has ever led in history. All human life today lives with organization—the factory, the trade union, the corporation, the civil service, parties and clubs and neighborhoods. The movement toward urbanization and the movement toward suburbanization are all forces that organize the life of man. The academic community is highly organized and unitary; it tends to be unified through its commitment, at least, to noncommittalism.

It seems to me that the threat today is not cultural disunity—the threat today is rather cultural uniformity and the menace it holds to the distinctness of personality and to the distinctness of the religious community within contemporary homogenized culture. And the danger is that both the person and the religious community will somehow be submerged in our growing undifferentiated mass culture whose structure is at once formless and rigid. I think, therefore, that the danger of some false or fictitious or fallacious national unities is not an illusory danger. It is real, it is clear, it is present. The existence of this danger gives a certain urgency to the problem of the kind and quality of national unity we shall seek to achieve.

I would suggest that the premises of any national unity that we want in this country are two: the first is the simple fact that there is no religious unity in this country. We exist in a state of religious division, a deplorable state, if you will, undoubtedly. Nevertheless, these religious divisions are not to be blurred, they are not to be transcended in the name of some common secular democratic faith and they are not to be reduced to some religious common denominator. This would, of course, be the end.

Secondly, regardless of our religious divisions, civil unity among us is necessary. Therefore, the only question that confronts us is this: What is civil unity in itself, and in its relation to religious pluralism in society? And secondly, how is it to be achieved?

Well, if this be the question, the outlines of the answer are not unclear. They are to be found quite readily in what we like to call the "liberal tradition of the West," the tradition that has dictated the norms for the creation of civil unity, the unity of a people. And it was said long ago by the Stoics, and even before them, that civil unity is based upon two things, first upon a constitutional consensus, and secondly, upon a community of interests. If you want the Latin, first, *consensus juris*, and secondly, *utilitatis communio*.

Civil unity, therefore, is established by two things. First of all, by the rule of law, the rule of common law, and secondly, by the rule of law that serves as a framework for the orderly pursuit of a common good. And when you speak of civil unity, the enemy to it is not the stranger nor the religious heretic; the enemy of civil unity is the outlaw, whether he exists in the criminal underground or in the areas of criminality that today are appearing overground—some great corporations, for instance. Or whether he exists in the international scene, like the Communist, who is, by definition, the outlaw—one who stands beyond the bounds, the horizons of civilized community as such.

If this be true, if civil unity is based upon the rule of law, a law that makes possible and regulates the orderly pursuits of the common good, then it follows, does it not, that civil unity is based on reason. I don't want to exaggerate, but I do maintain with all my strength and conviction that the forces of reason are basic in the creation of the civil community and its civil unity. If, and where, the forces of reason fail, civil unity becomes impossible.

I mean to speak of reason here in a multiple sense: there is moral reason and legal reason and political reason. It is, first of all, the moral reason to discern and to elect the ends and purposes of our national life: our domestic purposes and our purposes also within the wider community of nations. And a moral reason must discern and elect ends that are worthy, that are capable of calling forth the full energies of this still youthful people of ours.

Secondly, it is the legal reason to design and order a reasonable law which, because it is reasonable, will command the consents of the government, of the citizenry, and which, because it is a limited order of law—as the order of law must be—will leave room for all manner of legitimate freedom.

Thirdly, it is the political reason to master and to exercise the art of statesmanship and this art is forever architectonic. The art of statesmanship, the primary task of the statesman, is to organize; to organize the varying, the particular, the specific interests of the community into that community of interests that we call the common good, the good of the people which is always redundant to the good of the person. Political reason, to this end, must employ the canons of justice which are the canons of reason; political reason must observe the dictates of political prudence which are the dictates of reason; and political reason must utilize the high arts of persuasion.

Persuasion linked to passion, of course, is demagoguery; but persuasion linked to reason, persuasion that couches itself in high rhetoric—high rhetoric that embodies great meaning—this has forever been, and I hope still is, and always will be, the instrument of high politics. These are the tasks of political reason. If the political leader is gifted, then he has, I suppose, a "charism" which is hardly rational. How we produce this indispensable charism of leadership, and how we produce this type of man—these are other questions for another day.

Well, my suggestion is that it is in these resources of reason— moral, legal and political—that our hope of civil unity chiefly resides. Only I would add another resource, again a resource of reason. I would call it the "pedagogical" reason.

One of our greatest resources today is, and must be, the cultivated intelligence of the pedagogue, of the scholar, of the schoolmaster—the man who understands all that the Greeks meant by *paideia* (that is, the work of civilizing this strange creature called man, who is half angel and half beast, and who, especially in his youth, and even, mind you, in his age, always remains something of a barbarian, something of a tribesman at heart).

Savage, barbarian, tribesman though he be, he is somehow capable of the ideal that is Greek and also Christian, the ideal of living the life of reason, and living it within a city that is governed by the rule of reasonable law. Now this work of *paideia* (education is probably a most inadequate word to translate the Greek *paideia*—in any case, call it education if you want) is the work of reason. This is not a work of intelligence. The pedagogue, the scholar, the schoolman is not a prophet or a priest or a politician. Formally, he is a man of study, not a man of the Church nor of the state. He is not the herald of eternal salvation or the judge of theological truth; he is not a minister of grace; he is not an architect of the policies of state. He is only a scholar and only a teacher.

His ministry is simply a ministry of intelligence through intelligence; it is a ministry of the word, if you will, a ministry of the "logos," but a ministry of that word, that "logos," which is human, and which has been laboriously learned by man through long centuries. This is his dignity, a limited dignity, but a dignity high enough so that the scholar and schoolmaster can afford to recognize his own limitations. And if the pedagogical reason remains within its proper limits and, at the same time, discharges its proper responsibilities, then this reason of the schoolmaster will be a powerful ally of the moral and legal and political reason in fashioning the unity of the commonwealth.

So I say, if all these resources of reason are assembled and employed, they will together be able to lift our nation above the level of a tribal unity, above the unity of the war-making group. They will be able to lift it above the level of the sheerly mechanical unity, the unity of a sheerly technological order, and at the same time, they will make no pretense to fashion among us a religious unity.

Their goal will simply be a civil unity; their goal, if you want to use the other classical expression, will simply be the creation of civic peace. But they will be able to constitute us in our proper identity as a people temporal, existent within the liberal tradition of the West, a tradition that is at once rational and liberal, and liberal because rational.

This, my friends, is no mean goal—no mean goal!

And hence, having laid down a bit of doctrine, I will end, as I always like to do, with a question, because all that I have said leads us to the threshold of the famous question of John of Salisbury. His question was whether or not civilization, that is, civil order, civil unity, civil peace, is possible without what he calls in a beautiful phrase "the sweet and fruitful marriage of Reason and the Word of God."

On the Future of
Humanistic Education

JOHN COURTNEY MURRAY, S.J.

The issue of the future of humanistic education arises, I suppose, because the future of man himself has become an issue in our day. Is the present moment the portent of a new epoch of history, a new age of humanity, a new type of man? Must there consequently be a new kind of education, for which the tradition offers no model?

No one will deny that the signs of the times are portentous. It seems to be the fact that the crisis of history in which the whole world is presently engaged promises to be perpetual, at least in the sense that its duration and final resolution outdistance all possible fore- sight. The symbol of its perpetuity is the nuclear stockpile, here and also over there, undestroyed, perhaps indestructible, destined to per- manent presence, a hidden threat to the future of civilization. The modalities of the crisis and its manifestations will undoubtedly alter, as time alters all things, but only so as to make its root more plain and its nature more explicit.

There is also the problem of politics, or, more exactly, the prob- lem of scientific technocracy versus liberal politics. We already observe the phenomenon vaguely known as the "new politics," which is beginning to be visible in what is called, with equal vague- ness (whether in English, French, German, or Italian), the New Left. One cannot yet speak of a party; the phenomenon is still too amor- phous. It chiefly appears as a fact, the ubiquitous fact of collegial expertise in collaboration with government, directing the exercise of political power. Do we therefore stand on the threshold of Saint-

Originally published as 1964b: "On the Future of Humanistic Educa- tion" in *Humanistic Education and Western Civilization*, 231–47, ed. Arthur A. Cohen, in honor of the sixty-fifth birthday of Robert M. Hutchins (New York: Holt, Rinehart, & Winston, 1964); excerpted in *The Critic* 22 (February-March 1964):37–43.

Simon's "new regime"? "As long as governments exercise patronage over the learned, in theory and practice, we remain in the old regime. But from the moment the learned exercise patronage over government, the new regime really begins." Such a regime will, indeed, be new: but what will it be like? In any event, "socialism" will not be the word for it. Its new axiom of control seems likely to transcend all the principles of socialism, in any of its forms. Whatever is theoretically possible from a scientific viewpoint (it may well say) can be translated into political reality. Politics is only administration. The people are to be managed, not governed.

Again, there is the psychological problem that is the still undissipated legacy of Freud. The advance of civilization requires that man should sustain an unrelenting, rigidly controlled effort to master and organize the things of the world, including himself, by the techniques of conscious reason. He must therefore renounce the forces of instinct, deny them gratification, repress them. This, it seems, is not done with impunity. Its consequence is not self-fulfillment and happiness, but psychic misery and loss of personal identity. As civilization advances, the Marxist proletariat will, indeed, vanish, only to be succeeded by the new Freudian proletariat, chained in neurotic misery amid material abundance. Auden's phrase, "the Age of Anxiety," will be filled with meaning.

Furthermore, it may be that Ortega y Gasset touched the portentous meaning of the moment when he said that today "man has no nature, he has only his history." Technology promises at least to alter in radical fashion the contours of nature, if not to erase the once-sacred distinction between nature and artifice. Technology also promises to change the whole course of events, and perhaps, if Jacques Ellul is right, to make their course "self-determining in a closed circle." If Derek Price is correct in his projection of the exponential growth-curve of scientific activity since 1662 (the founding of the Royal Society), we shall eventually reach "a state where civilization is saturated with science." Then what? Will Kant have been proven wrong? Will civilization, which is an affair of the sciences, have overwhelmed culture, which is the moral state of man? In any case, we already confront the question that George A. Baker phrases: "Can science make history and make it orderly, provided that human beings are persuaded or coerced to act according to the precepts of order? Is proper technocratic organization, in effect, nothing less than the general will itself and a guarantee against the worst forms of coercion?"

The question might be put in another way if you admit, with Ellul, that a deterministic bent is inherent in technology. Will technology, which is man's own creation, eventually become his creator? Will it make man over into its own image, not free, but captive to the same determinisms to which the creator himself is subject? In the end, will man have lost, by undertaking to win, his perennial conflict with the energies of the material world and with the momentum of historical forces?

Perhaps Bruce Mazlish put the issue most sharply when he said, "Faustian man is everywhere on the stage of the world." His symbol—significantly not plastic, or even a thing of earth—is boundless space. It symbolizes his will to a limitless striving, supported by powers that are believed to be bottomless in their resources. The act to which he immediately aspires, as the evidence of his arrival in history and the announcement of his program, is to put a man on the moon. His motive seems not to be the wish to escape the human condition, as Hannah Arendt suggested, but, as Mazlish more correctly divines, the will to reveal the human condition and to fulfill its potentialities of power for the advancement of civilization.

Finally, there is the issue presently involved in the very notion of the advancement of civilization. It is not the old issues which Francis Bacon raised, which is the "elder" and which the "younger" age of the world. No one will now quarrel with his answer, that "our own times" are the elder, the "more advanced age." The new issue concerns the final meaning of the idea that was the morning star of modernity, the idea of progress. The idea has been newly qualified in conformity with the notion of progress in scientific knowledge and activity. Scientific progress is an unbrokenly continuous process, pursued for its sake, toward a truth that forever recedes in consequence of the very pursuit of it. The process is not animated by any vision of fixed and final goals in the form of eternal and unchanging truths; for science there are no such truths. As with the progress of science, so with the progress of culture. Culture is indeed the moral state of man; but its structure and substance, like the structure and substance of the state of material well-being which science provides, cannot be foreseen or determined in advance. Only in the pursuit of his goals does man discover what his goals are. He finds out what he wants to do, and must do, by finding out what he can do, and by doing it. The chase itself produces the quarry. And in the end man's only goal is—progress. The cultural concept of progress, like the technological concept, is open-ended. Progress is endless and it is its own end. This perhaps is what Ortega y Gasset meant. Man has no nature that is, no form, and therefore no finality. He is only history, progress, action— what the existentialists call an "ex-sistence" without an essence.

I do not know to what extent this Faustian ideology is explicit in the American mind. To some extent, however, it seems to be implicit in the general action of American civilization. It may be undergoing a pragmatic, not theoretical, evolution. To the same extent, there is evidence for the view of those who hold that an indigenous brand of Marxism is developing among us, with the consequence that American and Communist civilization are set on converging courses. (I am not speaking of forms of government, among which ours is still hardly more than an historical upstart, not yet tested in stern encounter with the newly emergent forces of history.) If this be the case, the end may be foreseen. There is no need or room in the world for two Doctor Faustuses.

These issues, and others of the sort, are brought up when there is talk of the New Age of Humanity. How one conceives them and wrestles with them in one's own mind depends, I suppose, on whether or not one is inclined to the tragic vision. More concretely, what matters is whether one is convinced that man is intelligent and free in the classical Christian sense, or not so convinced. More profoundly, what matters is whether or not one believes in God, Creator of the universe, Master of history, the End of man, who is only in the image of Pantocrator, not the Pantocrator himself.

The concern here, however, is with the bearing of the current prognosis of the New Man on the public institution of humanistic education. One's thought on this issue will be guided, I expect, by one's judgment on a prior issue. One can accept as a half-truth, because it is half true, Dr. Conant's weary definition of education as "what goes on in schools and colleges." The question then is, to what extent should education involve itself in all the cultural problems of the present moment, and with what function in mind, and to what end. Whether we need to be rescued from the New Man or rescued by him, to what extent may we look to education for rescue?

I take it that the day is long past when a Francis W. Parker could require of the citizen, as he did in 1894, that he "should say in his heart: 'I await the regeneration of the world from the teaching of the common schools [add: the universities] of America'." I further take it that none of us will address to American education the plea that it banish the Faustian man from the face of our fair country and halt the advance of his New Humanism. We might be content quietly to plead that education should not plunge into the business of producing the Faustian man and of fostering his dream. We might in consequence ask that the Deweyan premise of education be finally abandoned: "Since in reality there is nothing to which growth is relative save more growth, there is nothing to which education is subordinate save more education." In its own small way this is Faustianism. In reality human growth is relative to the ends of growth, which are inscribed in man's nature. Education is subordinate to the ends of education, which have been defined by the tradition of humanism.

For my part, I see nothing in the prognosis of a new age of humanity that would require us to abandon or radically to alter the fourfold structure of aims in terms of which the tradition of humanistic education has stated its ideal. The ideal has been to put the student in the way of developing a power of diction, a view of reality, a sense of values, and a sense of style.

By diction I mean, for the moment, all that traditional humanism, in dependence on Quintilian (A.D. 35-ca. 100), has meant by a finished power of utterance (*perfecta eloquentia*). In his *Institutio oratoria* (*The Training of an Orator*), Quintilian defined the majestic verb "eloqui" simply as the power "to utter, and to convey to the listener, what you have in mind." Diction in this sense means command of words, the ability to find in language the exact equivalent of the thought in mind, and the further quality of fluency. Diction, however, also includes the capacity to order discourse with a sense of logic and thus endow it with force, and to compose discourse with the care that issues in elegance, which is a thing of restraint, propriety, polish, grace. This art of utterance stands highest in the order of the skills which education seeks to develop. The mark of the humanist is the manner in which he uses his tongue, in the several senses of the word. Today we might speak of a power of communication, except that Quintilian would wince at the shallowness of meaning that the word has taken on. His orator was trained to fulfill Cato's definition, "a good man skilled in speaking," a man who had the public in mind, and who also had in mind something that needed utterance, because it was true, and therefore would serve the public good.

What the humanist is supposed to have in mind, needing utterance, is, in the end, a view of reality in Newman's sense of the word "view." In *The Idea of a University,* he contrasts the "genuine philosophical habit of mind," which is at once the possession and the quest for a view, with "that spurious philosophism which shows itself in what, for want of a word, I may call 'viewiness'." The contrast is between a grasp of things in their ordered intelligibility and what is pejoratively called "knowledgeability," which is a thing of bits and pieces, the property of the famous gentleman who "knew everything—and nothing else." This aspect of the ideal of humanistic education serves more often as the measure of its failure than of its success. In 1953-54 a survey of twenty-one colleges and universities, made for the Fund for the Advancement of Education, discovered that the "pervasive problem" was the problem of "coherence." The discovery was not new. Long before, Woodrow Wilson had spoken of "the feudal system of learning," in which "there is no common mastery, but everywhere separate baronies of knowledge, where a few strong men rule and many ignorant men are held vassals." My concern, however, is not with the factual state of education but with its ideal. The survey itself acknowledged the ideal in multiple references to the need for synthesis, integration, coherence, a unifying purpose and idea, a design, a synoptic view.

To achieve a view requires a certain comprehensiveness and versatility of intellect, a command over the mind's full range of powers, the faculty of entering with comparative ease into any subject of thought, the active power of insight that prompts one to ask the right questions, a flexibility of intelligence that enables one to assume a variety of viewpoints, the capacity to grasp the relations between things and to throw them into a system. The effort to build a view begins with the profound sense that intelligence is, as Aristotle said it was, *capax fieri omnia*, a universally responsive capacity for spiritual identification with, and therefore knowledge of, all that is real. To put it more simply, the quest for a view begins with the awakening of the spirit of wonder that is the root of the desire for understanding.

The spirit of wonder is man's native endowment. What is not an endowment but a most painful acquisition is an understanding of what Wilson called the "constitution of learning." Little success will attend any effort to order one's knowledge, unless one understands what the order of knowledge is and why it is an order. Therefore one must come to understand what understanding is, and what the ways of understanding are, and why there are several, not just one. From another point of view, one must come to understand the virtualities of man's intellectual consciousness—how they are multiple, not single.

In a metaphor, one must understand that truth is not a ranch-style structure, all on one level, with a single door of entry, but a many-storied edifice through which one ascends by those different modes of access which are the variant methodologies of inquiry. To say all this is, of course, to raise a whole spectrum of philosophical issues. They are precisely the issues that must be raised in the course of a humanistic education, because its aim is to put the student in the way of building a view of reality. The essential humanist refusal is to diminish the range of man's intelligence and thus contract the dimensions of reality.

I am implying, of course, that the subject matter of a humanistic education is the whole of reality, or, if you will, all truth, in its unity and in all the inner differentiations within its unity. Out of this implication a multitude of educational problems arise which cannot be touched here. I must, however, note that within the tradition of humanistic education the canon for the inclusion or exclusion of this or that subject matter or field of study was never considered to be relevance. The canon is too vague to serve as a heuristic principle. Relevance to whom? Why? When? Under what circumstances? How? And what precisely does relevance mean? The issue of relevance is best left to be solved *ambulando*. One must wait to discover by experience the uses of what one knows and the consequences of ignorance. The humanist is not greatly disposed to argue the issue of relevance. Not being a pedant, he is prepared to agree with Whitehead that all education is and ought to be useful, in the sense that all understanding is useful.

The tradition of humanistic education has never regarded the student as a naked intelligence inhabiting a world of concepts and propositions, in which the only issues are truth and error, certitude and probability, adequacy or inadequacy of formulation, logic or fallacy in argument. The student's attention was directed to the real world as it is, a world of good and evil, beauty and ugliness, order and disorder, in which man is called upon not only to think but also to act—to do things and make things. The aim, therefore, was to cultivate a power of moral judgment and the aesthetic sense that is called taste. Newman has the phrase for this aim: "the instinctive just estimate of things as they pass before us." The estimate, whether moral or aesthetic, is instinctive, but only because the sense of right and wrong, of the beautiful and the ugly, has been subjected to rigorous discipline and refined by the further necessary tutelage of experience. The estimate is just, because it is not merely visceral; valid reasons can be adduced for it, if need be. The right word here might be "appreciation," the capacity to set a just value on what presents itself, not only in the intellectual order of thought but in the practical orders of doing and making. The power of evaluation supposes the possession of a set of values, anchored in the order of reality and ordered in proper hierarchy. Humanistic education, therefore, has looked to the development of a set of values, moral and aesthetic.

Finally, the tradition has considered that humanistic education should somehow instill what Whitehead called "the most austere of all mental qualities," the sense of style. In the well-known passage in his Presidential Address to the Mathematical Association of England in 1916, he spoke of the sense of style as "the ultimate morality of mind" and also the final utility of education. "It is," he said, "an aesthetic sense, based on admiration for the direct attainment of a foreseen end, simply without waste." In all the affairs of men, certainly in all the affairs of intelligence, blindness or lack of focus with regard to the end in view, round-aboutness and muddle and wastage of effort in pursuit of the end assume somewhat the character of *hamartia*, sin. Where they are found, something essential is "missing" (the root meaning of *hamartia*), and the privation is a manner of evil. "Style," Whitehead concludes, "is the last acquirement of the educated mind; it is also the most useful. It pervades the whole being." Style is not, indeed, wisdom, which remains the highest of the intellectual virtues. Style is, however, a quality of wisdom as of the four other intellectual virtues—knowledge and understanding, art and prudence.

The foregoing may do as a highly condensed and generalized summary of the four traditional aims of humanistic education—diction, a view, values, and style. I maintain that this ideal, in its fourfold structure, will be as valid in the future as it has been in the past. The only objection to the ideal is that it may be impossible of attainment in the course of "what goes on in schools and colleges." The objection is irrelevant. The ideal always lay beyond reach; but one became an educated man in the process of reaching for it.

The whole issue, however, is not thus easily disposed of. There is some substance to the talk about the new epoch of history and the new man. Moreover, I happen to be a conservative who believes in innovation, as true conservatives must, lest in the end they find themselves with nothing worth conserving. Therefore, I further maintain that the educational tradition, in order to be true to itself, must undergo that organic process of change which is known as "growth." It only remains to know what the dynamism of growth is, what directions the progress in the tradition should take, and what new forms the development should show forth.

In the realm of doctrine or theory the dynamism of development is readily identified. It is the change of perspective that is brought about by the asking of either a new question, or of an old question in a new mode of statement or with a new note of urgency. The classical theological instance is Nicaea.[1] The new question asked by Arius altered the perspective in which the writings of the New Testament had viewed the Logos-Son. The New Testament question was asked in intersubjective categories, I and Thou, and formally raised the issue of presence and function: Art thou the Christ—the Lord-with-us, the Savior-of-us? The Arian question was asked in ontological categories and formally raised the issue of being and nature: Is the Son God or Creature? The Nicene answer, given in the famous *homoousion,* affirmed the scriptural doctrine but in the new perspective. Thus it was a development, a growth in understanding. Another theological instance confronts us today, as the polemical question (Who has the one true faith—Catholic, Protestant, Orthodox?) gives place to the ecumenical question (How shall Catholic, Protestant, and Orthodox move together toward unity in the true faith?). A change of perspective has occurred which affects almost every single theological issue and will surely result in an enrichment of the Christian tradition.

The same dynamism of development has operated in the field of political theory. There has been in the West a political tradition, a tradition of growth in the understanding and practice of politics. Its growth has been occasioned by changes of perspective; these in turn occurred as new questions arose, or, more exactly, as one or other essential political question took precedence over others; and this in turn happened in consequence of the changing experiences of particular cultures in different periods of history. For classical antiquity the political question was justice; for medieval times it was the political relationship, its origins and limits—that is, the question of authority; for modern times it was the freedom of the individual citizen. In our own times, as Hans Morgenthau tirelessly points out, the political question is power and the struggle for power.[2] The experience of total-

---

1. EDITOR NOTE: See "The Status of the Nicene Creed as Dogma" in Part 5, and references in that Section to Murray's 1964c: *Problem of God.*

2. Murray will later define the main problem of the time as one of "Community." See "Freedom, Authority, Community" (1966g) in Part 3.

itarianism has raised the question—that is, given primacy to it. And its primacy creates a new perspective within which the Western political tradition is given an opportunity for new growth in the understanding of itself.

The same complex of factors—new experience, new question, new perspective on an old problem—could furnish the dynamism for organic developments in the tradition of humanistic education. The new experience is easily identified; it prompts all the talk about the new age and the new man. It is the scientific experience, using the term in its broadest meaning. The new educational question, however, has not yet been formulated with clarity. A confused argument is, indeed, going on, but it seems to be hardly more that a reverberating echo of the seventeenth-century quarrel between the "ancients" and the "moderns," which was satirized by Jonathan Swift in *The Battle of the Books*. In Swift's version, which has the truth of caricature, the quarrel concerned occupancy of the higher and larger of the two tops of the Parnassus. Traditionally, it had belonged to the ancients; the Moderns coveted it. Hence they sent the demand, "either that the ancients would remove themselves and their effects down to the lower summit, which the moderns would graciously surrender to them, and advance in their place; or else the said ancients will give leave to the moderns to come with shovels and mattocks, and level the said hill as low as they shall think it convenient."

The same issue seems to appear in today's battle of the books, when the state of the question is conceived to be science *versus* the humanities. This conception of the issue releases only a sectarian quarrel, not a useful argument. The state of the question is altered when the positivist philosophers of science join the fray, as they enthusiastically do. (For the most part, scientists themselves are above the battle, or possibly beneath it; generally they want to get on with their work in the laboratory or at the desk, and not be bothered about education.) The positivist or pragmatist takes up the position that there are not two tops to Parnassus—the hill of true and certain knowledge—but only one, and now it is securely occupied by science. The humanities can make no valid cognitive claims for themselves; all such claims must be submitted to the test of scientific verification. In its extreme form, the position seems to assert that there is no Parnassus at all, but only a way of climbing it—that is, there is no definitive and universal truth, but only a method for its endless pursuit.

There are, moreover, those who attempt to reconcile the contending parties by saying that science deals with "facts," whereas the humanities deal with "values," and therefore there should be no quarrel. This position, of course, stultifies the humanist and makes the scientist quite rightly mad. His rejoinder is that science today is not value-free, that it is itself a value, and that it creates values for society as for the individual. The contention is true enough, but, so far from advancing the argument, it disguises or further confuses the real issue. And the confusion is worse confounded when the humanities are reduced to literature and the fine arts, under exclusion of philosophy, on the ground as Douglas Bush has pointed out, that "modern philosophy seems to be suspended somewhere between linguistics and mathematics," both of which, incidentally, are now considered to be scientific disciplines. Thus the old battle of the books, which was at least serious and even sprightly in its day, runs drearily down to the level of the trivial and nugatory, the partisan and the passionate.

The result is lamentable, because an issue of the highest importance lies somewhere buried beneath all the misstatements, confusions, and sectarianisms. If the issue could be unearthed and defined, we might come close to understanding the schism in the soul of our civilization which began to open sometime in the *quattrocento* and has been widening ever since—in more recent times, in consequence of the scientific experience. The issue, I suspect, is multifaceted; and it is by no means easy to define it in any of its facets. In so far as it is philosophical, it clearly involves a theory of knowledge and knowing. What is at stake is a metaphysics of cognition—the question of the dynamic structure of intelligence itself and of the processes whereby intellectual consciousness moves from the moment of wonder to the moment of attainment of truth. Consequently at stake is an ontology—the question of the structure of the real and its isomorphism with the structure of intelligence.[3] Finally at stake is an epistemology—the question of the criterion whereby to test the validity of insight and the certainty of affirmation.

---

3. EDITOR NOTE: In 1955 Lonergan had published an article that was eventually retitled "Isomorphism of Thomist and Scientific Thought (Bernard Lonergan, S.J., *Collection*, 142–51 (New York: Herder and Herder, 1967)). Again, Murray had led a CTSA workshop on the implications of Lonergan's thought for systematic theology in 1958.

If one could arrive at a view on these related questions, one would understand the meaning of the verb "to know" and of the correlative verb "to be," when there is a question of Aquinas, Aristotle, Lock, Spinoza, Newton, Einstein, Bohr, Gödel, Spengler, Shakespeare, Picasso, Mother Hubbard, and the man in the street, to cite random symbols of the modes of knowing: theological, philosophical, scientific, mathematical, historical, artistic, commonsensical. Here, I suggest, is the broad area in which the true lines of the philosophical battle of the books are to be drawn.

I do not think that this battle, which is only an engagement in a larger war, can be fought to conclusion in the course of "what goes on in our schools and colleges." (I really should not use the military image. The issue is a schism in the soul of civilization. And in a case of spiritual schism an image from the world of medicine, "healing," or from the higher world of religion, "conversion," would be more apt.) What, then, can education undertake to do, in response to today's dominant experience? What might be the directions and the forms of progress? Some few suggestions can be offered with regard to ways in which the four traditional aims of education may be enlarged and also brought to new focus.

A new issue of diction has arisen. If the Faustian man has arrived on the scene, it is important that the humanist should be able to talk to him. This means that his language must be learned. I do not mean his jargon, but his nonverbal language, which is mathematics, and his logic, which is the special logic of the scientific method of inquiry. As Ernest Nagel said, "To accept the conclusions of science without a thorough familiarity with its method of warranting them is to remain ignorant of the critical spirit that is the life of science." No educated man today can afford this ignorance. There is, moreover, the need to obviate the danger to which Margaret Mead has called attention, the danger of developing, as other civilizations before us have developed, "special esoteric groups," whose members can communicate only with one another. This development she says, is "schismogenic," self-perpetuating and self-aggravating. Again, if it be true that these esoteric groups, in combination, are fashioning a new age of man, the humanist cannot afford to be left out of their conversation. Its subject matter is his own—man and the world of men. Moreover, the scientific conversation is political in some Greek sense, as the scientific enterprise is a public enterprise. Scientists frequently flaunt the latter fact (though some of them made the disastrous mistake of supposing that humanism, like religion, is a purely private matter). The conversation ought, therefore, to be somehow open to the public. Furthermore, since the scientists are talking, not just about themselves and about what they are doing, but about the future of man, their conversation is of universal import. We the People should know what they are saying and what they are up to. There is, therefore, the problem of translation downward, so to speak, from the world of expertise to the world in which the rest of us live. The humanist, the man of diction, who is in command of all the forms of literary art, from the learned essay to the light theater-piece, and who is also the "good man speaking skillfully," should somehow let us know what is in store for us—in some more responsible ways than by scary stories of unsafe fail-safe systems.

Finally, there is the problem of diction as it touches the scientist himself. Privately, he may, indeed, be dealing with the ineffable, with what can be communicated only in nonverbal symbols. The ineffable is, however, useless to the political man, who lives in a world whose motive power is chiefly the power of speech. If, therefore, science is relevant to political man, as science says it is, the scientist must somehow learn intelligibly to use his tongue. Above all, he is not permitted to ascend to the arrogance of saying, as he sometimes does, "You would not understand." The rest of us would be tempted to the quick retort: "The trouble is that you do not understand what understanding is." We know today the scientific fact, verified in experiment, that a child of ten can be brought to understand almost anything if the teacher understands not only his subject but also the nature and process of understanding in any subject. Incidentally, the arrogant statement and the just retort embody an implicit statement of an aspect of our current cultural schism. Part of the trouble does seem to be that Science understands science, but it does not understand understanding.

In what concerns the second aim of education—the quest of a view of reality—the new perspective derivative from the scientific experiences makes possible a development. The central reality of which traditional humanism sought to fashion a view was man, taking "man" to mean "I-with-the-others-in-the-world," that is, the person, society, and the human environment in both its cosmic and in its humanly created aspects. In an older humanism man was simply the subject who undertook the inquiry. He was Ulysses, setting out "to gain experience of the world and of the vices and worth of men," pressing onward even into the "unpeopled world to be discovered by following the sun," and still further daring to pursue his quest into the transcendent world where God dwells in inaccessible light. Moreover, he had at his disposal, as his tool of research, only his intelligence, tutored in the logic of philosophical inquiry, stored with knowledge of what men had thought and said, made and done. Finally, what aroused his wonder was simply the world of common human experience; this was the world of which he had to render an account, in all the aspects of it that progressively aroused his curiosity. In our day, however, man is no longer simply the inquiring subject; he is also the object of inquiry. The inquiry is objective, skeptical, professionally neutral. And man has at his disposal, as tools of research, whole batteries of scientific instruments, new kinds of mathematics, new techniques of statistical estimate and so on. Finally, these new artificial hands, so to speak, have made accessible to man a whole new world of experience, the special experience, unknown to the old humanist, which is called "scientific."

The instant question is: What has science found out about man? The detailed and unfolding answer to this question needs to be made the common property of all educated men and women today. Therefore, as part of its aim to put the student in the way of acquiring a view of reality, humanistic education needs to develop what Robert J. Henle, S.J., calls a "program of cultural assimilation of science." It is not simply that the student must be exposed to the scientific experience by serious study of the scientific disciplines, to some depth at least in one or the other of them. It is a matter of conveying to the students—to adapt Henle's terms—the scientific "story" of the cosmos and the scientific "picture" of man in the cosmos, in so far as the story and the picture can presently be constructed out of the certified findings of all the sciences, from genetics to geopolitics. We know today how important the body-image is to the individual, how panic ensues when it is lost—in the course, for instance, of controlled experiments in the limited environment, so called. This body-image is largely an affair of the unconscious. For his own spiritual security man also needs a conscious image of himself and his world—the kind of image that every age has needed to construct for itself, if only by recourse to myth and fantasy. Science can now construct this image with a relative measure of factual accuracy. And the rest of us ought to know what it is; it belongs, as it were, to us, as a man's body-image is part of himself.

If the scientific view of man and his world were to become the common intellectual possession of scientist and humanist, expert and non-expert, some small step would have been taken toward the integration of science and humanism in our culture. There is, however, a more compelling reason why this effort at the cultural assimilation of science is imperative in education. Unless the student comes to know the scientific story of the world and the scientific picture of man (together, as I said, with a firm grasp of the method whereby the story was put together and the picture drawn, and thus of the level of explanation on which the picture and the story have their validity), he cannot intelligently get on toward his higher aim, which is the building of a view of *all* reality. That is to say, he cannot grapple with the question of whether the scientific perspective is the only perspective within which the truth about man comes into view; whether the scientific view is therefore the total view; or whether it is open to completion by inclusion within a wider framework of systematic understanding whose architecture is designed by philosophy and theology.

This question pertains to the pervasive issue with which humanistic education must continually concern itself—the spiritual and intellectual schism in our culture. I state the issue in the first instance as that of openness, in a reciprocal sense. Is the scientific story and picture of man open to, or closed against, the story and the picture which, in different ways, philosophy and theology have to tell or draw, and does this openness also reveal itself from the standpoint of philosophy and theology? Christian theology begins in biblical "recital-theology," so called, a telling of the story of the world and man—the story of creation and redemption—and a foretelling of the way in which the story will come out. Christian theology goes on to systematize the content and meaning of the story in the form of doctrine, which, in synthesis with such propositions about man and the world as philosophy may certify, presents a picture of man-in-his-world. There are, therefore, two stories and two pictures. How are they related? Does one cancel the other or complete the other? Is man to acquiesce in an irreducibly dualistic view of himself? Or is he to reduce the dualism to some sort of monism? Or can he account for the difference of views, render intelligible the diversity of perspectives, and compose the views into one, under respect for the respective character of the explanatory value of each? Here, I suggest, is a stimulating new focus for the second traditional aim of education. (I am supposing, of course, that theology will gradually find place in the higher education of the future.)

The third aim is the cultivation of the capacity to make valid judgments both of worth and of utility. Here the new focus would concern such judgments as they bear on science and technology, in themselves, and in their relation to other areas of intellectual achievement and moral aspiration. The sciences today present themselves for judgment in a variety of ways. They are systems of true statements, in the scientific sense of truth, which are conclusions of controlled investigation; these systems are part of the public knowledge. The sciences are disciplines that employ a distinctive logic of inquiry, by whose canons and criteria they evaluate claims to knowledge. They are disciplines whose pursuit forms the mind and imparts to it a special quality and a characteristic bent. They are sets of techniques whose import is pragmatic, in that they make it possible to manipulate, regulate, impart chosen directions to the energies of the cosmos and of man himself, and also to manage the course of events. They are collectively a massive enterprise within the liberal society, which profoundly affects its ethos and the whole moral as well as material conditions of man. In their ensemble they constitute a revelation of the spirit of man, a manifestation of his power over his own history and nature. In all these aspects science presents itself for value-judgment with regard to both its worth and its utility. Therefore, it becomes an aim of humanistic education to see that the student is equipped to pass this multiple judgment with discriminating nicety, in the light of both fact and rational standards.

The educated man is not permitted to be contemptuous of science, as if it were all an affair of "atoms and the void." Conversely, he will not permit himself to be seduced by science, as if it were the contemporary golden bull, symbol of divinity. In particular, he will stand against the temptation inherent in the contemporary climate, which is to be intimidated by science, as if it were Doctor Faustus.

Nothing need be added, I think, about the sense of style. Whitehead may or may not have been wholly right when he said, "Civilization advances by extending the number of important operations which we can perform without thinking about them." In any case, style is what you don't think about when in action, on penalty of awkwardness. Similarly, style is what you don't talk about when discoursing on education, on penalty of superfluity. In a true sense, style is not really an aim of education but a result. Aims need to be defined; but one must simply wait for results.

PART 3

Doctrines at the Cutting Edge

The articles in this section take up the development of doctrine and its implications for the internal life of the Church. In the last three, Murray attempts to restructure relationships between various subdivisions within the church, and to encourage attitudes (virtues) that are required, if the church is to respond adequately to the Second Vatican Council. The first two articles lay out the foundations for those recommendations. In "Freedom in the Age of Renewal," Murray speaks of the church's new (re)discovery of the importance of freedom. In "The Problem of Religious Freedom," he analyzes changes in the church's argument for religious freedom. By way of introduction, I will discuss what Murray meant by the term "doctrine," and changes in his understanding of that term.

Why focus on doctrine in a discussion of internal church discipline? First, for Murray, questions concerning discipline necessarily entail an adequate understanding of the doctrines that unite the church and direct its mission. His insistence on the necessary role of a public philosophy in directing civil society (part 1), applies analogously to the doctrines that the church affirms. Second, Murray used the term "doctrine" in both natural law and theological studies. The christological decrees of the great ecumenical councils, as well as the church's self-understanding (ecclesiology), are doctrines; and the truths of "We Hold These Truths" are doctrines of the natural order. Likewise, the East confronts the West most foundationally at the level of doctrine. The term, then, embraces general truth claims, whether they are grounded in nature or in redemption. Murray's treatment of doctrines bridges the natural and the redeemed.

What, then, is the nature of doctrine, as it designates both secular and sacred realities? Here I will discuss two distinct understanding of doctrine, as Murray shifted between them, in his natural law and theological writings. Within both realms, he moved from a definition of

doctrine (1) as general postulates of theoretical reasoning, to doctrine
(2) as judgments concerning either particular policies or general theoretical postulates. It is this move from an ahistorical notion of doctrine as
content to a historical notion of doctrine as judgment that makes the
recommendations of the last three articles possible and intelligible. The
articles in parts 4 and 5 will follow through the ethical implications of
this shift for relationships with those outside the church. Here I will first
trace Murray's discovery of the contingency of doctrines as content.
Then I will discuss how, on the basis of doctrine as judgment, he could
in principle make the recommendations that we find in the last three
articles.

THE CONTINGENCY OF THE DOCTRINES
THAT ARE NECESSARY FOR SOCIAL LIVING

As we saw in "The Construction of a Christian Culture," Murray initially
argued that only Catholic doctrines could offer sufficient groundings for
American freedoms. In that argument,"doctrine" signified general postulates or principles in the realm of theory—postulates that (1) define the
essential structures of existence, (2) guide judgments concerning specific actions, and (3) provide needed defence for specific social institutions.

When Murray eventually argued for the sufficiency of a natural
law consensus for international reconstruction, his notion of doctrine
was, again, theoretical. In his "cooperation" debates he examined three
bases for a cooperative rebuilding of the postwar world, and rejected
two of them.[1] First, common action cannot simply arise out of commonly affirmed goals or policies. Civil society needs a common doctrine or theory out of which it can argue for or against specific policies.
Second, Christians cannot rely on commonly affirmed theological doctrines or remnants of Christian symbols as frameworks within which
they may understand one another—for reasons that we will examine in
part 4. Finally, the doctrine that can and must serve as a common basis

---

1. For Murray's wrestling with the alternatives, see "Current Theology:
Christian Co-operation" (1942b); "Current Theology: Co-operation: Some Further
Views" (1943a); and "Current Theology: Intercredal Co-operation: Its Theory and
Its Organization" (1943b).

is natural law theory. Adoption of the natural law is the condition for the possibility of cooperation.

Two other arguments also highlight this notion that doctrine functions as the condition for the possibility of mutual understanding and action. In his first argument for religious liberty, Murray asserted that one could get to a defense of religious liberty from natural law and/or theological premises.[2] While he rejected the possibility of Catholics and Protestants reaching mutual understanding in the realm of theological truth, he insisted that they could find a common ground in natural law. In either case, that which allowed the church, in Murray's judgment, to adopt different stances toward various versions of the separation of church and state were changes in the temporal order of application, as guided by theoretical doctrines and mediated by prudential judgments.

Again, in the late 1950s, Murray argued that the East and the West were locked in a conflict concerning the doctrines by which each defined the world in which they lived. He maintained that their conflict could not be resolved through agreement at the level of policy, nor even at the level of the principles of justice. In his "Doctrine and Policy in Communist Imperialism" (1958c) he asserted that Soviet approaches to international relations were directed by a clear and consistent, if deadly, doctrine of "mystical Panslavic Messianism," a vision of the human person and human society that stood in absolute antithesis to the core commitments of the Western tradition, a doctrine whose purpose is the to put "an end to the history of the West." He therefore recommended types of action that would compensate for the impossibility of coming to a common doctrinal base with the East.[3]

Within these debates, then, doctrine is primarily a content of theoretical understanding that serves as the condition of the possibility (or

---

2. See "Freedom of Religion, I: The Ethical Problem" (1945b) and its original outline, "Notes on the Theory of Religious Liberty" (1945e). The latter was an April 1945 Memo to Archbishop Mooney.

3. In contrast, the West approached international relations with either no doctrine beyond pragmatism (see chapter 11, "The Uses of a Doctrine on the Uses of Force: War as a Moral Problem," *WHTT*, pp. 249–273)) or with a neo-orthodox irrationalism concerning the use of force (see chapter 12, "The Doctrine is Dead: The Problem of the Moral Vacuum," *WHTT*, pp. 273–294). Murray's main objective in these discussions appears to have been promoting natural law theory, using the incompatibility of East/West perspectives as a take-off point.

impossibility) of coming to common action and common understanding. Yet even in this conception of doctrine, Murray discovered that doctrines may and do develop.

In the interplay between Murray's American Constitutionalism and his arguments for Roman Catholic religious liberty his notion of doctrine as essentially timeless became more fluid.[4] While he was arguing (against American secularists and Protestants) for a natural law grounding to "the American Proposition," he was simultaneously defending the thesis (against some Roman Catholics) that a set of authentic moral and political insights had developed within the Anglo-American (natural law) tradition to which the church must be attentive. In both areas he had to argue that change had occurred at the level of principle (theory), not simply at the level of application.

This development in Murray's understanding of the contingency of (natural law) theory can best be grasped by contrasting his treatment of principles in "Freedom of Religion, I: The Ethical Problem" (1945b); "The Natural Law" (1950a; Chapter 13 of *WHTT*); "The Civilization of the Pluralistic Society" (1958a "Introduction" to *WHTT*); "Two Cases for the Public Consensus" and "The Origins and Authority of the Public consensus" (Chapters 3 and 4 of *WHTT*); and *The Problem of Religious Freedom* (1964e). In "The Freedom of Religion, I" (1945b), natural law is an ahistorical, asocial, complete body of general truth statements. By 1950, Murray recognized some movement in the tertiary principles of natural law, and by 1958, he was calling for a refounding of America's constitutionalism on critical, not naive, natural law premises. In WHTT, Chapters 3 and 4, he fully recognized the essentially social component of natural law affirmations. Finally, in 1964, in *The Problem of Religious Freedom*, natural law has become a set of affirmations that "emerge" from particular historical societies (consistent with the second meaning of "doctrine" discussed below).

Throughout these debates, then, doctrine signifies a comprehensive worldview, open to systematic formulation, that serves as a general framework within which conversations become mutually intelligible, out of which the goals of social action and the means to those goals can be argued. The primary driver of doctrinal development in this

---

4. See my outline of Murray's developing religious liberty argument in the "General Introduction to *Religious Liberty* (1993), pp. 27–37. On his Constitutionalism, see the introduction here to Part 1.

perspective is the moral will of the people—or at least of the elites. Murray's use of the term doctrine held this meaning until the publication of *We Hold These Truths.*

DOCTRINE AS PRACTICAL AND THEORETICAL JUDGMENTS

After the council, Murray repeatedly insisted the church was bound to the council's doctrine on civil religious freedom, not to the reasons that *Dignitatis humanae* advanced for that affirmation (see: "Religious Freedom" (1966i), 680, note 7).[5] By 1966 Murray had adopted Lonergan's notion that doctrine is an immediate product of judgment, and secondarily a product of understanding. Doctrine in this later sense can include both specific policy recommendations and generalized (theoretical) affirmations. In the case of *Dignitatis humanae*, doctrine designates an affirmation of a specific institutional arrangement. To get at church doctrine as an affirmation in the realm of theory we must expand this consideration to Murray's late treatment of specifically theological doctrines.

Throughout his life, Murray taught and studied the trinitarian theological doctrines of the Nicene councils. Murray always maintained that the use of Hellenistic theoretical reasoning in Christian theology is valid, especially regarding challenges to the faith, such as those posed by Arius. The faithful use of human reasoning is itself a participation in the redemptive action of Christ toward all that is human. Murray's eventual notions of historicity and the essentially social context within which natural law theory develops, prepared him well for Bernard Lonergan's conception of the development of specifically theological affirmations. Core to Murray's descriptions of both religious freedom and trinitarian doctrine is the notion of emerging questions within specific historical communities and the use of reason in answering those new questions.

Lonergan's description of the drivers of trinitarian doctrinal development profoundly augmented Murray's understanding. For Lonergan, Nicaea affirmed not only the consubstantiality of Father and Son, but also the use of the systematic differentiation of human reasoning in approaching the truths of faith. Not only can distinct new insights

---

5. Murray did not like the grounding for civil religious freedom that the final draft of *Dignitatis* put forward. For a discussion of this disagreement, see Hooper, 1983, pp. 147–56.

emerge that demand attention; also at play are differentiations of human consciousness—the commonsensical, the theoretical, the scientific, and, particularly, the historical. This notion of shifting from one cognitional stance to the next added increased specificity to the dynamic notion of human intelligence in Murray's idea of humanism and gave him better handles for distinguishing between types of doctrinal development.

Theological doctrine no longer advances simply in response to changes in the temporal, institutional order, or only in response to legitimate philosophical developments that are spurred by moral developments within the people. Murray now recognizes that doctrinal development can be instigated and justified by changes in what he calls perspectives—in the present case by changes in cognitional perspectives.[6] Systematic and historical consciousness effect the emergence of new doctrinal approaches—new approaches formulated in the phrase, "changing states of the question," that are not simply deductions from, or clarifications of, previous doctrinal declarations.

---

6. In the concluding paragraph of "Vers une intelligence du développment de la doctrine" (1967m, Murray Archives, file 7–517, pp. 51–52), Murray summed up the perspectival shifts that had painfully overtaken the church in the council. He described the growth in historical consciousness as at the root of all other shifts:

Development of doctrine was indeed the basic issue that underlay all other issues throughout the whole Council. The Council itself demonstrated, as perhaps never before in history, that the Church herself does not accept the fallacy of archaism, which lies in the desire to stop the growth of the Church's thought at some given stage of development—scriptural, patristic, medieval, modern, contemporary—and to reject the possibility of further growth. No other conciliar document represents so firm a rejection of this fallacy as the Declaration, *Dignitatis humanae*. This perhaps was the final reason why it met such opposition. This surely is its ultimate theological significance. And implicit in this significance is perhaps the significance of the whole Council—its manifold testimony to the growth of the Church in historical consciousness, and in a human consciousness of the dignity of man, and in an ecumenical consciousness of her ministry of reconciliation, and above all in an evangelical consciousness of herself and of the word that has been divinely entrusted to her, which is not only the "word of truth" (James 1:18) but also identically a word of freedom. Ultimately, the Declaration on Religious Freedom is "one of the major texts" of the council, as Paul VI called it, because as Part II of the text undertakes to show, it is a secular prolongation of "the word of this liberation which Paul announced at Antioch (Acts 13:26).

The articles of this section demonstrate Murray's use of both the understanding/judgment distinction and the notion of historical versus classical consciousness to reorder the church's internal life.[7]

---

7. Also indicative of this development and interest is a report of a talk that Murray gave shortly before his death, part of which dealt with the Majority Report of Pope Paul VI's Commission on the use of artificial contraception. That report is included in the Appendix to this volume.

Freedom in the Age of Renewal

JOHN COURTNEY MURRAY, S.J.

In this 1965 address, Murray begins to blend civil and theological notions of freedom (a task more fully outlined in the next article). He speaks more freely here of love in civil life than he had before the council. It was on this basis that he could work toward a redefinition of the church in the fourth article in this section, "Freedom, Authority, and Community".

This occasion invites some brief discourse on the new age into which the Second Vatican Council is striving to lead the People of God. This period is commonly called the Age of Renewal. The direction of our new and common Christian effort has already been clarified by the Council. It is to give new form, new expression, new vitality to traditional Christian doctrines and truths, values and virtues, institutions and modes of apostolic action. The profile of the New Age has not yet come clear, but one significant thing can be said with some confidence. Within the Church, and therefore throughout the length and breadth of mankind, Saint Paul's resounding message will be heard with new clarity: "For freedom Christ has set you free. . . . It was unto freedom, brethren, that you were called" (Galatians 5:1, 13). The significance of the message is heightened by the fact that it rings out at a particular juncture in history.

Originally published as "Freedom in the Age of Renewal" (1967d; *American Benedictine Review* 18 [September 1967], 319–24). An editorial note to the text reads:
This address is representative of the writing and countless speeches on freedom and secularity delivered by the late Father John Courtney Murray. The talk was originally presented at the commencement exercises of St. John's University, Collegeville, Minn, June 3, 1965.

It is said today that the word "freedom" has lost much of the political magic that it had in the nineteenth century. This seems to be true. But the truth needs to be carefully defined. Freedom remains today what Lord Acton in the nineteenth century said it was—the highest political end. Freedom also remains today what the liberal tradition of the West has always recognized it to be—the primary method of politics. However, within the context of today's world, the ancient simplicities of the Political Century are no longer available to us. We have come to understand better the complexity of the conditions required for the successful pursuit of freedom as a political end and for the practical application of freedom as the method of politics.

We know that freedom recedes beyond realization in a society which fails to reckon with the full truth about man—that man is a person, an ultimate value in the created order, and that all men are equal in their dignity as human persons. We also know that freedom is illusory in a society in which the essential exigencies of the order of justice among men are not met with some measure of human adequacy. We know, finally, that the noble phrase, "the free society," can have no more than an emptily formalistic meaning if love be lacking among the citizenry, if the body politic is rent with hatreds, whether racial or ethnic or religious. We understand, in a word, that freedom as the highest political end can be realized only in so far as society is based on truth, directed toward justice, and animated by love.

Secular experience, moreover, has given us a better insight into the nature of freedom itself. Freedom is indeed man's natural endowment as a person and his rightful claim as a citizen. But, more importantly, freedom is an achievement. More exactly, it is the goal of a striving, an endless striving which forever falls short of the goal. There is no sudden leap into freedom, whether personal or social. In order to be free a man or a society must undergo a process of liberation. The process is never complete, and it is always precarious, subject to deflection or defeat. Man is never more than an apprentice in the uses of freedom. Their mastery eludes him. The possession of freedom, like the possession of truth, is the term, always only proximate, of an arduous education.

Secular experience has taught us all this, as the era of modernity has run its course. And if there be any who have not learned these lessons, it is because they have been absent from class, truants from the school of history. The point is that political discourse on freedom today must have more substance than the nineteenth century dreamed of, if it is to be taken seriously. The era of slogans is ended.

The notion of human freedom as an absolute is today obsolete. Discourse on freedom must have some fullness of substance, if it is to be listened to. The practice of freedom must be disciplined by other values, if it is to be worthy of man.

It is at this historical juncture that the Council and the Church send forth again the Christian message of man's freedom. The message is as old as the Bible. The first thing that the Bible has to say about man is that he was made in the image of God. And Saint Thomas, following an exegesis that goes back to John Damascene and the Greek Fathers, interprets the phrase in the Prologue to his treatise on man and the moral life. Man, he says, "is made in the image of God; and by image here is meant that man is intelligent, free in his power of choice, and master of himself . . . the active source of what he does." The first biblical truth about man is that he is free. So too, in the New Testament, the first truth about Christ our Lord is that he is Liberator, the One who sets us free unto a higher freedom. Saint Paul says: "For the law of the Spirit of life in Christ Jesus has set me free from the law of sin and death" (Romans 8:2).

The Council and the Church today therefore are uttering a traditional truth. Nonetheless the utterance is new and it is made with no accent of triumphalism, for a good reason.

I should agree with Piero Barbaini that "the story of thought in general and of religious reflection in particular is there to demonstrate clearly how the arch of culture and the development of civilization in the last four centuries have been substantially nothing other than a movement toward freedom" (*La libertà religiosa*, p. 42). Man as a person has been on pilgrimage towards his rightful freedom, religious and civil. Society too has been moving, since the close of the Middle Ages, towards its rightful autonomy, that is, its proper secularity. On the other hand, it is also true to say that the Church has not joined this human pilgrimage. On the contrary, it has opposed man's historical movement toward freedom. In this matter, however, historical judgment must be nice. It must reckon with the concrete historical forms in which the problem of freedom has arisen. Two forms stand out, among others.

FREEDOM AND AUTHORITY

In the sixteenth century the problem of freedom arose within the Church, as the problem of the Church. The issue was the doctrinal authority of the Church and her right of pastoral guidance. Therefore the post-tridentine Church laid heavy accent not on the freedom of the Christian but on the authority of the Church. Again, in the nineteenth century the problem of freedom arose within society as the problem of God. The issue was whether the conscience of man and the power of the state were absolutely autonomous, subject to no higher law, emancipated from the dominion of God. It was the issue of the outlaw conscience and the totalitarian state. Therefore the ultramontane Church emphasized, not man's human and civil freedoms, but the due subjection of man and society to the ultimate Majesty, the Lord of creation and history, whose will sets limits to the freedom of man and to the reach of all human powers.

All this was right and necessary in the circumstances. The Church opposed the effort to lift man to the status of an idol, a divinity in his own right. She also opposed the effort to reduce man either to nature (naturalism) or to the plane of matter (materialism) or to the plane of society and history (nineteenth-century socialism and Marxism). All this opposition was a service to the dignity of the man, as all historians today are willing to recognize.

Catholic historians, however, are now beginning to recognize that there was also a failure on the part of the Church, her magistery and her people, chiefly the intellectuals. There was a failure to recognize the signs of the times, to look beneath the surface of error and deviation and to discern the genuine human aspiration that was at work—man's perennial aspiration to possess his birthright of freedom. Condemnations in abundance fell on the errors to the right and to the left. But there was no effort to discern the truth that always lies at the heart of error. Not until Pope Leo XIII, and then only hesitantly, was the effort begun to fashion a doctrine of freedom, human and Christian, out of the Church's own treasury of reason and faith, that would at once speak to the intelligence of man and also solicit his heart.

Looking back now, we can see that the teaching of the Church in the nineteenth and early twentieth centuries was one-sided, centered on the dangers of freedom, on the perils that the human person risks when he claims for himself a freedom that fails to recognize the limits set by truth, justice, and love. The perils were real at the time; in our time they still are real. The theme of warning is, in fact, traditional. In the same text in which he states the Christian call to freedom Saint Paul adds: "Only do not use your freedom as an opportunity for the flesh," that is, for the part of man that is ignorant and weak, proud and perverse. And Saint Peter: "Live as free men, yet without using your freedom as a pretext for evil, but live as servants of God" (1 Peter 2:16).

Nevertheless, for all its dangers freedom remains the first truth about man, a positive value, both personal and social, to be respected even when it involves man in error and evil. This, for long centuries, was the forgotten truth. The magistery of the Church hardly adverted to it, passed it over in silence, failed to impress it on the consciousness of the faithful.

FREEDOM AND HUMAN DIGNITY

The turning point came with Pius XII. It was his major merit to have placed at the very center of the Church's social teaching the human person, endowed with freedom, the subject of inalienable rights and duties. Then John XXIII in the Encyclical *Pacem in terris* at once summed up the development accomplished by his predecessors and laid the footing for further progress. "Freedom," he said, "is the highest attribute of the human person." Freedom is also a positive social value. Along with the traditional triad—truth, justice, and love—freedom takes its place as an indispensable social principle. More than that, [freedom is the principle that moves the][1] person towards his proper human perfection, and the progress of society towards a higher level of humaneness and sociability. Finally, in its turn Vatican Council II has affirmed, in act even more than in word, the positive value of freedom within the People of God. It is the principle of doctrinal progress, of the growth of the Church toward more perfect inner unity, and of the widening and strengthening of relations between the Church and the world, both religious and secular.

All these successively more explicit affirmations of the value of freedom have been traditional; for freedom is traditional truth. None-the-less these affirmations have also been new; for freedom has been the forgotten truth. The new age which the Church is entering is to be—such is our hope—the Age of Renewal of this truth.

---

1. EDITOR NOTE: At this point the original text is garbled. It reads:
   ... More than that,
   freedom have been traditional; for freedom is traditional truth. None-
   person toward his proper human perfection. . . .
The middle line ("freedom . . . None-) is repeated in the next paragraph. I have here added a line to connect the first and third.

I come then to you, on this day of your commencement. You will be the citizens of the Age of Renewal. You are to be the bearers of the new age, the agents of the renewal. Upon your ears falls the Pauline message, uttered with a fresh accent: "It is unto freedom, brethren, that you are called." What matters above all else is that you should understand, not misunderstand, the meaning of your call, the meaning of the freedom to which you are called.

Freedom, Saint Thomas said, is the mark of human dignity. But one does not achieve the fullness of this dignity overnight. One grows towards it in gradual stages. This too is Saint Thomas' insight. "This," he says, "is the highest degree of dignity in man, that he should be led to what is good, not by others, but by himself. The second degree is reached by those who are led to what is good by others, but under no coercion. The third degree is found in those who need to be coerced into being good. The fourth degree is proper to those who cannot be directed to the good even by coercion."

Freedom therefore is inwardness, spontaneity, the capacity of a man to find within himself the reasons and the motives of his own right decisions and action, apart from external coercion. Freedom therefore is authenticity, truthfulness, fidelity to the pursuit of truth and to the truth when found. In further consequence, freedom is experienced as duty, as responsibility—as a response to the claims of justice, to the demands of rightful law, to the governance and guidance of legitimate authority. In its intimately Christian sense, however, freedom has a higher meaning than all this. Freedom, in the deepest experience of it, is love. To be free is to be-for-the-others. The Christian call to freedom is inherently a call to community, a summons out of isolation, an invitation to be-with-the-others, an impulse to service of the others.

Contemporary philosophers say that freedom is man's very existence; to exist is to be free. They are not wrong, within the limits of their philosophy. But Saint Paul stated the higher truth: "It was unto freedom that you were called; only do not use your freedom as an opportunity for the flesh, but through love be servants of one another" (Galatians 5:13). Freedom is love; to be free is to serve the others. The experience of freedom is the experience of the new law of love whereby the children of God live. To this experience you are called in the Age of Renewal.

The Declaration on Religious Freedom

JOHN COURTNEY MURRAY, S.J.

Murray's conciliar argument for religious freedom in *The Problem of Religious Liberty* (1964e) was grounded in the notion of a proper autonomy of the sacred and the secular realms, that is, on the principle of Christian constitutionalism. There he mentioned, but did not develop, the claim that differences between the tolerance view and his own argument pivoted on a difference between classical vs. historical consciousness. In this essay (1966c), Murray treats both social dualism and historical consciousness as directing the church toward *Dignitatis*. He then adopts a call for the church to exercise a "self-denying ordinance." Of particular interest are his initial attempt to spell out an analogous notion of freedom, and his treatment of Modernism. In Murray's understanding, the turn-of-the-century Modernist movement first embodied the contemporary differentiation of historical consciousness.

The Declaration on Religious Freedom is a document of very modest scope. It is concerned only with the juridico-social order and with the validity, in that order, of a human and civil right to the free exercise of religion. The right is founded on the dignity of the human person; its essential requirement is that man in society should be free from all constraint or hindrance, whether legal or extralegal, in what concerns religious belief, worship, witness and practice, both private and public. The structure of a rational argument for this right is briefly sketched; norms for legitimate limitation of the exercise of the right are laid down; the duty of government to protect and foster the free exercise of religion in society is affirmed. Then the implications of reli-

---

Originally published as "The Declaration on Religious Freedom," in *War, Poverty, Freedom: The Christian Response*, 3–16 (New York: Paulist Press, 1966, *Concilium* 15).

gious freedom for all Churches and religious communities are set forth in some detail. Thereafter the human right to religious freedom is considered under the light of revelation.

The intention of this section is simply to show that a harmony exists between religious freedom in the juridico-social sense, and Christian freedom in the various senses of this latter concept as they emerge from Scripture and from the doctrine of the Church. The Declaration merely suggests that the two kinds of freedom are related; it does not undertake to specify more closely what their precise relationship is. The conclusion of the Declaration is a pastoral exhortation to the faithful and a respectful appeal to the conscience of mankind, urging the value of religious freedom, and of religion itself, in the world today.

The Declaration therefore does not undertake to present a full and complete theology of freedom. This would have been a far more ambitious task. It would have been necessary, I think, to develop four major themes: (1) the concept of Christian freedom—the freedom of the People of God—as a participation in the freedom of the Holy Spirit, the principal agent in the history of salvation, by whom the children of God are "led" (Rom 8:14) to the Father through the incarnate Son; (2) the concept of the freedom of the Church in her ministry, as a participation in the freedom of Christ himself, to whom all authority in heaven and on earth was given and who is present in his Church to the end of time (cf. Matt 28:18–20); (3) the concept of Christian faith as man's free response to the divine call issued, on the Father's eternal and gracious initiative, through Christ, and heard by man in his heart where the Spirit speaks what he has himself heard (cf. John 16:13–15); (4) the juridical concept of religious freedom as a human and civil right, founded on the native dignity of the human person who is made in the image of God and therefore enjoys, as his birthright, a participation in the freedom of God himself.[1]

---

1. EDITOR NOTE: Notice the initially and essentially social nature of Christian freedom as outlined here. Murray went to great pains to ground even civil religious freedom in the social aspects of human dignity (see "The Human Right to Religious Freedom" in *Religious Liberty*, [1993]). If Murray had developed this outline, it would have been grounded on a close study of salvation history, not on "essential" definitions of the church and God, as in his first religious liberty argument ("Freedom of Religion, I: The Ethical Problem" [1945e]).

This would have been, I think, a far more satisfactory method of procedure, from the theological point of view. In particular, it would have been in conformity with the disposition of theologians today to view issues of natural law within the concrete context of the present historico-existential order of grace. Moreover, the doctrine presented would have been much richer in content. There were, however, decisive reasons why the Council could not undertake to present this full theology of freedom.

1. The Declaration is the only conciliar document that is formally addressed to the world at large on a topic of intense secular as well as religious interest. Therefore, it would have been inept for the Declaration to begin with doctrines that can be known only by revelation and accepted only by faith.

2. What the world at large, as well as the faithful within the Church, wants to know today is the stand of the Church on religious freedom as a human and civil right. It would be idle to deny that the doctrine of the Church, as formulated in the 19th century, is somewhat ambiguous in itself, out of touch with contemporary reality and a cause of confusion among the faithful and of suspicion throughout large sectors of public opinion.

3. The theological structure of the argument, as proposed above, would give rise to historical and theological problems which are still matters of dispute among theologians. There is, for instance, the problem of the exact relationship between Christian freedom and religious freedom. There is, furthermore, the whole problem of the development of doctrine, from *Mirari vos* to *Dignitatis humanae personae*.

4. Christian freedom, as the gift of the Holy Spirit, is not exclusively the property of the members of the visible Church, any more than the action of the Spirit is confined within the boundaries of the visible Church. This topic is of great ecumenical importance, but the discussion of it would have to be nice in every respect, and therefore impossible in a brief document.

5. Finally, there was a serious consideration of pastoral prudence. Christian freedom is indeed asserted over against all earthly powers (cf. Acts 4:19–20; 5:29); in this sense it prompted the witness of the martyrs. It is, however, also asserted within the Church; in this sense it is the warrant for charismatic ministries, and it is also the basis of prudent protest when the exercise of authority goes beyond legitimate bounds. As everyone knows, however, the issue of freedom within the Church is neuralgic today, as indeed it was when Paul

wrote to the Galatians (cf. Gal. 5:13). The issue is also highly complicated. It would have been imprudent, therefore, to raise this issue
directly in a brief conciliar document. Hence the Declaration is at
pains to distinguish sharply the issue of religious freedom in the juridico-social order from the larger issue of Christian freedom. The disastrous thing would be to confuse the two distinct issues. Obviously,
the issue of Christian freedom—its basis, its meaning, its exercise and
its limits—will have to be clarified by free discussion, conducted carefully and patiently in a sustained dialogue between pastors and people over many years. However, this dialogue will be the more
successful now that the Declaration has settled the lesser issue of the
free exercise of religion in civil society.

Narrow though its scope may be, the Declaration is nonetheless
a document of considerable theological significance. This will become
apparent if the document is considered in the light of the two great
historical movements of the 19th century, both of which were bitterly
opposed by the Church.

THE SECULARITY OF SOCIETY AND STATE

The first movement was from the sacral conception of society and
state to the secular conception. The sacral conception had been the
heritage of medieval Christendom and, in a far more ambiguous
form, of the *ancien régime*. For our purposes here, two of its characteristics should be briefly noted. First, the Christian world—or at least
the Catholic nation—was considered to be somehow enclosed within
the Church, which was herself the one Great Society. Second, the religious prerogative of the prince extended to a care of the religion of his
subjects and a care of their religious unity as essential to their political
unity. (This religious prerogative of political rule was interpreted in a
variety of more or less arbitrary ways, but these details need not
detain us here.)

The 19th century saw the break with this conception of the sacrality of society and state, and a movement toward their secularity. As
everybody knows, the Church—both in Rome and in the so-called
Catholic nations—opposed this movement with all the forces at her
command. The reason was obvious. After the revolution in continental Europe (the new Federal Republic of the United States presents an
altogether different case), the term of the historical movement was
not a proper secularity of society and state. What emerged was the

laicized state of rationalist or atheist inspiration, whose function was the laicization of society. In effect, what emerged was the *ancien régime* turned upside down, as Alexis de Tocqueville noted at the time. One might property regard the Law of Separation (December 9, 1905) of the Third French Republic as the legislative symbol of the new order.

The Church could not in principle accept this new order in its premises, in its ethos, or even in its institutions, primary among which was the institution of the so-called "liberty of cult." Furthermore, the Church did not in fact do a work of discernment of the signs of the times in order to discover, beneath the transitory historical forms assumed by the new movement, the true and valid dynamisms that were at work.

The overt revolt was against the sacrality of society and state as symbolized by the union of throne and altar. Few historians today would deny that this conception and its institutional symbol, for all their venerable antiquity, had become archaistic in the world of modernity. However, the true underlying direction of the new movement was toward a proper and legitimate secularity of society and state. In the depths, where the hidden factors of historical change were operative, what was really going on was a work of differentiation, which is always a work of growth and progress. Civil society was seeking differentiation from the religious community, the Church. The political functions of secular rule were being differentiated from the religious functions of ecclesiastical authority. The trouble was that this work of orderly progress was disrupted and deflected, as so often happens in history.

Chiefly to blame was the disastrous law of contradiction—that desire to deny and destroy the past which was the very essence of Enlightenment rationalism (whereby it aroused the bitter antipathy, for instance, of Edmund Burke). What appeared on the surface, therefore, was not progress but simply revolution. Society as civil was not simply being differentiated from society as religious; the two societies were being violently separated, and civil society was being stripped of all religious substance. The order of civil law and political jurisdiction was not simply being differentiated from the order of moral law and ecclesiastical jurisdiction; a complete rupture was made between the two orders of law and the two authorities, and they were set at hostile variance, each with the other. Society and state were not invested with their due secularity; they were roughly clothed in the alien garments of continental laicism. At this horrid specter, stalking across the Europe of the Middle Ages, the Church in the person of Pius IX hurled her unmitigated anathema.

Leo XIII first began to discern whither the deep currents of history were setting. In response, he restored to its proper centrality, and also developed, the traditional truth that Gelasius I had sought to enforce upon the Emperor Anastasius in 494 A.D.: "Two there are, august Emperor, whereby this world is ruled by sovereign right (*principaliter*), the sacred authority of the priesthood and the royal power." However, Leo XIII transcended the historically conditioned medieval conception of the two powers in the one society called Christendom— a conception that, in debased form, had persisted under the *ancien régime*, with its Gallicanism and its famous device: "One faith, one law, one king." In a series of eight splendid texts, stretching from *Arcanum* (1880) to *Pervenuti* (1920), Leo XIII finally made it clear that there are two distinct societies, two distinct orders of law, as well as two distinct powers. This was the ancient affirmation in a new mode of understanding—an authentic development of doctrine. On this basis, Leo XIII was able to accomplish a second development. In scores of texts—more than a hundred in all, of which about one-fourth had to do with the Roman Question—he reiterated that the essential claim which the Church makes on civil societies and their governments is stated in the ancient formula, "the freedom of the Church." It was not possible for him to complete these two developments with a third—the affirmation of the freedom of society and of the duty of governments toward the freedom of the people. In any event, his doctrinal work cleared the way for further progress in understanding the rightful secularity of society and state, as against the ancient sacral conceptions.

This progress reaches its inevitable term in the *Declaration on Religious Freedom*. The sacrality of society and state is now transcended as archaistic. Government is not *defensor fidei*. Its duty and rights do not extend to what had long been called *cura religionis*, a direct care of religion itself and of the unity of the Church within Christendom or the nation-state. The function of government is secular: that is, it is confined to a care of the free exercise of religion within society—a care therefore of the freedom of the Church and of the freedom of the human person in religious affairs. The function is secular because freedom in society, for all that it is most precious to religion and the Church, remains a secular value—the sort of value that government can protect and foster by the instrument of law. Moreover, to this conception of the state as secular, there corresponds a conception of society itself as secular. It is not only distinct from the Church in its origin and finality; it is also autonomous in its structures and processes. Its structural and dynamic principles are proper to itself and proper to the secular order—the truth about the human person, the justice due to the human person, the love that is the properly human bond among persons and, not least, the freedom that is the basic constituent and requirement of the dignity of the person.

This is the true Christian understanding of society and state in their genuine secularity which appears in *Pacem in terris*. The *Declaration on Religious Freedom* adds to it the final clarity in the essential detail, namely, that in the secular society, under the secular state, the highest value that both state and society are called upon to protect and foster is the personal and social value of the free exercise of religion. The values of religion itself for men and society are to be protected and fostered by the Church and by other religious communities availing themselves of their freedom. Thus the Declaration assumes its primary theological significance. Formally, it settles only the minor issue of religious freedom. In effect, it defines the Church's basic contemporary view of the world—of human society, of its order of human law and of the functions of the all too human powers that govern it. Therefore, the Declaration not only completes the *Decree on Ecumenism*, it also lays down the premise, and sets the focus, of the Church's concern with the secular world, which is the subject of Chapter XIII. Not nostalgic yearnings to restore ancient sacralizations, not futile efforts to find new forms of sacralizing the terrestrial and temporal order in its structures and processes, but the purification of these processes and structures and the sure direction of them to their inherently secular ends—this is the aim and object of the action of the Church in the world today.

In its own way, the Declaration is an act in that lengthy process known today as *consecratio mundi*. The document makes clear that the statute of religious freedom as a civil right is, in reality, a self-denying ordinance on the part of government. Secular government denies to itself the right to interfere with the free exercise of religion, unless an issue of civil offense against public order arises (in which case the state is acting only in the secular order, not in the order of religion). On the other hand, the ratification of the Declaration by Vatican Council II is, with equal clarity, a self-denying ordinance on the part of the Church. To put the matter simply and in historical perspective, the

Church finally renounces, in principle, its long-cherished historical right to *auxilium brachii saecularis* (the phrase in Canon 2198 remains for the moment an odd bit of archaism). The secular arm is simply secular, inept for the furtherance of the proper purposes of the People of God. More exactly, the Church has no secular arm. In ratifying the principle of religious freedom, the Church accepts the full burden of the freedom which is the single claim she is entitled to make on the secular world. Thus a lengthy, twisting, often tortuous development of doctrine comes to a term.

Like all developments, this one will initiate a further progress in doctrine, that is, a new *impostazione* of the doctrine of the Church on the problem of Church and state, as it is called, in order to restore, and to perfect in its own sense, the authentic tradition. This, however, is a subject in itself, not to be dealt with here.[2]

HISTORICAL CONSCIOUSNESS

The second great trend of the 19th century was the movement from classicism to historical consciousness. The meaning of these two terms would require lengthy explanation, both historical and philosophical. Suffice it to say here that classicism designates a view of truth which holds objective truth, precisely because it is objective, to exist "already out there now" (to use Bernard Lonergan's descriptive phrase). Therefore, it also exists apart from its possession by anyone. In addition, it exists apart from history, formulated in propositions that are verbally immutable. If there is to be talk of development of doctrine, it can only mean that the truth, remaining itself unchanged in its formulation, may find different applications in the contingent world of historical change. In contrast, historical consciousness, while holding fast to the nature of truth as objective, is concerned with the possession of truth, with man's affirmations of truth, with the understanding contained in these affirmations, with the conditions—both circumstantial and subjective—of understanding and affirmation, and therefore with the historicity of truth and with progress in the grasp and penetration of what is true.

---

2. Editor Note: See, for example, "The Issue of Church and State at Vatican Council II" (1966h) *Religious Liberty*, in 1993, pp. 199–227.

The Church in the 19th century, and even in the 20th, opposed this movement toward historical consciousness. Here, too, the reason was obvious. The term of the historical movement was modernism, that "conglomeration of all heresies," as *Pascendi dominici gregis* called it. The insight into the historicity of truth and the insight into the role of the subject in the possession of truth were systematically exploited to produce almost every kind of pernicious "ism," unto the destruction of the notion of truth itself—its objective character, its universality, its absoluteness. These systematizations were false, but the insights from which they issued were valid. Here again a work of discernment needed to be done, and was not done. To be quite summary about it, this work had to wait until Vatican Council II. (I am not here speaking of the work of scholars.)

The sessions of the Council have made it clear that, despite resistance in certain quarters, classicism is giving way to historical consciousness. Obviously, neither of these theories has been debated, and perhaps they are not even understood as theories. The significant thing is that the Council has chosen to call itself "pastoral." The term has been misunderstood, as if the Council were somehow not concerned with truth and doctrine but only with life and practical directives for living. To so contrast the pastoral and doctrinal would be disastrous. The pastoral concern of the Council is a doctrinal concern. However, it is illuminated by historical consciousness: that is, by concern for the truth not simply as a proposition to be repeated but more importantly as a possession to be lived; by concern, therefore, for the subject to whom the truth is addressed; hence, also, by concern for the historical moment in which the truth is proclaimed to the living subject; and, consequently, by concern to seek that progress in the understanding of the truth demanded both by the historical moment and by the subject who must live in it. In a word, the fundamental concern of the Council is with the development of doctrine. The scholarly concern of the 20th century has become also the pastoral concern of the Church in the 20th century.

Viewed in this light, the second theological significance of the Declaration on Religious Freedom appears. The Declaration is a pastoral exercise in the development of doctrine. (This, it may be said in passing, is why it met some opposition; classicism—if not as a theory, at least as an operative mentality—is still with us, here and there.) Briefly, the Declaration bases itself on a progress in doctrine that has, in fact, occurred since Leo XIII. It also carries this progress one inevitable step further by discarding an older theory of civil tolerance in favor of a new doctrine of religious freedom more in harmony with the authentic and more fully understood tradition of the Church. Only a bare outline of this progress can be suggested here.

The remote theological premise of the Declaration is the traditional teaching of the Church, clarified by Leo XIII, with regard to the two orders of human life, the sacred and the secular, the civil and the religious. The immediate premise is the philosophy of society and its juridical organization—in this sense, a philosophy of the state—developed by Pius XII and given a more systematic statement by John XXIII in *Pacem in terris*. This philosophy is deeply rooted in tradition; it is also, by comparison with Leo XIII, new.

The Leonine doctrine, more Aristotelian and medieval in inspiration, rested on the conception of the common good as an ensemble of social virtues and values, chiefly the value of obedience to the laws. The Pian and Joannine doctrine, more profoundly Christian in inspiration, rests on the conception of the common good as consisting chiefly in the effective exercise of the rights, and the faithful discharge of the duties, of the human person. Correlatively, in the Leonine conception the function of government was primarily ethical, namely, the direction of the citizen-subject—who was considered more subject than citizen—toward the life of virtue by the force of good laws reflecting the demands of the moral order. In the Pian and Joannine doctrine, on the other hand, the primary function of government is juridical, namely, the protection and promotion of the exercise of human and civil rights, and the facilitation of the discharge of human and civil duties by the citizen who is fully citizen, that is, not merely subject to, but also participant in, the processes of government.

The insight of Pius XII, which lay at the root of the new development, was stated thus: "Man as such, so far from being regarded as the object of social life or a passive element thereof, is rather to be considered its subject, foundation, and end." In contrast, the customary focus of Leo XIII's doctrine was on the *principes* (his favorite word), the rulers who wielded in society the power they had received from God. In this latter conception, society is to be built and rendered virtuous from the top down, as it were; the rule of government is dominant. In the former conception, however, society is to be built and rendered virtuous from the bottom up, as it were; the role of government is subordinate, a role of service to the human person. Moreover, in Leo XIII's conception (except in *Rerum novarum*), government was not only personal but paternal; the "prince" was *pater patriae*, as society was the family writ large. In Pius XII's conception, on the other hand, government is simply political; the relation between ruler and ruled is a civil relation, not familial. This was a return to tradition (notably to Aquinas), after the aberrations of continental absolutism and the exaggerations of the Roman-law jurists.

Leo XIII's paternal conception owed much to historical fact and to the political culture of his day. The pivotal fact was the *imperita multitudo*, the illiterate formless masses which reappear time and again in his text. In contrast, Pius XII's political conception was a return to tradition, to the noble idea of "the people," a structured concept at whose root stands, as he said, "the citizen [who] feels within himself the consciousness of his own personality, of his duties and rights, and of his due freedom as joined with a respect for the freedom and dignity of others." This return to the tradition of "the free man under a limited government" (as someone has summarized the basic political insight of Aquinas) was likewise a progress in the understanding of the tradition.

Finally, in Leo XIII the traditional distinction between society and state was largely lost from view; its disappearance from history had been, in fact, part of the *damnosa haereditas*—the fateful heritage—of the *ancien régime*. It is a noteworthy fact that nowhere in the immerse body of Leo XIII's writings is there to be found a satisfactory philosophy of human law and jurisprudence. He was always the moralist, not the jurist. His concern was to insist that the juridical order of society must recognize the imperatives of the objective moral order. This emphasis was indeed necessary against the moral antinomianism and juridical positivism of continental laicism. However, in consequence of this polemic necessity, Leo XIII gave little if any attention to the internal structure of the juridical order itself—the structure, that is, of the state.

This became the preoccupation of Pius XII, as the menace of totalitarianism loomed large, threatening the basic dignity of the human person, which is his freedom. Pius XII revived the distinction between society and state, the essential barrier against totalitarianism. He also made it a pillar of his concept of the juridical state (the phrase is alien in English; we speak of "constitutional government"). The powers of government are not only limited to the terrestrial and temporal order. Since Leo XIII this had been clear doctrine, however much it may have been disregarded in practice. But even within this limited order, the powers of government are limited by the higher order of human rights, defined in detail in *Pacem in terris,* whose doctrine is completed by the *Declaration on Religious Freedom.* The safe-keeping and promotion of these rights is government's first duty to the common good.

Even this rapid comparison may help to make clear that, although Leo XIII's theory of civil tolerance was coherent with his conception of society and state, it is not coherent with the more fully developed philosophy of Pius XII and John XXIII. For Leo XIII the power of the ruler was *patria potestas,* a paternal power. The ruler-father can, and is obliged to, know what is true and good—the true religion and the moral law. His primary duty, as father-ruler, is to guide his children-subjects—the illiterate masses—to what is true and good. His consequent function is to protect them against religious error and moral aberration—against the preachments of the "sects" (that favorite Leonine word). The masses are to be regarded as children, *ad instar puerorum,* who are helpless to protect themselves. They must look to the ruler-father, who knows what is true and good and also knows what is good for them. In these circumstances, and given this personal conception of rule, the attitude of government toward what is error and evil could only be one of tolerance. Government permits by law what it cannot prevent by law. Moreover, this civil tolerance is no more than a dictate of necessity; it is practiced for the sake of a greater good—the peace of the community. This theory of civil tolerance may indeed be regarded as a counsel of practical wisdom. It can hardly be regarded as permanent Catholic doctrine, any more than the theory of government, with which it is correlative, may be so regarded. The roots of both theories are in the contingencies of history, not in the exigencies of abiding truth.

Therefore, the *Declaration on Religious Freedom* puts aside the post-Reformation and 19th-century theory of civil tolerance. The fault is not error but archaism. A new philosophy of society and state has been elaborated, more transtemporal in its manner of conception and statement, less time-conditioned, more differentiated, a progress in the understanding of the tradition. Briefly, the structural elements of this philosophy are the four principles of social order stated, and developed in their exigencies, in *Pacem in terris*—the principles of truth, justice, love and freedom. The declaration of the human and civil right to the free exercise of religion is not only in harmony with, but also required by, these four principles. The foundation of the right is the truth of human dignity. The object of the right—freedom from coercion in religious matters—is the first debt due in justice to the human person. The final motive for respect of the right is a love of appreciation of the personal dignity of man. Religious freedom itself is the first of all freedoms in a well-organized society, without which no other human and civil freedoms can be safe.

The Social Function of the Press

JOHN COURTNEY MURRAY, S.J.

In the "Forward" to *WHTT* (pp. ix–x) Murray claimed that any attempt to judge the church by criteria developed in the secular order would be "impertinent," for the Catholic "knows that the principles of Catholic faith and morality stand superior to, and in control of, the whole order of civil life." He therefore hesitated to import the ethical requirements for moral living, as developed by the Anglo-American tradition, into the internal life of the church. With the conciliar discussion of religious freedom well under way, however, he attempts, in the following address, an "analogous" application of democratic theory to the church. The stumbling block for such an analogy was, of course, a democratic people's right to "judge, direct, and correct" its government. No parallel right could be claimed for the faithful vis-à-vis the magisterium. Murray therefore shifts the grounding for free speech in the church to a right to correct information (at face value a rather passive right). Since the church is bound together by the meanings that its members share in common, church authorities acquire an obligation to encourage communication within the church. However, Murray had difficulty identifying who are to challenge abuses of that authority, and by what right or even obligation they might do so.

I fear that I am standing here this morning on rather narrow and shaky footing.

I spent only one year of my life as a journalist, between 1945 and 1946, at the Jesuit weekly *America*. Apparently I was not a great suc-

This essay is expanded from an address to the International Press Association, 1963. Originally published as "The Social Function of the Press," (*Journalistes Catholiques* 12 (Janvier-Avril 1964): 8–12). The text here is from "Information and the Church: The Function of the Catholic Press within the Catholic Church" (*Social Survey*. 13 [1964a], 204–8.

cess, because after one year, I was sent back to Woodstock as Professor of Theology where I have been ever since.

Gentlemen, you are approaching here a very difficult subject, when you undertake to discuss the function of the Catholic press within the Catholic Church, to discuss the service that the Catholic press is to render to the Church and to her members, to discuss the function that the Catholic press must play as the source of radiation of truth throughout the world. I suppose the basic difficulty arises from the fact that the Church is a unique society, a society *sui generis*. The Church is somewhat like and totally different from civil society. The Church has her own unique origin, her own unique purposes. She has her own structure of institutions, of government. She has her own order of law. There obtains within the Church a relationship between those who rule and those who are ruled, those who teach and those who are taught. And this relationship is somewhat like and totally different from the political relationship in the civil community. There obtains within the members of the Church a bond of union which again is somewhat like and totally different from the bonds of union that bind together civil society.

Nonetheless, I thought it might be useful to begin our discussion with a word or two about the political analogue, I mean the function of the free press as an institution of public information within civil society.

INFORMATION AND CIVIL SOCIETY

Today, as we all know, in every well-ordered, democratic society, political censorship of information and opinion is considered to be not only impossible but also imprudent and indeed unrightful. It is a violation of an objective right of the people. The reason is, that in every well-ordered society today, public information is a social necessity.

The premiss, the true premiss of the institutions of free speech and of free press is not of course that frightfully thin piece of rationalist ideology that was current at the beginning of the 19th century, namely, that a man has the right to say what he thinks, simply because he thinks it. This is about as silly a piece of nonsense as was ever foisted on the world. No, the premiss of the institution of free speech and free press is not an individualistic premiss, but a political and social premiss. These institutions are essential to the conduct of free, responsible and democratic representative government. These institutions find more particularly their bases in our true political tradition, the body of principles that are integral to the liberal traditions of the West. The true liberal tradition of the West which is a compound, as you know, of Greek, Roman and Germanic elements.

The first principle is that of the consent of the governed. The medieval principle held that the medieval monarch, unlike the absolute monarch of later times, was obliged to obtain the consent of his people to his legislation, very likely in those days, of course, financial legislation, fiscal legislation. And if this legislation was not just, the people possessed the right of resistance. This was the great Germanic contribution to the liberal tradition.

The second principle is that of the participation of the people in the processes of government. This too is an ancient principle as a principle, but only in modern times has it been so institutionalized as to be active or dynamic within society.

These two principles have been wedded together with the result that today in every well-ordered society the people are indeed governed, but they are governed because they consent to be governed and they consent to be governed because they govern themselves.

From these two principles there flows the fundamental right of the people in every well-ordered contemporary society. It is the right to judge, correct and direct the processes of government. I am using, you see, the medieval words: *judicare, corrigere, dirigere.* This right is inherent in the people as a people, as a body organized for action in history. And this right becomes a personal right through one's membership in the body politic. From this right there flows the social and political necessity of means of information of the people.

First, the people must be informed, need to be informed about public affairs, about what we usually call affairs of state. They need to be informed precisely in order that they may judge, correct and direct the actions of government.

The free press therefore is the vehicle, as it were, of a dialogue between the people and the government. It is the channel through which the government seeks the consent of the people and through which the people themselves give this consent.

Secondly, the people need to be informed and must be informed about the larger affairs of society, making the distinction—the classic distinction—between society and state. Therefore the free press is the instrument of a dialogue among the people themselves. The English Dominican Father Gilby said once that civilization is formed by men who are locked together in dialogue, in conversation. It is from this argument, this public argument that continually goes on, that the people become a political community in the strict sense. There is such a thing as the simple multitude and then there is the civil multitude. The multitude is civilized, made civil precisely by the fact that throughout the whole social body there is continually taking place this conversation among the people, this conversation between government and the people. This is the means for the integration of the people as the people, is the means toward the formation of a common mind and a common purpose in history.

What is the principle of limitation of public information in a well-ordered society today? The principle is simply the people's need to know. And the need to know of a free people, in a free and open society, is in principle unlimited. Indeed, this is why, of course, a political censorship is regarded, as I have said, as imprudent and also unrightful, a violation of right.

Repression of information may indeed be justified at times by grave reasons of state, such things as military security. But in the end, it is for the people to judge with regard to their need to know. It is not for government arbitrarily to decide what the people need to know and what they need not be told. This, I take it, is the contemporary theory. This, I also take it, is a sound theory. But you can see immediately the difficulty of applying it to public information, to the Catholic press within the Church.

INFORMATION AND CHURCH

The Church is not democratically organized. I do not need to delay upon this point, do I? This is a fundamental thing that we all are entirely familiar with. Within the church there exists among the people no right to judge, correct and direct the actions or the teaching of authority. Nonetheless, despite this fact, between civil society and the Church there exists this analogy. They are somewhat alike and totally different. There are points of resemblance and it might be useful to point them out.

In the first place, within the Church, as within civil society, public information is a social necessity. The press performs a social function and this function is indispensable. Is it necessary to linger on this? I hope not. The Catholic free press within the Church is not some sort of luxury that is really to be frowned on. It is not a nuisance that has to be tolerated. The quest of information by the professionals of the press, by you gentlemen and ladies, this quest is not a matter of idle curiosity and your publication of information that you collect is not pandering to curiosity. It is not a regrettable sort of indiscretion that we would rather like to stop but dare not. No, no. The Church for all her differences as over against civil society remains a society. And the societal character of the Church creates a public right to information about all that concerns the Church: about her teaching, about her discipline and law, about her policies, to call them that; that is to say, about the total action of the Church in history, in this present moment of history. What is the Church doing here and now today? The people of God need to know all this. The subject of this right to know is, first of all, the people as a people. And this right derives to you and me through our membership in the people of God.

Secondly, if the function of public information in the Church is a social necessity, then the discharge of this function must be free. This public information is a response to a public need. The need is basic, essential to the Church; and the need cannot be satisfied apart from the full validity of the principle of freedom. There ought to be no arbitrary limitations imposed upon the dissemination of public information within the Church.

The Catholic press, I take it, is not the organ of some class within the Church. It does not exist to further certain interests of the Church merely, especially if these interests be conceived in some narrow and rather sectarian sense. The Catholic press does not exist to glorify the clergy. The Catholic press does not exist in order to create a public image of the Church that will be untrue to the reality of the pilgrim Church, the wayfaring Church, the Church that trudges along the road of history and gets her feet dusty at times, the Church that has hands by which she takes hold of dirty stuff of history . . . because history is rather dirty stuff! (You remember what Péguy said about Kantianism: Kantianism has clean hands, because Kantianism has no hands.) If the Church is going to guide the course of history as indeed she must, sometimes the hands of the Church—of churchmen, perhaps I should say—get dirty. And therefore this public image of the Church must be the true image, the image of the pilgrim Church, the wayfaring Church, that we have discussed in this session of Vatican II. The Catholic press can be nothing but the vehicle of truth and of fact. Freedom therefore is the indispensable condition for the fulfillment of the social function of the Catholic press within the Church and for the Church. The freedom of the press to inform is nothing really but the other side of the rights of the people to be informed. And therefore, through these rights of the people the freedom of the press knows only one limitation, and that is the people's need to know. And I think within the Church, as within civil society, the need of the people to know is in principle unlimited.

Now we must leave the realm of general theory—in which discourse of course is always easy—and come perhaps to problems of application. This is always difficult. I might, however, touch upon just one practical problem of a certain general nature; it arises out of our own times, out of the tempo of our own times, which has been described both by Signore Manzini and also by Père Gabel. This tempo of the time was noted by Pius XII in his great Christmas allocution of 1944. "With respect to the State, with respect to governments, they (the people) have a new attitude: questioning, critical, suspicious. Taught by bitter experience, they oppose with increasing violence the monopolies of a power that is dictatorial, insidious, and untouchable, and they demand a system of government more compatible with the dignity and freedom of citizens." He said again in the same allocution: "In a people worthy of that name, the citizen senses in himself an awareness of his own personhood, of his sorrows and of his rights, of his own freedom linked with the respect and dignity of others."

This same phenomenon had been noted in a different style and tone by John XXIII, in his great testimonial encyclical *Pacem in terris*, in which he left us so much the legacy of himself. He speaks here of the desires that are abroad today. He says they are the manifestations that in our time men have become more and more conscious of their dignity. And for this reason, they feel the impulse to participate in the government of the state (that is of the republic). And also they feel the impulse to demand the rights that are their own, the rights that are inviolable. They demand that these rights be acknowledged and protected in the government of the city. Nor is this enough, nor is this all. Men today ask one thing more, namely, that those who rule the city should act according to the norms of a public constitution and that they should perform their functions within definite limits set by the constitution.

This is the political phenomenon of the day. It is a phenomenon whose appearance Pius XII greeted with joy and approval. He applauded the wakening of the people from their long sleep, as he called it. For so long the people, he said, had been simply the objects of the political and the social process. Now they realize that they are to be awakened to consciousness, that they are not simply subjects of rule; they are citizens.

This of course, as you know, is the great advance in Catholic theory made by Pius XII over Leo XIII. It is rather difficult to find in Leo XIII, for instance, the concept of the citizen, the concept of citizenship. He seems to regard the people as simply the subjects of rule. This, I say, is a political phenomenon. Call it the emergence of the will to self-direction on the part of people and also on the part of individuals. Together with this will to self-direction, there has emerged the will that government should be constitutional, that it is to be limited by law, limited by the consent of the people, that government—in a word—should be on the part of the people self-government. As a political phenomenon this is not to be deplored. It is a sign of growth, it is a sign of progress, it is a sign of maturity. It shows the flowering of the human person into a consciousness of his true dignity before God and men, and out of this consciousness of dignity there emerges the personal demand for freedom.

However, this political phenomenon, it seems to me, has larger implications to which the Church herself surely must be alert. You see, here is the active self-conscious citizen within the civil community, [the citizen who] cannot be expected to be simply a passive subject within the community of the Church. This ancient symbolism of the Gospel retains all its validity of course. This symbolism, I mean, of the sheep. But this symbolism is not today to be pressed too far. We cannot consent to any schizophrenia. Between civic life and Christian life, we recognize direct differences between the civil and ecclesiastical community; but these differences must not be allowed to effect a schism within the soul of the Christian today. Here in society is the mature man or woman who cannot be considered in the Church to be an infant or an adolescent.

The problem is to harmonize an affirmation of this new spirit of self-consciousness, this new will to self-direction, to harmonize this new spirit with the altogether permanently necessary affirmation of the principle of authority in the Church and with the Christian spirit of obedience.

There is not a sphere of life, it seems to me, in which this problem is not encountered. Not least, of course, in the classroom, where I spend my life. In classrooms of theology we meet this in a particular way. I am not going to discuss the problem. I shall merely suggest, ladies and gentlemen of the press, that the problem itself constitutes, offers, an opportunity for the Catholic press, an opportunity that must be grasped. This very problem itself makes your function, the function of public information in the Church all the more indispensable. The opportunity, briefly, I suppose, would be this: the situation now poses the necessity that the press should be the vehicle of dialogue between clergy and laity, among the laity themselves and of course between the local Churches across national boundaries. The premiss of this dialogue is evident, it seems to me. The personal will to self-direction is not incompatible at all with the principle of authority. But it is incompatible with such exercises of authority as might be arbitrary or capricious. This spirit of self-direction is incompatible with such exercises of authority as are not constitutional, that go beyond the limits that are always legitimately set to authority, so as to become an abuse of authority. Here the dialogic function of the press may do a service to the Church. The freedom of the press creates no right to stand against authority and its legitimate exercise. It does, however, create a responsibility to note abuses of authority, and thus to serve the true interests of authority. It is to the interest of authority that its method of exercise should be pure, free of all taint of the arbitrary.

Moreover, the press, as a function of information, serves the public advantage of the Church by offering a channel of communication through which the teaching of the church, her laws, and her policies in contingent circumstances may be explained and made intelligible to the people whose desire is to understand in order that their faith and obedience may be more profound and personal, in order that their solidarity as a people may be strengthened, in order that the sense of unity and spirit of confidence between the people and those who govern them in the name of God our Father may be more solid and operative.

Reference has already been made here by Signore Manzini to certain qualities of the time in which we live. It is a time in which many complex issues confront us all; a time of rapid change. And this complicated nature of the time in which we live makes more emphatic the need of the people of God to know. To know not only the doctrine of the Church more perfectly; that, of course. Primarily to know not only the laws and the disciplines of the church; that too, by all means is essential. But to know the pastoral directions in which the Church wants her people today to move.

These pastoral directions need to be made intelligible to the people, and here is where the press can play its purpose. Differences in such pastoral decisions are influenced by political considerations. The people and their pastors need to know this. If certain doctrinal orientations are considered to be dangerous—not wrong, but dangerous—the people need to know this, need to be told this.

Why? Very simply: in order that the faith and obedience may be more profound, more personal, more worthy of a Christian and more worthy of a man. The people need to know these things in order that a spirit of confidence may obtain between those who teach and rule the church and those who are taught and ruled. This spirit of confidence must be made more intimate in these troubled times, this spirit of confidence must not be disturbed by misunderstandings, by the intrusion of the emotional in any sense.

The people need to know, to understand the pastoral direction of the Church today in order that the sense of unity in the church may be all the stronger and more solid and more operative, in order that the church may be more and more fit for the perilous pilgrimage upon which she has set her feet.

It seems to me that the Catholic press lives and works upon, as it were, a border line, the border line between the Church and the world. The Catholic press occupies an exposed place and therefore a perilous place. If you stand on the border line between the Church and the world you must expect to be shot at from both sides. You will be; you have been, undoubtedly.

And what is your armor? I think it is twofold. First there is the armor of your Christian integrity, your faith and your loyalty to the Church. Secondly, there is your professional integrity, your devotion to the ideals of your profession. And perhaps these ideals were never more perfectly expressed than by Leo XIII, when he opened the Vatican archives and laid down that rule of the historian which is the rule of the journalist: to say nothing that is false and to conceal nothing that is true.

Freedom, Authority, Community

John Courtney Murray, S.J.

After the council Murray had declared that the very definition of the church, as employed by Pope Leo XIII, was incomplete. At issue was the ecumenical but divided reality of the church. Here Murray attempts another expansion of Catholic ecclesiology—a move beyond an exclusively hierarchical model of the church to a new understanding of the church as constituted by the meanings that all members can affirm. The dynamics of maintaining and developing common meaning recast the role of authority.

Some people today speak of a "crisis of authority" in the Church; others speak of a "crisis of freedom." For my own part, I should prefer to speak of a "crisis of community." The reasons for this description of the situation will appear, I hope, in what follows.

Vatican Council II did not create the crisis; its roots are deep in the past. But the Council brought the crisis into the open. In the first place, the Declaration on Religious Freedom (*Dignitatis humanae*) said, in effect, that in political society the human person is to live his relation with God, or even with his private idol, in freedom—within a zone of freedom juridically guaranteed against invasion by any form of coercion. This proposition, the Council added, is the product of a

This essay was originally published as "Freedom, Authority, Community" (1966g: *America* 115 (December 3, 1966): 734–41). Also published in *Freedom and Authority in the West*, edited by G. Shuster, 11–24 (Notre Dame: University of Notre Dame, 1967); in *Christian Witness in the Secular City*, edited by E. Morgan, 118–130 (Chicago: Loyola University, 1970); and in *Catholic Lawyer* 15 (Spring 1969): 158–68. Translated and published as "Libertà autorità e Communità Chiesa in un mondo in trasformazione," in *Verso il sinodo dei vescovi. I problemi.*, 173–81 (Brescia: Queriniana, 1967).

biblical insight, though centuries of secular and religious experience were needed in order to bring it to explicit conceptualization.

In the second place, the Constitution on the Church in the Modern World (*Gaudium et spes*) affirmed, in effect, that the relation of the Church to the world and of the world to the Church is to be lived in freedom. Freedom, Paul VI said in his momentous address to statesmen on Dec. 8, 1965, is all that the Church asks of the political world—freedom for its apostolic ministry, freedom for the Christian life, freedom for spiritual and peaceful entrance into the political world, there to make moral judgments when political affairs raise moral issues. In turn, the constitution generously acknowledged that the world too has its rightful freedom to live its own life—or rather, its many lives: political, economic, social, cultural, scientific—in accordance with autonomous dynamisms and structures. These respective claims of freedom, the Council implied, are likewise rooted in a biblical insight—that the Church is of God, and so too, though in a different way, is the world.

Having laid down these propositions bearing on freedom, the Council inevitably raised the next question, concerning freedom in the Church. Is not the Christian life within the Christian community to be lived in freedom? Even the essential Christian experience of obedience to the authority of the Church—is it not somehow to be an experience of Christian freedom in the evangelical sense? This is the question, not directly touched by the Council, which now commands serious theological consideration in the light of the doctrine of the Council and of its spirit—indeed, in the light of the Council itself as a splendid "event of freedom" in the ongoing life of the Church.

From a historical point of view, the need for new reflection on the relation between authority and freedom in the Church derives from the fact that presently this relation exhibits an imbalance. In order to grasp this fact, it will be sufficient for the moment to go back only as far as Leo XIII and to consider three aspects of his thought.

First, there is his retrospective reading of history, visible, for instance, in the famous "Once upon a time" paragraph (*Fuit aliquando tempus*) in *Immortale Dei*. Once upon a time there was a Golden Age, the medieval period. It was the age of Christian unity, of the alliance of the Two Powers, of the obedience both of princes and of peoples to the authority of the Church. Then came the Reformation. Essentially it was a revolt against the authority of the Church, and in reaction to it the Church laid heavy, almost exclusive, emphasis on its own authority. Later, by a sequence that was not only historical but also logical, there came the Revolution. It was essentially a revolt against the authority of God Himself, launched by the revolutionary slogan: "No one stands above man" (*homini antistare neminem*). Again in polemic reaction, the Church rallied to the defense of the sovereignty of God, of the "rights of God," of the doctrine that there is no true freedom except under the law of God.

Both of these reactions were historically inevitable and doctrinally justifiable. The Church fashions its doctrine under the signs of the times, and the Reformation and the Revolution were then the signs of the times. But the doctrine formed under them could not but exhibit a certain hypertrophy of the principle of authority, and a corresponding atrophy of the principle of freedom.

In the second place, there is Leo XIII's conception of the political relationship between ruler and ruled in civil society. It is a simple vertical relationship within which the ruled are merely subjects, whose single duty is obedience to authority. Only in the most innovative fashion does one find in Leo the notion of the "citizen," who is equipped with political and civil rights and protected in their exercise. His emphasis falls on political authority, which is invested with a certain majesty as being from God, and which is to be exercised in paternal fashion in imitation of the divine sovereignty. In turn, the submission of the subject is to exhibit a certain filial quality. Moreover, society itself is to be built, as it were, from the top down. The "prince" is the primary bearer and agent of the social process. *Qualis rex, talis grex*. The ruler is to be the tutor and guardian of virtue in the body politic; the whole of the common good is committed to his charge. The people are simply the object of rule. Leo XIII's political doctrine was plainly authoritarian. It was fashioned under the political signs of the state and the Jacobin conception of the sovereignty of the people. In that moment in the history of continental Europe, Leo could not assume the patronage of political freedom.

In the third place, there is Leo XIII's ecclesiology, as summed up, for instance, in the encyclical *Satis cognitum* (1896), in which he says: "We have faithfully depicted the image and figure (*imaginem atque formam*) of the Church as divinely established." The encyclical is, in effect, a lengthy, profound, magisterial commentary on the Vatican I constitution *Pastor aeternus*, which was the splendid sign of the theological times. The portrait of the Church that emerges is really a portrait of the role of the apostolic office, and in particular the Petrine office, in the Church. In consequence, the ecclesial relationship—to call it such, on the analogy of the political relationship—is the simple vertical relationship between ruler and ruled. The function of the faithful appears simply as obedience to the doctrinal and jurisdictional authority of the Church.

It was within these perspectives that the classical doctrine on the relation of freedom and authority in the Church was fashioned. Those who hold office make the decisions, doctrinal and pastoral. The faithful in the ranks submit to the decisions and execute the orders. The concept of obedience is likewise simple. To obey is to do the will of the superior; that is the essence of obedience. And the perfection of obedience is to make the will of the superior one's own will. In both instances the motive is the vision of God in the superior, who is the mediator of the divine will and the agent of divine providence in regard of his subjects, in such wise that union with his will means union with the will of God. The further motive, to be adduced when obedience means self-sacrifice, is the vision of Christ, who made Himself obedient even unto death.

The trouble is that this classical concept of the ecclesial relationship is today experienced as being true indeed, but not the whole truth—as being good indeed, but not good enough to meet the needs of the moment. The signs of the times are new. The age of anti-Reform polemic has gone over into the age of ecumenism. The will of the Church to break with the world of the Revolution has given way to a new will to effect that "compenetration" between the Church of today and the world of today of which *Gaudium et spes* has spoken. The perspectives in which history is now viewed open out not from a supposed Golden Age in the past (whose luster is now seen to be dulled with the tarnish of much immaturity), but from the present moment. They are set not by nostalgia for the past, visible even in Leo XIII's *Satis cognitum*, but by the solid doctrine of the eschatological character of the Christian existence, which requires it to look resolutely to the future—to the coming-to-be of the Kingdom.

New signs of the times have become visible and were fully recognized at Vatican Council II. The first is man's growing consciousness of his dignity as a person, which requires that he act on his own responsibility and therefore in freedom. The second is man's growing consciousness of community, of that being with the others and for the others which is revealed, for instance, in the phenomenon of "socialization" in the sense of *Mater et magistra*. The Church in Council assembled clearly assumed the patronage—though in no patronizing sense—of these two related ongoing movements in the growth of human consciousness. The Council further undertook the renewal and reform of Christian doctrine and life in the light of these new signs of the times. In particular, the times demand a reconsideration of the classical concept of the ecclesial relationship—a new development, doctrinal and practical, in the relations between authority and freedom in the Church.

The difficulty with the classical conception, as experienced at the moment, is clear enough. It is sometimes stated by saying that obedience is a bar to the self-fulfillment of the individual. The statement may conceal a fallacy—an individualistic concept of self-fulfillment, and a failure to realize that self-fulfillment is not simply an affair of freedom but also an affair of community. Briefly, self-fulfillment is the achievement of freedom for communion with others. Therefore it is also somehow an affair of obedience to authority; for in every kind of community there is always some kind of authority.

The fallacy aside, it must be said that the contemporary difficulty with the classical conception is rooted in a truth—in an experience of the truth that the signs of the times reveal. What is really being said is that sheer submission to the will of the superior and mere execution of his orders do not satisfy the exigencies of the dignity of the person. They do not call into play the freedom of the person at its deepest point, where freedom appears as love. Still less do they exhaust the responsibilities of the person, which are to participate fully in community and to contribute actively to community. Thus stated, the contemporary difficulty is seen to be entirely valid. It is not to be solved by methods of repression. Nor will it yield to mere reiteration of the principle of authority: that authority is to be obeyed simply because it is authority.

There is need, therefore, to view the issue of freedom and authority in the new perspectives created by the signs of the times—that is, to view the issue within the context of the community, which is the milieu wherein the dignity of the person is realized. Community is the context both of command and of obedience. Community is also the finality both of command and obedience. Authority is indeed from God, but it is exercised in community for the benefit of the others. Moreover, since both authority and freedom stand in the service of the community, they must be related not only vertically but also horizontally, as we shall see.

It may be well to remark here that there is no univocal definition of the ruler-ruled relationship, because there is no univocal definition of community. This latter term is analogous. The realities it
designates—the family, political society, voluntary associations, the
Church—are somewhat the same and entirely different, one from
another. In the case of the Church, which is at once a family and a
society and a form of voluntary association, the essential thing is to
attend to the *maior dissimilitudo*. Within the uniqueness of the Church
as a community, the uniqueness of the relation of Christian freedom
to ecclesiastical authority comes to view. Happily, Vatican Council II,
which raised the issue of freedom and authority in the Church, also
created the perspectives within which its resolution becomes newly
possible. Four aspects of conciliar ecclesiology are pertinent here.

In the first place, the Constitution on the Church (*Lumen gentium*) presents the Church in the first instance as the People of God.
The first characteristic of the People is that it "has for its condition the
dignity and the freedom of the children of God, in whose hearts the
Holy Spirit dwells as in a temple." The basic condition of the People
is therefore one of equality in dignity and freedom, established by the
common possession of the Spirit. A consequent characteristic of the
People is its charismatic quality as a prophetic, royal and priestly People. The Spirit "distributes special graces among the faithful of every
rank, and by these gifts he makes them able and ready to undertake
the various tasks and offices useful for the renewal and upbuilding of
the Church, according to the Apostle: 'To each is given the manifestation of the Spirit for the common good' (1 Cor 12:7)." In particular, as
the Constitution on Divine Revelation (*Dei Verbum*) says, God
through the Spirit "uninterruptibly converses with the Bride of his
beloved Son," and the Spirit continually "leads unto all truth those
who believe and makes the word of Christ dwell abundantly in
them." The dignity of the People and its common endowment of
Christian freedom importantly consists in the charismatic quality of
its members.

In the second place, the Council presents the Church as a communion (*koinonia*). Its infinite inner form is the Holy Spirit Himself,
the subsistent love of the Father and Son, therefore the gift of Father
and Son, who is the presence of God in the midst of His people. In
consequence, the Church is in the first instance an interpersonal community, whose members are united in love of the Father through
Christ and in the Spirit, and also united with one another by the Spirit

of Christ, through whom they have access not only to the Father but to one another. The consequence here is one of immense importance, namely, that as an interpersonal community the Church is an end in itself, an ultimate reality, [It is an] eschatological reality, or, more exactly, a temporal realization [of an eschatological reality]. As a communion *sui generis*, the Church has for its primary purpose simply to be a communion. As such it will endure beyond time, forever, in what is called the communion of saints.[1]

In the third place, precisely as an interpersonal communion of love, the Church has a service (*diakonia*) to perform toward all humanity. That is to say, the divine love that is the form of the People reaches out through the People, in witness (*martyrion*), to draw all men into the communion of love, so that they may participate in the response of faith and love to the love whereby the Father loves His own People, purchased by the blood of His Son. In other words, precisely as an interpersonal community *sui generis*, the Church is also a functional community, that is, a community with a work to do, an action to perform—the action of God in history, which is to "gather into one the children of God who are scattered abroad" (John 11:52). Moreover, the work of the community, which is a work of love, is not extrinsic to the thematic of the community; it is woven, as it were, into this thematic as an essential element of it. That is to say, the interpersonal community, united in love, is also united by the missionary work of love to which it is called by its very nature.

Regarded as a functional community, however, the Church is not an end in itself but a means to a higher end—its own growing self-realization and perfection as an interpersonal community. There will come a day when the Messianic function of the Church will have been finished—the Day of the Lord, when the gathering of the People will be complete and the reign of Christ definitively established: "Then comes the end, when he delivers the kingdom to God the Father" (1 Cor 15:24).

In the fourth place, the Church is not only a community of faith and love but also a visible society; it therefore exhibits a structure of authority and a juridical order. Moreover, the Church is an organized society precisely as a community of faith and love with a function to

---

1. EDITOR NOTE: The original *America* article read ". . . an ultimate reality, as eschatological reality in a temporal realization thereof."

perform in history. The societal aspect of the Church is not alien or extrinsic to its communal and functional aspects, but essential to both of them and inherent in each of them. That is to say, the organization of the society is required by the purposes of the community, both for the sake of its own unity as an interpersonal communion and also for the sake of its action in history. The hierarchically ordered society—its structure of authority and its juridical order—stands in the service of the community, to assist in perfecting its unity and in performing its function.

The structure of authority in the Church is unique, as the community it structures is likewise unique. It is both doctrinal and jurisdictional—a power of authoritative teaching and of imperative rule. Moreover, the structure is not merely a matter of political and sociological necessity, as in the case of the civil community. This latter is simply a functional community, which is therefore organized only in order to get its work done—its work being what is called the common good. Here the *maior dissimilitudo* appears. The Church is organized as a society *sui generis* in order that it may be what it is—a community *sui generis*, an interpersonal, eschatological communion of faith and love and a historical, missionary community whose work in history expresses its own inner reality.

These four themes in the ecclesiology of Vatican II are, of course, entirely traditional. The order of their arrangement, however, is distinctive: so too is the weight of emphasis distributed among them. For Leo XIII, for instance, the Church was both community and society, indissolubly; so it is presented in *Satis cognitum*. But the weight of his emphasis falls heavily on the societal aspect and on the structure of authority in the Church. It may be fairly, if rather broadly, said that Leo XIII comes to the notion of the Church as community through the notion of the Church as society. And in his construction, the functions of Christian freedom are not readily apparent; they are, in fact, obscured. Authority seems, as it were, to stand over the community as a power to decide and command. In contrast, Vatican II comes to the notion of the Church as society through the notion of the Church as community. Authority therefore stands, as it were, within the community, as a ministry to be performed in the service of the community. Within the perspectives created by this newly accented construction of traditional doctrine, the ecclesial relationship can be more adequately understood and therefore stated with a new nicety of balance. In particular, the functions of Christian freedom emerge

into new clarity, in themselves and in their relation to the correspondent functions of authority. The new clarity radiates from the notion
of the Church as community, now made newly luminous.

The functions of authority appear to be three, in hierarchical
order. And each of them is a function of service to the community.

The first function is unitive. Authority is to be and do what God
Himself, through Christ and in the Spirit, is and does. He gathers,
unites, establishes communion. This too is the primary function of
authority. Moreover, God gathers His Church by initiating and sustaining with men the "dialogue of salvation," brilliantly described by
Paul VI in *Ecclesiam suam*. God communicates with His People, elicit-
ing from them the response of faith and love. His call to them is an
imperative laid upon them, but it is an imperative because it is, in the
words of Paul VI, a "demand of love" (*domanda di amore*), to which the
response must be free. So, too, authority performs its unitive function
through dialogue with the charismatic body of the faithful. The purpose of the ecclesiastical dialogue, as of the divine dialogue, is to
build and strengthen the community: to guide it, under the guidance
of the Spirit, toward the full truth. About what? About itself, in the
first instance. The dialogue is to deepen that "self-awareness" on the
part of the community that was a major theme, and also a major
achievement, of Vatican II.

Authority therefore elicits from the charismatic community of
Christian faith the insights of each into the faith, for the enlightenment of all. (This function receives new emphasis in the new charter
of the reformed Congregation on the Doctrine of Faith; it was also
strongly advanced in the discourse of Paul VI on Oct. 1, 1966, to the
International Congress on the Theology of Vatican Council II, when
he spoke of the reciprocal dependency of the magistery upon the theologian and of the theologian upon the magistery.) Moreover, authority
stirs the love of the charismatic members of the community for the
community, to be shown in service of the community. Finally, authority solicits the informed concern of the community for the work of the
community—its relations with the world, its mission of salvation and
its spiritual mission in the temporal order. (This function is broadly
emphasized all through the Constitution on the Church in the Modern World, as well as in almost all the other conciliar documents.)

The primacy of this unitive function of authority, to be dis-
charged through dialogue, results from the primacy of the notion of
the Church as an interpersonal community whose conscious unity is

an end in itself. This primary dialogic function also depends for its performance on the reality of the People of God as a charismatic body, whose basic condition is one of equality in Christian dignity and freedom. It follows therefore that the unitive function of authority is to be carried out under respect for this basic condition. *Lumen gentium* is careful to provide room in the Church for all manner of legitimate diversities and pluralisms—in rites, theologies, etc.—which, so far from damaging the unity of the community, constitute an enrichment of it. The principle of the Declaration on Religious Freedom—that there should be in society as much freedom as possible and only as much restriction as necessary—applies analogously in the Church. Only "in necessary things" is unity itself necessary.

It may be remarked here that the modes and manners in which authority is to perform its unitive function through dialogue are still problematical today, in this era of *assestamento* (adjustment). New structures of communication need to be created (for instance, the Synod that will meet in 1967). Older structures need reformation, as in the case of the Roman dicasteries. Experiments are called for that will yield the necessary experience. The problem is not simply to conceptualize in theological terms the relation between authority and freedom in the Christian community, as it appears in new perspectives; this relation must be lived, in all concreteness and practicality. Thus the experience of life will give vitality to the theology.

The second function of authority may be called decisive or directive. It hardly needs lengthy description, since it already is a familiar thing, prominent perhaps to the point of undue emphasis in the classical conception of an older day. The decisive function is necessary because the Church is a community of faith, and it was to the magistery that the guardianship of the deposit of faith was committed. The directive function is needed because the Church is a functional community organized for action in history. It is to be noted, however, that the necessity of the function is not merely a matter of efficiency, to insure that the work of the Church gets done. The necessity is grounded in the very nature of the community. The point is to insure that the work done is the work of the Church, which it is when it is done under direction. The even more important point is to insure that the Body acts as one in the action of its members, singly and collectively.

Thus the decisive and directive function of authority is in a true sense a modality of its unitive function. Moreover, the performance of

this secondary function supposes that the primary function has
already been performed; that the dialogue, whether doctrinal or pastoral, has been afoot between the community and its decisions and
directives, without ceasing to derive their force from apostolic authority, are also the decisions and directives of the community, whose
common good they serve.

The third function of authority is corrective or punitive. It is an
accidental function, in the sense that it is necessary only because the
People of God, on its pilgrim way through history, is a sinful People.
It is also a function of service to the community, which needs to be
protected against the egoisms—whether of thought or of action—that
would destroy its unity or damage its work. Again, therefore, this
function of correction appears as a modality of the unitive function of
authority. What comes to the fore today is the need that the corrective
or punitive function of authority should be performed under regard
for what is called, in the common-law tradition, "due process." The
demand for due process of law is an exigence of Christian dignity and
freedom. It is to be satisfied as exactly in the Church as in civil society
(one might indeed say, more exactly.)

Three functions of Christian freedom in the Church correspond
to the three functions of ecclesiastical authority. They are likewise
functions of service to the community.

The primary function may be called, for the sake of a name, charismatic. It is the free response of the community and of all its members to the unitive function of authority, whose initial act is the
invitation to dialogue (on which the Council more than once laid
emphasis). The Spirit is given to the Christian not only for his own
sanctification and enjoyment, but also for the growth of the community in conscious self-awareness and for the fuller deployment of its
action in history. Concretely, the community uses the gift of the Spirit
by sustaining its part in the dialogue with authority, in that confidence of utterance that reveals—in our times, as in those of the Acts
of the Apostles—the presence of the Spirit.

This primary function of Christian freedom corresponds therefore to the nature of freedom in its most profound sense—to the
nature of freedom as love, as the capacity for self-communication, as
the spontaneous impulse to minister and not be ministered to, as the
outgoing will to communion with the others. "For you were called to
freedom, brethren," St. Paul proclaims (Gal 5:13). Whatever else the
call may imply, it is a call to love: " . . . through love be servants of

one another" (*loc. cit.*). The forms of service within the community are manifold, but the primary service to the community is to participate in the dialogue of salvation that is continually going on in the community. This participation is the first exercise of Christian freedom. It is also an exercise in obedience, in the horizontal dimension that obedience assumes when it is situated, with authority, within community, and therefore in dialogic relation to authority, united to authority in a ministry of love toward the community.

The second function of Christian freedom may be called, again for the sake of a name, executive. It corresponds to the decisive and directive functions of authority. It also corresponds to the formal moral notion of freedom as duty—the freedom whereby one does what one ought to do. Here, of course, obedience may occasionally appear as self-sacrifice. The act of obedience is not, of course, *per se* an act of sacrifice: it is simply an act of Christian freedom. Obedience assumes a sacrificial quality only when Christian freedom meets the resistance of what Paul calls "the flesh." And the premise of obedience as sacrifice is always the profound nature of freedom as love—the love whereby one freely engages oneself in the paschal mystery. Hence obedience, as an act of Christian freedom, even when it is sacrificial—especially when it is sacrificial—is always the way to self-fulfillment. It is the expression of one's self-awareness that one is called to be in the image of the Son Incarnate, who freely gave His life for the many, and thus "went His way" to the self-fulfillment that was His resurrection. Finally, whether sacrificial or not, the executive function of Christian freedom, which consists in acceptance of the decisions and directives of authority, is always performed within the community, in and for which He works. Therefore this secondary function of freedom is related to the primary function, the charismatic function, the charismatic function of love whereby I contribute in dialogue to the unity of the communion that is the Church. The dialogue is not an end in itself; it looks toward decisions and directives. In their issuance and acceptance, the community comes together in a new way.

The third function of Christian freedom may have to go without a name, unless one calls it self-corrective, in order to mark its correspondence to the corrective function of authority. It is the free act of Christian refusal to "submit again to a yoke of slavery" (Gal 5:1). More broadly, it is the Christian rejection of the temptation, inherent in the psychological notion of freedom as choice, to "use your freedom as an opportunity for the flesh" (Gal 5:13). One might call it the "mortifying" act of Christian freedom; the word may not be popular today, but the notion is still Pauline (cf. Rom 8:13). In any event, it is the act whereby Christian freedom stands forth in all its evangelical newness, unique among all the modalities of freedom that men have claimed or hoped for or dreamed of. "It was that we might be free" in this new way, says St. Paul, "that Christ has freed us" (Gal 5:1).

The aim of this brief essay has been simply to suggest how the rather fleshless skeleton of the classical conception of the ecclesial relation may be clothed with flesh and animated with blood. The skeleton remains; the classical conception of the vertical relationship of authority and freedom. But it needs to assume a more Christian and therefore more human form by standing forth in the living flesh and blood that is the Christian community. More abstractly, the vertical relationship of command-obedience needs to be completed by the horizontal relationship of dialogue between authority and the free Christian community. The two relationships do not cancel, but reciprocally support, each other.

This more adequate understanding of the ecclesial relationship does not indeed dissolve the inevitable tension between freedom and authority. But by situating this perennial polarity within the living context of community, it can serve to make the tension healthy and creative, releasing the energies radiant from both poles for their one common task, which is to build the beloved community.

A Will to Community

John Courtney Murray, S.J.

The following article was delivered to the Episcopal Church committee that was examining the problem of heresy. Relying on the distinction between understanding and judgment, Murray here places tight limits on the silencing of theological discourse. He also places restrictions on magisterial social criticism, based on his practical judgment/theology distinction. As best I know, Murray never gave serious attention to the thesis that the entire church was the proper forum for creative theological discourse. Yet note his difficulty in identifying the theological fraternity, a problem that plagued his identification of the wise in civil society.

THE CHURCH AND THEOLOGICAL INQUIRY

I suppose that the institution of the Church which bears primary responsibility for theological inquiry as such is the *studium*. It no longer exists in its medieval form, of course. It is more scattered in an age of general learning. To it now belong seminary faculties of theology, faculties in church-related colleges, Christian intellectuals (in universities, as writers, etc.), religious journalists (the latest accession). All are somehow engaged in "inquiry" in the wide sense that the word "theological" has today.

At that, I am not sure that the word "obligation" would be rightly used here. The spirit of theological inquiry is immanent in the very dynamism of Christian faith itself, chiefly in its aspect of assent

---

The address was originally published as "A Will to Community." Pages 111–16 in Stephen F. Bayne, Jr. ed., *Theological Freedom and Social Responsibility* (New York: Seabury Press, 1967n). Also published as "We Held These Truths," *National Catholic Reporter* 3 (August 23, 1967), p.3.

to the Word of God. Faith in this sense must seek understanding of itself.

The search, motivated by the love of truth, is the necessary prolongation of the "adhesion" of faith itself, which is an adhesion made in love, and made to a Message that, for all its mystery, is somehow intelligible—a true "word," with a meaning. Moreover, since the Word of God was spoken in history, and is not some sort of Platonic "eternal truth," the search must be for a historical understanding of the Word—its sources, the stages in its progressive understanding through history, etc. Moreover, since the Word of God is many words yet still one Word, the search must also be for systematic understanding of the kind that makes the Word intelligible in its unity.

Finally, complementing and further activating the impulse that issues from the interior of faith itself, there is the challenge *ab extra* which is constantly being put by the total complex reality of life itself, Christian and human, as history goes on. The deposit of faith is indeed a deposit, but new questions are constantly being put with regard to its meaning, its relevance, its general and particular relation to the developing problematic of human life. These questions (and often times the wrong or dubious answers being currently given to them) are the starting points of theological inquiry. Much more could be said about this aspect of the matter, but I presume it is not quite the point.

I presume the real point concerns the Church as somehow a structure of authority—more concretely, it concerns the bishops. They bear, of course, primary responsibility for the preaching of the gospel; and they normally discharge this responsibility through their priests. This, however, is a matter of Christian witness, not of theological inquiry as such. And the primary matter of episcopal concern is the integrity of the witness, the purity of the faith as preached to the people of God, pastoral zeal to declare the "full counsel of God," etc.

It is more difficult to define the responsibility of the bishop for theological inquiry. This dimension of the life of the Church has to do with the development of doctrine, with the "growing edge" of the tradition. The dynamism of this progress in theological understanding is, I take it, freedom, and not authority. Hence I assume that the first function of authority is to foster the freedom of theological inquiry. (This has not always been well understood in my own beloved Church; it is only now beginning to be understood.) The responsibility of the bishop is to be in a "communion" of thought and concern with his theologians (I am speaking here of the bishop in his office as bishop; he may himself be a theologian, but that is a personal charism or achievement). The theological fraternity, which is somehow a fraternity in its own right, looks to the bishop for encouragement, support, sustenance, appreciation of the theological function in the Church, trust—things of that sort.

I also suppose that it is the responsibility of the bishop at least to know where the theological difficulties lie today, what the religious preoccupations are and ought to be, what lines of inquiry need to be pursued, what questions the "world" is asking of the Church, etc. This is part of his pastoral concern, behind which lies his doctrinal concern, as doctrinal issues always underlie pastoral issues. In particular, the bishop ought to know about the inadequacy of traditional formulations of doctrine, if and as these inadequacies are brought to light in the variety of ways in which they are always brought to light, chiefly through the enlarging experience of the Christian as he exists with-the-others-in-the-world.

Finally, the bishop today is obliged to do something about setting up and perfecting some formal structures of collaboration with the theological fraternity—both for his own sake and for theirs. I also expect he is obliged to do something about providing for the continuing theological education of his clergy and thus stimulating the spirit of theological inquiry in the pastorate as such.

THE CHURCH AND SOCIAL CRITICISM

This is an even more difficult question. "Social criticism" is a large category, within which at least one distinction is altogether necessary. On the one hand, there is prophetic testimony, based on the Word of God and its exigencies, proclaimed in the first instance to the faithful but beyond them to the "world." This testimony, when rendered in the prophetic manner, has to do with issues of truth and falsity, right and wrong. This is surely "social criticism." But the phrase assumes another sense when it covers utterance (or action) within the temporal order itself, based on practical assessments of a situation, on prudent prognosis of variant outcomes, on pragmatic calculations of the better and the worse, etc. This manner of social criticism touches issues of policy—legislative policy, other public policies, the actions or omissions of government, etc.

This distinction is perhaps clear enough in the abstract; but it is very difficult to apply in the concrete, especially since the second range of utterance is or can be broad. In any event, what is at stake in the distinction is the competence of the Church as a spiritual authority in matters of the temporal order—a competence which is real, and also rather broad, but still limited. It includes the right to "pass moral judgments even on matters touching the political order, whenever basic personal rights or the salvation of souls make such judgments necessary" (Second Vatican Council, Declaration on Constitution of the Church in the World Today). The problem is to be sure that the judgments are properly moral judgments; that the Church is not just proposing one more public policy, one more political or economic position, alongside others, with the consequent danger that it be simply a partisan position.

The Second Vatican Council made much the same distinction when it said that it is "highly important" that there should be a "clear distinction between what a Christian conscience leads them [the faithful] to do in their own name as citizens, whether as individuals or in association, and what they do in the name of the Church in union with her shepherds." And there are other ways of formulating the distinction, e.g., between an engagement of the authority of the Church, and an engagement of the responsibility of the Christian. As you know, Paul Ramsey likes to formulate the self-denying ordinance, governing statements of the Church, in terms of what the whole Church can say for the whole Church, speaking to the whole Church, and speaking also to all men in the name of the Church, out of her own treasury of truth and wisdom. This canon would surely make for responsible utterance. The Church can always blunder and transgress, of course; but if this canon is not held in view, the mistakes will be in a maximalist direction. And this is dangerous today, not least because it tends to cheapen the authority of the Church. Flight from this danger should not be allowed to lead to "angelism," of course. The word today is "incarnationalism," but this route to relevance is something like the famous Irishman's "narrow path between good and evil"!

Incidentally, I think there is great need for ecumenical discussion among Christian communities, and with our Jewish brethren too, on the general issue of the mission of the Church in the temporal order. We are all more or less confused. And the confusions are being publicly dramatized in many ways. For my part, I rather like the general line struck out by Leo XIII, *scil.*, that it is not the mission of the Church to solve the social question, but that the social question will not be solved without the Church. One must go on from there, but

that is the place from which to go on. I also like to insist on the principle of parsimony, so called. There are always limits to evidence, and
utterance should not go beyond them. And the limits to the evidence
available to the Church (or to the theologian) turned social critic are
fairly stringent; they are to be defined in terms of what can honestly
be called Christian truth.

THE ISSUE OF HERESY

The word [heresy] is not popular today, even in the milieu—my
own—in which it was once vigorously brandished. Yet the issue
remains real enough. Perhaps the discussion of it ought to begin with
the peculiarities of the situation in which we all find ourselves in this
moment. The reality of contemporary life is rather brutally putting
altogether fundamental questions to the Christian conscience—all
multiple variants of the three famous Kantian questions. I need not
develop this point. But it leads to a distinction I like to make, *scil.*,
between adventurous answers, which may well be mistaken, and
hardened positions which deserve to be called errors. The former are
an affair of deficient intelligence; the latter, of deficiency in what can
only be called good will. Errors in faith are a matter of will.

Today there are abroad all sorts of tendencies, currents of
thought, climates of opinion. And many uncertainties attend the necessary business of a renewal of the personal structures of conscience
and the further business of a reform of the objective expressions of the
Christian faith. We all live in an unbelieving world. And a "credibility
gap" has opened between the doctrines and structures of the Church
and the sheer experience of the world as it is. The truths of the
Church and the forms of her life are supposed to interpret the experience of human life and to give it some saving structure. But is this
happening? Many say no, and not without reason. This answer seems
to have lain behind John XXIII's distinction between the "substance"
of Christian faith and the "forms" of its expression. The distinction
could be given a too simplistic meaning, as if only words were at
stake. But it points in the right direction, toward a task we must take
firmly in hand. We shall do the task badly, of course. There will be
lots of "mistakes," but they are readily dealt with, since they involve
no will to error. This latter thing is the danger. How to avoid it? I
think the corrective is a will to community—of thought and love. The
Christian community is not in error, whatever mistakes it may make.

PART 4

Christianity and Atheism

In Part 3, we saw that the term "doctrine" designates (1) theoretical truths that serve as the condition for the possibility of mutual understanding and action and/or (2) judgments concerning the moral value and the truth of anything that can be questioned—whether those questions intend particular acts, general commitments, or even God. There, too, we encountered shifts in Murray's recommendations for the internal life of the church. That is, we saw Murray moving between the different ethics that flow from these distinct conceptions of church doctrine. In this and the following section, two other areas of church interaction are transformed as Murray delves deeper into the implications of the historicity of, and role of human reasoning in, all truth claims. In the articles reprinted here, Murray refocuses his ethical concern on new structures, procedures, and virtues that are required for adequately living within fully historical churches and civil societies. In Part 4, we will discuss Murray's changing response to social atheism; and, in Part V, the changes in his ethical approach to ecumenism.

By the mid-1940s (see Part 2), Murray had admitted to the sufficiency of a natural law consensus for the task of social cooperation. He listed four essential principles of natural law that "all men of good will" could accept:

> (1) a religious conviction as to the sovereignty of God over nations as well as over individuals; (2) a right conscience as to the essential demands of the moral law in social life; (3) a religious respect for human dignity in oneself and in others—the dignity with which man is invested inasmuch as he is the image of God; and (4) a religious conviction as to the essential unity of the human race (*Pattern of Peace*, [1944b]).

In the same article he spelled out theism as the condition for the possibility of cooperation.

It is clear to whom [Pius XII's] invitation to cooperate was issued, namely, to all men who believe in God; for belief in God necessarily entails acceptance of the moral law and of human dignity and equality.

One presupposition that played through Murray's earliest arguments for cooperation and religious freedom, then, was the notion of a natural, readily apparent grounding for a reasonable belief in God. Without it, social cooperation was impossible. In this section, we follow Murray's movement toward the postconciliar Christian-Marxist dialogue, where the theistic premise becomes a question that demands a new response within new perspectives.

Throughout his publishing career, Murray encountered several forms of public atheism that continually challenged his positioning of natural law's theistic premise as an initial condition for entry into public ethical conversation. These included U.S. secular humanism whether it was scientific and positivistic or the more pragmatic variety that flows from exclusive focus on economic production (materialism); continental laicism born of the French Enlightenment; and Marxist-Leninism as exemplified by the Soviet state, or in its more theoretical incarnations. While all these types of atheism tended to blend together in his earliest arguments (see "Construction of a Christian Culture" in part 2), Murray sharply distinguished between secular humanism and French laicism in order to separate Pius IX's and Leo XIII's criticism of French Enlightenment democracy from his own increasingly positive evaluation of American democracy.[1] Only then could he claim that America was founded on a legitimate "great act of faith" in the moral powers of the people.

That still left the problem of American pragmatic and scientific atheism or secularism. Up to the Council, Murray found many pragmatic reasons for entering into a truce with American secularism.[2] Yet it

---

1. By "How Liberal Is Liberalism?" (1946a) Murray had clearly made this distinction, although its full impact on his religious liberty argument would not be felt until the early 1950s, in a series of articles on Leo XIII's arguments for establishment and intolerance. See especially "The Church and Totalitarian Democracy" (1952a) and "Leo XIII: Separation of Church and State" (1953c).

2. By "America's Four Conspiracies," WHTT [1958a], 5–24, Murray insisted that America's four "conspiracies" (Catholic, Protestant, Jew, secularist) must conspire together at least to limit national warfare. He had as yet, however, not advanced any principled reasons for inclusion of anything more than the pragmatic atheist (secularist).

was only during and after the council that he searched out principled reasons for advancing even theological discussions with the atheist or secular humanist.

The articles of this collection include most of these approaches to the social atheist. The first in this section, "The Right to Unbelief" (1962a; which was most likely written in the mid-1940s), fairly lumps together all forms of atheism, as did the passages quoted above. In his "Necessity for Not Believing" (1949c) Murray attempts a dialectic interplay with American scientific positivism. For Murray's treatment of American pragmatic atheism, see "The Return to Tribalism," in part 2. Finally, in the fourth article, "Religious Freedom and the Atheist" (1970), Murray asserts the principled legitimacy of the atheistic voice within both American and Christian constitutionalism.

There remains the problem of international atheism, particularly of the Marxist-Leninist variety. In "Things Old and New, in *Pacem in terris*" (1963j), Murray struggles with a suggestion that John XXIII might be opening the window to Communist-Christian dialogue. He rejects that possibility, but soon thereafter he suggested distinct perspectives for such a dialogue.

One beginning point for such a dialogue could be an examination of the behavior of Christians and atheists in actual historical societies. Such an examination would yield the admission by the atheist and the Christian that both have violated the principle of Christian dualism—both have attempted to reduce that dualism to a monism.[3] That is, Murray turned to the actual historical record for grounding of a new conversation.

This theme of the sinful violations of social dualism is developed in "The Declaration of Religious Freedom (1966c, pp. 190–94 of this collection). It is also central to his argument in *The Problem of God* (1964e). In the latter, however, Murray moved beyond common violations of social dualism to another source of modern atheism. That second source is human interiority or consciousness. Human consciousness, he argued, is structured toward the full comprehension of exist-

---

3. In a 1954 analysis of Pius XII's *Ci Riesce* talk to Italian jurists, Murray referred to those who held the Establishment/Intolerance view as "Catholic Jacobins," who were attempting to impose a monism on society no less than had the French Jacobins. Murray was instructed soon thereafter to cease writing on the church's stance toward religious freedom, a ban that was not lifted until the council.

ence (*gnosis*) but incapable of comprehending the ground of existence (*agnosis*).[4] The major temptation of the person who stands before the Otherness of God is, then, to claim full knowledge, or no knowledge, of God. It is a temptation to which the theist and the atheist can succumb (the atheist in the form of Marxism (*gnosis*) or existentialism (*agnosis*). Now, Murray argued, the common structuring of *gnosis* and *agnosis* consciousness gives a common ground for approaching the social arena with similar social and ethical concerns. By denying the dialectical nature of knowing, both the atheist and the theist can lock into a certitude that is inhuman or a skepticism that is debilitating. In either case, the denial of creatureliness in idolatry or despair results in social brutality.

The final article reprinted here, "Unbelief of the Christian" (1969), again explores violations of dualism and human interiority as sources of the conflict between Christianity and the modern atheist. Here Murray appeals to a notion of the church as a sacrament that is "already but not yet" a manifestation of God's kingdom, and he claims that the institutional (and not just personal) sinfulness of the church is a cause of social atheism. The *gnosis/agnosis* consciousness of his earlier argument has been replaced by the belief/unbelief that must be predicated of atheist and Christian alike. And social dualism has been extended to historical dualism (in secular and salvation histories that interpenetrate). Both these changes continue Murray's attempt to find in human consciousness and actual social history perspectives to bridge former polarities.

---

4. A forerunner of *gnosis/agnosis* consciousness can readily be found in Murray's description of the reach of intelligence in his discussion of Christian humanism (see part 2).

The Right to Unbelief

John Courtney Murray, S.J.

In 1962, a French translation of Murray's 1945: "Religious Liberty: The Ethical Argument" was published in seven issues of the Montreal-based *Relations*. The appearance of these translations leaves several open questions. By 1962 Murray had, of course, moved at least three steps beyond his 1945 argument, and the Council was just warming up to a full scale discussion of religious liberty.[1] Who initiated this resurrection of Murray's earlier (tolerance) argument, and why, appears to be lost to us.

Accompanying the French version of "The Ethical Argument" was a further brief article, under Murray's name, entitled "Le *droit a l'incroyance*" (1962a). This was not taken from the preliminary argument that Murray had sent to Mooney (1945e), nor is there any record in the Murray Archives of its English original, (although the French versions can be found there, indicating Murray's awareness of its publication). How and from whom *Relations* acquired it remains an open question.

Yet, on the basis of internal evidence the attribution of this article to Murray seems certain. "Le *droit*" operates within the premises of a natural law. It argues against any claim for immunity in the face of the state's curtailment of atheistic propagandizing. Murray was insisting in 1945 that a theoretical (philosophical) consensus was necessary for postwar international reconstruction. One necessary premise of that consensus was belief in God. In principle, though not pragmatically, the atheist had no valid claim to participation in that conversation.

Originally published as 1962a: "Le droit a l'incroyance" (*Relations* (Montreal*) 22 (Avril 1962): 91–92. See the entry for Murray 1945e for information on the *Relations* publication.

1. Editor Note: For my outline of the stages of Murray's religious liberty argument, see pages 27–36 of the "General Introduction" to *Religious Liberty* (Murray, 1993).

Those who attempt to set up a declaration of human rights will quite naturally inscribe there the right to freedom of religion, although it may be easier to praise religious freedom than to describe it, and easier further to describe it than to define it. One might proclaim that, in the name of reason and of conscience, the individual enjoys the right to believe in God, to render adoration to him, to live, to act according to his belief, to express it, to propagate it, to raise his children in it, to set boundaries for himself where, if he wants, he can abjure and change his religion.

Further, one could claim that a list of human rights also ought to include the right to not believe in God, and, consequently, the right to deny all religion, to act, to speak or persuade, to educate, and to associate in a manner conformable to this unbelief and to this atheism.

It would appear, then, that in the name of reason and of conscience, the right to believe and the right to not believe, are to be both legitimated, and that, in a fully adult democracy, the State not only will never make a law establishing or interdicting a religion, but that the law itself, as the "midday of justice" will extend the bounty of its impartiality as much on antireligious propaganda as on religious propaganda. The right to work for religion would imply the right to not work for religion; and the right of promoting it, the right of combating it.

Such is the paradox of tolerance in the heart of the entirely free city.

To demand thus without reserve, as rights of the individual and of associations, the right to unbelief and to atheism, is to sow a grave spiritual confusion, all the more inasmuch as one appears to measure these rights on the same footing as the rights of the true religious conscience. What principle might be formulated to justify this need of equality? None. In the fashion in which the problem is posed, it must be believed that the rights to unbelief and to atheism derive, in the same manner, from reason and from conscience as do other rights with which they would go as equals. Reason and conscience are taken in a very large sense, evidently. Far from being opposed to divine revelation, reason and conscience in the case of unbelief signify, as in the case of belief, a response of man to the call of God. But it is here an aberration. It is impossible that unbelief and belief would be equally legitimate human responses to the revelation of God, and that the voice of human reason and conscience would demand both atheistic zeal and religious zeal of the human person. To affirm that the human being, facing God and the moral law, has the right of not believing and of refusing obedience, is to deny that there is a God and a moral law. By the voice of conscience, the entire question of human rights does not hold up.

But can one not claim that unbelief and atheism have rights which can prevail upon the authority of the State? Quite certainly the conscience of the atheist, as erroneous as it may be, remains an inviolable sanctuary against all State sponsored intrusions or constraints. The atheist has the right to the private practice of atheism. This right, however, is uniquely founded on the law which limits the authority of the State to its proper end which is the common good of the human person.[2]

Let us push further. Has the atheist the right of diffusing his atheism within society by propaganda, teaching, and group activity? And does the State find itself in the moral obligation of abstaining from all repressive measures in his regard? Such a position would be intolerable. It would be equivalent to denying that the State has a moral function as well as a material function. To affirm that the State has a need to regard with equal satisfaction the public movements in favor of religion and morality, and the public movements which work to destroy them, is equivalent to saying that religion and morality are in no way relevant to the common good of society. It would follow from this that they are indifferent matters to the State.

Now, there is no one of sense in the world who could accept this conclusion. Ethics has always taught and experience confirmed as evident that the negation of God and of the moral law, the diffusion of anti-religious and anti-moral ideas are the most dangerous enemies of the social order. They tend to corrupt the virtue of the citizen in which repose, in the first place, the common good of society. They tend likewise to undermine the material and social conditions favorable to the practice of virtue and indispensable to the pursuit of the temporal common good. The freedom of religion is a political problem of immense implications. Unless you regulate the problem and regulate

---

2. EDITOR NOTE: Murray had not yet restricted the state to control over public order, not the common good. That distinction firmly entered his argument in 1951 in a heated exchange with Francis J. Connell and Joseph C. Fenton of Catholic University ("The Problem of 'The Religion of the State'") [1951b] and "For the Freedom and Transcendence of the Church" [1952b]. In the present essay, the following paragraph extols the moral function of the State. By 1964 Murray could rejoice that Pius XII had abandoned Leo XIII's moral state for the contemporary notion of the state as juridical (1964e, 65 [1993, 166]).

234   **Christianity and Atheism**

it well, you incite a grave disorder in the temporal order, as is evident in past and present history.

One cannot claim, then, that the State, to which falls the obligation of protecting the good order (even its moral values) of society, would leave the sphere of its mandate, if it would suppress—not certainly with an arbitrary violence but by the application of the law (by due process of law)—the public propaganda and teaching which strives to praise unbelief in God and in the moral law. And there exists no law which the atheist can invoke and which would confer on him the "rights" contrary to the legitimate rights of the State. In virtue of what would he be able to cry injustice if one restricted his plot of propaganda? Surely he can only plead that his reason and his conscience command him to similar initiatives because his reason and his conscience are clearly in error. And they cannot then be a source of valid juridical rights.

One must add here that if one claims as legitimate the right for the atheist to propagate his ideas, this claim is nonsense when one maintains at the same time that the State itself is responsible before the moral law and before God. Certainly, God and the moral law forbid open attacks against the foundations of religion and law. Does then the citizen not have the right to demand of the State that it conform to the law? Can he not insist, since it is within the limits of its mandate, that the State fulfill its strict obligation and, by the appropriate juridical means, place a restraint on the public initiatives which violate that law?[3] If such are the rights of the citizen and such are the

---

3. Editor Note: In Murray's last published article on the foundations for religious freedom, he imagines the following monologue by the state as a counter to the principal argument in *Dignitatis* that religious freedom is founded in the obligation to seek the truth:

We acknowledge and deeply respect the impulse to seek truth implanted in human nature. We acknowledge, too, your moral obligation to conform your life to truth's demands. But, sorry to say, we judge you to be in error. For in the sphere of religion we possess objective truth. More than that, in this society we represent the common good as well as religious truth—in fact religious truth is an integral part of the common good. In your private and in your family life, therefore, you may lawfully act according to your errors. However, we acknowledge no duty on our part to refrain from coercion in your regard when in the public life of society, which is our concern, you set about introducing your false forms of worship or spreading your errors. Continue, then, your search for truth until you find it—we possess it—so that you may be able to act in public in keeping with it.

Is this proclamation imaginary? Hardly! (1993: *Religious Liberty*, 235).

obligations of the State, they cannot be annulled by the fictitious rights of atheism.

Here, in very simply terms and in the point of view of ethics, the enunciated paradox is brought to an end.

In fact, there exists only one reason which can justify atheistic propaganda. And that reason is not founded in a moral right but on the legitimate considerations of practical order (the ground, not of moral right, but of legitimate expediency).

Political experience demonstrates, in effect, that, in our modern societies, the censure of the State and the measures of police are bad means of assuring the repression of ideas and activities, even those which work to sap the foundations of the common life. The worst evils which follow this type of repression are more grave than the evils one seeks to eliminate. In this conjunction, a government could not prefer to exercise its right to repress atheistic propaganda.

In our day and in my view, the general pattern ought to follow this practice. However, the motive guiding this decision does not derive from some moral obligation to respect the rights of atheism. No one can thus disarm a society in the face of its enemies. Its unique motive is that the State ought to pursue the common good by choosing between various political methods (none of which are without risk nor evil) that method which in fact is the most appropriate to the circumstances.

For a number of reasons, today, the defense of religion and morality ought to return, in large part, not to repressive measures of government, but to the pressure of the common conscience and of public opinion. I say "in large part" because I do not intend to allow the belief that the State ought to endorse a "neutrality" impossible in fact and immoral in obligation. The State has a positive obligation in regard to religion and morality. The direction stamped by its influence and its action ought always to tend toward their positive support. But the problem (precisely which we have addressed here) is limited to the repression of atheistic propaganda.

In order to avoid all unintended misunderstanding, let us remark yet one more time that I have treated this subject only from the point of view of morality and of natural law. This point of view imposes itself for an initial critical study of these matters. It is of sovereign importance, in this entire matter of religious liberty, to have clear and exact ideas. Such a critical study is imperative today since there is afoot a manner of treating the problem that presupposes, even from the point of view of morality and natural law, that religious liberty is unique and particular, a liberty which subsists by itself and for itself, absolutely untouchable and absolutely valid, when even its demands trouble the good order of society.[4] This separatist tendency seems to be colored by a Protestant dogma: that of the absolutism of private conscience.

A clear and exact idea of human rights requires that unbeliever and believers ascend to the realm of principle, and to the end of political society, and to the source of all authority among us. How can we move to erect a list of human rights, if we do not even know why these are rights?

---

4. Editor Note: In the mid- to late-1940s, any claim that religious liberty "subsists by itself and for itself" indicated to Murray a hidden theological underpinning. In his own manner of arguing, only the Roman Catholic Church could claim a right to religious freedom that had a source distinct from all other natural rights, or, in the terminology of the time, a *sui generis* right. The church's right was grounded in the redemptive will, not the creative will, of God. This led Murray to mistake any Protestant assertion that the American people conferred special and distinct importance on religious freedom as an appeal to the theological premise that all churches stood equally as instruments of God's creative will. For this exchange, see 1945a, 1946d, 1948b, 1949a. Also of interest, although not discussed here, is his response to Paul Blanshard's Protestant support (1951a).

On the Necessity for Not Believing
A Roman Catholic Interpretation

JOHN COURTNEY MURRAY, S.J.

In 1949, Homer W. Smith, Theodore M. Greene, and John Courtney Murray each addressed the question: Does our understanding of modern science rule out the possibility of religious belief? Murray's was the last of three essays that appeared in *The Yale Scientific Magazine*.[1]

In the first essay, Smith argued that modern science had eliminated the possibility of certain, metaphysical knowledge, and that the contingency and uncertainty of our knowledge ought to be embraced with enthusiasm, for now we have substantive grounds for approaching the social world in which we live with humility and tolerance.

In the second essay, Greene argued that, indeed, modern science has left us in the relativistic and humbling swamp, as described by Smith. But, he continued, we must be brave enough to make total personal commitments even with a lack of understanding.

Here Murray calls for a dialectic approach to the question of theistic affirmation and understanding. His concerns with Soviet Marxism are one reason why he claims the inadequacy of humble relativism or brave, blind commitment.

On entering this three-cornered ring I find that the other contestants have already taken their places; in fact, I find that a corner has already been assigned to me. I must be what Professor Greene calls

---

"On the Necessity for Not Believing: A Roman Catholic Interpretation." *The Yale Scientific Magazine*, 23, no. 5 (February 1949): 11, 12, 22, 30, 32, 34).

1. For the two other articles of this series, see Homer W. Smith, "Objectives and Objectivity in Science: A Naturalist Interpretation," pp. 7, 8, 16, 18, 28, and Theodore M. Greene, "The Middle of the Road: A Liberal Protestant Interpretation," pp. 9, 10, 20, 26, 28, both in *The Yale Scientific Magazine* 23 (February 1949).

the "authoritarian absolutist." However, when I think of the particular audience seated at this ringside, there comes the uneasy feeling that I have not so much been assigned a corner as laid flat on the canvas, with the gong already gone ten. Therefore the first thing I must do is to scramble to my feet and protest, on grounds that I was hit where I wasn't standing and hence that it wasn't me who was knocked out.

Less figuratively, I must begin by rejecting the adjective, "authoritarian." The reason is that, as far as I can see from the other two papers, this discussion is moving simply on a philosophical level. The basic issue seems to be the famous epistemological problem in which modern philosophy has been stuck for a hundred years: Can the human mind know reality, and how and what reality? Now, in the field of philosophy I am by no means authoritarian. My resources are singly those of intelligence and my method is solely that of rational, critical inquiry. My starting point is empirical, and at every step of argument my thought obliges itself to maintain contact with all the realities of experience—intellectual experience as well as sense experience. Moreover, since my philosophical aim is to explore and (as far as may be) explain all that is, I must reckon with all the data that the whole range of intellectual disciplines delivers as the materials of thought. No authority comes into the philosophical process save the authority of evidence—the perceived necessity that so things *are*. No principle external to reason commands any assent; only what I *see* to be "there," and therefore true.

Like anybody else, I have masters, of course. Their line begins in ancient Greece (importantly, with Aristotle) and ends with the last man who said anything he thought, and could prove, to be true. But the authority of these masters is only as good as the reasons they advance for their statements. In the course of this rational process of thought I do indeed arrive at some absolutely certain knowledge in the metaphysical order of being and in the intimately related moral order of values. Let this point go for the moment; I merely say here that this philosophical knowledge is not mediated by authority nor does it depend on authority for whatever absoluteness it possesses. The method of Scholastic philosophy is not an "easy way" to some pre-fabricated truth, antecedently proclaimed by authoritarian *apriorism* to be absolute. Nor, I may add, are the truths it reaches by a way as "hard" as scientific method ever devised, easy truths. It may not be easy for Dr. Smith to accept the discipline of scientific doubt; but does he suppose it is easier for me to accept the discipline of rational certainty? And if there is risk in Professor Greene's "life-long wager" that his "faith" lacks "certainty," am I staking nothing when I throw for the proposition that I have "certainty" in the philosophical order that is not "faith"? It would perhaps be well to rescue the question at the outset from involvement in any manner of false romantic heroics.

Being now on my feet (I hope), the orthodox thing would be to lead with a left. That is, I should label my position as the others have labelled theirs. However, this is hardly possible; for my position will not bear description by any other name than its own—Catholicism. As a reason for this, take, if you will, Adolph Harnack's description of Catholicism as *complexio oppositorum*, a synthesis of opposites. If you give it one label ("it is authoritarian"), you forget that it equally merits the opposite one ("it is the home of an immense intellectual freedom"). And so for all the other polarities in human life, it links each pair in the balance of a vital tension: faith and reason, authority and freedom, individual and community, flesh and spirit, the mind and the heart, the juridical and the mystical, law and love, tradition and progress, the historical contingent and the transcendent absolute, this world and the next, and so on. Of the three positions it is, I think, the most complicated and comprehensive, the least susceptible of a label.

In contrast, Dr. Smith readily falls into a philosophical category; he is quite forthrightly a monist of the materialist persuasion, on the ground that this is the only position defensible in terms of the methods and findings of the biological and physical sciences, which are the only valid methods of intellectual inquiry, leading to the only valid findings. His essential contention is that of the nineteenth century: "Science has destroyed the foundations of religion (and of metaphysics as well)." However, it seems that his mood is not exactly that of the nineteenth century: "I do not believe—hurrah! I am free!" There is about it just a touch of the twentieth century, Sartrean mood: "I cannot believe—alas! I am meaningless."Moreover, his roots are in the tradition of Huxley's biological materialism (minus its optimism), and not in that of Marx's dialectical materialism; consequently the tendency of his thought is atheistic in the agnostic sense, and corrosive of an old order of things. If I may use T. S. Eliot's phrase (respectfully, for Dr. Smith is my good friend), with him the nineteenth century goes out, "not with a bang but a whimper."[2]

Professor Greene's position is less readily categorized, if only for the reason that it is not so fully set out that its premises and implications can be clearly grasped. Perhaps he is an idealist, but only in the sense that Descartes was an idealist, as one who took a step to idealism by destroying the bridge between subject and object, intellect and reality. I have the impression that there is a suggestion of the Kantian critique in his distinction of "certitude" and "certainty," and in his bringing back through the hall door of "faith" the "absolute Truth" that he casts out through the kitchen window of "critical inquiry." However, I chiefly suspect that in the ultimate implications of his thought is the assertion that mind is the measure of being, and not being of mind; in this sense he would be a rationalist, understanding the term in a philosophical sense as a contrast to "realist." (Is not the prima[c]y of subject over object, of mind over being, latent, for instance, in the definition of absolute Truth as "the distinguishing characteristic of hypothetical omniscience"? A realist (like myself, who am what is called a "moderate realist") would formulate the relation between omniscience and absolute, i.e., infinite Truth with a different accent.)

At all events, for the purposes of this discussion I shall ask my friends to suffer—or perhaps suffer under—the appellations, respectively, of "scientific monist" and "critical rationalist." One denies all absolute values (metaphysical and moral) on grounds that both "knowledge" of them and "faith" in them are unscientific; the other asserts absolute values on grounds that, although absoluteness is impossible, faith in them is necessary. (And if my understanding of their positions is a misunderstanding, I heartily apologize.)

---

2. EDITOR NOTE: By the mid-1960s Murray sharply contrasted the atheisms that arise from nineteenth century scientism with twentieth century social atheism. In *The Problem of God* (1964c) he wrote off scientism as a quaint historical relic (pp. 86–101), while he searched for moral and cognitional roots of Marxism and existentialism (101–21). Murray tended to lump purely contractual notions of government under the Enlightenment/scientism label (see his "The Problem of Mr. Rawls' Problem" [1964d]). In his "The Death of God" (1967b) he also located death of God theologies as within the nineteenth century, scientistic state of the question, a problematic that has been transcended.

In the space available there can obviously be no question of full and fair critique of these positions. I could possibly undertake to distinguish my position from theirs by stating agreements and disagreements. This would be easy to do in negative terms. For instance, with Dr. Smith I am against easy ways to comfortable truths, pre-philosophical certitudes as the premises of philosophy, naive intuitions, the apotheosis of the unknown, anthropomorphic conceptions of God, the worship of progress as inevitable and of man as indefinitely perfectible, tolerance as meaning the ability to live with all manner of opinions while remaining committed to none, pantheism, Puritan morality, fundamentalist Protestantism, uncritical scriptural exegesis, legends, witchcraft, magic, and superstition. In a word, I am against all manner of ignorance, obscurantism, stupidity, error, and sin. As Dr. Smith is.

Conversely, with Dr. Smith I am for intellectual curiosity, full exploration of nature, scientific method, the satisfaction of biological needs, the progressive elimination of disease, honesty, the Bill of Rights, more dignity for man, politics as the science of the possible, leaving morality to moralists, and a life-expectancy of 64 years. In a word, I am for making this life as far as possible decently human, filled with some amount of moderately useful activity. As Dr. Smith is.

Finally, we have certain beliefs in common. I find, for instance, the lust of the flesh a sufficiently credible reality; and the loneliness of the soul—one knows something of that too. I find in myself all manner of things unworthy of a man, doubly unworthy of a Christian—is this the "essential indignity of man"? I believe that evil, statistically, predominates over good in this world. And it is altogether integral to my faith that the problem of evil is most real, most agonizing without adequate solution in the limited perspectives of unaided human reason. But with all these agreements listed (and I could list a like or greater number with Professor Greene), we are still nowhere; for the profound disagreement remains.

I am tempted to say that the disagreement is total. The reason is that I disagree with their very position of the problem. I think that each in his own way puts to himself a false problem. Dr. Smith's problem is that the advance of positive science have now made it *necessary* for man to dispense both with rational metaphysics and traditional Christianity in all forms. Professor Greene's problem is that the exigencies of critical reason now make it *necessary* for man—at least for mature men—to dispense with rational certainties in metaphysics (not with metaphysics itself) and more particularly with Catholicism (not with Christianity in general but only with the dogmatic principle, the principle of authority). In both cases the problem hinges on the posited *necessity*. If it is cogent, the ensuing philosophy has a basis and one could go on to scrutinize it; *y si no, no* (as the famous Aragonese phrase has it). Now in both cases I am prepared to say that the asserted necessity is illusory; and the result is a false problem. If man *must* live only by science, asks Dr. Smith, why live at all? And echo answers, Why? If man *must* relinquish, as childish, both the quest for certainty and obedience to authority, why not be content with "the faith that is actually available to him"? And echo answers, Why not? Only echo can answer, because the word "must" has loaded the question.

Here then would be the essential point of assertion for a critique. It would most effectively follow the principles of the so-called immanent critique. I should have first to assume, not my own standpoint but that of Dr. Smith, and ask two initial questions. The first concerns the evidence for the contested point: the necessity, to be proved by science, that science is All; have I collected all the evidence *pro* and *con*? The second concerns the interpretation of the evidence—has it been dictated by systematic consideration extraneous and antecedent to my actual problematic, or has it been objective (in the due measure possible; there is always an interplay of idea and fact, of theory and experience; what is important is that I should consciously know when I am applying ideas and theories, and be prepared to justify them either as resultant from the evidence before me or validly assumed from some other discipline).

I think Professor Greene has sufficiently indicated that Dr. Smith's fundamental position collapses under this type of critique. Dr. Smith's evidence is selected; he is not open to the evidence from man's "aesthetic, moral, and religious experiences," that tends to show that science is not All. Or when he does deal with these data, he interprets them systematically; religious faith, it seems, must be "either an attribution of transcendental significance to the ecstasies and miseries of the ephemeral biological organism (for the biological category is all-inclusive) or else an apotheosis of the unknown (for what biology does not know is unknowable)." Here we go off into a maze of conflicting scientific dogmatisms with reference to the origins of religion: the Freudians downing the classical ethnologists and their theory of the intellectual "hasty hypothesis," because religion quite obviously (in Freudian theory) rises out of the non-rational, biological category; and the Marxists furiously criticizing the Freudians, because quite obviously (in Marxist theory) religion is not a biological but an historical and social category, etc. etc. Meantime the scientists resolutely turn their backs on the meek little hypothesis that alone survives the buffetings of accumulated data, that religion has a religious origin; that it did not come out of animism or magic or some sort of pre-philosophical thought of the phenomenon of social oppression or economic struggle; that, more or less smothered in alien elements and unconscious of itself, it was always "there," as itself a primitive category, not a derived one.

One could pursue these scientific fallacies in this matter. The genetic fallacy, for instance, that priority in appearance means causal influence, and that there are no "inventions" or new beginnings and no radical transformations (e.g., the Hebrew prophets, Christianity). Or the fallacious equivalence of the "primitive" with the "essential," that enables the scientist to pass a judgement of value on all religion by simple inspection of its primitive forms ("originally religion was animism; but we know that animism is absurd; therefore all religion is absurd"). In all these cases the scientist is the victim of some systematic *a priori*, more or less philosophical in character. I shall not pursue the subject farther; let me only say in conclusion that the hypothesis of monist materialism is either a purely scientific hypothesis, adopted *ad hoc* for the severely limited purposes of scientific investigation of a particular set of phenomena, or else a piece of dogmatism. As the former it is acceptable (so, for instance, a theory of psychological determinism in a process of psychoanalysis that only aims at revealing compulsions). As the latter it is intolerable, even on purely scientific grounds; so, for instance, it is intolerable for a scientist to say that human life has no finality, simply because the concept of finality is not useful in exploring the biological organism.

This line of critique itself would show, if developed, that Dr. Smith is not under any proved necessity to live by science alone. After all his science has said all it has to say, the spiritualist and theist hypothesis is still open. In fact, science cannot close it save by illegitimate recourse to some non-scientific *a priori* absolute. This hypothesis therefore demands exploration, not indeed by scientific method in the narrow sense (for the data here are in another, though not less real, order of experience) but in the scientific spirit, under abnegation of arbitrary dogmatism about the nature of man and the limitations of his intelligence, and with good will—that is, with the will to accept whatever costly truths are encountered in the search.

There is not much room left for Professor Greene. My first task would be to show that he does not *have* to be a Kantian in philosophy. This would be an intricate argument: for the Kantian critique of reason and the Scholastic counter-critique are highly subtle. But the method would be the same as before. I think I could show that his philosophical position rests on a defective analysis of the data of intellectual experience (which are his express concern, as a philosopher), and that the analysis is defective because it is commanded (as with Kant himself) by a pre-philosophical postulate, the rationalist *a priori*—the decision, antecedent to thought, that it will be Professor Greene who shall determine what reality is, and that reality shall not determine what Professor Greene thinks.

This crudely put, because I must be brief. Actually, the analysis of the *a priori* is a highly delicate task; it raises the whole problem of the tradition within which a particular thinker stands—a tradition that has "authority" over him (it is vain to suppose that any philosopher is immune from such authority). Perhaps chiefly in view here would be the pervasive modern idea of freedom with its individualistic overtone—an idea that is the product not so much of a metaphysics as of a myth or a mood. And it is from this critique of the rationalist *a priori* that I would go on to show that Professor Greene does not *have* to reject the principle of authority in Christianity. After reason has deployed all its resources of critical inquiry, the Roman Catholic hypothesis still remains open, not to be closed by reason unless reason ceases to be merely critical of evidence and becomes dogmatic about its own autonomy.

There is another principle of the immanent critique that could be applied to these systems. It consists in asking whither these systems lead, by the necessary workings of their inner dynamism or by necessary reaction. As a system that leads to the abyss, Dr. Smith's scientific monism must give one pause; for in what is at least the extremely tenable hypothesis that it is not necessary thus to plunge into the nihilism of despair, it is not easy to see why anyone should choose to do so, much less invite anyone else to take the leap. On the same lines, the social destructiveness of the Smithian hypothesis of a completely autonomous science, operating to ends in whose choosing the scientist, even as a man, abdicates responsibility, has already been demonstrated in the world. A healthy society can tolerate this kind of scientism, but in the sense that an otherwise healthy mental structure can tolerate a neurosis; if it is not too violent in its autonomous operations, that are not collineated with the purposes of the organism, its very neuroticism can be turned to use.

On the same critical principle, Professor Greene's system gives me pause. The trouble with it is, not that it isn't good, but that it isn't good enough. Professor Greene attempts a *via media* between the integral Christianity of Roman Catholicism and the extreme rationalism that goes by the name of secularism. But his system has the two inescapable defects of any *via media*. The first is the inherent tendency of a *via media* to bifurcate into the two extreme paths between which it seeks to cut. The reason for this is (to change the metaphor) that it attempts to hold opposites in equilibrium, not by the inner vital tension between the extremes themselves, which are affirmed fully and in their reciprocal orderly relationship (as in a system of polarities), but by applying the "lore of nicely calculated less or more," by careful concession to each extreme. The result is always an unstable equilibrium, an uneasy ambivalence.

The intellectual history of Kantianism is instructive here. Kant attempted a *via media* between Hume's skepticism and German pietism, by conceding to Hume that the objects of religion (God, the soul, its immortality, its freedom) are not objects of knowledge, and by conceding to the pietism of his youth that nevertheless these objects must be affirmed on practical grounds. "I must," he said," get rid of reason to make room for faith." He wanted to eat the pietist's pie and the skeptic's cake—and have them both. The result was not an organic synthesis of reason and faith, but an artificial system in which both a rational and an irrational element were present, their incompatibilities not reconciled but screened from view by a rationalism that could at once deny the ability of reason to make religious affirmations that are rational, and affirm its need to make religious affirmations that are irrational. Time did the rest. Each of the unreconciled opposites worked itself out; the *via media* bifurcated, and then the two roads converged to a goal quite other than Kant's. The religious irrationalism worked itself out in Schleiermacher ("religion is mere feeling"), thence to irreligion ("I don't feel religious"), and thence full circle to an irreligious rationalism ("This world is my religion"). The rationalism worked itself out, through Fichte and Schelling, to the absolute idealism of Hegel—the Pandora's box whose lid was lifted by the "enlightened despots" (to release the Prussian nationalism with which Hitler did what we know) and by Marx (to release the dialectical materialism with which we are again gaining an increasing acquaintance). What began with critical reason ended with secularist myth.

The example is extreme, admittedly. My point, however, is that Kant's fatal error was the divorce of religion (ultimate truth and absolute moral values) from the order of rationally certain knowledge. This was indeed the stroke that constituted his *via media*: but this too was the thing that ultimately blew it up. It seems to me that Professor Greene (unless I misinterpret him) makes the same mistake. On a rationalist postulate, he denies the reach of reason to absolute truth, at the same time that he asserts that absolute truth *must* be "there." Is he playing Kant to some future Schleiermachers and Hegels (more likely Hegels; Schleiermachers are decidedly passé)? The fate of the Kantian noumenon (the ultimately intelligible thing that must be "there" but can't be known) is a hard one. Men say of it: "What good is it—this absolute Truth that, for all I know, I myself create? I do not need it. Here in the realm of the finite and fallible, the relative and contingent, the historically conditioned and culturally variable, I shall find all the truths, all the religion I need." This conclusion will be blatantly false, of course. However, *ex absurdo sequitur quodlibet*: it's a wise magician who knows what rabbits other people will pull out of his hat.

The second inherent difficulty with a *via media* is simply put: a *via media* is not a road that humanity can walk. An individual may indeed stay on it, or a group of individuals; but this is because of particularities of temperament or specially favored conditions of life—one is cultured, say, and of disciplined intelligence, the finished humanist. (The Non-Kantians who kept to the Kantian *via media* under development of its rational aspects, were university men in England and Germany.) But man as such, the ordinary man in the ordinary life, humanity at large, cannot be expected to slither carefully across the yawning chasm that is the world's despair, on the religious tightrope of a nicely critical rationalism. If there is a way to God, it must be a way that all men can walk. It is not indeed a broad highway. But it cannot be a *via media*.

In conclusion, what would be my estimate of the alternatives here? Dr. Smith's scientific monism is, I say, a false creed, vacuous, socially destructive, and—what is perhaps worse—altogether unnecessary. But it is rough and tough, and in the finished militant form that Dr. Smith has not given it, it is total. My creed is likewise rough and tough and total—rough enough to cope with rude adversaries, tough enough to stand up to the demonic forces that are always stirring beneath the troubled surface of this world, and total enough to challenge the total claims of an organized atheistic humanism, reinforced with the resources of science, that comes against it with all the irrational power of a myth. I think sometimes that Newman had a prophetic moment when he spoke of the "stern encounter" that history would see, "when two real and living principles, simple, entire and consistent, one in the Church, the other out of it, at length rush upon one another, contending not for names and words or half-views, but for elementary notions and distinctive moral characters." The two principles, he said, are "Catholic truth and Rationalism." They are not indeed today meeting for the first time; the encounter has been permanently engaged since the days of Celsus and Arius. But today it is, I think, particularly stern, now that rationalism has developed intellectual weapons and institutional armatures that would be the envy of the school of Antioch. And what I wonder is whether Professor Greene, who would occupy middle ground between these contending powers, does not risk being trampled—not by me, for he is greatly my ally, but by an enemy that is as contemptuous of his "relativist objectivism" as it is hostile to my "authoritarian absolutism."

Things Old and New in
"Pacem in Terris"

John Courtney Murray, S.J.

Murray found much that he liked in *Pacem in Terris*, not the least of
which was John XXIII's juridical theory and his addition of "freedom" to
the list of necessary social forces for a moral society (the others being
truth, justice, and love). Here, however, he bridles at John XXIII's suggestion that one can (and must) distinguish between the antithetical founding philosophy and the valid moral forces that drive modern social
movements. This essay might be compared to Murray's 1963f: "Good
Pope John: A Theologian's Tribute" in the last section of this collection.

An adequate interpretation of the encyclical *Pacem in Terris* must wait
on lengthy study, because the reach of the Pope's words, in its
breadth and depth, is greatly extensive. What follows are some comments on certain salient points of the encyclical, on the quality of the
Pope's thought and its major accents.

It is obvious, in the first instance, that the Pope here offers a shin-
ing example of everything that he means by his own word, *aggiorna-
mento*. He situates himself squarely in the year 1963. There is not the
slightest bit of nostalgia, nor of lament over the past course of history
or over the current situation that history has evoked here on earth.
The Pope confronts all the facts of political, social, economic and cultural change that have been the product of the modern era. Generously and ungrudgingly, he accepts those elements of historical
progress which can be recognized as such by the application of traditional principles as norms of discernment.

The Pope then proceeds to speak to the postmodern age, to a
new era of history that has not yet found its name but that is clearly

---

Previously published as 1963j: "Things Old and New in 'Pacem in Terris'" (*America* 107 (April 27, 1963): 612–14).

with us. His acute sense of the basic need of the new age is evident in the word that is so often repeated in the encyclical and that sets its basic theme. I mean the word "order." This does seem to be the contemporary issue. The process of ordering and organizing the world is at the moment going forward. The issue is not whether we shall have order in the world; the contemporary condition of chaos has become intolerable on a world-wide scale, and the insistent demand of the peoples of the world is for order.[1] The question is, then, on what principles is the world going to be ordered.

The basic principle of the Roman Pontiff is as old as Plato, for whom society was "man writ large." The "man" whom the Pope puts at the basis and center of a human world order is not the abstract human nature which is presented in certain older textbooks on ethics. His "man" is the man of today, that is to say, the human person upon whose structured nature history too has left its mark. This strongly personalist accent of the Pope should quiet the fears and win the sympathies of those to whom the phrase "natural law" is uncongenial.[2]

In dealing with the problem of political order, Pope John XXIII represents a development of the tradition. He leaves behind the predominately ethical concept of the society-state which was characteristic of Leo XIII. He adopts the more juridical conception of the state that was characteristic of Pius XII, and he carries this conception to new lengths. For instance, he clearly accepts the distinction between society and the state. His general conception of the political ideal is fundamentally that of St. Thomas, "the free man under a limited government." The Pope states, with a new firmness of accent, the three principles that constitute this ideal. The first is that society must afford men "the sphere of freedom." The second is the ancient principle of constitutionalism: that the state has its foundations in constitutional law, whereby the powers of government are limited. Even the

---

1. EDITOR NOTE: Murray's apocalyptic reading here stands in contrast to his definition of the order that, three paragraphs further down, he says contemporary people demand, namely, a juridical order that will protect and encourage human dignity. The chaos theme appears to apply to the East/West confrontation, spelled out in the last portion of this article. For Murray's earlier appeals for the creation of an international order, see the first two articles of Part I.

2. EDITOR NOTE: For a discussion of changes in Murray's understanding of natural law, see pp. 175f.

modern conception of the written constitution is endorsed by the Pope, for the first time (if I am not mistaken) in the history of papal utterances. The third principle is that of popular participation in the public administration. Though this principle is deeply rooted in the liberal and Christian political tradition of the West, the strong emphasis given it in this encyclical again represents a welcome newness.

One can hear in the Pope's words a contemporaneous echo of John of Salisbury and his broad definition of the function of the Prince, which is "to fight for justice and for the freedom of the people." Only here it is not the question of a Prince, but of the whole order of constitutional and statutory law of public administration. The first function of the state and of all its officers is to guarantee the juridical order, that is to say, the whole order of human rights and duties whose roots are in the human person as situated in the contemporary world.

One of the most striking aspects of the encyclical is the generosity, the breadth and the contemporaneity of the Pope's statement with regard to the rights and duties of the human person. An outstanding instance of his full acceptance of modern progress is his affirmation of the place of woman in society as conceived in the world of today. Even more important is his strong insistence on racial equality.

In the past, papal pronouncements on political and social order have always been suspended, as it were, from three great words—*truth, justice,* and *charity.* These three great words are repeated in this encyclical, and the demands of each are carefully particularized. But a fourth word is added, with an insistence that is new at the same time that it is traditional. I mean the word *freedom.*

Freedom is a basic principle of political order; it is also *the* political method. The whole burden of the encyclical is that the order for which the postmodern world is looking cannot be an order that is imposed by force, or sustained by coercion, based on fear—which is the most coercive force that can be brought to bear on man.

By sharply accenting this theme, the Pope clearly takes sides against movements on the march today that would organize the world and create an order in it on the basis of force and not on the basis of the principle, which we are proud to call American as well as Christian, that the ordering forces in the world must be the forces of "freedom under law." These forces of freedom and for freedom emerge from the depths of the human person, which in the end is *the* creative force in human affairs.

The summation of the Pope's thought is in the sentence which asserts that all order, if it is to be qualified as reasonable and human, must be "founded on truth, built according to justice, vivified and integrated by charity, and put into practice in freedom." Elsewhere the Pope makes clear that freedom is *the* method for the "realization" of order in human affairs as well as a goal of the order itself.

In another respect the Pope manifests his clear intention to be guided by the traditional axiom by which Leo XIII was likewise guided, *"vetera novis augere,"* the principle that the Catholic tradition is a growing tradition, a tradition of progress, which requires that the "old things" be constantly affirmed at the same time they are completed and complemented in organic fashion by "new things."

I refer here to the distinctions that the Pope draws between "historical movements that have economic, social, cultural or political ends" and the "false philosophical teachings regarding the nature, origin and destiny of the universe and of man" which originally animated these movements. The basis of the distinction is the fact that "those movements, insofar as they conform to the dictates of right reason and are interpreters of the lawful aspirations of the human person, contain elements that are positive and deserving of approval." It is therefore possible to divorce these movements, in all that is of practical merit in them, from the erroneous doctrines with which they were historically allied.

I am not sure just what "historical movement" the Pope chiefly had in mind. I suspect that it was Continental socialism, whose primitive inspiration was largely atheist. Perhaps the Pope's distinction has some relevance to the whole Marxist movement, but here its application would have carefully to be made. In any case, I should think that the distinction may be given full application in regard of the 18th- and 19th-century movements toward political freedom. So applied, the distinction dissolves the whole problematic of Leo XIII, whose great conflict was with Continental, sectarian Liberalism. In his time, he was not able to draw a distinction between the animating principle of this movement, which was that of the "outlaw conscience" that recognized no authority higher than itself and no law that was not of its own making, and the free political institutions of which this movement was protagonist.

At this distance from the 19th-century state of the question, which is now outworn, Pope John XXIII is able boldly to make this important distinction. The significance of its making will, I think, be

felt particularly in regard of an urgent problem that continues to face
us, namely, the problem of an organic development of traditional principles touching the relations of Church and State in such wise that we
may come into possession of what we still lack—a complete and unitary Catholic doctrine capable of prudent application in the political
and religious conditions of our own time. A further welcome contribution to this end is the Pope's unprecedently broad affirmation of
the "right to worship God publicly and privately" as a "right conscience" dictates.

I should say a word about the Pope's thought with regard to the
constitution of a world community. He is clearly in the tradition of
Pius XII, whose insistence on the need for a juridical organization of
the international community is well known. John XXIII seems to
develop the thought of Pius XII by his call for "a public authority, having world-wide power and endowed with the proper means for the
efficacious pursuit of its objective, which is the universal common
good in concrete form." This authority must, he adds, "be set up by
common accord and not imposed by force." Again the principle of
freedom, as a principle and as a method, is affirmed.

The Pope proposes this goal in the spirit of "confident hope"
that is the dominant spirit of the whole encyclical. But it will not be
clear to many, including myself, how this hope is concretely to be realized, given the fact that no moral or political consensus presently
exists within the total international community that would furnish
the basis for the existence of such a public authority and for the effective exercise of its powers. It is clear that the Pope is intimately aware
that our postmodern era is characterized by what he calls a "pro-
nounced dynamism" toward change of all kinds. It is also clear that
he has most correctly indicated the right direction of change toward
the remedy of a "structural defect" in the international community.
For the rest, it is clear that he puts his hope in the efforts of those, who
are still "not many" but whose numbers must grow, who are "scientif-
ically competent, technically capable and skilled in the practice of
their professions," and who will be able therefore to "create a synthesis between scientific, technical and professional elements on the one
hand and spiritual values on the other."

His hope, therefore, is not a utopian idealism. It is possible of
realization. It seems to be sustained, in the last analysis, by the confidence that breathes through the whole encyclical—a confidence in the
power of the human person, in association, to "insure that world

events follow a reasonable and human course." It is therefore a hope that no reasonable man can fail to share, no matter what the difficulties in the way may be.

The encyclical will be perhaps most closely scrutinized for the guidance that it may give to Christians and to men of good will in regard of all that we mean by the Cold War. There will be those who will think, as I do, that we have been given only limited guidance. The Pope did not choose to deal with an aspect of the matter that has been carefully covered by his predecessors, notably Pius XI. I mean the profundity of the current crisis of history out of whose depths the Cold War itself has arisen.

The Pope has indeed made it entirely clear that the future must not be permitted to belong to the conception of political and social order that is inherent in the Communist revolution. He declares himself openly against "political regimes which do not guarantee for individual citizens a sufficient sphere of freedom within which their souls are allowed to breathe humanly." The encyclical shows no disposition to come to terms, in some manner of false peace, with the doctrinal content of the world revolution, especially its conception of Promethean man as the creator of himself and the rightful single ruler of the world. There is no encouragement in the encyclical for those among us who take a shallow or mistaken view of the depths of evil that are inherent in Communist ideology. On the other hand, there may be some warrant for the thought that the spirit of confident hope which the Pontiff courageously embraces fails to take realistic account of the fundamental schism in the world today.

On this difficult subject, about which there will be much argument, I have only one suggestion to offer as a help toward an understanding of the encyclical. I think the Pope deeply understands the disastrous extent to which men today are gripped by the myth of history which the Marxists have so diligently inculcated. In many ways, a deterministic view of history has gained much ground among us. In this view, man has lost command of his own destiny on this earth; his destiny is determined by the events of history, and he is himself powerless to control these events. The conclusion is that history today is surely and certainly carrying man toward catastrophe with an inevitability against which man is helpless.

I think that the Pope wishes to take a strong stand against this myth of history as the master of man. I think this intention stands behind his confident assertion that, "the fundamental principle on which our present peace depends must be replaced by another." Today the principle of such peace as we enjoy is simply naked fear. No one will deny that this principle must be replaced by another. The difficulty arises when the Pope goes on to say that we not only must, but also can, move forward to a new and more solid basis of peace. We must not, he seems to be saying, feel ourselves to be trapped in history, unable to change its course, unable to control world events, unable to avoid the disaster that waits for us if the world continues on its present course. At least in this respect, the Pope will command the agreement of all men of good will who believe that there are energies in the free human spirit whereby man may fulfill his destiny on earth, which is to be, not God, but the image of God. All men who believe in God are agreed that He is the Master of history. Man, therefore, manifests himself as the image of God chiefly by his intelligent, confident efforts to master the course of historical events and direct it toward the common good of the peoples of earth.

Religious Freedom and the Atheist

John Courtney Murray, S.J.

After the council, in the context of the Christian-Marxist dialogue, Murray shaped two distinct arguments for entry into such conversations. Those two arguments will be discussed below. Here Murray affirms the valid entry that the atheist has within American constitutional law and within the Christian constitutional perspective of *Dignitatis humanae*. Previously, in his commentary to the latter, Murray had claimed that *Dignitatis* had included the atheist within the right of religious immunity (*The Documents of Vatican II*, [1966i], 678, note 5). And, in response to the reception of the "Thomas Jefferson Award for Conspicuous Service in the Cause of Religious Liberty," Murray called for a continuing conversation concerning human dignity, a conversation that "will be broadened to full ecumenical scope—to included Christians and Jews, humanists and atheists alike" ("Acceptance Speech" [1965a], 12). In the following article, Murray suggests that the sociological causes of atheist-Christian conflict must be fully examined, in order that the more theological roots of atheism and belief might be distinguished and dialectically examined.

During the tortuous passage of the *Declaration on Religious Freedom* through four years of conciliar procedure several efforts were made, notably by French bishops, to include in the text specific mention of the rights of the atheist. The efforts met opposition within the Council, and in the end they were defeated. The official reason given by the competent Commission, the Secretariat for the Promotion of Christian

First published as 1970: "La liberta religiosa e l'ateo." *L'ateismo contemporaneo* 4 (1970): 109–117. This text is taken from the English original, Murray Archives, file 4-327.

Unity, was that no explicit mention of the atheist was necessary. His immunity from coercion in religious matters was sufficiently guaranteed by the meaning that the successive schemata intended to give to the word "conscience" in the assertion that no one is to be forcibly constrained to act against his conscience or forcibly restrained from acting according to his conscience. The word was not to bear only the technical sense that attaches to it in ethical and theological literature, that is, moral conscience informed by specifically religious belief in God. It also bore a wider sense. It was meant to include any man's personal and intimate convictions or persuasions, whatever they might be, with regard to the ultimate questions of human life—questions that transcend the order of politics and of human society in general. Therefore it included convictions that were non-religious, simply humanist, or even atheist. Hence it was within the intention of the Council to proclaim the religious freedom, not only of the believer in God but of the atheist.

Behind this stated reason lay an unsteady and rather confused feeling that it was not seemly for a conciliar document of the Catholic Church to defend the rights of the atheist. In turn, this feeling seems to have been motivated by an unwillingness to affirm the equality of belief and unbelief even in civil society and in the face of human law and government. Would not this affirmation entail the further affirmation that the State—the order of law and government—should be neutral as between religion and atheism? This was the conclusion from which many of the conciliar Fathers shied away.

The long shadow of the Church's nineteenth-century struggle with Continental laicism and its deceptive conception of the religious neutrality of the State hung heavily over the whole conciliar argument about religious freedom. This is why the final text, at the instance of many Fathers, was amended to include this statement: "Civil government, whose proper purpose is to care for the common temporal good, ought indeed to recognize the religious life of the citizenry and to show it favor . . ." (n. 3). This is also why the final text includes the further statement that government is bound not only to protect religious freedom but also "to provide conditions favorable to the furtherance of religious life" (n. 6).

These statements are studiously vague. How should governmental recognition and favor of religion find transcription into constitutional law and legislative policy? What concrete actions should be taken by government toward the creation of conditions favorable to religious life in society? The Declaration deliberately refrains from answering these questions. Particular answers to them will depend on given historical circumstances, religious and social. These questions themselves concern the measure of cooperation that should obtain between government and religious forces in society. In this difficult issue the Council is content to state the broad principle that a flourishing religious life belongs to the common temporal good of society. It is necessary "in order that society itself may enjoy the benefits of justice and peace which flow from the fidelity of men toward God and toward his holy will" (n. 6). Consequently government, in virtue of its duty toward the common temporal good, has a duty toward religion in society.

So far the Council is merely recalling the traditional Catholic principle upon which Leo XIII, for instance, insisted endlessly and at length. However, the Council is also obeying, here as elsewhere, the maxim of Leo XIII: "*Vetera novis augere atque perficere.*" New norms are laid down for the discharge of the duty of government toward religion. First, from the context of the Declaration as well as from the whole context of the Council, especially its Decree on Ecumenism, it is clear that "religious life" in the statements cited must be understood in a broad ecumenical sense. Hence the Council goes beyond Leo XIII, for whom "religion" uniformly meant only the Catholic religion. Within his own historical context he defined the duty of government as a duty toward the Catholic Church as the true Church and as the one Church of the people in the Catholic nations so-called. Within the much broader historical context of Vatican II this understanding of the matter gives way to a much broader understanding.

Moreover, the Council lays down three further norms for the cooperation of government with religious forces in society.

First, government is not to exceed the limits of its own competence, which is confined to affairs of the temporal and terrestrial order (cf. n. 3). The Declaration does not draw out in detail the consequences of this political principle. (The conciliar Fathers were oddly reluctant to make much use of the political argument for religious freedom, scil., from the notion of limited constitutional government; they seem to have considered it "too American.") Nevertheless it is clear that the Declaration deprives government of the classical prerogative claimed by the Christian princes of old, call "*cura religionis,*" the care of religion itself—the care of religious truth, ecclesiastical discipline, and the religious unity of the people. These are affairs of the transcendental order; they are now put beyond the reach of government. The competence of government can extend only to what may be called the secular values of religion—such values as affect the common temporal good. It extends also, and primarily, to the freedom of religion; for freedom in all its forms, especially in the form of religious freedom, is a secular value. John XXIII made this clear in *Pacem in terris* when he expanded the traditional trinity of social values—truth, justice, and love—to a quaternity, by adding the value of freedom, both as a social goal and also as the political method par excellence.

It would be in accord with this development to say that the "conditions for the fostering of religious life" which government is bound to assist in creating are simply conditions of freedom in society—conditions within which, as the Declaration says, "citizens may effectively exercise their religious rights and fulfill their religious duties" (n. 6). So too government favors religion in its own proper way when it favors the freedom of religion. The Declaration does not explicitly say this, but the statement is within its total sense.

The second norm which limits governmental action in recognition and favor of religion is the principle of religious freedom, including the freedom of the atheist. It follows that the favor shown to religion is not to entail any discrimination against the atheist. This conclusion is enforced by the third conciliar norm which requires that government should see to it that "the equality of citizens before the law, which itself belongs to the common good of society, is not infringed, either overtly or covertly, for religious reasons, and that no discrimination among citizens is practiced" (n. 6).

It is hardly necessary to insist on the newness of these norms for governmental action in favor of religion. They are clearly a development beyond the doctrine of Leo XIII—a development occasioned by the new perspectives of Vatican II. In consequence of this development the doctrine of the Church places the atheist in a historically new legal situation within society. It should be immediately added, without further comment, that in this respect as in others the Declaration on Religious Freedom merely brings the Church abreast of the personal and political consciousness of civilized mankind today, which has long since accorded to the atheist, as also to the Jew, the full status of citizen in the body politic. Nonetheless, from the standpoint of the present need for Christian dialogue with atheists this development in the doctrine of the Church is important.

It would be easy to show that the new recognition of the legal status of the atheist corresponds to the new theological understanding of contemporary atheism which is exhibited in the Constitution, *Gaudium et spes*, and in the Encyclical, *Ecclesiam suam*. However, this topic lies outside the scope of this essay. It will be sufficient to add a few historical notes simply to illustrate the newness of *Dignitatis humanae* as a moment in a lengthy history.

In his magisterial work of scholarship, *Toleration and the Reformation*, Joseph Lecler thus summarizes the state of affairs in the post-Reformation period, when the issue of civil tolerance was actively argued:

> Lastly, during the seventeenth and eighteenth centuries, writers, theologians, and statesmen were practically unanimous in excluding from the benefit of tolerance all atheists and men without religion. The common opinion of the period was that an atheist was essentially "unsocial"; he rejected God, and had lost all sense of the absolute and the sacred, and therefore mocked at all moral law, promises, contracts, or binding agreements. Only two authors consented to tolerate him: the Dutch author, Dirck Coornhert, and the English Baptist, Roger Williams (II, 486).

This attitude towards atheists was common to Protestants and Catholics alike. Sir Thomas More, for all his gentleness of spirit, could find no place in his Utopia (the work was published in 1516) for materialists who denied the life of man hereafter, or for atheists who denied God and his providence. In his noted book, *De haereticis, an sint persequendi* (published in 1554), the great Protestant protagonist of tolerance, Sabastian Castiello, would extend no tolerance to atheists. In Bodin's *Colloquium Heptaplomeres* (ca. 1593) all of the seven participants, who were religiously divided one from the other, were unanimous in the view that there is no room in the State for the atheist. In 1648, in the reign of Charles I, the English Parliament enacted an ordinance which made Unitarians and atheists liable to the death penalty. And as late as 1689, the very year of the Acts of Toleration in England, the great philosopher of political freedom, John Locke, could write in his *Letter Concerning Toleration*: "Those are not at all to be tolerated who deny the being of God. Promises, covenants, and oaths, which are the bonds of human society, can have no hold upon an atheist. The taking away of God, though but even in thought, dissolves all." The reasoning is as old as Plutarch, who wrote: "There never was a state of atheists. Sooner may a city stand without foundations than a state without belief in the gods. This is the bond for all society and the pillar of all legislation."

It is well, however, to note that in the post-Reformation polemic against religious intolerance and persecution, whether exercised by Protestants or by Catholics, an interesting argument *ex consequentiis* began to be used about the middle of the sixteenth century—first, it would seem, by Jacques Bienassis, the Abbot of Bois-Aubry. Such persecution, he contended, drives men to atheism. Catholics are not converted to Protestantism or Protestants to Catholicism; both become atheists, and thus become a danger to the State. The argument became classic, along with the pragmatic argument that religious intolerance is a cause of economic ruin, and with the religious argument that intolerance imposes intolerable burdens on conscience. At that, the argument did not go uncontested. There were those who maintained that tolerance leads to religious indifference and finally to atheism. Nonetheless, in tracing the causes of contemporary atheism it is well to note the influence exerted by the intolerance of an earlier age, practiced by so-called Christian princes and approved by the Church and the churches.

The Continental European tradition was transplanted by the early American colonists to their new home. In the vast land later to be known as the United States of America a new history of religious freedom was to be lived and written. But it was a long time before the atheist came to be part of it. In early America he was socially unacceptable and legally disadvantaged. As late as 1789, when the Federal Republic was constituted, six of the states still had religious establishments (what European idiom calls a "religion of the State"), with consequent restraints on the freedom of dissenters. In most of the other states religious requirements for citizenship, and therefore for freedom, were imposed. Delaware required belief in the Trinity and in the inspiration of both Old and New Testaments; Maryland required the profession of "Christianity"; South Carolina required belief in God and in the future life; Pennsylvania required belief in God and in the Old and New Testaments. And in many states there was a religious requirement for public office.

In 1791 the First Amendment to the Federal Constitution proscribed any religious establishment on the Federal level and also guaranteed the free exercise of religion. Thus the new history was launched. It is not possible or necessary here to follow in detail its movement, much less to describe the peculiar genius of the great body of American constitutional law which regulates the relations between government and religion. For our purposes which have to do with the developing constitutional status of the atheist in society, it will be sufficient to note several aspects of the historical development that has taken place in the United States. This history has been in a sense paradigmatic.

In its original conception and intention the First Amendment declared a certain neutrality of government in matters of religion. It was not, however, a neutrality of indifference towards religion—the agnostic indifference of the French laicist republics which veiled a real hostility toward religion. The Federal government simply declared its neutrality in the face of the competing claims of the various Christian churches and sects on the American scene. This neutrality was no more than a denial of favoritism. The declaration of it was at the same time a declaration of general benevolence towards all religious forces engaged in the total enterprise of furthering the spiritual welfare of the American people. Therefore the First Amendment was not in any sense a declaration of governmental neutrality as between belief and unbelief, faith and skepticism. At the outset the First Amendment was not explicitly intended to provide constitutional security for the atheist, even though in fact and logic it did provide this security by its guarantee of the free exercise of religion. (There is a sort of analogy here between the First Amendment and the Vatican Declaration on Religious Freedom.) It was only in very recent years that the Supreme Court of the United States broadened the concept of neutrality to embrace a neutrality between religion and irreligion, and thus formally and explicitly affirmed the equality in constitutional status of the believer and the non-believer.

This significant development has taken place under a twofold judicial impulse on the part of the Supreme Court. The dominant impulse has been the general tendency to make "equality" the central objective of constitutional government. In more legal terms, the movement has been toward guaranteeing also to the atheist the "equal protection of the laws." The second impulse has been towards expanding the concept of "religion" so as to include, in effect, the contemporary religion of the religionless, and to set it on a footing of constitutional equality with traditional religion. There are in America constitutional lawyers and historians who deplore this latter tendency, not least on the ground that the expanding concept of religion will in the end come to embrace so much that it will have lost all real meaning. At the same time they approve the impulse to pursue the idea of equality and of the equal protection of the laws. They would prefer, however, that the constitutional security of the atheist should be grounded, not in the rule of neutrality stated in the First Amendment (which is, in effect, the American concept of separation of church and state) but in other constitutional prohibitions and implications—notably in the First Amendment's prohibitions regarding restrictions on freedom of speech and on the free exercise of religion, and in the implications of the legal and social concept of equality whose constitutional seat is in the Fourteenth Amendment.

The argument here is technical as well as historical. There is no need to pursue it further, but it was necessary to mention it, for several reasons.

In the first place, there is no doubt about the rightness of recognizing the immunity of the non-believer from coercion in religious matters. The recognition of his religious freedom in this sense represents a moment of progress in the personal and political consciousness of mankind. Moreover, it has already been said that this civilizational progress is consonant with the theological progress in the understanding of unbelief which is at least sketched in the Constitution, *Gaudium et spes*. Atheism is never the conclusion of an argument; in this respect it resembles Christian faith. Atheism, like faith, is a decision, a fundamental option, an act of freedom. Moreover, Vatican II strongly indicated that in the conditions of the contemporary world the free choice of atheism, in some form, might well be made without moral guilt. If this be so, it is fitting that the civil and social order should present conditions of freedom within which even the option against God could be made by the human person on his own responsibility. As a famous American jurist stated the matter with some humor: "If any American citizen chooses to go to hell, there is nothing in the Constitution to prevent him from doing so."

On the other hand, the ancient tradition which regarded the atheist as the enemy of ordered society has not been evacuated of all truth. An element of truth remains, although it has assumed a contemporary form, not known before the nineteenth century. In the post-Revolutionary era a school of atheist thought arose which contended that freedom of religion, especially freedom for the atheist, required—either as its premise or as its conclusion—an absolute separation of church and state, so called. That is to say, the functions of the state must be completely secularized; the state is to give no recognition or aid whatever to religion in any form; all the institutions of religion, including the religious school, are to be considered to exist completely outside the domain of public life and the common good; therefore their existence and functioning is a matter of no interest to the state, to the agencies of law and government. This, in an extreme form, was the ideology of Continental laicism. In a modified form, and with a different inspiration of a mixed kind, which cannot be described here, this ideology began to grow in the United States in the latter part of the nineteenth century. This secularism (which is its American name) has never gained the power which laicism acquired in Continental Europe, but it exists and it has influence.

The Christian must regard militant laicism or secularism as inimical to the orderly progress of society toward justice and freedom. In particular, its dogma of absolute separation of church and state is unacceptable, even on grounds of the common good of society. The principle of religious freedom does indeed demand a certain separation of church and state, in the sense that religious affairs are removed from the competence of the state. Similarly, the true secularity of society itself is to be recognized, as *Gaudium et spes* recognizes it, in the sense that the "good society" is to be regarded as an end in itself to be pursued for the sake of the earthly welfare of the human person as such, and in the further sense that the various orders of society—political, social, economic, cultural—possess their own respective dynamisms and laws of action, their own autonomy, an indigenous integrity which demands respect. On the other hand, no Christian can admit, what the Council refused to admit, that secular government may maintain a neutrality of indifference toward religion, or that secular society may excise religion from its concept of the common good.

The point here is that it belongs to the dialogue between Christian and atheist to convey the understanding that the fullness of religious freedom neither depends on, nor leads to, an absolute separation of church and state in the laicist or secularist sense. Historically, the atheist and the Christian have clashed on this issue; they now need to discuss it calmly and reasonably. On the other hand, in the contemporary world they should be able to agree on another issue of perhaps greater importance. They should agree that full religious freedom, whether the freedom of the Christian or the freedom of the atheist, cannot subsist except as an integral element and indeed the primatial element, in a larger order of political freedom, and within a

total structure of human and civil rights, all of which derive from the
dignity of the human person. One of the several weaknesses of the
Declaration, *Dignitatis humanae*, is that it fails to situate the right to
religious freedom within this more inclusive structure.[1] In this
respect, the Encyclical, *Pacem in terris*, presents a more complete and
satisfying picture. In any event, the mutual interdependence of the
right to religious freedom and all other human rights is a truth which
has been illuminated by the entire secular experience of the modern
world. The experience of Communism has confirmed it in a particular
way. Agreement between Christian and atheist on the truth of this
interdependence would be important in itself. It would also be the
necessary premise of further dialogue about, and of cooperation
toward, the creation of conditions of freedom and justice in the
human community. In turn, this latter conversation, prolonged into
cooperation, might help toward the resolution of the historic clash
over the meaning of separation of church and state.

There is a more profound significance which would attach to the
reciprocal recognition by Christian and atheist that they share a common human consciousness, both personal and political, with regard
to the values of religious freedom in society and likewise with regard
to the related values of a true concept of secularity as it touches both
the personal life of man himself and also the structures, processes,
and goals of society. This recognition might clear the way towards a
more fundamental dialogue of greater theological purity, so to speak.
It has been often pointed out that divisions among Christians have
had many non-theological causes. In the past, national prejudices,
class consciousness, economic interests, power conflicts, and social
tensions of all kinds have disguised themselves as religious differences. Theological divergences among Christians have indeed been
real enough; but almost every Christian division may be explained at
least partly in sociological terms. The same may be said of the more
radical division between believer and unbeliever. Moreover, it has
also been pointed out that today secular conflicts no longer have need
to clothe themselves in false religious garb, and religious conflicts can
no longer permit themselves to be confused with secular conflicts.

---

1. EDITOR NOTE: Murray's last article on religious freedom was just
such an attempt to fully ground that freedom in human dignity. See "The Human Right to Religious Freedom," in *Religious Liberty* (1993), 229–44.

The reason is that the lengthy historical process of the differentiation of the sacred and secular orders has advanced to a discernible term. Perhaps the major importance of the *Declaration on Religious Freedom* was that it marked the acceptance by the Church both of the historical process and of its contemporary term, which is, of course, like all historical achievements, only provisional.

If all this be true, it would follow that the real differences between Christian and atheist, as also among Christians themselves, may now begin to stand out with relatively greater purity than in the past. Presumably the differences between Christian and atheist would center on the whole concept of the sacred order—its existence, its relevance, the problem of its recognition. These differences could now perhaps be clarified and defined more closely, given the present-day sharper differentiation of the sacred and the secular and the termination of past adulterations of the sacred by the intrusion of alien elements of time-conditioned secular culture. It may well be that the atheist rejection of the sacred has been occasioned precisely by these adulterations. In any event, if this purification of the issues could be accomplished, the dialogue would profit greatly.

The Unbelief of the Christian

JOHN COURTNEY MURRAY, S.J.

As mentioned in the introduction to this section, Murray eventually looked for common perspectives within which Christians and atheists might begin to understand one another. He offered as beginning points (1) recognition of mutual violations by both sides of the principle of Christian dualism (constitutionalism) and, (2) gnosis/agnosis consciousness as posing to believer and non-believer alike the continual temptation to idolatry or despair. The first entailed a turn to historicity; the second to interiority. In this last article on the Christian-atheist dialogue, he again appeals to dualism and sinfulness, and to human interiority. Now, however, his language is shaped by an understanding of the church as sacrament. Dualism becomes two simultaneous histories, secular and sacred, that embrace both civil society and the church. The gnosis/agnosis structuring of human consciousness becomes the belief and unbelief that must be predicated of those in the church as well as of those outside, and of the church itself as well as of individual Christians.

I should like to begin with a somewhat general remark which is related to the theme of my discourse. There is one thing that has to be said about the massive phenomenon of contemporary unbelief, namely that the issue it presents to the Christian is not to be resolved by argument in the academy or by the academy. The issue can only be resolved in the order of action and history, by the whole people of God in dialogue and in cooperation with the whole people temporal. What we are confronted with today is not classical atheism, by which

---

First published as "The Unbelief of the Christian." In *The Presence and Absence of God*, 69–83 (New York: Fordham University Press, 1969).

I mean a simple denial of the existence of God on the ground that the whole concept of God is unintelligible. The Marxist, for instance, is quite willing to admit that the notion of God is conceivable and even intelligible. The whole contemporary problem rather arises from the fact that atheism has now found a positive basis. It is now based on an affirmation, an affirmation of the human person, his dignity and his freedom. And this affirmation is accomplished by a will to achieve the dignity of the person by achieving his autonomy, by liberating him from the indignity and misery to which he is subjected throughout large areas of the world. There is today a new confidence that man has within himself resources, purely human and secular resources, which are sufficient to organize the world in such wise that it will be a proper habitation for the man who is conscious of his dignity and freedom.

Therefore the Christian position today confronts a new counter-position. This counter-position is fairly simply stated. It says that there is only one history, the history that man makes and the history that makes man. The only forces operative in history, the only energies that galvanize history, are the energies immanent within man himself, his intelligence and his will, along with the modern prolongation of these energies which goes by the name of technology. And as for salvation, if there must be talk of salvation, the only form that man can hope for is a salvation to be achieved within history, by history, and by man himself, unaided.

Against this counter-position the Christian has to reaffirm the position that there are two histories. There is human secular history of which man is the agent, whose events are empirically observable and whose meaning is accessible to intelligence. But there is also, the Christian says, salvation history, whose operative principle is theandric, and whose basic agent is the Spirit of God. This Spirit, the Holy Spirit, is the power of God most high, who in this history summons men to be His co-workers, as Paul says in 1 Cor 3:9 and Col 4:11. The events of this sacred history are not empirically observable and their sense, that is to say, their direction, is not accessible to human intelligence but only to faith. These two histories the Christian says are distinct but not separate or separable. They are as it were two currents that flow through time together. They are coterminous in time. They began at the same moment and they run together, but they are not homogeneous in kind. One of them will end with the consummation of this world, the other is destined for a consummation beyond this world. Moreover, while the two histories run together, they are related in such wise (and this I think is the crucial point today) that the salvation of man even within the finite horizons of human history is mysteriously dependent upon another mode of salvation of which the theandric history is the bearer. In a word, if I had to state the issue that confronts us today in its broadest terms, I think I would be inclined to say that it could be put in this question: Are there two histories or only one?

Now within this large issue of the theological intelligibility of contemporary unbelief there is a narrower issue, at once more immediate and more urgent. For the Christian cannot simply regard unbelief as a brute fact to be accepted, to be faced, then perhaps to be forgotten. No, this phenomenon demands to be understood in the light of faith, and the immediate theological question is whether or not it can be integrated into the Christian understanding of the Church in the world, that is to say, of the two histories in their relation. It is to this question that I now wish to address myself.

I shall state a basic theme, and I would hope that this basic theme, if elaborated in two different directions, might lead us toward an answer to our theological question. I am very aware that I must speak in a somewhat tentative fashion because we are confronted today with a new phenomenon on which only recently theological reflection has been bent. My basic theme is that the Church is the sacrament of Christ. This notion of the Church was in a sense a conciliar ideal at Vatican II rather than a theme consciously developed, but it has indeed become a postconciliar theme. It was taken up rather importantly at the international meeting in Rome at the end of September, 1966, and was the subject of two major discourses, one by the Dominican theologian Edward Schillebeeckx, and the other by the Jesuit scholar, Juan Alfaro.

This theme of the Church as the sacrament of Christ has, of course, deep biblical roots in the Pauline epistles, in 1 Corinthians, Romans and especially in Colossians and Ephesians. The background of the idea is not, as many think, the medieval speculation on the nature of sacrament which led to the definition of the seven sacraments. The background is rather the biblical notion of *the* sacrament which is the "mystery" of Eph 3:3-4, where the Greek word μυστήριον is translated by the Vulgate *sacramentum*. In the earlier Pauline epistles the accent was on the eschatological fulfillment of the mystery of Christ, the mystery of God. In the captivity epistles, Colos-

sians and Ephesians the emphasis is upon the present, here and now,
history of what Paul in Col 2:2 calls the mystery of God, which is identically the mystery of Christ to which he refers in Col 4:3 and Eph 3:5.
This mystery is simply the divine plan of salvation as it unrolls in history from the first coming of Christ to the Parousia. It is identical with
the power and the action of God as operative for this salvation of
man. Hidden from eternity in God the Father, this mystery was
uttered in the eternal utterance of the Son and the eternal breathing of
the Spirit. Here in time, although still hidden by the veils that conceal
from man the face of God, it is nonetheless manifested in a sign, in a
sacrament. It is revealed, as Paul says in Eph 3: 10, through the
Church which is the manifestation of the manifold wisdom of God
and the epiphany of the salvific plan of God. The Church, therefore,
as visible and as historically active, is the sign and sacrament of
Christ who is here and now with us in the Spirit according to His
promise. The Church is the progressive realization of the divine plan
of salvation for mankind, that reconciliation of all things of which
Paul speaks in Col 1:20, and that fulfillment of all things of which he
speaks in Eph 1:10.

Now I think it is important to realize, certainly for the sake of
this discourse, that the Church about which we are speaking here is
the concrete, living Church, which is, as Vatican II made quite clear in
Chap. 7 of *Lumen gentium*,[1] an eschatological reality in which there is
an indissoluble tension between the "even now" and the "not yet."
Even now the Church is, and is one, and is holy, and yet the Church is
not yet one and is not yet holy. The Church indeed has been sanctified, washed by the blood of Christ, sanctified by the immolation of
Christ Himself on the Cross. But the sanctification of the Church still
remains an historical process which is not yet fulfilled, because the
Church, even now the one and holy, is still the pilgrim people of God,
capable at any moment of those betrayals that the original people of
God were guilty of after their rescue from Egypt. One must therefore
distinguish two aspects of the Church, but not dichotomize them.
One cannot divide the institutional Church from the people who
make it up, or, in more scholastic terms, one cannot divide the formal

---

1. *The Documents of Vatican II*, Ed. Walter M. Abbott, S.J., pp. 20–22
(New York: Herder & Herder and Association Press, 1966). EDITOR NOTE:
Most of these notes were supplied by the Fordham Press Editor.

from the material elements in the Church. And in this living, concrete, historical totality, the Church is the sacrament, the sign of Christ. It is the realization and manifestation of the mystery of salvation which is even now being wrought out, though it has not yet been fully wrought out.

This, then, very briefly is my basic theme. I suggest that this theme is capable of development in two directions both of which are pertinent to our present inquiry. It is the second direction which is more directly pertinent to the unbelief of the Christian, but I should like to go through the first development first.

The first development leads to a sort of dialectical tension which was completely unresolved by Vatican II. The Church, as we have said, is the sign of salvation for all men, the new humanity inaugurated by Christ, the existential realization of the deepest meaning of human history. On the other hand, the Church is simply the little flock. From a numerical point of view it is almost insignificant in comparison with the vast mass of men who do not know and do not recognize either the Church or the Christ of which the Church is sign and sacrament. This gives rise to the question of the relationship between this little flock which is already gathered and the literally innumerable multitude of men who are still scattered. Is the relationship simply extrinsic, between those who are inside and those who are outside? Or is there possibly an intrinsic relationship? In asking this question, I think we come to the heart of the theological intelligibility of contemporary atheism.

Here is the point, I think, at which to refer to the biblical problematic, because *prima facie* it would seem that the biblical problematic is stated in terms of those who are inside and those who are outside. On the one hand, there is the people of God, there is the people that God Himself knew, in the biblical sense, that is to say, the people whom He loved and chose and the people who in return loved Him and chose Him and entered into a covenant relationship with Him. And there are, on the other hand, what Paul in 1 Thess 4:5 calls the peoples who do not know God but reject Him and ignore Him, in the biblical sense of ignorance. They have chosen against Him and have thus become captive to what Paul calls in 2 Thess 2:7 the mystery of iniquity, that counter-action in the world which opposes the salvific action of God. These other peoples are thus under the power and rule of the kingdom of darkness. In the biblical problematic,

moreover, it seems evident that the ignorance of these peoples is
somehow culpable. They have somehow chosen to stand outside the
kingdom of light. We can see this in the Old Testament indictment of
the idolater, which is pitiless and even scornful. We can see it even
more clearly in the first chapter of Romans, where we find Paul's
indictment of the pagan idolaters which ends with the words: "Therefore they are themselves without excuse." Their ignorance was not
simply ignorance; it was an ignorance that was culpable. The same
problematic appears in St. John, in his classic statement of the contrast
between light and darkness. The light came into the darkness, he
says, and there were those who "loved the darkness better than the
light."

Now while this biblical problematic is perennially valid and
must not be dissolved, it was in fact the product of a polemic, or at
best, if you will, an apologetic. The prophetic indictment of idolatry
in the Old Testament and the passage in Romans directed exclusively
to the people of God. Neither Paul nor the prophets were talking to
the idolater. This polemic has had in fact a rather long historical life. It
was installed in ecclesiastical literature certainly after the Constantin-
ian settlement, and it has been maintained in papal literature right
through Leo XIII up to Pius XII. Only at Vatican II did the inadequacy
of this problematic begin to be appreciated and understood. Then the
Church became more aware of herself as situated in the interior of history and not above it, as situated in the world and not apart from it.
There was the consequent awareness that the relationship between
the Church and the world, the relationship between the two histories,
must be a dialogic relationship which implies a certain give and take.
The proclamation of the Word of God today, as Paul VI made very
clear in his encyclical *Ecclesiam suam*, must take the form of what he
called the dialogue of salvation.

Consequently we now feel the need to enlarge the biblical problematic without destroying or discarding it. To do so we have to take
very seriously a traditional doctrine that the order of grace is not
coterminous with the visible, historical, empirical Church. The frontier between the kingdom of light and the kingdom of darkness does
not coincide with the boundary, as it were, between the visible
Church and something we call the world. On the contrary, the order
of grace is pervasive through all humanity and the action of the Holy
Spirit which supports sacred history is also somehow supportive of

all human history including secular history. There is therefore a distinction to be made. The distinction is between the Church as the public manifestation of the mystery of Christ and the operative action of the grace of the Holy Spirit. The Church represents the fullness of Christian faith; the Church represents humanity in its consciously realized newness, and as such the Church is the sacrament, the sign, the manifestation of Christ. On the other hand, grace, and very notably the grace of faith, is somehow operative in all men, even in those we think of in terms of the biblical problematic as "those outside."

In consequence of this new conciliar awareness of the Church and of this newly realized distinction, a number of new theological themes have been cast up. There is the theme of the belief of the unbeliever, and the theme of the anonymous Christian. There is the theme of implicit faith, Christian faith that is implicit in all men of good will, in all men whose will is to the good, in all men who are animated by the spirit of love. There is the theme of the distinction between the manifest and the latent presence of the sacred in history. All these themes, all these theological theories, are pertinent to the issue of contemporary atheism because they serve to establish an intrinsic relationship between the Church and the world, between the two histories. These themes have, moreover, considerable theological fertility. They serve to enlarge and to deepen our notion of faith and to bring us back to a more biblical notion as over against the more intellectualized version of faith which was prominent in the scholastic tradition. These themes have besides a great pastoral significance insofar as they illustrate the necessity and possibility of dialogue; dialogue between the Church, which is the fullness of belief, and the world, in which there is indeed belief but a belief which has not come to a conscious conceptualization or even perhaps to an integrity of commitment.

Nevertheless, there is, I think, a danger today that these themes, especially the anonymous Christian idea, might lead to some dissolution of the biblical problematic. If you push these themes to their logical absurdity, you might be inclined to say that there are today no atheists, neither in foxholes nor anywhere else. You might be inclined to say that culpable unbelief is not a possibility, is not a viable option for man today, that there is no such thing really as conscious refusal or rejection of God. You might, if you pushed these themes to absur-

dity beyond the bounds of logic, be inclined to repeal the condemnation of Paul: "So that they themselves are without excuse in their
idolatry." This we cannot afford to do, for the biblical problematic
must stand.

Thus far I have been pursuing the first development of my basic
theme of the Church as the sacrament of Christ, namely the dialectical
tension between the institutional Church and those who have no visible relation to it. There is another line of development, however, one
more directly pertinent to the unbelief of the Christian. A hint of it is
to be found in Section 19 of the *Pastoral Constitution on the Church in
the Modern World*, where there is a discussion of the forms and roots of
contemporary atheism, and where explicit mention is made of the
responsibility of Christians themselves for this massive contemporary
phenomenon. Christians, the text says, "To the extent that they . . . are
deficient in their religious, moral or social life, must be said to conceal
rather than reveal the authentic face of God and religion," that is to
say, the presence of God here and now.[2]

Likewise in Section 8 of the *Dogmatic Constitution on the Church*
we read that the Church "faithfully reveals the mystery of its Lord to
the world, but under shadows, until finally the manifestation will be
complete in fullness of light."[3] Now these are very interesting statements and upon them hangs in a sense a kind of conciliar tail. For in
these texts there is explicit reference to the culpability of individuals
in the Church. There was a great resistance among the conciliar
Fathers against any notion that somehow or other guilt or sin or
defect or deficiency could be predicated of the Church herself. There
was great opposition to what finally got into the document on ecumenism, as to the fault of the Church. With regard to the document
on religious freedom, I can testify here personally to great opposition
on the part of the Fathers to any notion that the Church herself had
been guilty of default, defect and sin against the proclamation of that
Christian and human freedom which is inherent in the Gospel. It was
I who finally devised the formulation in Section 12: "even though
there were some people among the people of God who did not act up

---

2. *Documents of Vatican II*, p. 217.
3. Cf. *Documents of Vatican II*, p. 24. The translation here given is Fr.
Murray's own.

to the example of Christ in regard of Christian freedom."[4] That is the best we could get from the Fathers, and you have no idea what a strain it was to get this much into the documents, namely that somehow or other, here and there, now and again, one or another person in the history of the Church may not have lived up to the fullness of the Christian revelation.

I must say, with all due deference to the Fathers of the Council, that they were the victims of a defective ecclesiology, very Platonic in its implications, as if somehow the Church were some supernal entity hovering *above* history and not involved at all *in* history or in the people who make up the Church. They seem to have acquiesced too readily in some division between the formal and material components of the Church, between the Church as sacramental and institutional, and the Church as an historical and existential reality. They would have been well advised to return to a stream of patristic thought which as a matter of fact they themselves had found without

---

4. FORDHAM PRESS EDITOR NOTE: Cf. *Document of Vatican II*, p. 692. The sentence above appears in somewhat different fashion in this translation: "In the life of the People of God as it has made its pilgrim way through the vicissitudes of human history, there have at time appeared ways of acting which were less in accord with the spirit of the gospel and even opposed to it." In the Preface to *Documents of Vatican II*, p. xi, the following significant statement is found: "Although these translations are to major extent my own [Very Rev. Msgr. Joseph Gallagher], there is one exception. . .The translation of the Declaration on Religious Freedom was chiefly prepared by one of the architects of the Latin original, Father John Courtney Murray, S.J. for this volume, he slightly emended the translation he had prepared for the National Catholic Welfare Conference." In footnote 51 to the above version in *Documents of Vatican II*, p. 692, Fr. Murray wrote as follows: "The historical consciousness of the Council required that it be loyal to the truth of history. Hence the Declaration makes the humble avowal that the People of God have not always walked in the way of Christ and the apostles. At times they have followed ways that were at variance with the spirit of the gospel and even contrary to it. The avowal is made briefly and without details. But the intention was to confess, in a penitent spirit, not only that Christian churchmen and princes have appealed of the coercive instruments of power in the supposed interest of the faith, but also that the Church herself has countenanced institutions which made a similar appeal. Whatever be the nice historical judgment on these institutions in their own context of history, they are not to be justified, much less are they ever or in any way to be reinstated. The Declaration is a final renouncement and repudiation by the Church of all means and measures of coercion in matters religious."

fully knowing it. As you know, in Chapter 7 of the *Constitution on the Church* they picked up the great patristic theme of the eschatological character of the Church and as soon as you get into that you get into the tension that I spoke of a while ago between the "even now" and the "not yet." This tension is a vital tension—the "even now" and the "not yet" exist in unity and simultaneity in the concrete living reality of the Church that you and I belong to, the pilgrim Church making its way through history.[5]

If you take this theme of the eschatological character of the Church seriously, as we in the postconciliar age can do, then I think you are obliged to admit not merely that individuals in the Church can be sinners and sinful, but that the Church herself at any and all given moments of her earthly pilgrimage can also be a sinning and a sinful Church, even though at the same time the Church remains the one and the holy Church. While it is true that the Church incurs guilt only through her members, it is nonetheless also true that the guilt her members incur can rightly be predicated of the Church herself. In other words, you could apply to the Church in an orthodox sense the famous Lutheran dictum with regard to the individual: *simul justus et peccator*, at once just and a sinner. And this seems to me implicit in the explicit conciliar acceptance of the Lutheran dictum that the Church must always be reformed. In Chapter 8 of the *Constitution* there is mention of the Church as at the same time holy and always to be puri-fied;[6] and the Church is, as the text goes on to say, in continual quest both of conversion and also of renewal. This is what the Council said, and we in the postconciliar period are allowed to take it seriously.

It is at this point that I come back to my theme, namely that there is a certain ambivalence to the Church as the sacrament and sign of Christ. On the one hand, the Church is the explicit and visible manifestation of God's plan in history, of the divine salvific action, of the abiding presence of Christ in His spirit. On the other hand, the intelligibility of this sign and sacrament is darkened by the shadows that conceal rather than reveal the authentic face of Christ who is the image of the Father.

The first shadow that falls on the face of the Church and obscures its intelligibility as the sacrament of Christ is the disunity of

---

5. *Documents of Vatican II*, pp. 20–22 and n. 17.
6. *Ibid.*, pp. 22–24.

the Church herself. In John 17:21 the Lord said it was by the unity of
His followers that men were to know that He had been sent by the
Father. The disunity among His followers therefore is an obstacle to
belief in Him. This disunity blurs the message of the Church, confuses
her mission and obscures the significance of herself as sacrament.
Note that I am speaking of the disunity of the Church, because here
again Vatican II dissolved an older problematic. It used to be that you
had the one, holy, Roman, Catholic and apostolic Church over here,
then rather lamentably you had a group of separated brethren over
there. But this will no longer do. Obviously the Council here did not
follow out its own thought. In the Decree on Ecumenism[7] the Council
acknowledged that there are ecclesial realities outside the visible communion of the Roman Church. There is the reality of the Word, the
reality of baptism, the reality of faith, to some extent the reality of the
Lord's Supper. These realities are not merely realities that sanctify the
individual as such; they are also ecclesial, that is to say, they contribute to create and build the Church. In their ecclesial realizations outside the Roman Church, these realities play a role in the history of
salvation. It is not then simply a question of the true Church over here
and those unfortunately divided from the Church over there. No, the
Church herself is divided. She is not yet possessed of her full ecclesial
reality; she is not yet the one and holy, although she is even now the
one and holy. Here again we have the eschatological tension.

You will see, I think, that at this point I am once more touching
the ecclesial dimensions of the unbelief of the Christian. The Church
is sacrament of Christ, Christ is the sacrament of the Father. The
Church is the sacrament of Christ in the concrete totality of her presence and action in history. On the other hand, the concrete reality of
the Church in history obscures, dims, clouds the visibility and the
intelligibility of the Church as sacrament and sign of the mystery of
Christ. Christ is forever the *lumen gentium*, the light of the peoples. In
the opening words of the *Constitution on the Church*:[8] "Upon Christ as
the light of the peoples, the Church herself, who is to be the sign of
Christ, casts shadows." And it is in this ecclesial sense that I think I
would first speak of the unbelief of the Christian. It is the unbelief *in*
the Church and the *unbelief* of the Church. The basic notion here is the

7. *Documents of Vatican II*, pp. 341–66.
8. *Documents of Vatican II*, pp. 14–24.

notion of the Church as at once believing and unbelieving. It is the notion of the Church as at once realizing and signifying in history the divine plan, and in some sense being a negative realization of this plan and an obscuring of it. It is in such terms that I would in the first instance establish an intrinsic relationship between the Church, the world of belief, and those outside of it, the world of unbelief.

In some such terms I think one could reach a unified theological understanding both of the Church and of the world in their mutual relationship. There are of course the other factors mentioned by the Council itself: the faults of Christians, the neglect of education in the faith, misleading exposition of doctrine and defects of individuals in the Church. But you might raise this question: are there not also ecclesial defects, defects of the Church herself? Are not these related to defective structures in the Church, or to defective functioning of her institutions, whether these institutions be of divine law or of human institution? Do we not find defects in the organization of her prophetic ministry and its prolongation in theological education, defects in her pastoral mission, organized less in terms of love than perhaps simply in terms of efficiency? The *Constitution on the Liturgy*[9] notes defects even in the liturgical practice of the Church, in so far as the liturgy is a proclamation of the Gospel. The present funeral Mass, for example, is a complete misrepresentation of the fundamental Christian theology of death. Instead of proclaiming the ultimate meaning of death as the beginning of the fullness of life in Christ, what it proclaims is *dies irae* and all that kind of thing. This is somehow an ecclesial fault, for we cannot say it is the fault of the one who composed the Mass; we don't even know who he was. This liturgy is an instrument of the Church used kerygmatically to veil from the world the supreme message which the Church has to give to the world. Similarly the social practice as well as the social doctrine of the Church as such has as a matter of historical fact obscured her message of salvation. There is no need for me to develop this line of thought any further. The point is that the Church is a burden and a trial to the belief of the Christian as well as a help and a support to this belief.

The Church does indeed fulfill the great mandate of Matthew 28:18–20, her apostolic mission to teach. But the Church also forever

---

9. *Documents of Vatican II*, section III. Reform of the Liturgy, pp. 146–52 and passim.

falls short in fulfilling this mandate. The Church exists in the world as the sacrament of Christ, and does indeed reveal by her existence and her action the mystery of Christ; but she does this in a shadowed and darkened kind of way, *fideliter sed sub umbris,* as the Council says.[10] By her own unbelief the Church bears an intrinsic relationship to the unbelief of the world, as well as a responsibility for this unbelief, insofar as she herself, destined to be the sign and sacrament of the mystery of Christ, conceals instead of reveals the face of Christ. Yet the dialectic still holds because the Church is the revelation of the mystery of Christ, she imposes upon the unbeliever a responsibility for his own unbelief. Thus we rejoin the biblical problematic: "So that they are inexcusable" who fail to recognize and acknowledge Christ in the sign of Christ. This biblical problematic is at root an affirmation both of the accessibility and the obscurity of faith. It is an assent to mystery, an assent that is given not on evidence but on the Word of God. Faith therefore contains within itself the seeds of its own imperfection; belief itself contains the seeds of unbelief.

In my opening remarks I underlined what I feel to be the central issue in the contemporary phenomenon of unbelief, namely whether there is something else in human life besides the history that makes man. For the Christian affirmation is that there is indeed another history, the history which God makes, and which takes place in and through the events of human history. This history of salvation can be seen only with the eyes of faith and its external manifestation is a sign, the sacrament which is the Church. Yet this instrument of Christ's revelation has, in cold historical fact, obscured His face and failed to proclaim His message. This the Church has done not through malice but simply because she is human. Her members are therefore themselves in some sense unbelievers, and must share responsibility for the unbelief of the world around them. This world in turn cannot be absolved from its own guilt, for there will always be men who freely choose to live in darkness rather than in light. Yet what the Christian must guard against, when he and his Church present themselves to the world in which they live, is that this world should not encounter in them that portion of darkness which is theirs. This we all pray for, that the light which is Christ may break through our darkness, and that contemporary unbelief may find in the Church a sacrament of Christian faith.

---

10. *Documents of Vatican II,* Decree on Ecumenism, 6, p. 350.

PART 5

Ecumenism

In 1933, while still preparing for ordination at Woodstock College, Maryland, Murray wrote that the radical break caused by the Reformation left no basis whatsoever for the discussion of theological truth claims between Catholics and Protestants. In 1943, he recommended a systematic avoidance of interfaith, theological discussion. Theological discourse was impossible, he clarified, because the severe Reformation break rendered impossible even an analogical understanding of the truths by which the various churches' grasped the mysteries of Christian redemption.[1]

After the council Murray discussed the ecclesiological implications of doctrinal development with Anglican bishops and traced through the intricacies of Roman Catholic trinitarian theology with the Lutherans.[2] He declared that the Roman Catholic church would not be able to come to new truths about the content of Christian faith unless it entered into dialogue with Protestants.

As contrary as those actions and recommendations appear, in both positions the possibility, impossibility, or range of ecumenical interaction hinges on Murray's prior judgments concerning human reasoning in the realm of faith. The articles in this section focus on the possibility of theological—not simply ethical or even natural law theistic—discourse between the churches. By extension, they suggest the possibility of theological discourse between all social sectors within a

---

1. The 1933 article is the first in this section. See the introduction to that article for references to Murray's mid-1940s claims against mutual understanding based in theological affirmations or symbols.

2. In this section Murray's "The Status of the Nicene Creed as Dogma" (1966j) was delivered at a Lutheran-Catholic Dialogue, Baltimore, Maryland, July 1965, and his "A Will to Community" (1967n) was presented to an Episcopal Church committee on the study of heresy.

religiously pluralistic society. Two factors—one internal to Murray's own faith tradition and the other native to American society—did not allow the issue of public theological languages to disappear from his thought and these same factors, I suggest, offer some resources for our contemporary approach to the possibility and nature of public theological discourse. They are (1) the complexity of natural and revealed reasoning, and (2) the presence of active religions in America's public discourse.

THE COMPLEXITY OF NATURAL AND REVEALED REASONING

Why did Murray insist on natural law discourse within pluralistic America? In Part 1 we saw one reason: namely, the need for public discourse to extend beyond the pragmatic, institutional, and practical. A society needs to discuss its general value commitments so that it can determine goals of social action and evaluate means toward those goals. A second reason for that insistence was his rejection of the possibility of theological discourse, taken up in this section. A third reason focused on the complexity of the issues that contemporary society faces, and the ability of natural law to deal with that complexity. Ethical complexity demanded adoption of natural law methodology.

For example, Murray's claims for the just war tradition were based, in large part, on its ability to clearly identify, evaluate, and control the multiple forces that are involved in the possession of nuclear weapons. If America did not find a way to understand adequately those forces, the use and even nonuse of nuclear deterrence would be abandoned to the realm of the irrational, with consequent confusion and brutalization of international relations. Only the "tradition of reason," he contended, could sufficiently factor the values and possibilities alive in contemporary international relations.[3]

Likewise Murray's insistence that the church pay attention to natural law arguments for religious liberty had one grounding in the complexity problem. Murray began his first religious liberty argument with the claim that the church could not forgo a natural law argument for religious liberty, prior to a theological argument, and that conclusions

---

3. Another appeal to natural law for its complex handling of social forces can be found in Murray's juridical writings, as presented in Part 1. See particularly his "Memo to Cushing on Contraception Legislation."

from the natural law argument would not be reversed (merely "humbled") in the theological argument. One reason given was the need for clear, essential definitions of the realities at play in the world ("conscience," "state," "God").[4] When Murray later argued that the church must be attentive to the valid moral and political insights that arise even in the face of the church's own opposition, this claim was based on the proper autonomy, but also the validity, of some complex, secular conceptions of the world in which we live (here, primarily, the dignity of the human person and the juridical state). In all these cases, human inquiry had to search through complex institutional and theoretical realities that humans newly face. Those realities could not be deductively or apodictically drawn from revelation, nor even from foundational principles of natural law. To ignore those realities ran against the moral demands for human attentiveness.

As will be evident in the later articles of this section, it was again the complexity of human inquiry that shaped Murray's understanding of what was at stake in ecumenical, theological discourse. But now he focused not simply on the complexity of social, ethical issues, nor on the general value commitments that grounded the American experiment. That which the Roman Catholic church brings to ecumenical dialogue is the redemption of human systematic reasoning.[5] In that understanding of ecumenism, Murray could claim that the future of ecumenism rested on responses to the question "What think ye of Nicaea?"—a question that led, in his understanding, immediately to questions of the use of reasoning in matters of faith.

Behind Murray's insistence on the adequacy of natural law reasoning and his later claims for Catholic systematic theology is his belief in the compatibility of nature and grace. In Murray's view, to deny the possibility of a natural law or the place of systematic thought in theological discourse runs against the theological claim that God—as Creator and as Redeemer—is present to, and knowable in, the contemporary world.

---

4. See "Freedom of Religion, I: The Ethical Problem" (1945b), pp. 234–36. The additional terms for which the theological argument required clear definition were "Christ," "law of the Gospel," and "Church" ("Notes on the Theory of Religious Liberty" 1945e, p. 15).

5. An early forerunner of this insistence is Murray's discussion in the 1940s of the theology that priests should study, their role in redeeming human intelligence. See "Toward a Theology for the Layman: The Problem of its Finality" (1944d), pp. 56–57.

Further, his notion of compatibility entailed not simply the claim that
the conclusions reached in secular reasoning could not, in principle,
contradict conclusions reached in the realm of faith. The compatibility
Murray was arguing involves the deep compenetration of reasoning and
faith, as initially developed in his discussions of Christian humanism.

AMERICA'S ACTIVE RELIGIOUS VOICES

A second factor that forced Murray to face public theology was the
nature of public discourse in mid-century America. Within the ongoing
conversation that constituted America, theological truth claims repeatedly emerged; they refused to remain hidden behind a "purely" natural
philosophical argument or behind even a natural theism.[6] In his earliest
reactions to Protestant definitions of religious freedom, for example,
Murray claimed that Protestant reactions to the "Catholic position" had
the bad habit of importing theological principles into the debate. Princi-
pally these entailed the ecclesiological claim that all churches stood
equally before God. The second article in this section deals with Murray's reaction to such an importation. Again, by 1960, Murray had to
admit that Protestant theological stances did in fact continue to shape
the civil, political community. Among other forces that tended to undermine the people's faith in reasonable ethical discourse, Murray fought
Protestant, neoorthodox theological stances, with their claim of ambiguity and paradox, as a major force in the collapse of American civil discourse (see chapter 12, "The Doctrine is Dead, *WHTT*, pp. 275–94).

If America's theologically based disagreements would not disappear, neither, on the other hand, did Murray want them to entirely

---

6. Of course the quality of those truth claims might be questioned. Against
Will Herberg's claim that the equal respect paid to Catholic, Protestant, and Jewish claims was superficial (*Protestant, Catholic, Jew* [New York: Doubleday,
1955]), Murray chose to focus, in *WHTT*, on their equality, then insist on their
inclusion in public education. Stephen L. Carter appears also to admit the general acceptance of religious languages in America, but also claims that their
usage is superficial (*Culture of Disbelief* [New York: Basic Books, 1993]). At the
very least, religious languages emerge as trump claims, much as do rights languages. They are treated differentially to the degree that they are not imposed on
others, although they often close down public argument. Late in his life Murray
was concerned to show that religious languages open up public argument.

recede into a neutral deism or into the purely personal. After a series of exchanges with Robert MacIver (dealing with censorship within public universities),[7] Murray eventually insisted that theology be taught in public universities. Students have a right to know something about the faiths held by the American people. But even here, the epistemological spinoff of his nature-grace compatibility claim reasserted itself. Now the university was defined as a neutral forum in which questions of ultimate meaning could be examined fairly and fully, exposing the "logics" of those faiths.[8]

During and after the council, Murray endorsed *theological* discourse between the churches. This is not yet theological discourse within the full body politic. Yet perhaps here we can find some grounds for claiming the importance of such a discussion, the virtues necessary for public theological discourse, and some of the contours of a particularly Roman Catholic contribution to that discussion. In any case, these late, postconciliar approaches to ecumenical discourse are extensions of his earlier treatment of Christian humanism, as outlined in Part 2.

---

7. See "Correspondence with Robert MacIver (1954a), dating from 1952 through 1954." Murray Archives, files 2–156.

8. Murray's best presentation of his case for public education as a neutral forum in which competing "logics of faith" can and ought to be brought into public discussion is Chapter 5, "Creeds at War Intelligibly: Pluralism and the University," of *WHTT*, pp. 125–39.

A Crisis in the History of Trent

JOHN COURTNEY MURRAY, S.J.

In this essay, Murray explores the role of Charles of Guise (b. 1525, d. 1574; Cardinal of Lorraine, 1547–1574) in a debate that preceded the third session of the Council of Trent. At issue was whether the council should abandon its doctrinal and internal focus, perhaps thereby encouraging Protestant participation. The New Catholic Encyclopedia describes Guise as "[e]xtremely intolerant[. H]e tried to bring the Inquisition to France and was responsible for the cruel suppression of the Huguenot conspiracy of Abroise against the Guises (1560)" (vol. 6, p. 858). However, Murray faults Guise for his tolerance—for failing to understand that "the rupture with the heretics is easily seen to have been from the outset irremediable." What Murray judged true of the sixteenth century he also appears to have maintained in the mid-twentieth. In his first extensive discussions of intercredal cooperation, he rejected any possibility that Christian doctrines or common commitments to Christian symbols could unite Catholic and Protestant laity in their common laboring for just social structure (see his "Current Theology: Christian Co-operation" [1942b] and "Current Theology: Co-operation: Some Further Views" [1943a]). As the next article in this section will suggest, the principal focus of Murray's theological concern became doctrines on the church.

I

During the last fifty years the labors of historians, largely under the inspiration of Leo XIII, have been powerfully focused on the Council of Trent, the central point of that most complicated, most fascinating,

Originally published as 1932: "Crisis in the History of Trent." (*Thought* 7 (December 1932): 463–73).

most misunderstood epoch in Church history, the Catholic Reformation. The research done has been prodigious in its extent, profound in its scholarship, and all impregnated with that spirit of insistence on integral presentation of the truth that was the great Leo's ideal in historical writing. And the result has been a remarkable clarification of the relations that existed between the Council and the Popes, and a complete vindication of the ideals that underlay the Papal reform policy as formulated by Paul III and brought to fruition by Pius IV. The ghost of Fra Paolo Sarpi, which had prowled down the centuries right into our own times through the pages of Le Courayer, Ranke, Drüffel, Brandi, and even Döllinger, has at long last been effectually laid; and similarly, the shade of the sturdy Jesuit, Pallavicini, must now certainly rejoice at the happy fulfillment of the task which he strove so mightily and failed so signally to accomplish.

However, in spite of all the light let in upon the Tridentine era, several prominent figures have remained hitherto rather shadowy, notably the tall, handsome, aristocratic figure of Charles Guise, second Cardinal of Lorraine. Pastor several years ago termed his attitude toward the Holy See "a mystery,"[1] and remarked that "a biography complying with the requirements of modern science, of the Cardinal, who was a man of most complex character, is still very much wanted."[2] Dr. Richard, too, in his recent definitive history of Trent,[3] points out the lack of an adequate study of Lorraine as one of the few remaining lacunae in the Tridentine documentation.

Obviously, then, the recent volume of Mr. H. Outram Evennett[4] has been awaited. It forms the first part of the complete reinterpretation of Lorraine undertaken by the distinguished Cambridge don. And though its first and most eminent success consists, of course, in the decisive manner in which it rescues the great French Cardinal from the thicket of historical misunderstanding in which he has so long wandered, alone and almost friendless, yet it has besides a wider significance. For the solidity and sense of the Papal ideals concerning the orientation of the Counter-Reform movement are set in relief

---

1. *History of the Popes*, ed. Kerr, Vol. XVI, p. 158, note 3.
2. Ibid., p. 154, note 1.
3. Hefele-Leclercq, *Histoire des Conciles*, t. IX, Concile de Trente, par P. Richard, Ire Ptie, p. 17.
4. *The Cardinal of Lorraine and the Council of Trent, A Study in the Counter-Reformation*, Cambridge, 1930, pp. xvii–517.

more luminously than ever by contrast with the hollowness and impossibility of another set of ideals that found their last personification in Lorraine. Upon this single aspect of Lorraine's significance it might be interesting briefly to dwell.

II

At the outset we must recall that there was among Catholics themselves in the early and middle sixteenth century a lamentable lack of unanimity as regards the proper method of meeting the Protestant menace, and more especially as regards the relative emphasis that ought to be put on attempts at reunion and efforts for reform. The Papal attitude, though always paternal and not seldom weak, was nevertheless fundamentally intransigent; it never seriously envisaged the possibility of reunion with the dissidents; and this fact gave the handle to one of Fra Paolo's chief complaints against the Council of Trent, and consequently, against the Popes to which it was supposedly "enslaved," namely, that by its "gratuitously unnecessary dogmatic definitions" it had widened irreparably the rift in the unity of Christendom.

History, however, supreme arbiter of all contemporary differences of opinion, has abundantly established the rightness of the Papal attitude; viewed in retrospect, the rupture with the heretics is easily seen to have been from the outset irremediable. Yet not all had the vision to see or the courage to accept this fact at the time. And from this lack of vision and courage there arose, at least in large part, the so-called continuation controversy between France and the forces of Pius IV. The controversy raged during the interval between the latter's election in 1559 and the reopening of Trent in 1562, and the point at issue was[5]

whether Trent should be resumed, or whether an attempt should be made to summon an entirely new council, one so constituted as to win the good will of the Christians who had seceded from the obedience of Rome, and thus to hold out hope of restoring the broken unity of Christendom.

5. Evennett, op. cit., p. xiv.

The resumption of Trent meant the definite abandonment of hopes of reunion; a new Council might serve as fuel to keep those hopes faintly flickering yet a while longer.

In France feeling against the resumption of Trent ran high, and on its crest rode Charles Guise. And as he was the coryphaeus of the anti-continuationists, so also and most naturally he was the sponsor of a National Council for an autonomous settlement of French religious difficulties, with which project was in turn associated the search after formulae of reunion with the Calvinists. These, together with the question of toleration (upon whose many thorns, however, Lorraine was too circumspect to rend his scarlet robes), were the issues of the day and by his stand on them Lorraine found himself at odds with the saner, more ecumenical ideals of Pius IV, and at the head of a school of thought that neither moved nor spoke with Rome. He undertook to pit Gallic logic against Roman grasp of facts, with the future course of the Counter-Reform hanging on the issue of the combat. Naturally one asks the reason for such hardiness, and in the answer lies the reason why Lorraine simply had to be worsted. He was fighting for a cause already lost before he so much as entered the lists; Gallic logic was far too fragile a weapon with which to stem the onrush of history. All of which needs some explanation.

III

First of all, what was the motive of Lorraine's opposition to Rome?

Personal vanity, ambition, the vision of himself as patriarch of a schismatical France, a subterranean inclination toward heterodoxy—all these were at the time alleged, and since then have been widely believed. Now, however, it must be recognized that Lorraine's campaign against Trent and more especially his support of the National Council were based on a set of principles that he really held with great sincerity. These principles he had inherited from the past, his own and that of France; their soundness was apparently confirmed by the exigencies of circumstances; their hold on him was strengthened by their congeniality with certain peculiar elements of his own character; they determined his course, and held him in it even though it might cut across the path plotted out by Rome.

In the first place, when in the famous memorandum he prepared for the Lutheran princes in 1561, Lorraine stated that his "main object was the reestablishment of Christian unity, which is vital for the preservation of Christianity itself, and is demanded alike by the honor of God and the safety of the State," he was undoubtedly speaking from the heart, whatever we may think of the ingenuousness of other parts of the document. Christian unity, to be sought under the double formality of a religious *desideratum* and a political necessity, was the ideal set in the center of all his activity. And the ideal was certainly traditional enough to be quite legitimate. But Lorraine, like Charles V before him, egregiously erred in his choice of methods wherewith to pursue that ideal; and, in fact, he was wrong in his initial judgment upon the possibility under existing circumstances of the ideal itself.

Still, his reasoning, however erroneous, was clear enough. The Calvinist *Réforme* had, in 1558, leaped almost overnight into a serious threat against the political and social fabric of the French nation. Persecution had been tried, but, as always, had proved a weapon that broke in the hands of those who used it. Toleration, on the other hand, was altogether illogical; if there were only one true religion how could it consistently allow any other to stand by its side? Nevertheless, some sort of a solution of the problem was imperative. And in arriving at it no help was to be looked for from beyond the Alps; the salvation of the unity of France was not a matter that could safely be trusted to the hands of Italian lawyers. Obviously then, concluded Lorraine, reunion with the Calvinists was the only possible remedy; reason and experience (and prejudice) excluded all others.

Moreover, his own peculiar character added its weight to the balance. He was a congenital opportunist, gifted by nature with an extraordinary facility for adapting himself to circumstances; he had been brought up in the atmosphere of the old *Réformisme* of the reign of Francis I, that smacked so much of the idealism of Contarini and of an Erasmian spirit of compromise; he had been educated by a theologian of the stamp of Claude d'Espence who was well known and not a little suspected for his conviction that heresy was to be met with argument and persuasion and a willingness to minimize dogmatic differences. Being thus what he was, it is not hard to see why Lorraine should have done what he did, why he should have shrunk from hard-and-fast definitions and from "contentious disputations," and have trusted to "eirenic conferences" to wield the magic needle that would repair the rent in the seamless robe.

We are tempted at our distance to smile at the pathetic absurdity of such hopes and at the blindness they display to the realities of the time. But Lorraine was not blind. His only difficulty was that he stood too close to the wall to be able to read on it the handwriting that to us stands out so boldly. He was centuries before the [First] Vatican Council and only thirty years after the Diet of Augsburg. And just as his views on the Papacy as the instrument of Catholic unity lacked the precision so natural to us, so also and with more disastrous results he labored under a vast delusion as to the whole nature of Protestantism and of the forces that were driving it. In this latter respect he was not alone; Contarini, for instance, had done the same before him.[6] And Lorraine in 1561 had not glimpsed the revelation that was vouchsafed at length even to Contarini at Ratisbon, that "the differences with Protestants were differences about *things*, and that therefore no unification could be found in words. . . ."[7] Lorraine did not realize that what had happened was not a split on any specific problem of theology which could readily be patched up by a little sweet reasonableness on both sides and by a little clever manipulation of formulae, but that it was a complete revamping of man's whole relation to God, a subversive questioning of the very foundation principles of all religious life.

IV

Furthermore, in his attempt at the Colloquy of Poissy to use the Eucharistic doctrine of the Confession of Augsburg as a middle ground on which Catholic and Calvinist could join hands and begin to advance toward understanding, Lorraine showed how little he had profited by the lessons of history. It was precisely on this rock, Catholic Eucharistic faith, that the Conference of Ratisbon, after perilously skirting the cape of Justification, had been wrecked and had gone down in wrangling and abysmal failure. The Eucharist is the *sacramentum unitatis*, Lorraine argued, with a piety quite commendable; but he apparently forgot the concluding verses of the sixth chapter of St. John.[8]

---

6. Cf. Pastor, Vol. XI, pp. 433–4.

7. Ibid, p. 447.

8. EDITOR NOTE: The final verses of John's sixth chapter read:

After this many of his disciples drew back and no longer went about with him. Jesus said to the twelve, "Do you also wish to go away?" Simon Peter answered him, "Lord, to whom shall we go? You have the words of eternal life; and we have believed, and have come to know, that you are the Holy One of God." Jesus answered them, "Did I not choose you, the twelve, and one of you is a devil?" He spoke of Judas the son of Simon Iscariot, for he, one of the twelve, was to betray him (John 6: 66–71, the *New Oxford Annotated Bible*).

At Poissy also, and later by his meetings at Saverne with the Duke of Wurttemberg and his theologians, Lorraine betrayed how hopelessly he had misread the relations between Germany and Geneva. He failed to see that dogmatic rapprochement with the Lutherans was now a chimera. Indeed, it had never been anything else, as the wretched outcome of the Hapsburg experiments in *Konkordia* might well have taught him. And furthermore, even if the impossible could have been brought to pass and Augsburg made the common measure between Geneva and Rome, the situation would not have been appreciably changed. The control and direction of the Reformation had as long ago as 1536 passed from the hands of Lutheran theologians. What they had wounded they could not heal.

At Rome on the other hand all this was clearly understood. Back in 1540, the Papal judgment on the futility of round-table discussions with the Protestants had been distinctly enunciated in the *Consilium* of Cardinals Farnese and Cervini laid before Charles V in an endeavor to dissuade him from holding the Diet of Spires. Typically Roman in its clear-eyed contact with practical reality, this document traces the history of former discussions of this kind. At Augsburg, for example:[9]

> . . . on account of the sinuous evasions of our opponents no conclusion could be reached. . . . They are slippery as eels, and hence no decisive advantage can ever be gained by Catholics from religious debates with them.

The Frankfort negotiations in 1539 had taught a similar lesson:[10]

> . . . at the very outset [of the deliberations] our adversaries again brought up against a snag. It was evident that they had no slightest wish to arrive at a composition of differences, since, having

---

9. *Ehses, Concilium Tridentinum IV, Actorum Pars la, p. 184: . . . proper tortuosos recessus adversariorum nihil concludi potuit . . . . Igitur si cum iis tractandum erit de religione, cum sint tamquam anguillae lubrici, nihil omnino certi in manibus Catholicorum haberi poterit.*
10. *Ibid.: . . . in primo limine iterum adversarii in lapidem impegerunt, ostendentes quam alienum animum habeant a concordia, quippe qui, excusso semel jugo obedientiae, non reformatum Romanum Pontificem sed nullum, non remotos abusus aliquos a Sede Apostolica sed Sedem ipsam destructam velint. Ex quo principio quae potest concordia sperari. . . .?*

once and for all thrown off the yoke of obedience, they now desire not a reformed Pope but no Pope at all, not the extirpation of Papal abuses but of the Papal office itself. Starting from such a premise, can any hope of composing differences be held out. . . ?

Peace had also been sought at Ratisbon and Worms, and with what result?[11]

During the very truce itself, by writings and threats and plots they go on daily seducing men from all ranks of society; since it is easy, once charity has grown cold, to win men over from the stricter to the softer mode of life, wherein continence gives way to low pleasures, and obedience to freedom from restraint.

So the conclusion follows inexorably.[12]

One cannot therefore hope for any stable and enduring peace from these "eirenic conferences," unless indeed one wishes such a peace as would completely undo the prestige of the Apostolic See, trample under foot the Catholic religion, and overturn and destroy all ecclesiastical hierarchy.

These were the Roman ideas. But they lay quite beyond the mental horizon of Lorraine. He could not see, much less face the fact that the disruption of Christian unity, as the past had understood it, was a *fait accompli*. The world could never again be what once it had been. And the time had come when the Church had no other choice but that, after one last sorrowful glance at her lost children, rebellious but beloved still, she should turn her hand to strengthening her defenses against their confirmed contumacy and to preparing the ways of a fuller life for her faithful ones. Lorraine could not grasp this fact, and

---

11. *Ibid.*, p. 185: *Durante ipse pace, tum libris tum minis tum practicis aliquos quotidie seducunt ex omni hominum genere, cum facile sit ubi religio refrixerit, evocare homines e duriori vita ad molliorem, e continenti ad voluptuosam, ex obedientia ad libertatem.*

12. *Nulla igitur spes firmae diuturnaeque pacis ex his amicis tractationibus haberi potest, nisi eam pacem velimus quae et omnem dignitatem Sedis Apostolicae imprimis opprimat, et catholicam religionem conculcet, et omnem ordinem eccelesiasticum confundet ac destruat.*

in his pursuit of the will-o'-the-wisp reunion he had to come into forcible collision with the realism of Pius IV. Of course, granted the legitimacy of the French ideal, the logic of their position was unassailable. If the purpose of a General Council was to be reunion, and not reform and the precision of doctrinal formulae, then the continuation of Trent was certainly unthinkable. The great decrees of its earlier sessions— on the Scriptures, Original Sin, Justification, the Sacraments—had dug an impassable chasm between Rome and the Reformers. The fundamental positions of the Reform had been thoroughly examined and categorically rejected. Consequently, over a continued Trent would brood the forbidding shadow of its own past, a shadow which Lutheran and Calvinist alike would shrink from entering. Consequently again, an entirely new Council must be summoned, in which the dissidents might sit without feeling prejudged and in which the former decrees could be thrown open to "rediscussion" (no one, indeed, was quite so hardy as to say "refashioning").[13]

V

It ought to be added, of course, that the French opposition to the continuation of Trent was not wholly based on their idealistic concept of what the General Council should be and do. For them to accept a continued Trent would have also been to recognize retroactively the ecumenicity of its sessions under Julius III against which Henry II had protested so vigorously, and this was a pie much too humble for the Gallican palate. Again, they were reluctant to imperil their dear Gallican liberties, the defense of which was the whole reason for the presence of French ambassadors at the second period of Trent. An international assembly gathered beyond the Alps and under the domination of a Pope whose centralizing tendencies were well known— what crippling reefs it might put in the sails of His Most Christian indeed, but also most Gallican, Majesty!

Certainly the French had a very definite set of values, religious as well as national, to stress. But in spite of all the force behind their

---

13. It is a nice point whether or not this *retractatio* would have been at all legitimate. The General of the Jesuits, Lainez, (*Disputationes Tridentinae*, ed. Grisar, pp. 8*–10*:1–17; 21–23) argued strenuously and acutely against it, and won his point to the extent of having the phrase *ab integro indicimus* struck out of the Bull of Convocation.

case, supported as it was by the prestige and eloquence of Lorraine, by the diplomatic skill of that "faithful disciple of Machiavelli and past mistress of mendacity,"[14] Catherine de'Medici, and by the at times only half-concealed sympathy of the unstable Emperor Ferdinand I, yet it was from the outset doomed to ultimate failure. All its fine logic was shattered between the anvil of facts and the hammer of an irresistible purpose swung vigorously and at times perhaps rather vengefully by the arm of Pius IV. With a persistence and an optimism in which we must recognize something more than human he beat away; and on January 26, 1562, when the weary Bull "Ad Ecclesiae Regimen" at last had done its work and 109 Fathers assembled in the Seventeenth Session of the *Sacrosancta Tridentina Synodus*, the victory of the Papal ideals was completely assured, and the channels of the Counter Reformation quite finally and unalterably cut.

VI

This was soon apparent. For almost at the same time that Lutherans and Calvinists alike were scornfully rejecting the extremely liberal safe-conducts issued to them by the Council on March 4 and flatly refusing to have anything to do with any Council summoned by a Roman bishop, the Fathers at Trent fell into the long and heated debate on the nature of the episcopal obligation of residence, and thus on their part gave token of where their interests lay. With that debate the inner history of the third period of Trent really began; the threats and jeers of the heretics faded into the distance as the Spirit of God descended upon the Trentino and the Council's energies gradually orientated themselves in accordance with the wishes of the Holy Father toward completing the renovation of the Church's interior discipline and life and toward perfecting the formulation, in terms forever unequivocal, of her ancient beliefs.

On the other hand, in France the inevitable soon came to pass. The Calvinists, who would not be conciliated, finally had to be fought, and amidst the din of civil war, France, too, turned a corner in her history, and entered upon bitter days. Thus do ideals perish when they are divorced from contact with the real, and thus too do they conquer when the blood of actuality is in them.

---

14. The epithets are Pastor's, op. cit. Vol. XVI, p. 159.

The Catholic Position: A Reply

JOHN COURTNEY MURRAY, S.J.

In 1948 *The American Mercury* invited W. Russell Bowie and John Courtney Murray to address "the widening gulf between Protestants and Catholics." In his "Protestant Concern Over Catholicism,"[1] Bowie outlined concerns ranging from Catholic control of hospitals to Catholic doctrine on religious establishment and intolerance. The tone of Murray's response speaks for itself, although it must be remembered that Bowie was also a founder of Protestants and Others United for the Separation of Church and State (a group Murray referred to as "PU"). Murray eventually abandoned this polemical style. Yet the article does highlight his concern that Protestants kept insisting on a theological (i.e., ecclesiological) grounding for intercredal cooperation and for the First Amendment.[2]

I

When I was asked to comment on an article, which I had not yet seen, dealing with Protestant concern about Roman Catholicism, it occurred to me—a wry thought—that I could very well sit down and

---

First published as "The Catholic Position: A Reply in *The American Mercury* 69 (September 1949): 274–83.

1. EDITOR NOTE: See *The American Mercury* 69 (September 1949), 261–73. For Bowie's response to Murray's article, see *The American Mercury* 69 (November 1949), 636–37.

2. EDITOR NOTE: In two earlier works, ("Current Theology: Freedom of Religion" [1945a] and "*Review of Religious Liberty: An Inquiry*, by M. Searle Bates" [1946d], Murray had responded to the much more serious work of M. Searle Bates *Religious Liberty An Inquiry* [New York: International Missionary Council, 1944]). Between the two articles, the tone and centrality of concern with Protestant ecclesiologies developed in the direction of this present article. See also his "Dr. Morrison and the First Amendment" (1948b).

myself write the Protestant article. The formula has become entirely familiar: some introductory pious platitudes, a superficial advertence to the Catholic theological doctrine of the Church, the stock tags from a few Catholic documents on Church and State, the allegations of the "horrible example" (the "Catholic State" on the Spanish model), a selection of the stock incidents purporting to show that the horror begins to dawn in the United States, a rhetorical flight on the unparalleled contributions of Protestantism to the growth of democracy, and the final concluding plea that Catholic and Protestant leaders should sit down together and discuss their differences. This familiar formula allows certain variations in vocabulary and emotional tone; there will, for instance, be a more or less liberal sprinkling of epithetical qualifications of the Catholic Church ("ecclesiastical arrogance," "clerical tyranny," etc.), and a more or less indignant arraignment of the Catholic Church for the ultimate immorality—the quest of power for the sake of power. Finally, Protestant writers always throw in the two distinctions that are classic in the Communist polemic against the Catholic Church: first between Catholicism as a faith and as an institution; secondly, between the Catholic laity and the Catholic hierarchy.

Dean Bowie faithfully follows the familiar formula, with a literary accent that is, of course, quite Union Theological Seminary rather than Southern Baptist or Boston Methodist.

In my comments I have been asked to be "specific." It will be a bit difficult, given the sweep of some of Dean Bowie's generalizations, which could only be met with statements of similar sweep. He asserts, for instance, that it was the Protestant majority which founded this nation that "has given to it its particular genius of liberty." To this the only brief answer is to say: Historical nonsense. Again, he asserts that the Church of Christ is "that larger and unstereotyped fellowship of the spirit which includes Christians of different names." To this one can only reply: Theological nonsense. Again, he asserts that "the dignity of all human souls and . . . liberty of mind and spirit [are] the only guarantee of truth." And to this one must simply answer: Epistemological and ethical nonsense. To go beyond this two-syllabled word would be to write a three-volume work. . . . At all events, I shall be as specific as possible in the circumstances, and on a subject in which ideas and assumptions, rather than what are called "facts," are determinant of conclusions.

I am in agreement with Dean Bowie when he says that the issue of Catholic-Protestant relationships should be "clearly faced with no smokescreen of evasive works." And this leads me to suggest that he is using an evasive word when he describes this issue in terms of "tension." In the United States there are indeed tensions, properly so called, in the interracial and economic fields, and between religious and secularist forces, and between Jew and non-Jew. But between Protestants and Catholics we cannot properly speak of "tension." To have a tension, both parties (not one) must be tense, as, for instance, are white and colored in certain sections. But today in the United States, and elsewhere, Catholicism is not tense, not polarized against Protestantism. In fact, every intelligent Catholic I know would agree that, in the contemporary spiritual state of the world, a polemic against Protestantism is practically an irrelevance, except insofar as this or that Protestant position manifests an alliance with secularist tendencies. Between Catholicism and secularism one may indeed speak of a proper "tension"; but if Protestantism is caught in it, the reason is that it has itself entered the field between two poles.

One would therefore be less evasive if one said that what is happening today is simply another resurgence of the anti-Catholic feeling on the part of Protestants which has been a sociological phenomenon in the United States since, and even before, the repeal of the Maryland Act of Toleration. One would be still more forthright if one admitted that this phenomenon is itself the product of a necessity inherent in Protestantism, especially of the American, "left-wing" type. It is not, in fact, possible for Protestantism to situate itself historically, to define itself as a religious system, or to deploy itself as a cultural dynamic except, fundamentally, in terms of opposition to the Catholic Church. What Newman called "the anti-Roman bias" is of its essence. In contrast, an anti-Protestant bias is in no sense of the essence of Catholicism, which does not need to situate or define itself in negative, critical terms—terms of "protest."

Moreover, this anti-Roman bias has always had social repercussions. I do not doubt that individual Protestants would wish it otherwise; the question is whether it can possibly be otherwise. A Protestant minority is by necessity aggressively anti-Catholic, as Pastor Brutsch has said of Spanish Protestantism. A Protestant majority is by necessity oppressively anti-Catholic, as in the First and Second German Reichs and in contemporary Norway and Sweden. Even in the United States the necessity has worked itself out, as readers of Billington's *Protestant Crusade* and Myers' *History of Bigotry in the United States* are aware. And I suppose the necessity will continue to operate.

II

To put the matter, with Christopher Dawson, in psychological terms, it seems that hostility to the Catholic Church is profoundly lodged in the Protestant collective unconscious, in consequence perhaps of some natal trauma. The outbursts are periodic, as in the Colonial period, in the 1830s, after the Civil War, after World War I, and most recently in the last five years or so. Each has had its special social context and particular quality. Erick von Kühnelt-Leddihn has suggested that the latest one is a display of "defensive aggressiveness." Actually, in the judgment of Professor Paul Tillich, in today's cultural situation and in the face of the dynamic forces that are shaping it, for good or ill, "Protestantism is merely on the defensive." Inevitably, there is a reaction to this situation. And I suppose it is equally inevitable that the reaction should take the form of what Dr. Bowie rather evasively calls "concern" about Roman Catholicism. For here is the old enemy, at which alone Protestantism knows how to strike. Against other enemies—the real ones today—its arm is somewhat palsied. I say all this simply in the interests of being specific. The thing that needs specifically to be understood about Protestant "concern" is its profoundest motivation. And nothing is gained by being evasive on this point.

My second specific comment concerns Dr. Bowie's central thesis. It is contained in the sentence he approvingly quotes from Avro Manhattan's book, *The Catholic Church Against the Twentieth Century*, to the effect that "the Catholic Church [is] a ruthless and persistent enemy of our century and of *all* that individuals and nations are laboring and sweating to attain." The italics are mine; they indicate the breath-taking sweep of the thesis. At that, it is but part of the larger, traditional Protestant thesis that the Catholic Church has been the enemy of *every* century since the sixteenth when, on the Protestant account, the centuries began to have a friend (Protestantism) as well as an enemy.

I think it will be agreed that Dr. Bowie has undertaken to prove a good deal. In fact, this thesis would instantly be declared unprovable by any intelligent man of good will who knows our century, and a few other centuries, and who is even slightly acquainted with the religious and social activity of the Catholic Church. To such a man the mere casting up of this resounding thesis will be evidence enough that something besides logic, idea and fact is operating in the mind of its proponents. Such a man will also see the identity between the thesis adopted by Dr. Bowie and the thesis being proclaimed at the moment by Mr. Cepicka in Czechoslovakia. It is likewise the identical thesis recently sustained by Mr. Paul Blanshard, the undiluted secularist who has just been coopted into the ranks of the Fathers of the Protestant Church. (His book, *American Freedom and Catholic Power*, seems to have been published with the silent *Imprimatur* of a multitude of Protestant clergymen; and Dr. Bowie reverently quotes it.)[3]

There is, of course, the difference that, in choosing to be against the Catholic Church, Mr. Cepicka (quite clearly) and Mr. Blanshard (up to a point) know what they are *for*. The former is for a Communist world order; that latter is for the democratic social-welfare State as the single and ultimate vehicle of whatever salvation is available to man—a State within which secularism will be the established religion, publicly professed and supported, with a grant of freedom of private worship and practice to the outworn traditional religions. However, it is not easy to know what Dr. Bowie is for. He does indeed believe three things: "That every soul is accountable to God, that religion can only be real when each man espouses that which he himself believes, and that, in the long run, where there is spiritual independence, truth can be trusted to emerge." But this is not helpfully specific. Every religious man believes the first thing; any rationalist will subscribe to the second; and the third sounds like one of the clichés of nineteenth-century liberalism which I thought we had all seen through by this time. At all events, we know what Dr. Bowie, like Mr. Cepicka and Mr. Blanshard, is against—the Catholic Church. It is, in his view, the enemy of the twentieth century, of the State, of religious and civil liberties, of "civic morale," of democratic culture—in fact, "of all that individuals and nations are laboring and sweating to attain." What are his specific proofs?

III

After what he admits are "general assertions," he says, "let us particularize." Analysis reveals that the particularizations fall under three main heads: the conduct of Catholic teachers in public schools; the Catholic position on government aid to education; and an alleged

---

3. EDITOR NOTE: For Murray's thoughts on Blanshard, see "Review of *American Freedom and Catholic Power*, by Paul Blanshard" (1949h) and "Paul Blanshard and the New Nativism" (1951a).

"attempt to set up a censorship that reaches into the whole field of our public life." This is the sum of his indictment. In the inadequate space remaining let me make some brief and specific comments.

The first statement alleged is by a Catholic moralist, to the effect that when a religious, moral or social problem is being discussed in a public school, a Catholic teacher ought to state his or her position— that of the Catholic Church.[4] So—I inquire inelegantly—what? Are we to suppose that the Catholic teacher could only be a true friend of the twentieth century by keeping his or her mouth shut in those circumstances? And can it be that Dr. Bowie gives Protestant benediction to the "singular phenomenon" pointed out by Professor Frank Gavin of Princeton that "in the modern secular American university [the same goes for the public school] attacks upon religion and its fundamental theses can be delivered and accepted by society without demur, and yet a vigorous defense—in anything like so able a fashion—of the root principle of religion [the same goes for any religious and moral position] immediately arouses opposition and antagonism"? Or is there an action inimical to democracy simply because a *Catholic* position is stated? I suspect that this is it. It is entirely "democratic" for one public school teacher to tell her pupils (with all her teacher-authority): "I am in favor of divorce, euthanasia, birth control, etc." But it is "undemocratic" for another to say: "The Catholic Church is against these things, as forbidden by the natural and divine law—and so am I." This, I take it, is Dr. Bowie's position. To state it is to show its absurdity.

The second count in the indictment concerns the Catholic assertion that the religious school which serves a public purpose is entitled in terms of moral right and political principle to a fair proportion of public support. This is an enormously complicated issue, not to be settled in a sentence. Dr. Bowie settles it in a sentence; he is against having "a divisive religious influence supported by public taxes." In other words, he settles the issue by begging all the leading questions involved in it. I have no space to argue the whole issue here; hence I shall make one point.

---

4. Editor Note: Bowie quoted Francis J. Connell (*Morals in Politics and Professions*) (see W. Russell Bowie, "Protestant Concern Over Catholicism" *The American Mercury* [September 1949], 264). Murray himself tangled with Connell on the religious freedom issue (see "For the Freedom and Transcendence of the Church" [1952b].

Dr. Bowie attempts to force the Catholic position, asserted in the Federal-aid debate, into a pattern conceived by himself, of Catholic aggression. On the contrary, a fair-minded survey of the educational situation would reveal it to be what in fact I know it is—a necessary piece of defensive strategy. From the Protestant and secularist assertion, "You have no right to aid," viewed in the light of the reasons and feelings behind it, it is but a step to the declaration, "You have no right to exist." And powerful forces are urging that the step be taken. Professor Childs of Teachers College was recently their spokesman when he urged obligatory public-school education for all American children, at least for a portion of their school life. (The "at least" is the nose of the camel of secularist Statism in the tent of American education; and aren't Protestants very familiar with what happens to tents when camels' noses get into them?) Mr. Max Lerner was also their spokesman when he said that the Oregon school case decision in 1925, vindicating the right of parents to send their children to a school of their own choosing, was the first step in the wrong direction—the first breach in the wall of separation between State (*i.e.*, education) and church. It is against this parental right that today's educational aggression moves; it is in its defense that the Catholic position is taken. We are indeed aggressively opposed to the idea of the State as the primary educator and to the institution of the single State school. But this is no aggression against religious and civil liberties; it is a rally to their defense. And if we are charged with being in this respect the enemy of the twentieth century, in which the single State school has had, and is having such horrid success, we do not hesitate to plead guilty.

The third main count in the indictment concerns an alleged Catholic attempt at a "censorship" over "the whole field of our public life." Again the sweeping charge ("whole field"). And again the scanty premises—seven incidents or utterances. I cannot deal with them in detail. Let me say, first, that every utterance is taken out of context, and every incident is reported with such a lack of factual detail as to quite misrepresent its significance. For instance, Dr. Bowie cites an article written in *America* in 1928 on boycotting offensive newspapers; this is somehow to prove us the enemy of "free speech." What he fails to note is the significance of the date, 1928. Does he expect his readers to have forgotten that in 1928 the campaign of misrepresentation, calumny and vilification, launched against the Catholic Church because a great American who happened to be a Catholic was seeking the Presidency, was about at its height? (Incidently, would it be ungracious to venture the understatement that the campaign did not proceed without Protestant assistance?) Does Dr. Bowie wish to maintain that this ugly campaign was justified in the name of "free speech"? And what were the Catholics supposed to do—stand smiling at the crossroads while the dirty work went on?

We were angry in 1928, not without reason; the situation was such as to call for means of last resort. And a metaphorical horsewhip was here and there used. (There is something of a tradition that when a man deliberately and continually insults your bride or mother the principle of free speech does not forbid use of a horsewhip.) The facts of 1928 are freely admitted; but when, twenty years later, they are recalled, I should like to see them *all* recalled. If they are, no fair-minded man will draw from them the implications that Catholics are the enemies of free, responsible, democratic discussion of all issues affecting the public weal. We are, if you will, opposed to a poisoning of the public mind by the spread of lies and slander about ourselves or anybody else. But does this fact stigmatize us as enemies of the twentieth century?

IV

Another instance of Dr. Bowie's slapdash reporting is his one-sentence reference to the famous banning of the *Nation*. It is "well known," says he, that Catholic pressure did the trick; you see how Catholics are the enemies of free speech. What does one do with this sort of back-of-me-hand-to-you thing? A one-sentence swipe serves his turn, which is further to fasten the hold of a myth on the public mind. It would take me five pages to marshal the facts and principles relevant to forming a fair judgment on the *Nation* incident. The fair judgment would by no means have the deceitful simplicity of Dr. Bowie's myth; he could trust it not to have the same impact on the public mind. I confess, therefore, that Dr. Bowie has the advantage of me. I must deal in nice conclusions from complex premises of fact and premises; he can use what the logicians call the fallacy of progressive assertion (Say it often enough and everyone will believe you").

The same technique of accusation characterizes his rapid enumeration of other incidents. For instance, certain Protestant and Jewish doctors are dismissed from the staff of private Catholic hospitals for their advocacy of birth control. You see, says Dr. Bowie, how the

Catholic Church is the enemy. (Enemy of what? It's not at all clear; suffice it that we are the enemy.) But what is omitted is any suggestion of a reason why they should *not* have been dismissed. Granted their sincere conviction that birth control is ethically right, what possible moral or legal right have they to practice in a private hospital whose ethical code asserts that it is wrong? or has it somehow got to be undemocratic for a hospital to have an ethical code?

However, enough of all this small stuff. Dr. Bowie is quite aware that these stock-in-trade incidents are completely inadequate to explain what he chooses to call Protestant "concern." Actually, they are to him like the bone or two out of which the Sunday-supplement archaeologist constructs the museum-piece prehistoric monster. Only Dr. Bowie wants to exhibit a monster of the future, not the past. This future monster is, of course, a "Catholic America." And what Dr. Bowie at bottom is saying is this: "A future Catholic America would be exactly like contemporary Catholic Spain. How monstrous! Americans, beware!"

This is the very heart of the Protestant line being plugged today. One cannot, of course, do anything with it in a page. It is always a bit difficult to convince anyone that a bogey-man does not exist. And the difficulty is greater here because (to return to the previous metaphor) Dr. Bowie does indeed have his few scattered bones. He has Cavalli's article,[5] a tag or two from Leo XIII, a proposition from the *Syllabus*, a fragment from a Spanish catechism, etc. What one would have to do, therefore, would be to prove that it is impossible or illegitimate to construct out of them his fearsome monster—a United States of the future that, if inhabited by a Catholic majority, would have the political structure and the mode of religio-social organization visible in contemporary Spain.

If this is what Dr. Bowie would wish me to prove, I quite frankly give up. For one thing it is like being asked, "When are you going to start beating your wife?" For another, as a Catholic theologian who knows a bit about political history, I have more sense than to regard past Catholic documents on Church and State as so many crystal balls

---

5. EDITOR NOTE: Bowie referred to an April 1948 article in *La Civiltà Cattolica*, concerning religious freedom. In it, Cavalli defended the Catholic support of religious freedom where they were minorities, and suppression of Protestant public voice where Catholics were the majority.

in which to discern the exact shape of things to come. Even if one looked at these documents in their entirety and immense number, and not (with Dr. Bowie) at a few splintered fragments, they do not contain political prophecy or a preview of constitutional history. If, for instance, one had attempted in 1076 to explain to Gregory VII the future constitutional concept, "religion of the State," which took shape in the nation-States of post-Reformation Europe, he would have been exceedingly puzzled; for he could not have understood the idea of a "nation-state" or of a "constitution." I am afraid, therefore, that I shall have to leave the crystal-gazing to Dr. Bowie; he seems to be much more authoritative about it than I should care to be. However, if I were to venture a prophesy, it would be that the development of the genuinely Catholic and democratic State will mean the end of the concept, "religion of the State" (on the Spanish or Cavalli model), as the constitutional form in which the doctrinal idea of the "freedom of the Church" has historically found its expression. I could explain this statement in roughly fifty pages.

V

There is another more profound reason for my unwillingness to follow Dr. Bowie onto his unsubstantial ground—the future of the United States Constitution in a hypothetically Catholic America. The reason is that this is not really what "concerns" him—what really gnaws at Protestant religious vitals. I should wish to put the matter delicately because it is a delicate matter. Protestants are not really afraid lest one day they become "second-class" citizens in the United States, as they maintain their coreligionists are in Spain today. This is what the psychologists call a "secondary affect." There is something deeper. They are wounded and angry because the Catholic Church considers Protestantism to be a second-class religion. They are wounded because they are conscious of being first-class people—better, some of them, than their Catholic neighbors. And they are angry at what must be taken by them as a disparagement of something they hold sacred. What they really want, as Dean Bowie implies, is the repudiation by the Catholic Church of "the flat assertion of her sole prerogative" of being the one true Church of Christ. At bottom, they are not seeking official papal assurance that Catholicism will never become in the United States "the religion of the State" in the Spanish sense; they seem to want the Pope himself to take his seat, as an equal among equals, at the table of the World Council of Churches. This, if I understand it, is the heart of the matter—the refusal of the Church to acknowledge the equality of the churches.

Here, however, is the point of irreducible difference. This refusal will continue to be made; for it is the obverse of an affirmation cardinal to Catholic faith. It is quite literally an awful affirmation to make; and for a Catholic to make it with the slightest touch of arrogance would be irreligious in the extreme. However, make it he must, with humility, with the tools of rational reflection and historical investigation, under the illumining influence of God's grace sought by prayer.

And for the rest, there remains a secondary question in another and lower order of ideas and life; I mean that of the equal friendship of men of different faiths in the political order of society. Modern developments have revealed this to be a political question separate from the theological question of the equality of religious faiths in the light of God's revealed law. The political question can be solved affirmatively, with that always limited measure of satisfaction that attends all human solutions. I know that the Catholic can give assurance that, whatever may have been historical situations of fact, there is nothing in any element of Catholic faith that requires the religious dissenter to be accounted a "second class citizen" in a society of Catholics. Reciprocally (to voice at the end a Catholic concern about today's Protestant "concern"), he would wish the assurance that the anti-Roman bias inherent in Protestantism should not issue in pro-secularist attitudes and policies in the civil order that will, he rightfully thinks, result in a society from which religion itself shall have been ruled as irrelevant.

❖   ❖   ❖

A Statement by Fr. Murray

The American Mercury allowed Bowie to respond to Murray's comments. Bowie expressed surprise at the "tone" of Murray's piece, but continued: "The one clear fact which does emerge from [Murray's] words is the admission that the Roman Catholic Church makes the totalitarian claim to be the only church of Christ; and the arrogant corollaries in the wholefield of public affairs which have flowed and do flow from that have already been pointed out."

Apparently most responses to the *Mercury* editorial board ran against Murray. They then gave him the opportunity for the following response.

Sir: In reply to your request for an "over-all comment" on the 52 letters you sent me, let me make four points.

First, controversy is a dreary business and (as several correspondents remarked) largely a profitless one; I had thought to maintain a certain lightness of tone. It was therefore disconcerting to learn that I had been supercilious, sarcastic, arrogant, slippery, disparaging, cavalier, haughty, disdainful, glib, cocksure, tricky, contemptuous, smug (these are some of the epithets with which your correspondents adorn me). Apparently my attempt at lightness misfired rather badly. Only one correspondent seems dimly to have glimpsed the point, when he "wondered" whether my piece "was intended as a rare bit of exceedingly dry humor or . . . as a serious-minded statement." Actually, the whole subject—like life itself—is much too serious to be taken too seriously.

Secondly, I frankly could not manage to take too seriously Dr. Bowie's thesis of "the Catholic peril." I suggested, and am prepared to maintain, that Protestants take it so seriously because of the "anti-Roman bias" inherent in their position. I cannot match their seriousness for a reason suggested in one or other way in the fifteen letters from atheists or secularists. They say in effect, "A plague on both your houses! The future of America belongs to us." One of them asserts that "the influence of American Clergymen (he means both Protestant and Catholic) has sunk almost to the level of astrologers and chiropractors." The contemptuous exaggeration serves to empha-

"A Statement by Fr. Murray," *The American Mercury* 69 (November 1949): 637–39.

size the core of sobering truth in the statement. The peril of "a Catholic America" is a chimera; the real peril is other.

Were I to identify it, I should point of course to Mr. Blanshard. His name, as he himself knows, is Legion; and his creed, as he likewise knows, is shared by millions of Americans. He and they are significant, not because of what they are against (the Catholic church) but because of what they are for. I have elsewhere called it the "New Nativism." Men more learned than Blanshard have given it a philosophical armature which they call evolutionary scientific humanism. Other men more practical than he are endeavoring to give it political expression in what I should call "our Holy Mother the State," almighty (by democratic means, of course), creator of all things visible and invisible, even the dignity of man. Here, I think, is the enemy, all the more dangerous because it comes bringing gifts—gifts that are doubly "Greek." In the presence of this enemy I consider (as I said and still maintain) Catholic-Protestant polemic to be an irrelevance. And this perhaps is why there appeared in my article a note of impatience—a refusal to take the Protestant polemic as seriously as it takes itself. This is not to say that I do not take seriously the dynamism of the polemic—the pervading fear of Catholicism which, my Protestant friends tell me, has gripped the Protestant community. However, here one is dealing with an emotion, not an argument; the problem is not refutation but exorcism. And despite a concern about it, I confess myself at a loss.

Thirdly, the only troubling accusation is that of having been evasive (sophistry and Jesuitical casuistry, some called it), because I said that in the space allotted I could not argue the issue. However, I can only repeat this statement. On the matter of Catholic doctrine with regard to Church-State relationships I flatly refuse to be what is called "simple," because the subject, historically and doctrinally, is enormously complex. Padre Cavalli was "simple," in the article cited by Dr. Bowie; I reject his theory of "unblushing intolerance" as a ruthless simplification that distorts the truth by ignoring the whole political dimensions of the problem. Other Catholic polemists are "simple" when they seem to assert that the whole issue is settled by the axiom, "Error has no rights." I reject this false simplicity; the axiom is at best politically inoperative (it settles nothing about governmental repression of error) and at worst ethically meaningless (it merely asserts that error is error). I likewise reject all simplistic interpretations, whether Catholic or Protestant, of the Syllabus of Errors, which is a notoriously difficult document, and of the utterances of Leo XIII, whose doctrine is greatly complex and delicately adjusted to a special historical context. I reject the simplifications of Protestant polemists who allege the Golden Rule as singly decisive in the whole matter, or who argue that an authoritarian Church cannot be reconciled with a democratic society, or who assert (as indeed do some Catholic apologists) that the constitutional concept, "religion of the State," on the Spanish model, represents a "Catholic ideal," necessarily to be realized by inherent exigence of Catholic faith wherever there is a Catholic majority.

I refuse therefore to "sum it all up in a few words," however much I wish I could! This is not dishonesty, as one correspondent implies, but its exact opposite.

For the rest, if any of your readers wish to see the problem dealt with at length I refer them to three articles of mine in *Theological Studies* (of which I am Editor), for December 1948 (pp. 491–535), June 1949 (pp. 177–234), and September 1949 (pp. 409–32).

Finally, I was dismayed to learn that some readers understood me to be making a personal attack on Dr. Bowie. I profoundly regret this mistaken impression. It seemed to me sufficiently clear from my opening paragraph that I was aiming not at him but beyond him at the whole contemporary Protestant offensive against the Catholic Church. I deplore personal attacks, no matter who makes them. At the same time I maintain the right to deal sharply with an argument. If perhaps any of my language made it too difficult for my readers to make the distinction I myself had made—between a man and his argument—I am sorry.

Hopes and Misgivings for Dialogue

John Courtney Murray, S.J.

In 1961, with the Second Vatican Council on the horizon, *America* elicited eight Protestant and Catholic evaluations of ecumenism. Murray's essay (1961c) was the most skeptical response. Note Murray's insistence on the centrality and value of reason in the two areas that he distinguishes for possible dialogue.

There are two possible areas of dialogue. In the first area the general issue would be the bearing of religious faith on "public affairs" in the widest sense—the matters that concern the commonwealth, whether as problems in public policy or as more theoretical problems in the public philosophy. In the second area the general issue would be the analogous relationship between the religious faiths themselves, to be discerned through direct confrontation on the properly theological level. In both areas there are grave difficulties.

In the second area the major difficulty has long been known. There is not much use in arguing the question of whether Protestant and Catholic hold in common certain articles of the traditional Christian creed, at least in some analogous fashion, when both parties to the dialogue must admit that they differ radically about the meaning of the word with which the traditional creed begins, "Credo," "I believe." On this antecedent issue the two universes of theological discourse part company, each to assume its own irreducibly different style and content. At that, there would be value in having it made clear, in argument, that the two universes do thus differ. This achievement would at least eliminate one of the possible dangers—that of a false irenicism.

Originally published as "Hopes and Misgivings for Dialogue," *America* 104 (January 14, 1961): 459–60.

For the rest, there might be some hope of reciprocally useful confrontation, if the issues on the table concerned biblical themes, to be discussed under strict regard both for their properly exegetical content and for the distinctively biblical mode of conception and statement in which the themes are cast. It is sufficiently evident today that in the field of biblical scholarship the possibilities of agreement between Protestant and Catholic are considerable. The two roads diverge in the yellow wood only when the question rises as to whether it be legitimate to transpose the "functional theology" of Scripture (as it is sometimes called today) into the conciliar "metaphysical" mode of conception and statement.

The Catholic moves easily from the New Testament to Nicaea and Chalcedon, knowing that he has not added to his faith, but only altered and improved his mode of understanding it. To the Protestant, however, Nicaea and Chalcedon are still at bottom "Hellenization," a deformation of the Christian faith itself, whose final mode of statement must always remain scriptural. In this divergence of view the ancient—and to the Catholic—false dilemma, "Holy Writ or Holy Church," makes itself most sharply felt today. At that, there would be value in experiencing, in argument, the sharpness of the divergence.

In the first area of possible dialogue, mentioned above, the difficulties are likewise formidable. One might perhaps best plumb their depths by contrasting, in content and especially in style of construction, all that a Catholic means by a rational ethic and all that a Protestant means by a biblical ethic. The real argument here concerns the value of reason, and its limits, as the force directive of public affairs. The Catholic assumes that "religion," for all its indispensability as the basic energy of civilization, is not a force directive of public affairs, except in so far as its truths and imperatives are transmitted to society and to the state through the medium of the public philosophy that has been elaborated by human reason over centuries of reflection and experience. The Protestant does not seem to share this assumption. Nor does he seem to regard the concept of the public philosophy as even theoretically valid. Thus, in the absence of common premises, dialogue on the deeper aspects of public affairs proves desultory.

Good Pope John:
A Theologian's Tribute

JOHN COURTNEY MURRAY, S.J.

Murray wrote this essay (1963f) in response to Pope John XXIII's death on June 3, 1963. The Second Vatican Council had already met for its first session (October 11–December 8, 1962). After not being invited to the first session, Murray was preparing to serve as a *peritus* (expert) at the second session (September 29–December 4, 1963). The more positive attitude toward ecumenism in this piece contrasts to that in the preceding articles, and its evaluation of John XXIII also advances beyond Murray's earlier troubled response to *Pacem in terris*.

The office of the papacy is the one and only public office that is permanent in history; its occupants are destined to permanent presence in history. No Pope simply makes his private passage through death to his eternal personal reward, as all men must. Every Pope must also make, as few men do, a passage into history, not to become a figure of the past, but to remain a force in the ongoing present, an active participant in the church's permanent presence in the historical process.

One aspect of the abiding historical presence of John XXIII is immediately apparent. He will be present in the further sessions of Vatical Council II. The precise scope of the Council's work still remains to be defined. But in the process of definition, John XXIII will be present as the insight of genius is present in the later minds that strive to factor it out in concepts.

He made the premise of the council plain enough. It is the perennial, if sometimes hidden, premise of all the Church's thinking about herself and about her mission of bringing salvation to men in the moment when they need salvation, which is always today. The Latin

First published as "Good Pope John: A Theologian's Tribute," in *America* 108 (June 15, 1963): 854–55.

maxim of Leo XIII states the premise: *"Vetera novis augere"* ("to make new things grow out of the old things").

John XXIII will be present in the utterance of the "old things" that the Council may say; for in them the collective voice of the centuries will be heard. He will, however, be more intimately present when the "new things" are said, whatever they may be. For even at this too early date, the historian, whose role for the moment is no more than necrological, can readily find the relative clause that states the significant deed: "John was the Pope who started something new."

What the "something" will be has not yet appeared in detail. But the basic component of the new thing has already caught the attention of all the world. He started the bishops talking, not privately to Rome in terms of question and answer, but publicly to one another in a free interchange of argument. He restored Rome to its traditional function, which is to be the apex of doctrinal and disciplinary decision, not the first source of theological thought and pastoral directive. Out of this new thing, which is also very old, there will issue— one is inclined to think—whatever newnesses the Council will bring forth. John XXIII will be in a true sense their author, present in their accomplishment.

One glimpses a future paradox. John XXIII was no great scholar; his purpose was fixed on being the pastor of souls. But he may live in history, not as the "theologian's theologian" (a title that might fall to his predecessor, Pius XII), but as the "theologian's Pope," who affirmed the uses and value of the theological function in the church, at the same time that he asserted the full dignity of the papal office. He raised some questions himself—notably the great, sprawling ecumenical question—to which he returned no definitive answers. He encouraged the raising of other questions, both old and new, both theological and pastoral—and even political. The symbol of him might well be the question mark—surely a unique symbol for a Pope.

He has left the questions behind him. They are a witness to his continuing presence among us, now that he is gone. They cannot be avoided. They are not to be summarily settled. Above all, they are not to find any answer without prior argument, catholic argument. For it remains true that to this sort of argument John XXIII summoned the whole Church—cardinals and bishops, priests and laity, pastors and professors, and not only the learned but also the simple, who are the "greater part of the faithful," today as when St. Thomas so named them.

The theologian's Pope, who listened while the theologians freely talked, had an even keener ear for the voice of the simple faithful, for whom alone the theologian undertakes to speak, and by whom, too he must be understood.

After John XXIII certain things are no longer possible. Chiefly, it is not possible abruptly to impose silence on any of the parties to the talk in the Church concerning old things and new. It is also not possible impatiently to turn away from the voices, within or without the Church, of whom it can now be said that a Pope once listened to them.

The Pope is dead—long live the Pope! The ancient cry of grief and gladness has multiple meaning. At the moment, it voices our sorrow that John XXIII no longer converses among us, listening, speaking. It also voices our joy that he will be long present in our midst, as the very spirit of the new conversation that he started.

The Status of the
Nicene Creed as Dogma

John Courtney Murray, S.J.

In a discussion of the second conciliar text on religious liberty, Murray wrote:

> We are living in an age in which a great ecumenical hope has been born. The goal of Christian unity lies, of course beyond the horizons of our present vision. We do, however, know that the path to that goal can lie only along the road of freedom—social, civil, political and religious freedom. Hence the Church must assist in the work of creating conditions of freedom in human society; this task is integral to the spiritual mission of the Church, which is to be herself the spiritual unity of mankind and to assist all men in finding this unity.[1]

The church's mission entailed a changed attitude on the part of the church. The eventual decree on religious freedom should undertake "to define the attitude that Catholics ought to maintain and exhibit toward their fellow Christians and toward all men. This attitude is based on the Catholic doctrine with regard to the necessary freedom of the act of Christian faith."

In a discussion of the implications of the decree on Ecumenism, he wrote:

> . . . the rules of dialogue must be such that "each can treat with the other on a footing of equality" (n. 9). This reciprocity in the ecumenical dialogue is a matter of love and respect, not only for

---

Originally published as: "The Status of the Nicene Creed as Dogma." *Chicago Studies: An Archdiocesan Review* 5 (Spring 1966): 65–80.

1. Editor Note: "On Religious Liberty" (1963j), p. 704. By Murray's count there were five conciliar texts leading to the final decree (*Dignitatis humanae*). The first two were on hand before Murray's arrival. The third and fourth followed his own line of argument. For a discussion of the texts and the final results, see Richard Regan, S.J., *Conflict and Consensus: Religious Freedom and the Second Vatican Council* (New York: Macmillan, 1967).

the other as a person, but also for the truth as possessed by each, to be understood by both (1966h, "The Issue of Church and State at Vatican Council II," 592).

As to the content of discussions with fellow Christians, Murray's *The Problem of God, Yesterday and Today* laid out his most extended treatment of the development of Christian trinitarian thought, from the biblical witness through the problem of modern, social atheism. The main concern in *The Problem of God* is with atheism, though it may also be read for the Lonergan background of the next article. In this article, Murray places the Catholic manners of preserving and developing faith at the core of ecumenical discussion.

During the course of time, it is true, the Church, guided by the Holy Spirit, comes to understand these truths more perfectly and declares and explains them more explicitly in applying them in the new historical situations which Divine Providence furnishes.

— Cardinal Meyer
Lenten Pastoral on Ecumenism
January 25, 1967

There is a preliminary issue of method. For my part, I do not think it useful, at the outset of ecumenical dialogue, for a Catholic to propose to a Lutheran Catholic questions that emerge from a Catholic theological problematic. The converse likewise holds. Such questions might be considered unanswerable, or possibly peripheral, or even irrelevant. The basic question concerns the very problematic which gives rise to particular questions. In what follows, therefore, I shall attempt to state the major questions which the Catholic theologian puts to himself with regard to the Nicene faith (N and NC)[2] and to indicate the lines of answer.

Historically, this has been the primary question. It still is. In a context dealing in general with the fallacy of archaism, the primary function of the theologian was thus stated by Pius XII:

It is also true that the theologian must constantly return to the sources of divine revelation. It is his function to show how (*qua*

---

2. N: Nicene Creed (325); NC: Nicene-Constantinople Creed (381).

ratione) the truths which are taught by the living magistery are contained in Sacred Scripture and in the divine tradition, be it implicitly or explicitly. Moreover, both of these sources of revealed doctrine contain treasures so varied and so rich that they are in fact inexhaustible. Consequently, the theological sciences are kept forever young by the study of their sacred sources. In contrast, as we know by experience, speculation becomes barren when it neglects an ever more profound investigation of the sacred deposit. For this very reason, however, positive theology, as it is called, may not be equated with merely historical science. The reason is that, together with these sacred sources, God has given to his Church the living magistery in order that the truths which are contained in the deposit of faith only obscurely and in some implicit fashion may be brought to light and formulated. The divine Redeemer entrusted this deposit to the magistery of the Church alone, not to the individual Christian or even to theologians.

When therefore, as it has often happened throughout the ages, the Church exercises this function of hers, whether the exercise be ordinary or extraordinary, it is clear that a full method would be brought into play if what is clear were to be explained by what is obscure. On the contrary, the converse method is plainly imperative. Hence when our predecessor Pius IX taught that the most exalted office of theology is to show how the doctrine defined by the Church is contained in sources, he added, with good reason, "in the very sense in which it was defined" (*Humani generis*, DB 2314).

With regard to Nicaea, the basic relationship between the dogma and the Scriptures appears in Athanasius' famous statement of the councilor intention in his letter, *De decretis nicaenae synodi* (350/351). The original intention had been to adhere to the creedal tradition and therefore to use the "confessional words of Scripture" (n. 19: MPG 25, 448). However, the scriptural words (especially *ek tou patros*) were twisted by the Eusebians to their own sense. Hence "the fathers, perceiving their craft and their impious cunning, were forced to state more distinctly what is meant "from (the) God" and to write that the Son is "from the essence" (*ousias*) of God, in order that 'from (the) God' might not be considered common and equal in the Son and in things originate, but that all other things might be acknowledged as creatures and the Word alone as from the Father" (449).

Similarly, the fathers had wished to adopt the scriptural theme that the Son is "the true power and image of the Father, in all things like (*omoios*) and exactly like (*aparallaktos*) the Father." Again, however, these phrases proved inadequate as the safeguard of scriptural doctrine against the Eusebian evasions. Hence the fathers "were again compelled to gather up the mind (*dianoian*) of the Scriptures and to state and write again more clearly what they had said before, that the Son is consubstantial (*homoousion*) with the Father, in order that they might make clear that the Son is not merely like but is from the Father as the same in likeness (*tauton tê homoiôsei*)" (451). Therefore the anti-Arian formulas of the creed state the "mind" of the Scriptures. Between Scripture and dogma there is an identity of sense. The dogma defines what is revealed in the word of God.

What then is the mind of the Scripture that is identically the mind of Nicaea? Again Athanasius makes the classic statement in his third *Oratio contra Arianos* (356–362, during the Egyptian exile?): "Thus, given that they (Father and Son) are one, and given that the divinity itself is one, the same things are said (in the Scripture) about the Son that are also said about the Father, except that the Son is not said to be Father" (MPG 26, 329). This is the famous Athanasian rule of faith. It is a synthesis of scriptural doctrine; it is likewise a statement of the mind of Nicaea—the sense of *ek tês ousias tou patros* and *homoousion*. The Son is all that the Father is, the one God; but he is not the Father, he is from the Father.

The polemic intention of Nicaea was to outlaw the Arian "impiety" as contrary to the mind of the Scriptures. The doctrinal intention was to make a positive statement of the Christian faith by gathering up the mind of the Scriptures. The Council had to give a positive answer to the Arian question in its first form: "Is the Son Son or a creature?" In response it affirmed the full divinity of the Son, who is God in the fullness of the sense in which the Father is God. It also affirmed the mysterious uniqueness of the origin of the Son; it is as Son that he is "begotten" (*gennetos*), and only in this sense is he originated (*genetos*). Finally, it affirmed the unity of the Godhead in Father and Son. (It did not, however, explicitly specify the nature of this unity. This specification had to wait until the Arian question was asked in its second form, in the late Eunomian phase of the controversy). This threefold positive affirmation was made as a statement of the mind of the Scripture.

Hitherto it has chiefly been a question of the relationship of material identity in content between the Nicene dogma and the Scripture. There is the further question of their formal relationship—the question of Scripture as the norm of the dogma defined by the Council.

It is evident that the Nicene Church considered the relationship between the Scriptures and the magistery to be reciprocated. The word of God in the Scriptures was regarded as the norm of the faith of the Church. Even Arius, and later Eunomius, felt it necessary to appeal to this norm, though their doctrinal systems owed nothing to Scripture. The Arian formulas were judged by this norm and condemned as false. Judged likewise by this norm, the Nicene formulas were put forth as the true faith; this is clear from the Athanasian rule. At the same time, the Nicene Church considered it to be the magisterial function of the Church to interpret the Scriptures and to declare their sense in formulas that were to be accepted by faith on pain of exclusion from the communion of the faithful. The word of God therefore is the norm for the magistery in declaring the faith of the Church. At the same time, the magisterial interpretation of the word of God and its declaration in the word of the Church is normative of the faith of the Church.

This is substantially the theology stated by Pius XII in the citation given above. It may be doubted whether it is possible fully to conceptualize the reciprocal relation between the word of God and the word of the Church, precisely because it is a question of a polar tension. One can at best undertake to give an adequately balanced description of a relationship which, like all relationships, in the end escapes exact definition.

The essential error would be a theological idealism, so called, which would assert that either the individual consciousness of the Christian or the collective consciousness of the Church is the norm of faith; that neither consciousness is bound on the word of God as a norm which confronts it; that the content of belief therefore is derived solely from the inward teaching of the Holy Spirit. The opposite error would be a biblical positivism, which would posit the word of God as "already out there now" and assert that the content of faith is to be derived from it by the methods of rational hermeneutic. Both errors have in common the same vice; each of them in different ways separates the Word of God from the Spirit of God.

Perhaps the analogue for a true understanding of the reciprocal relationship between Scripture and magistery is, in the ultimate instance, the indivisible Trinity itself, in which, as the Athanasian Creed states, there is *nihil prius aut posterius*. Differing in their modes or origin, the Word and the Spirit are absolutely correlative (*simul sunt*). The same correlation exists between Word and Spirit in the history of salvation amid a difference of function. The Word of God, Christ the Son, stands, as it were, over against and above the Church, seated at the Father's right hand as the Lord-of-us. In contrast, the Spirit of God, the Father's Gift to the Church through Christ Jesus, abides hiddenly in the Church (cf. John 14:16) as the Lord-with-us (cf. Acts *fere passim*).

The relationship between Word and Spirit is conveyed by John (cf. 16:13–15) through the image of the relationship between Yahweh and his people—a speaker-hearer relationship (the analogy is deficient but valid). The Word spoke to men from outside them, as it were, in deed and word (cf. John 15:26 "all that I have said to you"). The Word still speaks to the Church through the written word of God which is also somehow outside-of-us, above the Church, like the Word himself, containing a revelation that is at once definitely given to the Church and never fully to be comprehended by the Church. The Spirit in turn, indwelling in the Church, is the true hearer of the Word, as they are the true people of God who faithfully hear his word (cf. Ezekiel; cf. Luke 11:28). He is "the Spirit who is from God," who has been "received" by the people of God, "that we might understand the gifts bestowed on us by God" (1 Cor 2:12). It is the Spirit-with-us who gives understanding of the Word-above-us, both in himself and in the written word which is itself a gift to the Church and not, in the end, a work of the Church. The forbidden thing therefore is to separate Word (or word) and Spirit (or spirit, the charism of the Church) or to confuse them by mistaking their respective functions.

Authority of the Nicene Faith

The authority of N and NC as the rule of faith derives formally from the authority of the magistery of the Church, "whose function it is to judge with regard to the true sense and interpretation of the sacred Scriptures" (Council of Trent, sess. 4, DB 786). This function of judgment is a function of certification. In the case, N and NC, in virtue of the assistance of the Holy Spirit, the true hearer of the word of God, certify as true the three affirmations noted above, together with the fourth in NC (the expansion of the article on the Holy Spirit in N). It is to be noted that, when the affirmations are certified as true, the understanding contained in the affirmations is not certified as adequate.[3]

It is hardly necessary to add that the authority of N and NC does not depend on the fact that the material identity of sense between Scripture and dogma can or cannot be established by the methods of rational hermeneutic. To say this would be to make biblical scholarship the norm of the faith of the Church—*quod absit.* Finally, in accord with what has been said above, the fact that the status of N and NC is dogma formally from the act of the magistery in no wise derogates from the authority of the word of God, the Scriptures, as the source of revelation. Nicaea certified the *homoousion* as a true statement of faith because the Scriptures say of the Son whatever they say of the Father, *excepto Patris nomine.* On the other hand, the word of God, somehow "already out there now," does not certify itself as the word of God. Still less does it wait on scholarship for such certification of its sense as scholarship may provide. Judgments of certainty belong to the magistery. And such judgments are certain because it is true to say of the Church—analogously, of course, and *proportione servata*—what is said of the Spirit himself: "He will not speak on his own authority, but whatever he hears he will speak" (John 16:13).

Immutability of the Nicene Dogma

Immutability, like certainty, attaches to judgments, to affirmations, and to the sense in which the certain judgment or affirmation is made. On the other hand, the immutability of an affirmation, again like its certainty, does not preclude development—that is, fuller understanding—of the sense in which the affirmation is made.

In the first place, therefore, it will be forever immutably true to say that the Son is consubstantial with the Father, that he is all that the Father is, except for the name of Father. Moreover, it will be forever forbidden so to understand the Nicene dogma—so to "interpret" it, so to "develop" its sense—as, in the end, to affirm that the Son is not consubstantial with the Father, not all that the Father is, except for

---

3. EDITOR NOTE: Throughout this argument Murray distinguishes between doctrine as judgment and theology as understanding. For a discussion of this distinction and its role in Murray's later thought, see the Introduction to Part 3.

the name of Father. Finally it will be forever forbidden to say that the Nicene dogma is mutable in the sense that it has or may become irrelevant, of no religious value or interest, no longer intelligible *suo modo* as a formula of faith. No such menace of irrelevancy hangs over the scriptural revelation, that the Son is all that the Father is, except for the name of Father. Similarly no such menace threatens the *homoousion*. The pertinent citation here would be Vatican I, Constitution on Faith, c. 4, "On Faith and Reason" (DB 1800).

In the second place, however, no less pertinent is the canon of Vincent of Lerins, cited in the same chapter, which urges the Christian and the Church to growth in understanding, knowledge, and wisdom *in eodem scilicet dogmate, eodem sensu, eademque sententia*. The historical fact is that the Nicene dogma underwent development.

First the *homoousion* was applied to the Holy Spirit, explicitly by Gregory Nazianzen, later implicitly by Constantinople I, still later commonly. Second, what was only implicit in the original Nicene affirmation about the divine unity came to explicit statement in the latter phase of the Arian controversy. Following on this, the *homoousion* was applied to the Trinity, the *triada homoousion* of Constantinople II (can. I). In the course of this development, the word lost the connotations of "origin from," which it had in the original Nicene text. It came to be simply a statement of the numerical identity of the Three in the one divine substance. In this sense the notion was foundational to the systematic Trinitarian formula first struck off (it seems) by Anselm and later canonized by the Council of Florence, "All things are the one thing, where no opposition of relations intervenes." Every notion acquires fuller meaning when it becomes an organic part of a systematization.

The question, however, may be asked, whether the Nicene dogma admits further development today, whether it can be stated in other categories. The answer is no. Nicaea answered the Arian question, "Is the Son Son or a creature?" The answer was necessarily cast in the categories of the question, God or creature, from the Father as begotten or from the Father as made. There are no other categories in which the answer can be cast. And the question itself, in the categories of its asking, is not time-conditioned, the product of a particular culture; it is perennial, the product of the human mind as such.

Many other questions may indeed be asked about the Son; but they would have to be answered in their own terms, not by a reinterpretation of Nicaea. The Nicene answer to the Nicene question is final and definitive. There is no going beyond it, since it brings the believer to the very edge of the abyss of the mystery of the eternal Son, who is God of God. In this sense, the *homoousion* is a "limit-concept."

Obviously, this is not the place to enter the enormous area of theological development to which Nicaea opened the way. Every mystery of faith creates a problem for the theologian. In this case, the problem inheres in the mysterious affirmation that the Son is "God of God." But if he is God, he exists *a se*; if he is God of God, he exists *ab alio*. A contradiction seems to appear. This is the problem to which Augustine addressed himself and to which Aquinas fashioned the solution, in so far as a solution is available. The key to the solution is the psychological analogy, glimpsed by the intuitive genius of Augustine, formulated by the philosophical intelligence of Aquinas, and—it may be added—re-stated with newly profound understanding by Bernard Lonergan.[4]

The appeal is to human interior intellectual and moral experience, that is, to the experience of the procession of the inner mental word (concept) from the act of understanding (insight) and to the experience of the procession of the act of moral choice (love) from the intellectual estimation and desire of the good. The analogy is metaphysical, because man is the image of God. It is not therefore merely a matter of metaphor. One can be admitted to a measure of analogical, imperfect, obscure understanding of the processions of the Word and the Spirit in the inner trinitarian life of God. All this, of course, is theology, not dogma. The premise of the Augustinian and Thomist theology, however, is the Nicene dogma under its ontological aspect. In certifying the scriptural truth, the dogma also certified that human intelligence under the light of faith can and should go on to an analogical understanding of what God is—the one Being who is subsistent Intelligence—and how God is Triune: God the Father, the God who speaks; God the Son, the Word uttered by the Father, who is begotten

---

4. EDITOR NOTE: As editor of Theological Studies Murray had published, in 1942, Lonergan's dissertation under the title "St. Thomas' Thought on Gratia Operans" (TS 3 (1942): 69–88, 375–402, 533–74). In 1958 Murray led a workshop at the annual Catholic Theological Society of America meeting in which he discussed the implications of Lonergan's *Insight* for an understanding of Trinitarian doctrine. The use of the procession of the inner word from the former and the distinction between naive and critical realism play throughout this article.

because uttered. God the Holy Spirit, procedent from Father and Son as their Love and Gift.

Religious Value of the Nicene Dogma

The dogma was consciously formulated as a test of orthodoxy. As someone has said, it was not a creed for catechumens but for bishops. Here is its first religious value; for orthodoxy is a religious value. This value, however, is extrinsic. The essential inherent value of the dogma lies in its certification of what God is in himself, antecedent to whatever he may be to us. The question, what is God, is not the appropriate subject for idle musing on a summer afternoon. However unanswerable it may be in the end, it is the first and last of all religious questions. Nicaea gave the certified answer—that God is the Father and that the Son is Son. Thus Nicaea also answered the other urgent religious question, whether we are redeemed or not. The premise of its asking can only be the basic Old Testament conviction that only God can redeem us. Nicaea answered by certifying that the Son is God of God; therefore he could save us and he did and does. This is, of course, the soteriological argument so called that was incessantly alleged by the protagonists of the Nicene faith (about the Spirit as well as about the Son). In a word, Nicaea explained what John meant when he said, "God is love" (1 John 4:16).

The Nicene Faith and Human Intelligence

It is presumably too late in the scholarly day to bother discussing the question, whether Nicaea initiated the process of *die Hellenisierung des Glaubens*. The categories of the Nicene argument—God or creature, begotten or made—were not Hellenic but biblical. Moreover, the *homoousion* is not a category at all. A category is an abstract classifying concept which furnishes the essential definition of a number of individual instances The *homoousion*, however, first defined with complete concreteness what the Son is, what only the Son is. Later it defined, again concretely, what the Spirit is. Finally, it defined, still concretely, what the Trinity is—"the one nature or substance (*ousian*), the one power and authority (*exousian*), the consubstantial Trinity, the one divinity to be adored in three subsistences (*upostasesin*) or persons (*prosopôis*)" (Constantinople II).

If there was any "categorizing" here, it was simply the collocation of Father, Son, and Spirit in the order of the Godhead. And "God" is not a category. Finally, the use of the word *homoousion* did

not involve the Church in the endless argument about the metaphysical concept of substance—the concept which contemporary philosophy is desperately struggling to thrust out with a pitchfork, and
which always returns (to paraphrase the Horatian tag: *naturam expelle-*
les furca, tamen usque recurret). The *homoousion* is not a metaphysical
concept. It is a dogmatic coinage whose content is the mind of the
Scripture with regard to what the Son is.

All this, however, only clears the way for the real argument.
Nicaea said the very same thing that the Scriptures had said, but it
certainly did not say it in the same way. The notorious accusation that
the *homoousion* was "unscriptural" did not lack foundation. The first
series of post-Nicene synods, beginning with the Dedication Council
at Antioch in 341, refused to use the word. The second series, beginning with the third synod of Sirmium (357), explicitly forbade its use.
The real issue, however, was not simply one of words. It concerns the
ontological aspect, so called, of the Nicene dogma and the warrant for
making the transition from the scriptural mode of conception and
utterance to a different mode. There are three questions—historical,
dogmatic, theological.

Historically, on the witness of Athanasius, the transition was
made for reasons of polemic necessity. Moreover, the new usage was
defined as an exception, not as an instance of a general principle. The
Nicene fathers would have been enormously astonished, had anyone
told them that they were engaging in the development of doctrine.
This fact, however, is itself not astonishing. In what concerns the process of art, whereby things are made, a man must know what he is
going to do before he does it. In contrast, in what concerns movements of intelligence whereby knowledge is acquired, a man must
first reach the term of the movement—the knowledge itself—before
he can know what the term is, much less understand the process
whereby he reached it. This is why the great issue today—in our case,
the development of trinitarian doctrine—was no issue at all while the
development was going on. This would be true even apart from the
energizing fact of the moment, the rise of historical consciousness and
the blessed decline of "classicism."

Dogmatically, the transition was certified as valid by the authority of the Church as the authentic interpreter of the mind of the Scriptures. The certification falls both on the term of the transition—the
Nicene dogma as a statement of revealed truth—and on the validity
of the mode of the statement.

The theological question is much more difficult. It is not an issue of certainty but of intelligibility. And it is twofold. First, is there an intelligible relationship between the scriptural and the dogmatic modes of conception and utterance which would explain their homogeneity of sense? Second, is the historical process of movement from one to the other intelligible? Evidently, the second question is the more difficult. It raises the issue of the intelligibility of history—and indeed in its most complicated form, which concerns the history of thought.

It is obviously impossible in this paper to explore both of these questions or either of them. It may suffice briefly suggest some considerations relevant to each in turn.

Ontological Aspect of the Nicene Dogma

It was a providential dispensation that Christianity was born in the world of Hebraic culture and grew in the larger world of Hellenistic culture. The providential character of the definition is seen in the fact that in both of these cultures the mythical consciousness, characteristic of the primitive, had been transcended, at least in principle, through a differentiation of the mythical and the intellectual consciousness. The transcendence was, of course, effected in different ways.

In the Hellenic world the mythical consciousness was transcended by virtue of the metaphysical impulse, resultant in the Platonic insight, whereby man was admitted into the world of theory, distinct from the world of community; theory became the norm and measure of man's dramatico-practical life. Contributory also were the scientific impulse, of which Aristotle may here serve as the example, and the humanistic impulse, visible chiefly in the great Greek dramatists and historians. In the Hebraic world, on the other hand, the mythical consciousness was transcended by virtue of the prophetic word of God.[5] The "speaking God" notified himself to the people as their Lord and Creator, he who is with the people, he who is the Holy

---

5. EDITOR NOTE: In this closing discussion, Murray appeals to scriptural texts for their sense of "dogmatic realism." In the *Problem of God* (particularly chapter 1, "The Biblical Problem: The Presence of God,") Murray covered much the same ground, there, however, in terms of the existential awareness of God's action in history (1964c). The two approaches are compatible, though this present argument highlights cognitional stances rather than dramatic historical action.

One. In the conception of Yahweh anthropomorphisms and symbols abounded. There was, however, a true knowledge of God, a profound consciousness of the reality proclaimed in the text of Osee: "I am God and not man" (Os 11:9). There was, consequently, a fuller liberation from the mythical consciousness in religion than was achieved in any other ancient culture.

To be brief, implicit in the Old Testament understanding of the word of God was a certain dogmatic realism. That is, there was the consciousness that the word of God is true and therefore it notifies that which is: God is God and not man. This realism was dogmatic in the sense that it was unreflective, a matter of direct consciousness that went unanalyzed. God was simply believed to be God and not man, and that was an end of the matter. The realism in consequence was only implicit. It was not thematized by explicit distinction between the mythical and the intellectual consciousness. The latter was simply manifested in the act of faith itself.

To be even more brief, the same dogmatic realism was implicit in the New Testament word of God. Thence it carried over into the apostolic kerygma and didache; and thence further into what Origen identified as "the certain line and the manifest rule" of faith, which required that "the preaching of the Church must be adhered to, that which has been handed on (*tradita*) from the apostles through the order of succession and abides in the churches up to the present moment" (*De principiis*, praef., 1,2). Further witness to the realism in the preaching of the Church as in the word of God was, for instance, the exclusion of heretics from communion. Even more striking witness was the witness of the "white-clad army of martyrs" who died, not for myths or ideas or religious experience, but for their adhesion to reality for their faithful affirmation of truths endowed with ontological reference, for their love of him whom they believe to be Lord and Father, who had not spared him who is the Only-begotten but really sent him for man's redemption.

The conclusion here is that the Nicene dogma, under the aspect of its ontological reference, did not represent a leap, as it were, into an intellectual world alien to the Christian message—a leap from religious experience to ontology. The word of God itself, which becomes the apostolic kerygma and then the preaching of the Church, is a matter of true affirmations to which corresponds reality as it is—the reality of God and his saving counsel in man's regard. There is no more "ontology" in the Nicene dogma than there is in the word of God itself. In both there is the same dogmatic realism. It was always implicit in the word of God; it becomes explicit in the Nicene dogma. Therefore the word of the Church is homogeneous in its sense with the word of God. In the dogma there is no new sense, alien and heterogeneous to the sense of the word of God, accruing to the dogma by reason of the transition from the scriptural consideration of the "God who acts" to the dogmatic consideration of the "God who is" (or, in technical terms, from the *prius quoad nos* to the *prius quoad se*, from what is prior in the order of experience to what is prior in the order of being).

Movement From Didache to Dogma

There is no question that Hellenistic culture played a part in the formulation of the consubstantiality of the Son and Spirit. Had there been no Gnostics and Marcionites, no Sabellians, and especially no Arius and Eunomius, there would have been no need to draw up the "bishop's creed." And had it not been for Hellenistic culture, there would have been no Gnostics, Sabellians, Arians. Hellenistic culture, from which these errors derived, was simply the occasion and cause, under the providence of God, which enabled and obliged the Church to render explicit what had always been implicit in the word of God— its ontological aspect, its dogmatic realism.

The long process which led to the explicit realism of the Nicene dogma was dialectical. The whole of the "ante-Nicene problem" so called, consists in the exploration of this dialectic. It will have to suffice here to indicate simply the structure of the dialectic, under omission of citation from ante-Nicene authors which would illustrate its content.

The material principle was the objective set of contradictions, either explicit or implicit, evident in ante-Nicene thought (e.g., in Origen, between his firm adhesion to the affirmations of this rule of faith and the subordinationism in his trinitarian theology, owing to the influence of Middle Platonism). These contradictions were possible and inevitable because the realism of the word of God was merely dogmatic and implicit. It is quite possible for the dogmatic realist, precisely because his position is unreflective, to make true affirmations— in this case, the affirmations contained in the word of God—and then proceed so to explain his affirmations as to contradict their sense, without perceiving the contradiction (as Origen did not).

The dialectical process was the elimination of the contradictions, which required that they first be perceived and made explicit (in this respect, Arius performed the major service by his flat and altogether correct statement of the problem of the Son).

The formal principle of the dialectical process was the thinking subject—or more concretely and historically, the whole series of ante-Nicene thinkers who wrestled with the problem of the Son (now as then, no one man can be the bearer of the process of development of doctrine, which is normally dialectical).

The term of the dialectic was the Nicene dogma, a development of the doctrine in the word of God—the affirmation that the Son is Son (the affirmation long contained in the word of God and in the rule of faith) and the affirmation that the Son is Son because he is from the substance of the Father, consubstantial with the Father, begotten and not made (the development of the rule of faith). From the dogma all the previous contradictions were removed, chiefly Sabellianism and Subordinationism. It had been seen that they were contradictions, incompatible with the word of God which says of the Son all that it says of the Father, except for the name of Father.

This was the term of the dialectic when the process was conducted by intelligence under the light of faith. Another term, however, was possible, and in fact it was reached—the heresy of Arius and Eunomius, for whom the formal principle of the dialectic was human reason alone and for whom therefore its term was the evacuation of the mystery announced in the word of God. It only remains to say that none of the men engaged in the dialectic understood the dialectic in which they were engaged. This, as has been said, is in the nature of an intellectual movement. Its intelligibility, as a movement, is hidden from its participants. But when the Holy Spirit is present in a movement men build better than they know.

A final remark is necessary. It must remain only a remark, since it really begins a whole new subject. Nicaea contains no philosophy and it canonizes no philosophy—no metaphysics or epistemology. Nevertheless, it laid the foundations of a philosophy. It accomplished the definitive transcendence of the mythical consciousness in philosophy and religion. It carried Christian thought beyond a [naive][6] real-

---

6. EDITOR NOTE: The *Chicago Studies* version of this text had the term "critical realism" here. I have substituted the term "naive" to match the contrasting use of "critical realism" in the last sentence of this paragraph. Murray is arguing a realism to biblical language that became critical, but still realism, with Hellenistic thought. This transition in his Trinitarian studies matches a transition from naive to critical realism that he called for in the "Introduction: The Civilization of the Pluralistic Society" of *WHTT* (pp. 5–6). Again we have a cognitional structure common to reasoning in civil society and in the realms of faith.

ism, in which imagination substitutes for intelligence, for which the final categories of understanding are space and time, and in which the real is, in the end, the experience of the real. It also carried Christian thought around, as it were, the sublimities of Platonic idealism, which does not heed the injunction made by the word of God and obeyed by the word of God itself: "Let what you say be simply 'yes' or 'no'" (Matt 5:37). Nicaea made explicit the dogmatic realism implicit in the word of God. By so doing, it laid the foundation of the philosophical movement towards a critical realism, for which that is real which can be intelligently conceived and reasonably affirmed—in which therefore the axiom obtains, *Ens per verum*: I know what is when I affirm what is true.

Our Response to the
Ecumenical Revolution

JOHN COURTNEY MURRAY, S.J.

This article, which was published a few months before Murray's death, brings together his earlier recommendations for public university education with the notion that ecumenical discourse must be explicitly theological. By this time, Murray has admitted that the definition of the church as used by Leo XIII is no longer sufficient to the reality of the Christian church (see "The Issue of Church and State at Vatican Council II" [1966h], 582–83), and has focused on the church's need for ongoing theological reflection (see "A Will to Community" in Part 3).

The ecumenical movement has not only had a genesis; it has also had a palingenesis. It has been twice-born. It was born many decades ago within the Protestant community, out of deep Christian faith, hope, and love, which launched the movement toward Christian unity along the twin roads of "faith and order," "life and work." Recalling the fact, one should not lose the opportunity to render tribute to the men of vision and dedication who brought the movement into being. Recently the movement was born again—in 1964, in consequence of the Vatican Council Decree on Ecumenism, *Unitatis redintegratio*. The movement now has a new scope, a new depth, an added seriousness, in consequence of the Roman Catholic commitment to its furtherance. The fullness and depth of the commitment may best be measured, I think, in terms of the acknowledgment, made in the Decree on Ecumenism and also indicated elsewhere, that properly ecclesial realities, forming part of the history of salvation, exist outside the visible boundaries of the Roman Catholic Church. This acknowledgment

Originally published as "Our Response to the Ecumenical Revolution." *Religious Education* 42 (March–April 1967): 91–92.

was something new. Its theological implications—especially for the very concept of Christian unity itself—are extensive. This, however, is not the place to discourse on them.

It was entirely in the logic of the Decree on Ecumenism—in the logic of its doctrine and also in the logic of the document itself as a historical event—that it should have raised other issues within the Council. Primary in importance, for obvious reasons, both doctrinal and historical, is the relation between Christian and Jew. Hardly less inescapable is the issue of the relations between the Christian Church and the vast world of the religions of the East. Finally, there is the altogether formidable issue of the relation between the Christian and the characteristic phenomenon of modernity, the atheist—whether in his classical or in his more recent Promethean form.

Simply by stating these issues, I am brought to the proposition that I want to present to you, in the belief that it is of importance to the members of the Religious Education Association. However, I must first state the proximate premise of my proposition.

The *premise* was asserted or suggested time and again in the course of the deliberations of Vatican Council II. It is also explicit in the encyclical of Paul VI, *Ecclesiam suam*. It is the affirmation that the proclamation of the Gospel today must be made *from within history, not from above it, and must therefore be made in dialogue*—in dialogue within the Church, among the Christian churches, between the Church and the synagogue, between the People of God and the world which is increasingly choosing to be without God.

The simple *conclusion* from this premise would seem to be that *theological education*, which is the preparation for the proclamation of the Word of God, must likewise take place in dialogue. The necessity of the conclusion would seem to be obvious. The men of my generation have been converts to ecumenism; we were not brought up as ecumenists. Now we have to see to it that theological students are, as it were, born ecumenists. Moreover, even at the moment, not to speak of the past, ecumenism appears as a dimension added to theology from without. We have to see to it that ecumenism becomes a quality inherent in theology, as it is an impulse intrinsic to Christian faith itself. We have to develop a new style of theology and a new style of theologian.

Obviously, theological education in the high sense of the word, which lifts it above the level of sheerly academic learning, must take place at the interior of a religious commitment to a tradition of faith, and should seek to strengthen this commitment. However, the tradition itself will become more vital and relevant, and the commitment to it more personal and profound precisely because it is studied, learned, and lived in dialogue with other traditions and with other men of religious commitment.

It has been argued—most recently and cogently by Mr. Walter Wagoner—that there is no longer any future for the denominational seminary existing in isolation. For the denominational seminary—yes, but not in isolation from a larger center of learning and experience. The future of theological education lies with an ecumenical community of scholars—teachers and students.

Is that the whole of the matter? Hardly. This ecumenical community must somehow become *a presence in the secular university.* The signs of the times call not only for dialogue between Catholic and Protestant, Christian and Jew, but also between the Christian and the secular world. This "world" is made up of many worlds. Among them the secular university occupies a place of central significance, whence its influence radiates into all the other worlds. There must therefore be dialogue with the Academy, with the Republic of Letters, from which religion and theology have much to learn, to which they surely have something to communicate. Along the way of this dialogue one might even look forward to the reconstitution of the medieval *Studium*—to a renewal of that ancient institution in a form adapted to our ecumenical age and to the pluralistic society in which we live.

It has been remarked that the modern world looks much like the medieval world turned inside out. In medieval times the world—the small and circumscribed "inhabited earth" known as the *oikoumeme* was Christian. The secular world existed at the interior of this Christian world, largely in the form of the secular power. Now, however, the world, grown to vastly greater dimensions, is secular. And the religious thing, in all its forms, exists at the interior of this secular world.

This fact of contemporary life was recognized by the Vatican Council II, speaking for the Catholic Church. The fact was not merely accepted as a fact; it was also acknowledged to be in conformity with the right scheme of things. The sacred at the interior of the secular— that is the way things should be. The Christian call is to exist within a world that has "come of age," that is, come to its rightful secularity. This vocation is to be fulfilled by Christian presence in the Secular

City—this we all recognize today. But the vocation has a farther reach, toward presence in the secular university.

This presence is becoming a possibility today, as it was not a few years ago. The ecumenical dialogue has caught the attention of the world of secular learning, as it has also caught the attention of the civic community. Obviously, the ecumenical movement is much more than a movement of ideas, but it is also that. Hence it is a valid object of university interest. High talk about religion, not only as a human concern but as a body of knowledge capable of validating itself in its own terms, is becoming a possibility within the Academy. Thus one might hope that the ecumenical movement could serve to give some new quality and substance to the university enterprise, at the same time that the university could serve to sustain and invigorate the ecumenical movement.

If this development were to occur, the consequences would be manifold. It might help for instance, to rescue the ecumenical movement from a *cul de sac* into which it might possibly head. I mean the trap of being simply an affair of the churches, or if you will, an affair of the church and synagogue. The ecumenical movement would be untrue to itself, if it were to fall into this trap. Certainly we Christians are not called simply to witness to one another. The call is to witness to the world—to all the worlds of human life, in the appropriate form which witness should take within each of them. There is a form appropriate to the university, namely, theological scholarship imbued with the ecumenical spirit. It has nothing to do with propaganda; it is directed to intelligence and it looks simply to create understanding. What is more, this form of scholarly theological witness cannot take place except in dialogue with the university, wherein the *genius loci* is the pursuit of truth.

I suggest that our response to the challenge of ecumenism must include a willingness to move forward into this new area of dialogue.

Appendix: Toledo Talk

John Courtney Murray, S.J.

On May 5, 1967, Murray delivered a talk in which he explored the changes brought on by the Second Vatican Council. Among other issues, he discussed the majority and minority reports of the Vatican commission that Paul VI had asked to study the question of artificial birth control. The most complete report of the talk was published as "Birth Control Report 'Leak' Called an Act of Genius," *The Catholic Chronicle* (May 5, 1967) pp. 1, 5. This, and all other reports focused on the birth control issue, reducing the other issues and the general orientation of the talk to secondary positions. Although a note in the Murray Archives claims that an audio tape of the talk exists, no tapes, notes, or manuscripts have surfaced. This article is compiled from all available newspaper sources.[1]

I have tried to restore, as suggested by internal evidence, the general structure of Murray's argument. The portions that directly quote Murray are permeated by Lonergan's contrast between historical and classical consciousness.[2] Even more remarkable, however, the original reporter, in the indirect discourse sections, preserved much of Lonergan terminology that must have been in the original address. That terminology had to be alien to the reporter's normal style. I have left that original language intact, neither developing nor weakening it.

---

1. EDITOR NOTE: Other available reports of the talk appear dependent on the *Catholic Chronicle* story. See "Murray Says Church Was Too Sure," *The National Catholic Reporter* (May 17, 1967), p. 3; *The Tablet* (May 20, 1967), pp. 66–567; *The Advocate* (May 26, 1967).

2. EDITOR NOTE: Several months earlier Murray received a draft of what eventually became Lonergan's "The Transition from a Classicist World View to Historical-Mindedness" (*A Second Collection*, edited by William F.J. Ryan, S.J. and Bernard J. Tyrrell, S.J. (Philadelphia: The Westminster Press, 1974), 1–10.) That paper was presented to the Canon Law Society of America in 1966 and first published in 1967.

Jesuit Father John Courtney Murray, a Vatican II expert, spoke to an ecumenical group of priests and ministers concerning the external and internal problems facing the church. Many of these problems, while not new, must be faced by the church in new ways, since "the Council moved the church squarely into the world of history," ending the church's attempt, over several centuries, to operate as if it were outside history. Within history the church faces three major external problems.

First, the church has had to adjust to the now two-century old transition of civil society conceived as sacred to a society that is secular. *The Declaration on Religious Liberty* and *The Church in the Modern World* defined the church with its own proper transcendence and the world with its own proper secular autonomy. With the recognition of this sacred/secular distinction, the problem now is how to reunite the sacred and the secular, without collapsing one into the other.

Second, the church—in acknowledging a rightfully secular society—also faces a world that is an unbelieving world. "The problem of the world today is the problem of God. . . . The Church is not the focus of interest today—but the issues of God, faith, revelation, belief, unbelief." This shift of focus from the church as institution to the truths of Christian faith is recently new for both the church and the world.

Third, there is the deep cultural crisis caused by the transition from "classical to historical consciousness." To the classicist, he said, truth is so objective that it can exist apart from anyone's possession of it. It is Platonic truth—with "ideas always up there in Heaven." In this view of truth, there is no such thing as an historical dimension to truth, no development, no growth.

By contrast, "historical consciousness" holds to a certain notion of truth that, while recognizing that it is objective, yet also insists that truth must be intelligently conceived and rationally affirmed.

"Truth is an affair of history and is affected by all the relativities of history. Truth is an affair of the human subject. Truth, therefore, is an affair of experience. The question of truth as possessed brings into the whole problem the question of the human person who must personally possess truth.

"And in the perception of truth the human intelligence has a function that must be conceived as being creative. This is the truth in the philosophical error of idealism. Somehow the mind creates truth in a sense. There is a truth here as there is in all errors."

Another characteristic of classicism, said Father Murray, is the cult of certainty which developed especially in the Cartesian era, resulting in an excessive development of the notion of papal infallibility.

Father Murray explained that historical consciousness assigns the primacy not to certainty but to understanding. The immediate criteria governing historical consciousness, then, are not certainty and doubt, but rather adequacy and inadequacy.

"The war here is not against doubt. The war here is against the incomplete, the partial, the unilateral, the simplistic.

"Today there is a distrust of the ready-made certainties, of the certainty that is too easy. In fact there is a distrust of certainty itself. And this crisis of certainty is related to the crisis of authority which is or has been the source of certainty. If you bring certainty into question, you also bring authority into question."

As a community now consciously situated within history, the church faces internal difficulties that in part reflect those external problems. Father Murray suggested that the present manner in which the church is dealing with the birth control issue clearly exemplifies those internal difficulties. In his judgment the publication of the majority and minority opinions of the members of the papal birth commission was "an act of genius." He even ventured that if the leak was deliberate, he would be inclined to attribute it to Pope Paul himself.

He discussed birth control as one of three areas that used to be of the most unquestioned certainty. (The others are the liturgy and obedience-authority.)

Teaching on birth control, said Father Murray, had been "very clear and very certain." The trouble, he said, was that "The church reached for too much certainty too soon, it went too far. Certainty was reached in the absence of any adequate understanding of marriage. This, many would hold—I would hold—is today no longer theologically tenable. . . . It is also psychologically untenable.

"We are seeing a new systemization. The other was only theology; it was not dogma. It was system, not faith.

"In the absence of an adequate understanding of marriage, there was an inadequate understanding of the marital act and an inadequate understanding of the total situation of the problem of reproduction, especially in its demographic dimension. Also there was an inadequate understanding of the authority of the church as exercised in the field of natural morality.

"There was a little too much exuberance for a Church whose dynamism was not within the Christian faith itself but in the classicism which had infiltrated into Christian faith. In itself it is not Christian but Platonic."

This is evident, said Father Murray, in the majority and the minority opinions.

He said the majority clearly was in quest of new understanding that would be in continuity with the past and representative of progress.

For the minority, the issue is not one of control but certainty. Those of the minority view, he said, are still classicists in search of certainty, raising an issue of authority related to certainty. They transferred the problem of birth control from moral grounds—not arguing about birth control at all—to argue about certainty and the authority of the Church. These are two different problems—related but to be distinguished.

Father Murray admitted that one must distinguish between the moral norm itself governing marital intercourse and adherence to the norm. To find out about adherence to the norm is a sociological problem. Surveys can be made, he said, to find out how many are not living up to the norms of *Casti Conubii* (Pius XI, 1930).

However, noting that the question of the moral norm itself is a theological problem, Father Murray also suggested that the social might have something to offer to our understanding of the theological.

"Perhaps the sense of the social is reshaping the norm itself. . . . They are forcing us, the official Church, to reflect on the authority that was in the former norm."

At worst, he said, what's going on is that the historical consciousness of the faithful is expressing itself rather confusedly, not seeing what it is in the technical sense. But it is the mentality of the moment that the majority have grasped, and the minority apparently have not.

"It is very difficult for the classicist to accept what is going on— is it only because he doesn't like what is going on or thinks it wrong?

"He does not understand the mentality behind it and the fact that this mentality, whether you like it or not, is at the moment the great dynamic historical force. It is a good force—a force for good. Yet like all forces it is somewhat ambivalent and can do a fair amount of harm."

Further, Father Murray said that the discussion about birth control is not the only issue caught in transition from "classicism to historical consciousness."

The big divider between the two mentalities was, he said, the modernist crisis—between faith and history, the absolute and the relative, Christianity as doctrine and Christianity as event.

Father Murray said the council fathers rejected classicism and embraced historical consciousness.

"They conceived the renewal of the Church to mean a turn to the sources of the life of the Church—the sources in history which are also trans-historical; the event of Christ and the Word of Christ in the Gospel. This is where the renewal must start."

This reform, he said, is taking place also in the realms of theology or faith or ecclesiastical structure. Theology itself is caught in a crisis of understanding.

"The traditional affirmations of faith are still being made. The question is whether or not their historical content is adequate, whether we have had an adequate understanding of faith. This is what the theological fraternity is up to today.

"Questions about almost everything—about original sin, the order of grace and its relation to the visible Church, about the Eucharist as sacrament and sacrifice, about the notion of sacrament itself, about trans-transubstantiation, about the Church, about the Trinity, above all about God.

"The question," Father Murray continued, "is not, is the Catholic Church the one true Church. The answer is yes, that is our belief. The question is what is the church, what is the true church which is one.

"The theological way of putting the question today is not how certain are we. The question today is how much have we really understood, how much more is there to be understood in the traditional affirmations of faith, and, above all, how are these traditional affirmations to be related to my human interest and experience—the relevance.

"The question is not how certain is that truth out there. The question is what does it mean, and above all, what does it mean to me."

Father Murray said the Church is newly aware of the situation it always has been in, that it must exist at the interior of the world, of history.

To do this, however, means that the Church must exist in a state of multiple revolutions. History is at a turning point where new directions have to be seen and followed. Human consciousness is deeply troubled, especially in the case of the young.

The council's insistence that the Church see itself in history was consistent with Pope John. Pope John's idea, he noted, was to get into history and guide it in terms of discernment of what is going on, what is right and true and good in what is going on, and of how to get everyone into this current—what is salutary for the Church, the world, for all.

Pope Paul, he said, sees real values in both the old classicism and the historical consciousness. Apparently still attractive to Pope Paul is the classicist view of being able to stand outside the world and somehow exercise control over history, to guide it according to pre-given concepts.

"Paul cannot quite make up his mind which to do—stand outside, come down inside. And who would know?"

What is the source of reform that is sweeping the church, as well as the world? It has changed, said Father Murray. He appealed to a distinction, made by sociologists, which he believes to have theological validity—a distinction between religious and ecclesiastical reform.

Religious reform has to do with values, norms, goals, types of experience. It is rather personal and interpersonal. Ecclesiastical reform has to do with doctrinal formulations, structures, procedures. The council was watchful of both types, but the dynamism of each is different.

"The dynamism of Christian reform is the Christian himself—the Christian and the Christian community, ongoing Christian experience. This reform takes place from the bottom up. The source of ecclesiastical reform for us Catholics is authority, its sanctions and changes in structure. . . . This type proceeds from the top down. One might entertain that these two forms should go hand in hand. And we might assume that the ecclesiastical reform ought to be in charge of the religious. I am afraid this assumption just really is not true.

"First, the pace is very distinctly different—the religious reform goes very rapidly, the ecclesiastical very slowly. Bureaucracies do not move rapidly. They are not supposed to. I do not indict them for not doing that, but you see what the result has been. The religious reform advances with great rapidity—the reform in attitudes and values and norms and what not. The existing structures cease to be functional at all. They seem to the Christian community, especially the avant-garde, to be quite irrelevant."

He illustrated this development in terms of the rapid changes overtaking the church's liturgical life. Without inferring a negative evaluation of the church's preconciliar liturgical practices, he said, one could fairly claim that a principal motivation for Mass attendance included the obligation imposed by law on Catholics of weekly attendance. Also demanded was some mental attention to what was going on, although that attention was passive and highly individual.

Today, especially for youth, Mass is a function of community and the emphasis is on creative participation. Today, there is new interest in understanding the Eucharist, so that one does not go to Mass without going to Communion, essentially a community act. The liturgical movement is now primarily a religious movement, only secondarily an ecclesiastical movement.

Father Murray said one thing is clear in the distinction between religious reform and ecclesiastical reform—the religious changes that are going on are beyond the control and even the responsibility of the Chancery.

"I think this is recognized by bishops, pastors, priests, all of us. We know that you cannot sit on the lid. You cannot stop these things even if you tried.

"The dynamism, the quest for Christian experience, is remote from our control. These things are going on and will go on and we recognize it. At the same time the chancery does not recognize it because the chancery is not the agent of change. The church stands for stability and continuity. It does not stand for alteration and progress. It is not supposed to."

Father Murray said it is not the function of a bureaucracy to change itself but that institutions are only changed in one of two ways—pressure from without or by some sort of dialectical process from within. It is hoped that the institutional changes can be brought about through an internal dialectic process, which by another name is dialogue.

"It is certainly not that one or other side should try to win—the Church beat the people or the people beat the church. That is silly! What is needed is a work of discernment and reconciliation.

"It is up to both people and chancery to do the work of discernment and reconciliation . . . to do the work of discernment on what is going on and try to cooperate to bring as many as possible of the people into the good things and the right things and the true things that are going on. There will always be a fringe on both sides—right and left. But try to get as many as possible into the mainstream of the life of the Church today."

This, said Father Murray, was the mind of Pope Paul in a recent statement on liturgical extremism. He was saying: "Why can we not get into the middle where the real action is supposed to go on?"

The worst thing that could happen, said Father Murray, would be to deny there are conflicts. There must be recognition that conflicts are inevitable. The best thing, as sociologists say, would be to institutionalize the conflicts, set up forums in which conversation can take place. "Let us have confrontation on both sides."

He said that bishops have yet to learn how to talk with priests, priests with each other, Catholic Christians with other Christian brethren. Dialogue is in its infancy.

"[Dialogue] would be at once to a religious people the agent and mechanism—what all we Christians always wanted to do—to maintain our continuity with the past and at the same time know we must progress in the new world, the only world we have."

Works by
John Courtney Murray, S.J.

The following bibliography of Murray's works is arranged chronologically, with items of the same year marked with lettered extensions. I have kept the date-letter references consistent with the bibliographies of Murray, 1993, *Religious Liberty*. Two further items have surfaced since the compilation of that bibliography. They are here properly listed according to their publication year, but their letter positioning is out of alphabetical sequence for that year. All Murray Archive material can be found in Special Collections, Lauinger Library, Georgetown University.

1929. "Governmental Supervision of Schools in the Philippines." *Woodstock Letters* 58: 48–53.

1932. "Crisis in the History of Trent." *Thought* 7 (December): 463–73.

1937. *Matthias Scheeben on Faith: The Doctrinal Dissertation of John Courtney Murray*, edited by D. Thomas Hughson, S.J. Vol 29, Toronto Studies in Theology. Lewiston, NY: The Edwin Mellen Press, 1987.

1938. "Taken from Among Men." *Jesuit Seminary News* 12 (June): 3–5.

1940a. "The Construction of a Christian Culture: I. Portrait of a Christian; II. Personality and the Community; III. The Humanism of God." Three talks given in February 1940 at St. Joseph's College. Murray Archives, file 6–422.

1940b. "Necessary Adjustments to Overcoming Practical Difficulties." In *Man and Modern Secularism: Essays on the Conflict of the Two Cultures*, edited by the National Catholic Alumni Federation, pp. 152–57. New York: National Catholic Alumni Federation.

1941a. "The Christian Fulfillment." Murray Archives, file 5–577.

1941b. "Toward a Christian Humanism: Aspects of the Theology of Education." In *A Philosophical Symposium on American Catholic Education*, edited by H. Guthrie and G. Walsh, pp. 106–15. New York: Fordham University Press. Presented at the 17th Annual Convention of the Jesuit Philosophical Association of the Eastern States, September 4–6, 1940.

1942a. "Book Reviews: New Periodicals." *Theological Studies* 3 (May): 290–93.

1942b. "Current Theology: Christian Co-operation." *Theological Studies* 3 (September): 413–31.

1942c. Review of *The Layman's Call*, by William R. O'Connor. *Theological Studies* 3 (December): 608–10.

1943a. "Current Theology: Co-operation: Some Further Views." *Theological Studies* 4 (March): 100–111.

1943b. "Current Theology: Intercredal Co-operation: Its Theory and Its Organization." *Theological Studies* 4 (June): 257–86. Also published as *Intercredal Co-operation: Principles*. Washington DC: Catholic Association for International Peace, 1943.

1943c. "Descriptive Notes." *Theological Studies* 4 (September): 466.

1943d. Review of *Principles for Peace: Selections from Papal Documents*, edited by Harry C. Koenig. *Theological Studies* 4 (December): 634–38.

1943e. "To the Editor." *Theological Studies* 4 (September): 472–74.

1944a. "The Juridical Organization of the International Community." *The New York Law Journal* (October 9): 813–14. A sermon given at a Red Mass at St. Andrew. Also published as "World Order and Moral Law." *Thought* 19 (December 1944): 581–86.

1944b. *The Pattern for Peace and the Papal Peace Program.* Washington, DC and NY: Paulist Press, Pamphlet from the Catholic Association for International Peace. Another version of this article, with some alterations, can be found as "Co-operation Among All Men of Good Will," Murray Archives, file 12–764. This latter was in turn published as "La Cooperacion Interconfessional Para la Pax," *Verbum* [Guatemala] (January 9, 1945), and in *Vida: Revista de Orientacion* 7 (1944): 757–71.

1944c. "Toward a Theology for the Layman: The Pedagogical Problem." *Theological Studies* 5 (September): 340–76.

1944d. "Toward a Theology for the Layman: The Problem of Its Finality." *Theological Studies* 5 (March): 43–75. This and the last article appeared in a condensed form in "Toward a Theology for the Layman," *Jesuit Educational Quarterly* 11, no. 4 (March): 221–28.

1944e. "Woodstock Wisdom." *Woodstock Letters* 73 (December): 280–84.

1945a. "Current Theology: Freedom of Religion." *Theological Studies* 6 (March): 85–113.

1945b. "Freedom of Religion, I: The Ethical Problem." *Theological Studies* 6 (June 1945): 229–86. This was much later translated and published in *Relations* [Montréal] 22 (Mai 1962): 118–20; (Juin 1962): 151–53; (Juillet 1962):179–82; (Août 1962):207–10; (Septembre 1962): 234–38; (Novembre 1962): 301–04; (Décembre 1962): 33–35; 23 (Janvier 1962): 2–4. A further article, "Le droit à l'incroyance" (Avril 1962): 91–92, was part of this French series but not part of 1945b.

1945c. "God's Word and Its Realization." *America* 74 (December 8, supplement): xix–xxi.

1945d. "Memorandum" and April 30, 1945 letter to Zacheus Maher (Jesuit American Superior) on the racial issue at St. Louis University. Murray Archives, file 8–585.

1945e. "Notes on the Theory of Religious Liberty." April 1945. Memo to Archbishop Mooney, Murray Archives, file 7–555.

1945f. "On the Problem of Co-operation: Some Clarifications: Reply to Father P. H. Furfey." *American Ecclesiastical Review* 112 (March): 194–214.

1945g. "The Real Woman Today." *America* 74 (November 3): 122–24.

1946a. "How Liberal Is Liberalism?" *America* 75 (April 6): 6–7.

1946b. "Operation University." *America* 75 (April 13): 28–29.

1946c. "The Papal Allocution: Christmas." *America* 74 (January 5): 370–71.

1946d. Review of *Religious Liberty: An Inquiry,* by M. Searle Bates. *Theological Studies* 7 (March): 151–63.

1946e. "Separation of Church and State." *America* 76 (December 7): 261–63.

1947a. "Admonition and Grace." In *The Fathers of the Church: Writings of St. Augustine II,* pp. 239–305. New York: Cima, 1947.

1947b. "The Court Upholds Religious Freedom." *America* 76 (March 8): 628–30.

1947c. "Separation of Church and State: True and False Concepts." *America* 76 (February 15): 541–45.

1948a. "Belief in Life." Three talks given on "The Catholic Hour" and published in pamphlet form with the specific titles: *The Assault of Fear,* March 7, 1948; *The Desert and the Garden,* March 14, 1948; and *The Supreme Sorrow,* March 21, 1948. Washington: DC: National Council of Catholic Men. Also published in *Catholic Mind* 80 (April 1982): 2–7.

1948b. "Dr. Morrison and the First Amendment." *America* 78 (March 6): 627–29; (March 20): 683–86.

1948c. "Government Repression of Heresy." *Proceedings of the Third Annual Convention of the Catholic Theological Society of America Chicago,* pp. 26–98. Bronx, NY: Catholic Theological Society of America. This article and 1948g, 1949e, and 1951c were then collected as "A Church-State Anthology: The Work of Fr. Murray" in *Thought* 27 (1952): 6–43, then translated and reprinted as "Kirche und Demokratie" in *Dokumente: Zeitschrift für übernationale Zusammenarbeit* 12 (February 1956): 9–16.

1948d. "On the Most Blessed Trinity." In *The Summa Theologica of St. Thomas.* Vol. III, pp. 3153–63. New York: Benziger Brothers.

1948e. "Religious Liberty: The Concern of All." *America* 78 (February 7): 513–16.

1948f. "The Role of Faith in the Renovation of the World." *The Messenger of the Sacred Heart* 83 (March): 15–17.

1948g. "The Roman Catholic Church." *The Annals of the American Academy of Political and Social Science* 256 (March): 36–42. Also published as "What Does the Catholic Church Want?" *Catholic Digest* 13 (December 1948): 51–53 (abbreviated); and "The Roman Catholic Church," *Catholic Mind* 46 (September 1984): 580–88.

1948h. "The Root of Faith: The Doctrine of M. J. Scheeben." *Theological Studies* 9 (March): 20–46.

1948i. "St. Robert Bellarmine on the Indirect Power." *Theological Studies* 9 (December): 491–535. This article and 1948c, 1949b, and 1951b were translated and reprinted as "Kirche und Demokratie," *Dokumente: Zeitschrift für übernationale Zusammenarbeit* 12 (February 1956): 9–16.

1949a. "The Catholic Position: A Reply." *American Mercury* 69 (September): 274–83; (November): 637–39.

1949b. "Contemporary Orientations of Catholic Thought on Church and State in the Light of History." *Theological Studies* 10 (June): 177–234. Also published in *Cross Currents* (Fall 1951): 15–55. This article and 1948c, 1948h, and 1951b were translated and reprinted as "Kirche und Demokratie," *Dokumente: Zeitschrift für übernationale Zusammenarbeit* 12 (February 1956): 9–16.

1949c. "Current Theology: On Religious Freedom." *Theological Studies* 10 (September): 409–32.

1949d. "Law or Prepossessions." *Law and Contemporary Problems* 14 (Winter): 23–43. Also published in *Essays in Constitutional Law*, edited by R. G. McCloskey (New York: Alfred A. Knopf, 1957), pp. 316–47.

1949e. "On the Idea of a College Religion Course." *Jesuit Educational Quarterly* (October): 79–86.

1949f. "On the Necessity for Not Believing: A Roman Catholic Interpretation." *The Yale Scientific Magazine* 23, no. 5 (February): 11, 12, 22, 30, 32, 34.

1949g. "Reversing the Secularist Drift." *Thought* 24 (March): 36–46.

1949h. Review of *American Freedom and Catholic Power*, by Paul Blanshard. *The Catholic World* 169 (June 1949): 233–34.

1949i. Review of *Free Speech in Its Relation to Self-Government*, by Alexander Meiklejohn." *Georgetown Law Journal* 37 (May): 654–62.

1950a. "The Natural Law." In *Great Expressions of Human Rights*, edited by Robert M. MacIver, pp. 69–104. New York: Harper. Also published as "Natural Law and the Public Consensus," in *Natural Law and Modern Society*, edited by John Cogley (Cleveland, Ohio: World Publishing, 1962; reprint Freeport, NY: Books for Libraries Press, 1971), pp. 48–81. Forms the concluding chapter, "The Doctrine Lives: The Eternal Return of the Natural Law," of *WHTT*, pp. 295–336, with only slight revisions.

1950b. "One Work of the One Church." *The Missionary Union of the Clergy Bulletin* 14 (March): 5–11. Also published in *Catholic Mind* 48 (June 1950): 358–64.

1951a. "Paul Blanshard and the New Nativism." *The Month* New Series 5 (April): 214–25.

1951b. "The Problem of 'The Religion of the State.'" *The American Ecclesiastical Review* 124 (May): 327–52. Also published as "The Problem of State

Religion," *Theological Studies* 12 (June 1951): 155–78. This article and 1948c, 1948h, and 1949b were translated and reprinted as "Kirche und Demokratie," *Dokumente: Zeitschrift für übernationale Zusammenarbeit* 12 (February 1956): 9–16.

1951c. "School and Christian Freedom." *National Catholic Educational Association Proceedings* 48 (August): 63–68.

1952a. "The Church and Totalitarian Democracy." *Theological Studies* 13 (December): 525–63.

1952b. "For the Freedom and Transcendence of the Church." *The American Ecclesiastical Review* 126 (January): 28–48.

1953a. "Christian Humanism in America." *Social Order* 3 (May-June): 233–44. Slightly edited and republished as chapter 8, "Is It Basket Weaving? The Question of Christian and Human Values," in *WHTT*, pp. 175–96.

1953b. "Leo XIII on Church and State: The General Structure of the Controversy." *Theological Studies* 14 (March): 1–30.

1953c. "Leo XIII: Separation of Church and State." *Theological Studies* 14 (June): 145–214.

1953d. "Leo XIII: Two Concepts of Government." *Theological Studies* 14 (December): 551–67.

1953e. "The Problem of Free Speech." *Philippine Studies* 1 (September): 107–24.

1953f. Sermon given at a Red Mass, Washington, DC, February 1953. Murray Archives, file 2–294.

1954a. Correspondence with Robert MacIver, dating from 1952 through 1954. Murray Archives, file 2–147.

1954b. "Leo XIII: Two Concepts of Government: Government and the Order of Culture." *Theological Studies* 15 (March): 1–33.

1954c. Notes to Murray's *Ci Riesce* talk at Catholic University. March 25, 1954. Murray Archives, file 5–402.

1954d. "On the Structure of the Church-State Problem." In *The Catholic Church in World Affairs*, edited by Waldemar Gurian and M. A. Fitzsimons, pp. 11–32. Notre Dame, IN: University of Notre Dame Press.

1954e. "The Problem of Pluralism in America." *Thought* 24 (Summer): 165–208. Also published in *Commonweal* 60 (1954): 463–468 and in *Catholicism in American Culture* (New Rochelle, NY: College of New Rochelle, 1955). Republished, with less positive affirmation of American society, in *The Catholic Mind* (May-June 1959): 201–15; and as chapters 1 and 2, "E Pluribus Unum: The American Consensus" and "Civil Unity and Religious Integrity: The Articles of Peace," *WHTT*, 27–78; and as "The Problem of Pluralism in America," *Thought* (Sesquicentennial Issue), 323–59.

1955a. "Catholics in America—a Creative Minority—Yes or No?" *Epistle (New York)* 21: 36–41. Also as "Catholics in America—a Creative Minority?" *Catholic Mind* 53 (October 1955): 590–97.

1955b. "The Christian Idea of Education." In *Eight Views of Responsibility in Government, Business, Education and the Church*, pp. 372–84. St. Louis: St. Louis University. Excerts published as "The Unity of Truth," *Commonweal* 63 (January 13, 1956): 381–82. Extended with a different conclusion and published as "The Christian Idea of Education" in *The Christian Idea of Education* (New Haven: Yale University Press, 1957), pp. 152–63. Then republished as "The Catholic University in a Pluralistic Society," *Catholic Mind* 57 (May-June 1959): 253–60.

1955c. "Leo XIII and Pius XII: Government and the Order of Religion." In *Religious Liberty: Catholic Struggles with Pluralism*, edited by J. Leon Hooper, S.J., pp. 49–125. (Louisville, KY: Westminster/John Knox, 1993.) Original publication in *Theological Studies* blocked by Rome in 1955. Galley pages in Murray Archives, File 7–536.

1955d. "Special Catholic Challenges." *Life* 39–40 (December 26): 144–46. Also published as "Challenges Confronting the American Catholic." *Catholic Mind* 57 (May-June 1959): 196–200.

1956a. "The Bad Arguments Intelligent Men Make." *America* 96 (November 3): 120–23. This and the Fischer article that provoked it were published as appendixes in *Catholic Viewpoint on Censorship*, edited by Harold C. Gardiner, S.J. (Garden City, NY: Hanover House, 1958), pp. 157–92.

1956b. "Die Katholiken in der americanischen Gesellschaft." *Dokumente: Zeitschrift für übernationale Zusammenarbeit* 12 (August): 287–92.

1956c. "Freedom, Responsibility and Law." *The Catholic Lawyer* 2 (July): 214–23, 276. Reprinted in *Catholic Mind* 56 (September-October 1958): 436–47.

1956d. "The Next Liberal Task for America." September 29, 1956. Murray Archives, file 3–295.

1956e. "The Quality of Reverence." *Journal of the Newman Club of the University of Minnesota* (June). A manuscript copy in Murray Archives 5–390.

1956f. "Questions of Striking a Right Balance: Literature and Censorship." *Books on Trial* 14 (June-July): 393–95, 444–46. Reprinted as "Literature and Censorship," *Catholic Mind* 54 (December 1956): 665–77; and slightly edited for chapter 7, "Should There Be a Law: The Question of Censorship," *WHTT*, pp. 155–74. Translated and published as "Literatur und Zensur," *Frankfurter Hefte: Zeitschrift für Kultur und Politik* 17 (December 1962): 824–33.

1956g. "Remarks on Theological Method." Murray Archives, file 4–324.

1956h. "The School Problem in Mid-Twentieth Century." In *The Role of the Independent School in American Democracy*, edited by William H. Conley, pp. 1–16. (Milwaukee: Marquette University Press.) 1956. Reprinted as "The Religious School in a Pluralistic Society," *Catholic Mind* 54 (September 1956): 502–11, and slightly reedited for chapter 6, "Is It Justice? The School Question Today," *WHTT*, pp. 143–54.

1956i. Sermon for a Red Mass at Boston College, Chestnut Hill, Mass. September, 1956.

1956j. "St. Ignatius and the End of Modernity." In *The Ignatian Year at Georgetown*. Washington, DC: Georgetown University Press. Mimeographed version in Murray Archives, file 5–410.

1956k. "The Thesis Form as an Instrument of Theological Reflection."In *Proceedings* of the Eleventh Annual Convention of the Catholic Theological Society of America, pp. 218–24. Bronx, NY: Catholic Theological Society of America.

1957a. "Church, State and Political Freedom." *Modern Age: A Conservative Review* 1 (Fall): 134–45. Also in *Catholic Mind* 57 (May–June 1959): 216–29; as "The Freedom of Man in the Freedom of the Church," in *Modern Catholic Thinkers*, edited by A. Robert Caponigri, (New York: Harper, 1960), pp. 372–84; and in *The Essentials of Freedom: The Idea and Practice of Ordered Liberty in the Twentieth Century*, edited by Raymond English, (Gambier, OH: Kenyon College, 1960), pp. 151–166; and as chapter 9, "Are There Two or One? The Question of the Future of Freedom" in *WHTT*, 197–217.

1958a. "America's Four Conspiracies." In *Religion in America*, edited by J. Cogley, pp. 12–41. New York: Meridian Books. Reprinted in *Catholic Mind* 57 (May–June 1959): 230–41 and in *Readings in the Philosophy of Education*, edited by M. Carron, (Detroit: University of Detroit Press, 1960), pp. 84–86. Also appeared as "Introduction: The Civilization of the Pluralistic Society," in *WHTT*, pp. 5–24.

1958b. "Church and State: The Structure of the Argument." Murray Archives, file 6–490.

1958c. "Confusion of U.S. Foreign Policy." In *Foreign Policy and the Free Society*, edited by John Courtney Murray and Walter Millis, pp. 21–42, with a discussion between Millis, Murray, and others, pp. 53–116. New York: Oceana Publications. This was sponsored by Fund for the Republic. Excerpt published as "Confusion of U.S. Foreign Policy," *Catholic Mind* 57 (May–June 1959): 261–73. Also published as chapter 10, "Doctrine and Policy in Communist Imperialism: The Problem of Security and Risk," *WHTT*, 221–247.

1958d. "How to Think (Theologically) about War and Peace." *Catholic Messenger* 76 (December): 7–8. Also as "U.S. Policy vis-à-vis the Soviet Union." Catholic Association for International Peace *News* 19 (December 1958): 8–10.

1958e. "The Making of a Pluralist Society." *Religious Education* 53 (November-December): 521–28. Reprinted as "University in a Pluralist Society," in *Religion and the State University*, edited by Erich A. Walker (Ann Arbor: University of Michigan Press, 1958), pp. 13–26. Reprinted as "State University in a Pluralist Society," *Catholic Mind* 57 (May–June 1959): 242–52. Edited for chapter 5, "Creeds at War Intelligibly: Pluralism and the University," in *WHTT*, 125–39.

1958f. Talk on religious knowledge and the university, given at Loyola. Murray Archives, file 6–423.

1959a. "The Liberal Arts College and the Contemporary Climate of Opinion." November, 1959. Murray Archives, file 6–480.

1959b. *Morality and Modern War.* New York, NY: The Church Peace Union. Pamplet, from a paper delivered before the Catholic Association for International Peace, October 28, 1958. Printed as "The Morality of War," *Theological Digest* 7 (Autumn 1959): 131–37; as "God, Man and Nuclear War," *Catholic Mind* 57 (May-June 1959): 274–88; as "Remarks on the Moral Problem of War," *Theological Studies* 20 (March 1959): 40–61; as "Theology and Modern War," in *Morality and Modern Warfare,* edited by William Nagle (Baltimore: Helicon Press, 1960), pp. 69–91; as "Der Krieg als sittliches Problem" *Dokumente: Zeitschrift für übernationale Zusammenarbeit* 4 (August 1959), 275–90; and slightly edited as chapter 11, "The Uses of a Doctrine on the Uses of Force: War as a Moral Problem" in *WHTT,* pp. 249–73.

1959c. "The Next Task for America." Sermon given at a Red Mass in Baltimore, MD. September, 1959. Murray Archives, File 3–296.

1959d. "Unica Status Religio." Murray Archives, file 7–558.

1960a. "Morality and Foreign Policy, Part I & II." *America* 102 (March 19): 729–32; (March 26): 764–67. This two-part article appeared as chapter 12, "The Doctrine Is Dead: The Problem of the Moral Vacuum," in *WHTT,* pp. 273–94

1960b. "On Raising the Religious Issue." *America* 103 (September 24): 702.

1960c. *We Hold These Truths.* New York: Sheed & Ward, 1960. Made up of previously published articles: Introduction, 1958a; chapter 1 and 2, 1954d; chapter 5, 1958c; chapter 6, 1956j; chapter 7, 1956f; chapter 8, 1953a; chapter 9, 1957b; chapter 10, 1958c; chapter 11, 1958f; chapter 13, 1950a. Also includes new additions: chapter 3, "Two Cases for the Public Consensus: Fact or Need," 79–96; chapter 4, "The Origins and Authority of the Public Consensus: A Study of the Growing End," 97–123; and 1960a (published the same year).

1961a. "The American Proposition." *Commonweal* 73 (January 20, 1961): 433–35. Transcription of an interview on "The Catholic Hour."

1961b. Foreword to *In a Spirit of Wonder: A Christmas Anthology for Our Age,* by M. L. Shrady (New York: Pantheon Books), pp. ix–xi.

1961c. "Hopes and Misgivings for Dialogue." *America* 104 (January 14): 459–60. Also part of a pamphlet published as *One Fold, One Shepherd* (New York, NY: America Press).

1961d. "What Can Unite a Religiously Divided Nation?" *Catholic Messenger* 79 (May 4): 4. Republished as "The Return to Tribalism," *Catholic Mind* 60 (January 1962): 5–12, and in *Readings in Social Theology,* edited by E. Morgan (Dayton, OH: Pflaum Press, 1961), pp. 191–201.

1962a. "Le droit à l'incroyance." *Relations* [Montréal] 227 (Avril): 91–92.

1962b. "Federal Aid to Church Related Schools." *Yale Political: A Journal of Divergent Views on National Issues* 1: 16, 29–31.

1962c. Foreword to *The Encounter With God: Aspects of Modern Theology* by Joseph C. O'Neill (New York: Macmillan), pp. vii–x.

1962d. "Letter to Archbishop L. J. Shehan, August, 1962." Murray Archives, file 18–1008.

1962e. "Remarks on Theological Method." Murray Archives, file 4–324.

1963a. "The Church and the Council." *America* 104 (October 19): 451–53.

1963b. "The Elite and the Electorate: Is Government by the People Possible?" 7–8. Center for the Study of Democratic Institutions, by the Fund for the Republic, Santa Barbara, California. An occasional paper on the role of political process in the free society: Murray comments on an article by J. William Fulbright.

1963c. *Encyclopaedia Britannica*. 11th ed, S.v., "Extreme unction," "Holy Spirit," "Nuntio."

1963d. Foreword to *American Pluralism and the Catholic Conscience* by Richard J. Regan S.J. (New York: Macmillan), pp. xii–xv.

1963e. Foreword to *Religious Liberty and the America Presidency: A Study in Church-State Relations* by Patricia Barret. (New York: Herder), v–vii.

1963f. "Good Pope John: A Theologian's Tribute." *America* 108 (June 15): 854–55.

1963g. "Kirche und Staat in Nordamerika." *Dokumente: Zeitschrift für übernationale Zusammenarbeit* 19 (December): 423–33. Republished as "Das Verhältnis von Kirche und Staat in den USA," in *Das Verhältnis von Kirche und Staat: Erwägungen zur Vielfalt der gerschichtlichen Entwicklung und gegenwärtigen Situation* (Wurzburg: Echter, 1965), pp. 51–71. English original in Murray Archives, file 11–703.

1963h. "Make the News Good News!" *Interracial Review* 36 (July): 130–31, 134–35. Also published in *What Do They Want Now? Questions and Answers on Race*, edited by C. J. McNaspy (New York: America Press, 1964), pp. 33–39.

1963i. "On Religious Liberty." *America* 109 (November): 704–6. Also published in *American Catholic Horizons*, edited by Eugene K. Culhane (New York: Doubleday, 1966), pp. 219–26. Also published as "Religionsfreiheit als Konzilsthema," in *Das Konzil: Zweiter Bild- und Textbericht*, edited by Mario von Galli (Olten, Switzerland, 1964), pp. 138–40; as "Liberté religieuse: la position de l'épiscopat américain," *Choisir* (1964): 14–16: in *Etudes et Documents* [Secrétariat conciliaire de l'Episcopat Français, Paris] N.S. no. 2 (4 Fevier 1964); and as "En torno ala 'Libertad Religiosa'," in *Libertad Religiosa: Una Solucion Para Todos*, edited by Rafel López Jordan, S.J. (Madrid: Ediciones Studium, 1964), pp. 45–52; by Rafel López Jordan, S.J., in *Problematica della libertà religiosa* (Milano: Ancora, 1964), pp. 29–37; and as "Due documenti al Concilio sulla liberta religiosa," *Aggiornamenti sociali* 15 (1964): 57–62.

1963j. "Things Old and New in *Pacem in Terris. America* 108 (April 27): 612–14. Also published in *American Catholic Horizons,* edited by Eugene K. Culhane (New York: Doubleday, 1966), pp. 188–94; and as "Key Themes in the Encyclical *"Pacem in Terris"* in *Peace on Earth* (New York: America Press, 1963), 57–64.

1964a. "Information and the Church: The Function of the Catholic Press within the Catholic Church." *Social Survey* 13: 204–8. Expanded form of an address to the International Press Association, 1963. Also published as "The Social Function of the Press," *Journalistes Catholiques* 12 (Janvier-Avril 1964): 8–12.

1964b. "On the Future of Humanistic Education." In *Humanistic Education and Western Civilization,* edited by Authur A. Cohen, in honor of the sixty-fifth birthday of Robert M. Hutchins, pp. 231–47. New York: Holt, Rinehart, & Winston. Excerpted in *The Critic* 22 (February-March 1964): 37–43

1964c. *The Problem of God, Yesterday and Today.* New Haven: Yale University Press. An earlier and shorter version of this study appeared as "On the Structure of the Problem of God," *Theological Studies* 23 (March 1962): 1–26. Translated and published as *Il problema di Dio ieri e oggi* (Brescia: Morcelliana, 1971) and as *Le Problème de Dieu de la Bible á l'incroyance contemporaine* (Paris: Centurion, 1965).

1964d. "The Problem of Mr. Rawls' Problem." In *Law and Philosophy,* 29–34. Edited by Sidney Hooks. (NY: New York University Press, 1964.)

1964e. *The Problem of Religious Freedom.* Woodstock Papers, Number 7. Westminster, MD: The Newman Press, 1965. An earlier, briefer form was published as "The Problem of Religious Freedom," *Theological Studies* 25 (December 1964): 503–75. Also published as "De kwestie van de godsdienstvrijheld op het concilie" in *Documentation Hollandaise du Concile* dossiers 9, 7–83 (Hilversum/ Antwerp, 1965); as "Le probleme de la liberté religieuse au Councile," in *La liberté religieuse: exigence spirituelle et problème politique* (Paris: Centurion, 1965), pp. 9–112; as "Die religioese Freiheit und das Konzil," *Wort und Warheit* 20 (1965): 409–30, 505–36; as "Il problema della libertà religiosa al concilio," *Il Nuovo Osservatore* 54 (1966): 686–734; and as "La libertà religiosa: Un grave Problema di oggi ereditato dalla storia di ieri" in *Cattolicesimo e libertà,* edited by F.V. Joannes, 157–254 (Milano: Mondadori, 1969). Reissued as "The Problem of Religious Freedom" in John Courtney Murray, *Religious Liberty: Catholic Struggles with Pluralism,* edited by J. Leon Hooper, S.J. (Louisville, KY: Westminster/John Knox Press, 1993), pp. 127–97.

1964f. "The Schema on Religious Freedom: Critical Comments." Murray Archives, file 18–986.

1964g. "Today and Tomorrow: Conversation at the Council: John Courtney Murray, Hans Küng, Gustave Weigel, Godfrey Diekmann, and Vincent Yzermans." *American Benedictine Review* 15 (September 1): 341–

51. Also published in somewhat different form under the same title in *Ave Marie* 100 (1964): 10–11.

1965a. *Acceptance Speech.* New York: Unitarian-Universalist Association, 1965. A pamphlet of a talk on Receipt of the Second Annual Thomas Jefferson Award, March 22, 1965.

1965b. "Commentary on the Declaration." Murray Archives, file 18–1005.

1965c. "The Conciliar History of the Declaration." Murray Archives, file 18–1005.

1965d. Foreword to *Freedom and Man*, edited by John Courtney Murray, S.J. (New York: P. J. Kenedy), pp. 11–16.

1965e. Foreword to *A Theology of Mary* by Cyril Vollert. Saint Mary's Theology Series No. 3, pp. 9–11. New York: Herder & Herder.

1965f. Memo to Cushing on Contraception Legislation. No month cited. Murray Archives, file 1–43.

1965g. "Osservazioni sulla dichiarazione della libertà religiosa." *La Civiltà Cattolica* 116 (December): 536–54. Also published as "La déclaration sur la liberté religieuse," *Nouvelle Revue Théologique* 88 (1966): 41–67.

1965h. "Religious Freedom." In *Freedom and Man*. Edited by John Courtney Murray, S.J., pp. 131–40. New York: P. J. Kenedy.

1965i. "Remarks on the Schema on Religious Liberty." Murray Archives, file 18–1000.

1965j. "This Matter of Religious Freedom." *America* 112 (January 9): 40–43. Published as "La 'libertà religiosa': Materia di dibattito conciliare," *Aggiornamenti Sociali* 16 (Aprilo 1965): 303–10.

1966a. "Conference on the Development of the Doctrine of Religious Liberty." In *Council Day Book*, edited by Floyd Anderson, pp. 14–17. Washington: NCWC Press, 1966. Also published as "The Issue of the Development of doctrine," *DO-C, Documentation Hollandaise du Concile* V. III, H. 206

1966b. "The Declaration on Religious Freedom." In *Vatican II: An Interfaith Appraisal*, edited by John H. Miller, article, pp. 565–76, and discussion, pp. 577–85. Notre Dame: Association Press. Translated and published as *La teologia dopo il Vaticano II*, edited by J.H. Miller (Brescia: Morcelliana, 1967), 710–33.

1966c. "The Declaration on Religious Freedom." In *War, Poverty, Freedom: The Christian Response*, pp. 3–10. New York: Paulist Press. *Concilium* 5, no. 2. Also published as "La Déclaration sur la Liberté Religieuse. *Concilium* 15 (1966): 7–18.

1966d. "The Declaration on Religious Freedom: A Moment in Its Legislative History." In *Religious Liberty: An End and a Beginning*, edited by John Courtney Murray, pp. 15–42. New York: Macmillan & Company.

1966e. "The Declaration on Religious Freedom: Its Deeper Significance." *America* 114 (April 23): 592–93. Also published as "The Vatican Declaration on Religious Freedom: An Aspect of Its Significance," in *The*

University in the American Experience (New York: Fordham University Press, 1966), pp. 1–10.

1966f. "Fairfield Address." June 5. Murray Archives, file 6–463.

1966g. "Freedom, Authority, Community." *America* 115 (December 3): 734–41. Also published in *Freedom and Authority in the West*, edited by G. Shuster (Notre Dame: University of Notre Dame, 1967), pp. 11–24; in *Christian Witness in the Secular City*, edited by E. Morgan (Chicago: Loyola University, 1970), pp. 118–30; and in *Catholic Lawyer* 15 (Spring 1969): 158–68. Translated and published as "Libertà autorità e Comunità Chiesa in un mondo in trasformazione," in *Verso il sinodo dei vescovi. I problemi.* (Brescia: Queriniana, 1967), pp. 173–81.

1966h. "The Issue of Church and State at Vatican Council II." *Theological Studies* 27 (December): 580–606. Republished under the same title in John Courtney Murray, *Religious Liberty: Catholic Struggles with Pluralism*, edited by J. Leon Hooper, S.J. (Louisville, KY: Westminster/John Knox Press, 1993), pp. 199–227.

1966i. "Religious Freedom." In *The Documents of Vatican II*, edited by Walter M Abbot and Joseph Gallagher, introduction, p. 673–74, and text with commentary, pp. 674–96. New York: America Press.

1966j. "The Status of the Nicene Creed as Dogma." *Chicago Studies: An Archdiocesan Review* 5 (Spring): 65–80. Delivered as a talk on ecumenism in a Lutheran-Catholic Dialogue, Baltimore, Maryland, July 1965.

1967a. "The Danger of the Vows: An Encounter with Earth, Woman and the Spirit." *Woodstock Letters* 116 (Fall): 421–27.

1967b. "The Death of God." January 10, 1967. Address at the University of Connecticut. Murray Archives, file 6–462.

1967c. "Declaration on Religious Freedom: Commentary." In *American Participation at the Second Vatican Council*, edited by Vincent A. Yzermans, 668–76. New York: Sheed & Ward.

1967d. "Freedom in the Age of Renewal." *American Benedictine Review* 18 (September): 319–24. A talk given at St. John's, June 1965.

1967e. Introduction to *One of a Kind: Essays in Tribute to Gustave Weigel*, pp. 11–22. Wilkes-Baare, PA: Dimension Books.

1967f. "Mentalità moderna e problemi attuali dell'uomo nella Chiesa." In *Verso il sinodo dei vescovi. I problemi*, pp. 173–81. Brescia: Queriniana.

1967g. "Murray Says Church Was Too Sure." *Toledo Catholic Chronicle* 33, no. 29 (May 5): 1, 5. See also NC News service "Jesuit Priest Calls Minority Birth Control Report 'Classicism'," *National Catholic Reporter* (May 17, 1967): 3

1967h. "Our Response to the Ecumenical Revolution." *Religious Education* 42 (March-April): 91–92, 119.

1967i. "Religious Liberty and Development of Doctrine." *The Catholic World* 204 (February): 277–83.

1967j. Review of *Academic Freedom and the Catholic University*, by Edward Manier and John W. Houch. *AAUP Bulletin* 53 (1967): 339–42.

1967k. Review of *The Garden and the Wilderness: Religion and Government in American Constitutional History*, by M. D. Howe. *Yale Law Journal* 76 (April 1967): 1030–35.

1967l. *Selective Conscientious Objection.* Huntington, IN: Our Sunday Visitor, Inc. Pamphlet of an address at Western Maryland College, June 4. Republished as "War and Conscience" in *A Conflict of Loyalties: The Case of Conscientious Objection*, edited by James Finn (New York: Pegasus, 1968), pp. 19–30.

1967m. "Vers une intelligence du développment de la doctrine de l'Église sur la liberté religeuse." In *Vatican II: La Liberté Religieuse*, edited by J. Hamer and Y. Congar, pp. 111–47. Paris: Cerf. Also published as "Zum Verständnis der Entwicklung der Lehre der Kirche über die Religionsfreiheit," in *Die Konzelerklärung: über die Religionsfreiheit: Lateinischer und Deutscher Text* (Paderborn: Bonifacius Druckerei, 1967), 125–65. English original in Murray Archives, file 7–517.

1967n. "A Will to Community." In *Theological Freedom and Social Responsibility*, edited by Stephen F. Bayne Jr., pp. 111–16. New York: Seabury Press. Also published as "We Held These Truths," *National Catholic Reporter* 3 (August 23, 1967): 3.

1968. "De argumentis pro iure hominis ad libertatem religiosam." In *Acta Congressus Internationalis de Theologia Concilii Vaticani II*, edited by A. Schoenmetzer, pp. 562–73. Rom, Vatikan. Translated and published as "The Human Right to Religious Freedom, in *Religious Liberty: Catholic Struggles with Pluralism.* edited by J. Leon Hooper S.J. (Louisville, KY: Westminster/John Knox Press, 1993), pp. 229–44.

1969. "The Unbelief of the Christian." In *The Presence and Absence of God*, edited by Christopher Mooney, pp. 69–83. New York: Fordham University Press, 1969.

1970. "La liberta religiosa e l'ateo." In *L'ateismo contemporaneo*, pp. 109–17. Torino: Società Ed. Internazionale, 1970. English Original in Murray Archives, 4–327.

1993. *Religious Liberty: Catholic Struggles with Pluralism*, edited by J. Leon Hooper, S.J. Louisville, KY: Westminster/John Knox Press. Publication of 1955c and 1968; reissuing of 1964e and 1966h.

Works on
John Courtney Murray, S.J.

The following vary in their use of, or appeals to, Murray. Some are close textual analyses of his work, while others consciously attempt to move beyond his thought. Some are simple obituaries. Some make passing reference to his attempts to reconcile (or challenge) the church and American society.

Allitt, Patrick. 1990. "The Significance of John Courtney Murray." In *Church Polity and American Politics: Issues in Contemporary American Catholicism*, edited by Mary C. Segers, 51–65. New York & London: Garland Publishing.

Bacik, James J. 1989. "John Courtney Murray: Living as a Christian in a Pluralistic Society." In *Contemporary Theologians*. Chicago: Thomas More Association.

Barr, Stringfellow. 1960. Review of *We Hold These Truths. New York Herald Tribune Book Review* (October 30): 4.

Barrionuevo, Cristobal M. 1956. "La teoria del P. Murray sobre las relaciones entre la iglesia y estado." Ph.D. Dissertation, University of Granada (Granada, Spain).

Benestad, J. Brian. 1991. "Catholicism and American Public Philosophy." *Review of Politics* 53 (Fall): 691–711.

Bennett, John Coleman. 1958. "A Protestant View of American Catholic Power." In *Christians and the State*, 252–68. New York: Charles Schribner's Sons.

_____. 1967. "John Courtney Murray." *Christianity and Crisis* 27 (September 18): 198–99.

Brandt, Lawrence E. 1983. *John Courtney Murray and Religious Liberty: An American Experience*. Roma: Pontificia Università Lateranense.

Broderick, Albert. 1967. "From a Friend Who Never Met Him: Tribute to John Courtney Murray." *America* 117 (September 9): 246–48.

Burgess, Faith E. R. 1971. *Ecclesia et Status: The Relationship between Church and State According to John Courtney Murray, S.J.* Düsseldorf: Stehle.

Burghardt, Walter J., S.J. 1967. "A Eulogy." *Woodstock Letters* 96 (Fall): 416–20.

_____. 1967. "He Lived with Wisdom: Tribute to John Courtney Murray." *America* 117 (September 9): 247–48.

_____. 1968. "A Tribute to John Courtney Murray." *Catholic Mind* 66 (June): 29–31.

_____. 1968. "Unity through Ecstasy: A Tribute to John Courtney Murray." *Dominicana* 53 (Spring): 3–5.

_____. 1969. "From Certainty to Understanding." *Catholic Mind* 67 (June): 13–27.

_____, editor. 1976. *Religious Freedom: 1965-1975*. New York: Paulist Press.

_____. 1985. "Who Chilled the Beaujolais?" *America* 153 (November 30): 360–63.

_____. 1989. "Consensus, Moral Witness and Health-care Issues: A Dialogue with J. Bryan Hehir." In *Catholic Perspectives on Medical Morals*, edited by Edward Pellegrino et al., 223–29. Boston: Kluwer Academic.

Burke, Eugene. 1980. "A Personal Memoir on the Origins of the CTSA." In *Proceedings of the Thirty-Fifth Convention of the Catholic Theological Society of America, June 11- 14, 1980, San Francisco*, 35: 337–45. Bronx: Catholic Theological Society of America.

Cahill, Lisa Sowle. 1987. "The Catholic Tradition: Religion, Morality, and the Common Good." *The Journal of Law and Religion* 5 (1): 75–94.

Canavan, Francis J., S.J. 1982. "Murray on Vatican II's Declaration on Religious Freedom." *Communio* 9 (Winter): 404–5.

_____. 1993. "Apostle of Religious Freedom: John Courtney Murray and the Council." *Crisis* 11 (May): 31–36.

Carrillo de Albornoz, Angelo Francisco. 1965. "Religious Freedom: Intrinsic or Fortuitous?" *Christian Century* 82 (September 15): 1122–26.

"City of Man and God." 1960. *Time* 76 (December 12): 64–70.

Cogley, John. 1956. "In Praise of Father Murray." *Commonweal* 65 (December 7): 253.

Coleman, John A. 1976. "Vision and Praxis in American Theology: Orestes Brownson, John A. Ryan, and John Courtney Murray." *Theological Studies* 37 (March): 3–40.

_____. 1978. "A Theological Link between Religious Liberty and Mediating Structures." In *Church, State, and Public Policy: The New Shape of the Church-State Debate*, edited by Jay Mechling, 22–48. Washington, DC: American Enterprise Institute for Public Policy Research.

Cox, Harvey. 1961. Review of *We Hold These Truths*. *Cross Currents* (Winter): 79–83.

Cross, Robert D. 1958. *The Emergence of Liberal Catholicism in America*. Cambridge: Harvard University Press.

Cuddihy, John Murray. 1979. "John Courtney Murray, S.J." In *No Offense: Civil Religion and Protestant Taste*, 64–100. New York: Seabury Press.

Curran, Charles E. 1982. "Civil Law and Christian Morality: Abortion and the Churches." In *Abortion: The Moral Issues*, edited by E. Batchelor, 143–65. New York: Pilgrim Press.

———. 1982. "John Courtney Murray." In *American Catholic Social Ethics: Twentieth-Century Approaches*, 172–232. Notre Dame, IN: University of Notre Dame Press.

Daly, Simeon, O.S.B. "John Courtney Murray, S.J. and Giovanni Cardinal Morone Connected." In *Christian Freedom: Essays by the Faculty of Saint Meinrad School of Theology*, edited by Clayton N. Jefford, 41–57. New York: Peter Lang.

Deedy, John. 1978. "John Courtney Murray." In *Seven American Catholics*, 123–53. Chicago: Thomas More Press.

Dionne, J. Robert. 1987. *The Papacy and the Church: A Study of Praxis and Reception in Ecumenical Perspective*. New York: Philosophical Library.

Dougherty, Jude. 1990. "Dean Dougherty on Separation of Church and State." *Wanderer* (October 25): 6–7.

Drinan, Robert F. 1965. Review of Thomas T. Love, *John Courtney Murray: Contemporary Church-State Theory. Journal of Church and State* 7 (Autumn): 444–46.

Dumortier, Francois-Xavier. 1988. "John Courtney Murray revisité: la place de l'eglise dans le débat public aux Etats-Unis." *Recherches de Science Religieuse* 76 (4): 499–531.

Douglass, R. Bruce. 1989. "Public Philosophy and Contemporary Pluralism (or, The Murray Problem Revisited)." *Thought* 64 (December): 344–61.

Faherty, William Barnaby, S.J. 1988. "American Freedom: John Courtney Murray (1904–1967)." In *Rebels or Reformers? Dissenting Priests in America*, 91–97. Chicago: Loyola University Press.

Fallon, Thomas L., O.P. 1990. Review of *Matthias Scheeben on Faith*, by John Courtney Murray, edited and with an introduction by D. Thomas Hughson, S.J. In *Critical Review of Books in Religion*, 441–43. Atlanta: Scholars Press.

Finn, James. 1983. "Pacifism and Just War: Either or Neither." In *Catholics and Nuclear War*, edited by P. Murnion, 132–45. New York: Crossroads.

Flaherty, Daniel L. 1966. "Christian Marxist Dialogue." *America* 115 (December 17): 805.

Formicola, Jo Renee. 1987. "American Catholic Political Theology." *Journal of Church and State* 29 (Autumn): 457–74.

Ferguson, Thomas P. 1994. *Murray's Analysis of the Problem of Religious Freedom*. San Francisco: Sheed & Ward.

Garrett, James Leo. 1961. Review of John Courtney Murray, *The Problem Of Religious Freedom. Journal of Church and State* 3 (November): 200–3.

Gilby, Thomas. 1961. Review of *We Hold These Truths. Thomist* 24 (January): 111–13.

Goerner, Edward A. 1959. "John Courtney Murray and the Problem of Church and State." Ph.D. Dissertation. University of Chicago.

_____. 1965. *Peter and Caeser: Political Authority and the Catholic Church.* New York: Herder and Herder.

Gonnet, Dominique, S.J. 1994. Le liberté religieuse à Vatican II: La contribution de John Courtney Murray. Paris: Les Éditions du Cerf.

Gould, William. 1992. "The Challenge of Liberal Political Culture in the Thought of John Courtney Murray." *Communio* 19 (Spring): 113–44.

Gremillion, Joseph. 1982. "Religious Freedom and the Local Church's Responsibility for Mission: The Regional Church of North America." In *Mission in Dialogue: The SEDOS Research Seminar on the Future of Mission*, edited by Mary Motte and Joseph R. Lang, 459–70. Maryknoll, NY: Orbis.

Guroian, Vigen. 1987. "Between Secularism and Christendom: Orthodox Reflections on the American Order." *This World* 18 (Summer): 12–22.

Harrison, Brian W. 1988. "Annexe: John Courtney Murray: sur l'eglise et l'etat." In *Le développment de la doctrine catholique sur la liberté religieuse*, 166–79. Grez en Bour: Dominique Martin Morin.

Hastings, C. B. 1988. "Huges–Félicité Robert de Lamennais: A Catholic Pioneer of Religious Liberty." *Journal of Church and State* 30 (Spring): 321–39.

Hehir, J. Bryan. 1976. "Issues of Church and State: A Catholic Perspective." In *Issues in Church and State: Proceedings of a Dialogue between Catholics and Baptists*, edited by Claude U. Broach, 81–95. Winston-Salem, NC: Ecumenical Institute.

_____. 1985. "The Unfinished Agenda." *America* 153 (November 30): 386–92.

_____. 1989. "Religious Pluralism and Social Policy: The Case of Health Care." In *Catholic Perspectives on Medical Morals*, edited by Edward Pellegrino et al, 205–21. Boston: Kluwer Academic.

Higgins, George G. 1969. "John Courtney Murray and the American Bishops." *The Priest* 25 (March): 175–79.

_____. 1985. "Some Personal Recollections." *America* 153 (November 30): 380, 382, 384, 386.

Hock, Raymond Anthony. 1964. "The Pluralism of John Courtney Murray, S.J., and Its Relationship to Education." Ph.D. Dissertation. Stanford University (Menlo Park, CA).

Hollenbach, David. 1976. "Public Theology in America: Some Questions for Catholicism after John Courtney Murray." *Theological Studies* 37 (June): 290–303.

_____. 1985. "The Growing End of the Argument." *America* 153 (November 30): 363–66.

_____. 1987. "War and Peace in American Catholic Thought: A Heritage Abandoned?" *Theological Studies* 48 (December): 711–26.

Hollenbach, David, Robin W. Lovin, John A. Coleman, and J. Bryan Hehir. 1979. "Theology and Philosophy in Public: A Symposium on John

Courtney Murray's Unfinished Agenda." *Theological Studies* 40 (December): 700–715.

Hooper, J. Leon, S.J. 1986. *The Ethics of Discourse: The Social Philosophy of John Courtney Murray*. Washington, DC: Georgetown University Press.

———. 1993. "General Introduction." In *Religious Liberty: Catholic Struggles With Pluralism*, by John Courtney Murray, edited by J. Leon Hooper S.J., 11–48. Louisville, KY: Westminster/John Knox Press.

Hughson, D. Thomas, S.J. 1987. "Introduction." In *Matthias Scheeben on Faith: The Doctrinal Dissertation of John Courtney Murray*, by John Courtney Murray, edited by D. Thomas Hughson S.J, 1–54. Volume 29, Toronto Studies in Theology. Lewiston/Queenston: Edwin Mellen Press.

———. 1993. *The Believer as Citizen: John Courtney Murray in a New Context*. New York/Hahwah, NJ: Paulist.

Hunt, Robert P. 1989. "Murray, Niebuhr, and the Problem of the Neutral State." *Thought: A Review of Culture and Idea* 64 (December): 362–76.

Hunt, Robert P., and Kenneth L. Grasso, editors. 1992. *John Courtney Murray and the American Civil Conversation*. Grand Rapids, MI: William B. Eerdmans.

"J.C.M.—R.I.P." 1967. *Commonweal* 86 (September): 540.

"John Courtney Murray." 1967. *Ave Maria* 106 (September 2): 4.

"John Courtney Murray, S.J.: Obituary." 1967. *Tablet* 221 (August 26): 915.

Kerwin, Jerome G. 1960. *Catholic Viewpoint on Church and State*. Garden City, NY: Doubleday and Company.

Komonchak, Joseph A. 1993. "The Coldness of Clarity, The Warmth of Love: The Measure of John Courtney Murray." *Commonweal* (August 14): 16–17.

Kossel, Clifford George, S.J. 1984. "Religious Freedom and the Church: J.C. Murray." *Communio* 11 (Spring): 60–74.

Krause, Edward C. 1975. "Democratic Process in the Thought of John Courtney Murray and Reinhold Niebuhr." Ph.D. Dissertation. Boston University (Boston, MA).

Larrey, Martin F. 1972. "John Courtney Murray: A Reappraisal." *Triumph* 7 (December): 20–23.

Lawler, Peter Augustine. 1982. "Natural Law and the American Regime: Murray's *We Hold These Truths*." *Communio* 9 (Winter): 368–88.

"Life Issues After the Election." 1984. *America* 151 (November 10): 285.

Lindbeck, George A. 1961. "John Courtney Murray, S.J.: An Evaluation." *Christianity and Crisis* 21 (November 27): 213–16.

Lindsey, William D. 1992. "Public Theology as Civil Discourse: What Are We Talking About?" *Horizons* 19 (January): 44–69.

Little, David. 1989. "Conscience, Theology, and the First Amendment." *Soundings* 72 (Summer-Fall): 356–78.

Love, Thomas T. 1965. "Contemporary Conservative Roman Catholic Church–State Thought." *Journal of Church and State* 7 (Winter): 18–29.

_____. 1965. *John Courtney Murray: Contemporary Church-State Theory.* New York: Doubleday.

_____. 1965. "John Courtney Murray: Liberal Roman Catholic Church-State Theory." *Journal of Religion* 45 (July): 211–24.

_____. 1966. "De *Libertate Religiosa*: An Interpretive Analysis." *Journal of Church and State* 8 (Winter): 30–48.

_____. 1967. "John Courtney Murray." In *Modern Theologians: Christian and Jews*, edited by T. E. Bird, 18–39. Notre Dame, IN: University of Notre Dame Press.

Lovin, Robin W. 1978. "The Constitution as Covenant: The Moral Foundations of Democracy and the Practice of Desegregation." Ph.D. Dissertation. Harvard University.

_____. 1979. "The Constitution as Covenant: The Moral Foundations of Democracy and the Practice of Desegregation." *Harvard Theological Review* 72 (July-October): 318.

Marquez, Antonio. 1959. "Catholic Controversy on Church and State." *Theology Today* 15 (January): 531–41.

Marshner, William H. 1983. "*Dignitatis Humanae* and Traditional Teaching on Church and State." *Faith & Reason* 9 (Fall): 222–48.

Marty, Martin E. 1960. Review of *We Hold These Truths*. *Christian Century* 77 (November 9): 1315–17.

May, Joseph R. 1958. *The State and the Law of Christ.* Rome: Ponta Grossa.

McCann, Dennis P. 1987. "The Good to be Pursued in Common." In *The Common Good and U.S. Capitalism*, edited by O. Williams and J. Houck, 158–78. Lanham, MD: University Press of America.

_____. 1990. "Natural Law, Public Theology and the Legacy of John Courtney Murray." *Christian Century* 107 (September 5–12): 801–3.

McDonough, Peter. 1990. "Metamorphoses of the Jesuits: Sexual Identity, Gender Roles and Hierarchy in Catholicism." *Comparative Studies in Society and History* 32 (April): 325–57.

_____. 1992. *Men Astutely Trained: A History of the Jesuits in the American Century.* New York: Free Press/Macmillian.

McElroy, Robert. 1988. "Revisiting John Courtney Murray: The Question of Method in Public Theology." *New Catholic World* (July/August): 179–83.

_____. 1989. *The Search for an American Public Theology: The Contribution of John Courtney Murray.* New York: Paulist.

McEvoy, Raymond Owen. 1973. *John Courtney Murray's Thought on Religious Liberty in Its Final Phase.* Rome: Pontifical Lateran University.

McManus, Robert Joseph. 1987. *Ecclesial Loyalty in Political Responsibility: A Critical Reading and Evaluation of the Discussion in the American Arena from 1960 to 1985.* Roma: Pontifical Gregorian University.

McManus, William E. 1985. "Memories of Murray." *America* 153 (November 30): 366–68.

McNearney, Clayton Leroy. 1970. "The Roman Catholic Response to the Writings of Paul Blanshard." Ph.D. Dissertation. University of Iowa.

Miller, William Lee. 1987. *The First Liberty: Religion and the American Republic.* New York: Alfred A. Knopf.

Moser, Mary Theresa. 1988. "Revising the Constitution: The Problem of Religious Freedom."*Journal of Religious Ethics* 16: 325–44.

Most, William G. 1983. "Religious Liberty: What the Texts Demand." *Faith & Reason* 9 (Fall): 196–209.

"Murray Dies of Heart Attack in Taxi at 62." 1967. *National Catholic Reporter* 3 (August 23): 1.

Neuhaus, Richard John. 1984. *The Naked Public Square: Religion and Democracy in America.* Grand Rapids, MI: Eerdmans.

_____. 1987. *The Catholic Moment: The Paradox of the Church in the Postmodern World.* San Francisco: Harper & Row.

Novak, David. 1992. "John Courtney Murray, S.J.: A Jewish Appraisal." In *Jewish Social Ethics*, 67–83. New York/Oxford: Oxford University Press.

Novak, Michael. 1983. *Moral Clarity in the Nuclear Age.* Nashville: T. Nelson.

_____. 1984. *Freedom with Justice: Catholic Social Thought and Liberal Institutions.* San Francisco: Harper & Row.

_____. 1985. "Economic Rights: The Servile State." *Catholicism in Crisis* (October): 8–15.

_____. 1993. "Public Arguments: Murray After 26 Years—The Founders' Religious Wisdom versus Today's Secularist Folly." *Crisis* 11 (May): 4–10.

O'Brien, David J. 1972. "American Catholicism and American Religion." *Journal of the American Academy of Religion* 40 (March): 36–53.

O'Collins, Gerald, S.J. 1984. "Murray and Ottaviani." *America* 151 (November 10): 287–88.

Palmer, T. Vail. 1965. "Eschatology and Foreign Policy in the Thought of Reinhold Niebuhr, William Ernest Hocking, and John Courtney Murray." Ph.D. Dissertation. University of Chicago Divinity School.

Pavlischek, Keith J. 1990. "The Real John Courtney Murray." *First Things* (October): 46–49.

_____. 1992. "John Courtney Murray, Civil Religion, and the Problem of Political Neutrality." *Journal of Church and State* 34 (Autumn): 729–50.

Pawlikowski, John T. 1979. "Human Rights in the Catholic Tradition: Some Theological Reflections." In *The American Society of Christian Ethics, 1979: Selected Papers*, edited by Max Stackhouse, 145–66. Waterloo, Ontario: Council on the Study of Religion.

_____. 1989. "Catholicism and the Public Church: Recent U.S. Developments." In *The Annual of the Society of Christian Ethics 1989*, edited by D. M. Yeager, 147–65. Washington, DC: Georgetown University Press.

Pelotte, Donald E. 1976. *John Courtney Murray: Theologian in Conflict.* New York: Paulist Press.

Porter, William. 1993. "Inculturation as Transformation: The Case of Americanism Revisited." *U. S. Catholic Historian* 11 (Summer): 107–24.

Regan, Richard J., S.J. 1967. *Conflict and Consensus: Religious Freedom and the Second Vatican Council.* New York: Macmillan.

"Religious Liberty: A Jesuit View." 1945. *Christian Century* 62: 878–80.

Rielly, J. E. 1961. "Contemporary Catholic Thought on Church and State: An Analysis of the Work of Jacques Maritain and John Courtney Murray." Ph.D. Dissertation. Harvard University.

Rohr, John A. 1966. "Murray and the Critiques." *Continuum* 4 (Spring): 147–50.

————. 1978. "John Courtney Murray's Theology of Our Founding Fathers' 'Faith': Freedom." In *Christian Spirituality in the United States: Independence and Interdependence*, edited by Francis A. Eigo, 1–30. Villanova, PA: University of Villanova Press.

————. 1985. "John Courtney Murray and the Pastoral Letters." *America* 153 (November 30): 373–79.

Sanders, Thomas G. 1958. "A Comparison of Two Current American Roman Catholic Theories of the American Political System with Particular Reference to the Problem of Religious Liberty." Ph.D. Dissertation. Columbia University

————. 1965. *Protestant Concepts of Church and State.* Garden City, NY: Doubleday.

Scharper, Philip. 1967. "Grace Under Pressure: A Salute to John Courtney Murray, S.J." *Catholic Mind* 65 (February): 29–31.

————. 1977. "John Courtney Murray: Belated Hero." *Commonweal* 104 (March 4): 150–52.

Schuck, Michael J. 1991. "John Courtney Murray's Problematic Interpretations of Leo XIII and the American Founders." *Thomist* 55 (October): 592–612.

Sebott, Reinhold. 1977. *Religionsfreiheit und Verhältnis von Kirche und Staat: Der Beitrag John Courtney Murrays zu einer modernen Frage.* Rome: Università Gregoriana Editrice.

Segers, Mary C. 1990. "American Catholicism: The Search for a Public Voice in a Pluralistic Society." *Conscience* 9 (May/June): 1–7.

Sheridan, Michael P. 1967. "Honor to Fr. John Courtney Murray." *America* 117 (September 2): 208.

Shrady, Maria. 1967. "John Courtney Murray, S.J., Some Memories." *Thought: A Review of Culture and Idea* 42 (Winter): 485–87.

Smith, E. A. 1969. "Fundamental Church-State Tradition of the Catholic Church in the United States." *Church History* 38 (December): 486–505.

Spann, Edwin Russell. 1956. "The Freedom of the Church and the Freedom of the Citizen." *Bibliography for Religious in Life* 25 (Spring): 205–16.

Sullivan, Andrew. 1987. "Cross Purposes: A Review of: Eric O. Hanson, *The Catholic Church in World Politics* (Princeton University Press); George Weigel, Jr., *Tranquillitas Ordinis* (Oxford University Press); John Courtney Murray, S.J. *We Hold These Truths* (Sheed & Ward)." *The New Republic* 196 (June 1): 30–34.

Tinnelly, J. T. 1961. "The Challenge of John Courtney Murray: Can an American Public Philosophy Be Stated." *Catholic Lawyer* 7 (Autumn): 270–96.

Traffas, John Raymond. 1983. "John Courtney Murray's Theology of Political Right: An Analysis of Murray's Theory of Religious Liberty in Terms of the Teaching of *Dignitatis Humanae."* Masters Thesis, University of Dallas.

Van Allen, Roger. 1982. "Review Symposium: *American Catholic Social Ethics: 20th Century Approaches*, by Charles E. Curran." *Horizons* 9 (Fall): 323–47.

Villaroel Carmona, A. 1967. *Libertad religosa signo de nuestro tiempo.* University of Santiago (Santiago, Chile).

Wallace, Marilyn. 1988. "The Right of Religious Liberty and Its Basis in the Theological Literature of the French Language (1940–1988): An Analysis and Critique of the Contributions of Guy de Broglie, René Coste, Philippe Delhaye and Louis Janssens." Ph.D. Dissertation, Catholic University of America (Washington, DC).

Weigel, George S. 1985. "John Courtney Murray & The American Proposition." *Catholicism in Crisis* (November): 8–13.

_____. 1986. "John Courtney Murray and the Catholic Human Rights Revolution." *This World* 15 (Fall): 14–27.

_____. 1987. "The National Interest and the National Purpose: From Policy Debate to Moral Argument." *This World* 19 (Fall): 75–100.

_____. 1987. *Tranquillitas Ordinis: The Present and Future Promise of American Catholic Thought on War and Peace.* New York: Oxford University Press.

Weithman, Paul J. 1993. "Review of John Courtney Murray and the American Civil Conversation, edited by Robert P. Hunt & Kenneth L. Grasso." *New Oxford Review* 60 (May): 28–29.

Weston, William. 1987. "Michael Novak's Pluralistic Religion." *This World* 19 (Fall): 14–26.

Whelan, Charles M. 1985. "The Enduring Problems of Religious Liberty." *America* 153 (November 3): 368–72.

Whitmore, Todd David. 1993. "Immunity or Empowerment? John Courtney Murray and the Question of Religious Liberty." *Journal of Religious Ethics* 21 (Fall): 247–74.

Wolf, Donald, S.J. 1966. "American Catholic Theories of Church–State Relations." In *Current Trends in Theology*, edited by Donald Wolf and James Schall, 191–210. Garden City, NY: Image Books.

Wolf, S.J., Donald J. 1968. "Historical Consciousness and the Contemporary Church-State Problematic." In *Toward Consensus: Catholic and Protestant Interpretations of Church and State*, edited by James Shall and Donald Wolf, 3–35. New York: Doubleday.

Yanitelli, Victor. R. 1951. "A Church-State Controversy." *Thought* 26 (Autumn): 443–51.

_____. 1952. "A Church-State Anthology: The Work of Father Murray." *Thought* 27 (Spring): 6–42.

Index

Afterlife, as warrant for moral life 120, 122, 227. *See also* Ecclesiology, church as eschatological

American culture 102–5, 109f, 119–21, 142f, 149–53, 171, *282f. See also* Catholics in America

Analogy, use of: between individual/family/government 32, 36f; between civil and ecclesial societies 201, 203ff, 212, 214, 216, between faith and reason *173*, between First Amendment and *Dignitatis* 261; between denominational beliefs *279, 309*, in trinitarian studies 322

Anti-Roman bias 297f, 306f

Anti-intellectualism 103–4, 142f

Arius 165, 317f

"As much freedom as possible. . ." *see* Jurisprudential principle

Atheism, defined 262, 270f, 278; dangers of 16, 121, 151, intolerance toward 137, 230–36, 259–61; expediency toward 234f, 260, and social rights 233f, 255f, 258, positive base for 267; in new problematic 262f, 271f; Christian causes of 273; dialogue with 264f, 332–35. *For general discussion, see xi*, 43, 227–30. *See also* Scientism, Laicism, Unbelief

Augustine 129, 322

Authority, *see* Church authority; Civil authority

Authorization principle *82 note 3*, 65, *200*, 202, 206

Autonomy, of secular society 183, 210, *263, 281, 335*; of laity *ivf*; as aspect of human dignity 110, 267; false of human reason 144, 244; from God 184; of church 193

Belief, in human solidarity/dignity 11, *82 note 3*, 103, 113, 119; in reason, *see* Reasoning and faith; in God 15, 17, 113, 228; in God of history *331*, in Christ 16, 109; in afterlife 119. *See also* Indifferentism; Unbelief; Faith, *and under* Reason

Benedict XV 33–34

Birth control 81–86, 300–3 *passim*, 336–38

Bishops, role in social issues 18–20, 24f, 224–26, and theologians 223–24, 226, transformed by council *312, 340*

Blanshard, Paul 299, 307

Bourke, Vernon J. 72f

Bowie, W. Russell 295–305

Normal font page entries refer to Murray's work, *italicized* page entries refer to editor comments.

CPSIA information can be obtained at www.ICGtesting.com

230739LV00001B/104/A